THE FRENCH HOME FRONT
1914–1918

THE LEGACY OF THE GREAT WAR

A series sponsored by the Historial de la grande guerre Péronne-Somme

General Editor
JAY WINTER

F o r t h c o m i n g

Antoine Prost
IN THE WAKE OF WAR
'Les Anciens Combattants' and French Society

Stéphane Audoin-Rouzeau
MEN AT WAR 1914–1918
National Sentiment and Trench Journalism in France during
the First World War

Gerald D. Feldman
ARMY, INDUSTRY, AND LABOR IN GERMANY 1914–1918

Rosa Maria Bracco
MERCHANTS OF HOPE
British Middlebrow Writers and the First World War, 1919–1939

THE FRENCH HOME FRONT 1914–1918

EDITED BY
PATRICK FRIDENSON

BERG

PROVIDENCE / OXFORD

English edition
first published in 1992 by
Berg Publishers, Inc.
Editorial Offices:
165 Taber Avenue, Providence, RI 02906, U.S.A.
150 Cowley Road, Oxford OX4 1JJ, UK

English Edition, © 1992
Originally published as *L'autre front.*
Second edition from the French by permission of the publishers
Les Éditions Ouvrières, Paris.
Chapters 1, 2, 3, 4, 7, 8, and 9, translated by Bruce Little.
Chapter 10, translated by Helen McPhail

A CIP catalogue record for this book is available from the British Library.

Library of Congress Cataloging-in-Publication Data
1914–1918, l'autre front. English.
 The French home front 1914–1918 / edited by Patrick Fridenson.
  p.   cm. — (Legacy of the Great War)
 Translation of: 1914–1918, l'autre front.
 Includes index.
 ISBN 0-85496-693-5 — ISBN 0-85496-770-2 (pbk.)
  1. World War, 1914–1918—France. 2. France—History—1914–1940.
I. Fridenson, Patrick. 1944–   . II. Title. III. Series.
D516.A17   1992
940.3'44—dc20   92–13235

iv

CONTENTS

Contents

THE POLITICS OF DAILY LIFE

Introduction:
A New View of France at War

Patrick Fridenson

There is a conventional wisdom on the French home front during World War I. It says that for the French economy and society this war is both a parenthesis – the major trends at work in prewar France are suspended, all the more as industrial regions like the North and the East are soon occupied by German troops – and a catastrophe – there one thinks of the 1.2 million male war-related deaths, of the wounded and amputees, of the decline of the French birth rate, of the destruction of many rural and urban areas, of inflation. This view is still very present in most works. For instance, the most authoritative survey of the French economy in the twentieth century says that "by far the negative consequences were the most important. The stimulus of war orders did not make up for the losses caused by the invasion."[1]

On the contrary, the aim of this book is to show that not only most major changes already taking place in the French economy and most conflicts dividing French society continued during the war, but also that the war was the theater of deep transformations, some of them still having consequences on today's France. To be sure, the book duly takes into account the destruction and disruption caused by what was the first war of attrition. But it argues, in keeping with recent works by British historians,[2] that war is a contradictory phenomenon, whereby short-term and long-term damages may coexist with a pursuit of growth by unusual means.

This argument is applied in four directions: there is in 1914–1918 a second front, the home front; the dynamics of the war economy matter; the State carries new functions; and society undergoes a strong upheaval. The consequence of these four points is drawn in conclusion: the seeds of change had been planted, and it was impossible for France to go back to normalcy.

Notes to this chapter can be found on page 10.

1

The Two Fronts

Apparently, in 1914–1918, as in earlier wars, there is only one front, i.e., on the battlefield. Among the civilians unity prevails, the famous *Union sacrée*. It is even felt in those parts of France which are occupied by the enemy.[3] The truce of political divisions, born in Paris in Parliament, is "relayed to the populations of towns and villages" by the mayors, the primary school teachers, and the priests.[4] Individuals accept war, not in a fit of bellicose enthusiasm, but, as Jean-Jacques Becker's chapter shows, in a combination of mental resignation and will of self-defense.[5] Political forms and trade unions accept war and the *Union sacrée*. The impact of this shelving of political and social differences (at least until 1916) is highly differentiated. The major benefits are reaped by the right wing, which regroups the nation at war behind its program, as the chapter by Serge Berstein argues. Therefore the loser is the radical party, which then loses its identity. Yet the *Union sacrée* also gives the French socialist party for the first time access to political power. It thus learns of the potential and constraints of governmental action. As for the trade unions, they share a parallel experience by joining various kinds of bipartite and tripartite committees with State officials and the employers. The most visible embodiment of this union is the intense mobilization of almost the entire French economy, here analyzed in the chapters by Gerd Hardach and Alain Hennebicque. Years later, its memory still prompted the socialist Albert Thomas, who had been the first Minister of Munitions during the Great War, to mourn for the metallurgy tycoon Camille Cavallier in the following terms: "How could I have been insensitive to the lucidity of his mind, the authority of his long experience and, over and above, his love of public good?"[6]

The *Union sacrée*, naturally, brings grist to the mill of an interpretation of the Great War as a parenthesis. Indeed it "was an extraordinary interlude, a *sursis glorieux* in a period of social and political strife which culminated in the bitter divisions of the 1930s."[7] Nevertheless, as the war progressed it appeared that exhortations to rally together masked persisting antagonisms less and less, especially between employers and workers. During the war employers' strategies, of which the chapters by Gerd Hardach, Gilbert Hatry, Mathilde Dubesset *et al.* give different examples, modify the labor process, the recruitment of personnel, wages and allowances, and even the leisure facilities and activities of the workforce. As a result, employers' differences with a large part of the labor force increase, despite the conciliatory attitudes of numerous national union leaders. Gradually workers, men and women, French and foreigners, once more display their pugnacity. In front of this open resistance of various types and groups of workers, French employers can bargain with unions or shop stewards, but their last resort, once again, is repression. There is, then, among French civilians, a second front, the home front. Its main battles are waged from 1916 to 1918. But the First World War ends before any decisive victory is won on the home front.

The Dynamics of the War Economy

What balance can we strike, first, about the war's effects on economic life on the home front? In this domain those who think of the Great War in terms of temporary deflection or of negative impact have much evidence in support of their views. To the evidence of destruction and to inflation a number of points may be added: the wearing out of the railways and of the coal mines;[8] the discontinuance of civilian product lines; the loss of export markets; the interruption of normal channels of labor supply; the disruption of the sources of materials supply; the hyperspecialization and quick wearing down of many war factories; the hegemonic position of the army as customer; and the complexity of the interallied agencies which were set up to regulate international commerce and shipping.[9]

Nevertheless, the available case studies in business behavior also point in the opposite direction, as the chapter by James M. Laux suggests. Most large corporations supplying the army invent new products and devices or buy new licenses. They are able to make sizeable investments. They develop their managerial hierarchies. They apply several methods of "scientific management" of labor in workshops or factories hitherto untouched by Taylorism.[10] Some companies manage to export or even to invest abroad,[11] all the more as – see Robert Paxton's chapter – international links between firms often persist. Those corporations which do not work for war orders have moderate growth, but it is real growth. As for small and medium sized enterprises, most of them grow – and take part in the war effort. These features characterize old industries such as metallurgy,[12] machine-tools,[13] shipbuilding,[14] chemicals, glass,[15] as well as new industries such as the pharmaceutical industry,[16] the aluminum industry,[17] the automobile industry,[18] and the nascent aircraft industry, which has the largest production in the world during the Great War.[19]

Simultaneously interenterprise cooperation develops, taking a variety of paths: cartels, buying or selling pools, and consortia, all institutions which in fact reinforce the role of large firms.[20] In comparison, neither small and medium-sized enterprises nor anticapitalist currents are able to reach a countervailing position of power in politics or in the economy, as evidenced by Robert Paxton's chapter. Moreover, during the war some firms, whether large or medium-sized, already dream of worldwide alliances for postwar times.[21] The industrial, commercial, and social role of trade associations grows, too. Furthermore, the first national interprofessional association of French employers, the Association Nationale d'Expansion Economique, is created in 1915 and soon takes an active part in public affairs.[22]

Therefore some industrialists begin to see their new place within the nation in glowing colors. One of the leaders of the chemical industry in Lyons, Emile Guimet, writes: "The politics of the current war are dominated by commercial matters and by the interest attached to industry. It is the industrialist who is at the center of the action. It is for him that people fight. It is he who will later gain the economic victory."[23]

However, the dynamics of the war economy do not result only from the decisions of business leaders. They also depend on a radical alteration of the relationship of private industry to the State.

The Expansion of the State

What has been rightly called "the exuberance of the State"[24] during the Great War can easily be ascribed to temporary circumstances, i.e., the difficulties of making the war economy work, the necessity of consolidating French society, and the pressures of the British government on its ally. "To satisfy both civilian and military needs, the French government was obliged not only to provide factories with raw materials . . . but also to direct production, to initiate industrial programs to meet the strategic demands of the army, and to furnish the civilian population with basic consumer goods which would otherwise have been quite unobtainable."[25] In parallel, both the logic of the war and labor's demands considerably enlarged the prewar interventionist tendencies and the action of the State over working conditions, welfare, and industrial relations.

Are these new functions of the State a simple adaptation to hard times? The unceasing clashes between bureaucrats, industrialists, and politicians, to which I would add the pressures of labor or other strands of public opinion, can give this impression. Yet this book suggests that the wartime expansion of the French State is not purely opportunistic, or merely motivated by short-term strategies. Alain Hennebicque's chapter shows that politicians and bureaucrats begin to dream of a controlled capitalism. Contrary to their counterparts in Germany, they are able to devise methods to restrict the power drawn by capitalists from their increased strength and thus to preserve the interests of both the consumer and the State. John Horne's chapter, similarly, shows that labor leaders do not limit themselves to dealing with the war as a social emergency. Soon trade-unionists, socialists, and *coopérateurs* concert to draw the long term implications of both the expansion and the sophistication of the French State and to prepare the "economic reorganization" of postwar France.

Let us take a case in point: the development of a research policy by the State during the Great War. It bears all the signs of a wartime innovation. In 1915 the Minister of Education creates a "Direction of Inventions which are interesting for national defense," and in 1916 it becomes a junior ministry within the Ministry of Munitions. This is not a unilateral move by the State. In fact, there had been an outburst of individual inventions, and they had met with inertia by the War Ministry. Deputies had then mobilized to have the State encourage and organize the work of inventors. So, the role of the new administration is to test the findings of individual private inventors, to support the good ones, and to coordinate their activities. But further research shows that inventors' lobbying for State action long predated the war, and it is not surprising to see that the new institution is not dismantled when war ends. It is even one of the origins of the French Centre National de la Recherche Scientifique.[26]

Taking this line of interpretation leads us to assess the two components of this expansion of the State: the ministers and the civil servants. What are the real differences between the views of the ministers about the growing role of the State? The recent literature on the major statesmen who directed the transformation of the French State – Etienne Clémentel, the Minister of Commerce and Industry,[27] Albert Thomas, the Minister of Munitions,[28] his deputy and successor Louis Loucheur,[29] the Prime Minister Georges Clemenceau[30]– offer striking contrasts. This literature opposes Albert Thomas and Clémentel: "less interested in long-term reforms than solving immediate problems," Thomas "initially moved less boldly than Clémentel against the industrialists" and was less successful.[31] In turn Clémentel the *dirigist* is differentiated from Loucheur the laissez-faire man.[32] Both comparisons need revisions. The negative picture of Thomas' policies ignores his prewar political thinking and much of his postwar action.[33] Thomas' statism never disappears entirely during his early years at the Ministry, and it evolves toward "a permanent system of collaboration between businessmen and representatives of the community at large" and a deployment of the State as an arbiter between industry and labor.[34] Similarly, the differences between Clémentel and Loucheur have been exaggerated and some similarities overlooked. Loucheur is not the traditionalist liberal often depicted, nor is Clémentel a bureaucratic doctrinaire. Both associate "a preference for the autonomous initiatives" of businessmen and a measure of economic management, and both find a vigorous State and "industrial self-government" complementary.[35] Such are the real differences between these men, and the paradoxical common feature to all – an anti-bureaucratic approach to State action.

A larger role for the State brings about an increase in the number of civil servants. Surprisingly though, this question has not drawn historians' attention, and accurate statistics are not yet available. A tentative estimate is a twenty-five percent growth of the French civil service in four years. Given the simultaneous needs of agriculture, army, and industry, this is no small achievement. It means that like the industrial workforce, the civil service develops by calling on newcomers, women for instance, or "freshly graduated students, scientists, engineers, or industrialists" and by transferring skilled personnel to other sectors, for instance teachers and professors to economic ministries.[36] The State also calls women to replace conscripted male teachers.[37] The State tries to increase the productivity of its servants by introducing several methods of management, notably Taylorism, and to check expenses by improving accounting methods.[38] Like industry, it faces problems of labor relations. This process of bureaucratization, although by no means particular to France,[39] contributes to the transformation of French society.

The Transformation of Society

Some of the changes which occur are clearly ephemeral. This is the case of the material prosperity of peasant families, a topic now so well researched that we did not find it necessary to deal with it in this book.[40] Also evidently temporary is the hiring of disabled persons, foreign refugees, and prisoners of war, and the increased mobility of labor prompted by the relocation of industry. For instance, the Viseux family, coal miners sent to the Carmaux mine in the Southwest, comes back to the North as soon as the War finishes.[41] Similarly, only one-sixth of the establishments which instituted shop stewards during the war still have delegates in 1921–1924.[42]

6

But the war also produces lasting changes. Those pertaining to the social composition of the working population and to the collective consciousness of its main groups are the more salient. A first element of social change is the decline in domestic labor. From 930,000 in 1911, this category falls to 784,00 in 1926. This shift had probably begun before the war. Once again we can distinguish short-term causes: conscription, inflation, housing problems, and shortage of labor; and long-term influences: prolongation of women's education and the opening of more attractive industrial or tertiary jobs.[43]

Conversely, as in Britain, women's work undergoes "a marked increase . . . both absolute and relative, in trade, banking, and insurance,"[44] and, I would add, in the civil service. As for women in industry, the chapter by Mathilde Dubesset, Françoise Thébaud, and Catherine Vincent shows that after a marked, but uneven increase during the war, it then declines in some sectors, and in others, such as metallurgy, remains at a slightly higher level than prior to the war. The idea of a "secular decline in women's employment" from 1918 to 1970 is widely held. It has been challenged and at least qualified by two French historians, who contest the exhaustiveness and the interpretation of available statistics.[45]

A third element is the importance of foreign labor. The war leads to an introduction of half a million immigrants. Moreover, their ethnic composition diversifies markedly. The reception of immigrants by their French neighbors or comrades oscillates between ambiguous recognition, distrust, and outright rejection – latent xenophobia lurks.[46] It is for these immigrants that the French State invents in 1916 the identity (ID) card, which in 1917 is generalized to other foreigners. Thus the ID card originally allows its holder to stay in France. For French born citizens, the ID card becomes compulsory only in the 1950s.[47] Since World War I, immigration remains a key feature of French society and a major concern for the State which regulates it.

The Great War also modifies the collective representations of social relations. Here the first shift clearly is the development of unionization among civil servants, which progresses during the war. This results from a feeling of greater strength inspired by the growth of the State and from the frustration provoked by the quasi-stability of civil servants' wages in an era of rising prices and inflation. After the war their unionization continues to increase: those civil servants who were deprived of the right to unionize conquer it, and unions obtain the right to discuss wages.[48] During the war more organizations affiliate to the confederation of workers' trade unions, the C.G.T., and its majority leaders

7

actively cultivate relations with the other associations of State employ-ees.[49] This signals a durable rapprochement of workers and civil ser-vants, by which white collar workers are going to turn into the back-bone of French trade unions.

As for workers, they change, too. Gerd Hardach's chapter shows that on the home front they gain a triple experience: a society entirely com-mitted to production, which Albert Thomas later called "the great industrial family of France"[50]; a powerful State, able to direct the econo-my, to protect workers and consumers, and to coerce labor; and a series of financial and material sacrifices concerning their incomes and their working conditions. The first and the third of these features actually converge, to reinforce among skilled workers, though not all, and among some semi-skilled workers a productivist vision and an appetite for consumption. The three features combined bring about a swelling of the two opposite wings of the French labor movement. John Horne's chapter demonstrates that reformists have not only established a durable program, they are also henceforth well implanted "in the more tradi-tional segments of the working class as well as in the public sector." Gilbert Hatry's chapter makes us understand how revolutionaries' par-ticipation in the wave of social movements which swept over the indus-trial nations from 1916 to 1920[51] gives them both a real sense of mass action and a new credibility, which the now crucial role of the State favors. They are better represented "in the sectors and localities domi-nated by war production," such as metallurgy and the railways.[52] The bifurcation of workers' attitudes and of French labor has retained much of its relevance to at least the 1970s. It has weakened since, with the decline of communism, but has not disappeared.

Finally, the political and social consciousness of the petty bourgeoisie is also shaken and altered by the Great War. Shopkeepers and artisans resent economic concentration, as Robert Paxton's chapter shows. Small proprietors and holders of government securities – the *rentiers* – are threatened by inflation. Therefore much of the petty bourgeoisie shifts to the right for a long time, as evidenced by the evolution of the radical party analyzed in Serge Berstein's chapter.

The Seeds of Change

Nobody has ever argued that after World War I France went back to "normalcy." The real question was whether there was a continuity between the experience of the home front and the experience of the fol-lowing years. Here historians split into three groups.

The first stresses discontinuity. Significantly, Gerd Hardach's chapter concludes that after the war the Socialist Party failed to obtain a majority, unions declined, and in politics pre-war ideologies and institutions loomed large. Other historians underline the importance of postwar decontrol and of the drive for a return to the status quo or the dominance of neo-liberal policy.[53] Jean-Louis Robert's chapter on Paris cooperatives shows that their striking wartime growth contrasted both with their prewar difficulties and with a postwar activity which attracted fewer members. It also argues that the real progress of the cooperative spirit among trade unionists was limited.

The second stresses continuity in the long term. In 1974 I already suggested that the First World War had been the laboratory for many economic and political innovations of post-World War II France.[54] Today John Horne writes that "in the case of the First World War, it may well be that the more substantial, if indirect legacy of French and British labor reformism should be sought not in the first but in the second après-guerre."[55] Adrian Rossiter finds some connections with the Vichy regime and corporatist tendencies: "Many potent ideas made their first significant appearance during the Great War, and were either enacted temporarily or at least came close to fruition – obligatory grouping of businessmen, compulsory labour arbitration, a central organization for the Chambers of Commerce, a national corporatist assembly, concerted interaction between professional associations in order to achieve a national direction of the economy."[56] Indeed the oral history of people on the home front of the Great War can confirm that none of them forgot the ideas or solutions drafted in 1914–1918.

The third argues that there were some elements of continuity even in the 1920s. The chapter in this book on the end of article 419 of the Penal Code on coalitions of enterprises would be a case in point. Adrian Rossiter, the staunchest proponent of this idea, thinks that the "scaffolding of corporatist politics" was in fact extended in the 1920s.[57] A similar approach could be taken to account for the birth of Social Security in the 1920s by linking it to the birth of family allowances during the Great War and to the proliferation of welfare schemes which was characteristic of life on the home front. The interpretation of the 1920s undoubtedly needs further revisions.[58]

The debate is fully open. This book, which first appeared in French but has been entirely updated and revised by all its authors (and includes two chapters that were not in the French edition), which also weaves the approaches of historians working in different countries (France, Germany, Ireland, United States), has been intended precisely

9

as a tool for debate. In many a respect, the home front of the Great War is still close to us.

Notes to the Introduction

1. J. Bouvier and F. Caron, "Guerre, crise, guerre," in *Histoire économique et sociale de la France*, ed. F. Braudel and E. Labrousse (Paris: P.U.F., 1980), vol. 4, book 2.

2. J.M. Winter, ed., *War and Economic Development* (Cambridge: Cambridge University Press, 1975). A. Milward, *The Economic Effects of the Two World Wars on Britain*, 2nd ed. (London: Macmillan, 1984).

3. L. Köll, *Auboué dans la Grande Guerre* (Paris: Karthala, 1983).

4. P.J. Flood, *France 1914-18: Public Opinion and the War Effort* (London: Macmillan, 1990), p. 22.

5. See also J.J. Becker, *The Great War and the French People* (New York-Leamington Spa: Berg Publishers, 1986) and Y. Pourcher, "Un quotidien des années de guerre. Les signes d'une rupture du temps, des habitudes et des normes dans *Le Journal* d'Indre et Loire (1914–1918)," *Sociétés*, September 1991, p. 275-283.

6. Archives of the late Pierre Waline, letter by Albert Thomas to Alfred Lambert-Ribot, vice-chairman of the Union of Metallurgical and Mining Industries, 13 June 1926.

7. Flood, *France*, p. 17. Also J. Cavignac, *La classe ouvrière bordelaise face à la guerre (1914–1918)* (Bordeaux: Institut Aquitain d'Études Sociales, 1976), pp. 90–102.

8. F. Caron, *Histoire de l'exploitation d'un grand réseau: la Compagnie du Chemin de Fer du Nord 1846–1937* (Paris: Mouton, 1973). D. Reid, *The Miners of Decazeville* (Cambridge: Harvard University Press, 1985).

9. M.M. Farrar, *Conflict and Compromise: the Strategy, Politics and Diplomacy of the French Blockade 1914–1918* (The Hague: De Gruyter, 1974). P. Guillen, ed., *La France et L'Italie pendant la Première Guerre mondiale* (Grenoble: Presses Universitaires de Grenoble, 1976). A. Kaspi, *Le temps des Américains. Le concours américain à la France en 1917–1918* (Paris: Publications de la Sorbonne, 1976). Y.M. Nouailhat, *France et États-Unis: août 1914–avril 1917* (Paris: Publications de la Sorbonne, 1979). S.D. Carls, "Louis Loucheur: a French Technocrat in Government, 1916-1920" (Ph.D. diss., University of Minnesota, 1982). J.F. Godfrey, *Capitalism at War. Industrial Policy and Bureaucracy in France, 1914–1918* (New York-Leamington Spa: Berg Publishers, 1987), pp. 80, 99–101.

10. G.C. Humphreys, *Taylorism in France 1904–1920* (New York-London: Garland, 1986). P. Fridenson, "Un tournant taylorien de la société française (1904–1918)," *Annales E.S.C.* (September-October 1987), pp. 1046, 1051–1053. A. Rabinbach, *The Human Motor. Energy, Fatigue and the Origins of Modernity* (New York: Basic Books, 1990), pp. 261, 266. A. Moutet, "La rationalisation du travail de 1900 à 1939" (thèse de doctorat d'État, University Paris X-Nanterre, 1992).

11. M. Lagana, *Le Parti colonial français* (Sillery: Presses de l'Université du Québec, 1990), pp. 105–106, 109, 111, 125–127. P. Cayez, *Rhône-Poulenc 1895–1975* (Paris: A. Colin/Masson, 1988), pp. 65, 70.

12. J.P. Baccon, "La sidérurgie française (août 1914-décembre 1915)" (MA thesis,

University Paris I, 1971). J.C. Mauffre, "Un aspect de la mobilisation industrielle au cours de la Première Guerre mondiale. La fabrication des obus en France" (MA thesis, University Paris I, 1971). C. Beaud, "Les aciéries Holtzer à Unieux, 1914–1918," *Bulletin du centre d'histoire économique et sociale de la région lyonnaise*, 1975. J.N. Jeanneney, *François de Wendel en République* (Paris: Le Seuil, 1976). R. Colinet, "Un site industriel: Nouzonville. Une dynastie industrielle de la métallurgie ardennaise: les Thomé" (MA thesis, University Nancy II, 1979). Godfrey, *Capitalism*, pp. 239-288. T. de la Broise, *Pont-à-Mousson* (Paris: Inter Editions, 1988), pp. 62–67. J.P. Borgis, *Charles Morel, constructeur dauphinois sous la Troisième République* (Grenoble: Presses Universitaires de Grenoble, 1990).

13. J.C. Guillaume, *Guilliet. Histoire d'une entreprise 1847–1979* (Auxerre: Société des Sciences Historiques et Naturelles de l'Yonne, 1986), pp. 97–99.

14. E.H. Lorenz, "The Labour Process and Industrial Relations in the British and French Shipbuilding Industries from 1880 to 1970" (Ph.D. diss., Cambridge, 1983). J. Domenichino, *Une ville en chantiers. La construction navale à Port-de-Bouc 1900–1965* (Aix: Edisud, 1989).

15. J.P. Daviet, *Un destin international: la Compagnie de Saint-Gobain de 1830 à 1939* (Paris: Éditions des Archives contemporaines, 1988), pp. 426, 443, 456, 481, 549, 555–557, 567–570. Godfrey, *Capitalism*, pp. 157–179.

16. Cayez, *Rhône-Poulenc*, pp. 57–74.

17. H. Morsel, *Histoire d'une grande entreprise: la Société d'électrochimie et d'électrométallurgie et des aciéries électriques d'Ugine (SECEM et AEU)* (Paris: LaRuche, 1972).

18. P. Fridenson, *Histoire des usines Renault* (Paris: Le Seuil, 1972), vol. 1. G. Hatry, *Renault usine de guerre 1914–1918* (Paris: Lafourcade, 1978). G. Declas, "Recherches sur les usines Berliet (1914–1949)" (MA thesis, University Paris I, 1977), pp. 3–11, 123–125. B. Pérot, *Panhard la doyenne d'avant-garde* (Paris: E.P.A., 1979), pp. 77, 80, 115. Y. Cohen, "Ernest Mattern, Les automobiles Peugeot et le pays de Montbéliard industriel avant et pendant la guerre de 1914–1918" (thèse de 3e cycle, University of Besançon, 1981). S. Schweitzer, *Des engrenages à la chaine. Les usines Citroën 1915–1935* (Lyons: Presses Universitaires de Lyon, 1982).

19. J.M. Laux, "The Rise and Fall of Armand Deperdussin," *French Historical Studies* (Spring 1973). E. Chadeau, *L'industrie aéronautique en France 1900-1950. De Blériot à Dassault* (Paris: Fayard, 1987).

20. N. Plutino, "Un aspect de l'intervention de l'Etat pendant la guerre de 1914–1918: les consortiums" (MA thesis, University Paris X – Nanterre, 1969). Godfrey, *Capitalism*, pp. 106–143. F. Hachez, "L'Aluminium Français et sa politique de vente de l'aluminium (1911–1939)" (DEA thesis, University Paris IV, 1990), pp. 72–82.

21. Daviet, *Un destin*, pp. 387–388. A. Baudant, *Pont-à-Mousson (1918–1939)* (Paris: Publications de la Sorbonne, 1980), pp. 264–266.

22. H.D. Peiter, "Institutions and Attitudes: the Consolidation of the Business Community in Bourgeois France, 1880-1914," *Journal of Social History* (June 1976), pp. 510–515. Godfrey, *Capitalism*, pp. 49–50, 221–238, 244–245. G. Kerouredan, "Un aspect de l'organisation patronale au XXe siècle: l'Association Nationale d'Expansion Économique (décembre 1915–mars 1951)" (thèse de 3e cycle, University Paris I, 1986).

23. É. Guimet, *Après la guerre. Notes d'économie politique* (Fleurieu-sur Saône: Imprimerie de l'Usine Guimet, 1916), vol. 3, p. 10.

24. F. Bock, "L'exubérance de l'État en France de 1914 à 1918," *Vingtième Siècle* (July 1984), pp. 41–51.

25. Godfrey, *Capitalism*, p. 289.

26. Y. Roussel, "De la science et de l'industrie, Ministère de Clémentel 1915–1919" (DEA thesis, École des Hautes Études en Sciences Sociales, 1985). Roussel, "L'histoire d'une politique des inventions 1887–1918," *Cahiers pour l'histoire du C.N.R.S.* (September 1989).

27. Godfrey, *Capitalism*, pp. 85–105, 186–191.

28. B.W. Schaper, *Albert Thomas': trente ans de réformisme social* (Assen: Van Gorcum, 1959). M. Fine, "Albert Thomas: A Reformer's Vision of Modernization, 1914–1932," *Journal of Contemporary History* (October 1977), pp. 545–564. Godfrey, *Capitalism*, pp. 184–194, 257–288. J.N. Horne, *Labour at War. France and Britain 1914–1918* (Oxford: Clarendon Press, 1991), *passim.*

29. J.M. Chevrier, "Le rôle de Loucheur dans l'économie de guerre (1914–1918)" (MA thesis, University Paris X – Nanterre, 1972). Carls, "Louis Loucheur."

30. J.B. Duroselle, *Clemenceau,* Paris, Fayard, 1988.

31. Godfrey, *Capitalism*, p. 292.

32. R.F. Kuisel, *Capitalism and the State in Modern France* (Cambridge: Cambridge University Press, 1981), pp. 37–58.

33. M. Fine, "Towards Corporatism: The Movement for Capital-Labor Collaboration in France, 1914–1936" (Ph.D. diss., University of Wisconsin, 1971). M. Rebérioux and P. Fridenson, "Albert Thomas, pivot du réformisme français," *Le Mouvement Social* (April-June 1974), pp. 85–97.

34. A. Rossiter, "Experiments with Corporatist Politics in Republican France, 1916-1939" (Ph.D. diss., Oxford University, 1986), pp. 19, 27–30, 33.

35. Rossiter, "Experiments," pp. 34, 39, 54, 82–83.

36. Godfrey, *Capitalism*, p. 292.

37. J. Wishnia, *The Proletarianizing of the Fonctionnaires: Civil Service Workers and the Labour Movement under the Third Republic* (Baton Rouge: Louisiana State University Press, 1990).

38. S. Rials, *Organisation et administration 1910–1930* (Paris: Éditions Beauchesne, 1977).

39. R. Torstendahl, *Bureaucratisation in Northwestern Europe, 1880–1985* (London-New York: Routledge, 1991).

40. P. Barral, "La paysannerie française à l'arrière," in *Les sociétés européennes et la guerre de 1914–1918*, ed. J.J. Becker and S. Audoin-Rouzeau (Nanterre: Publications de l'Université Paris X, 1990).

41. A. Viseux, *Mineur de fond* (Paris: Plon, 1991). For a general view of mobility and stability after the end of the war, J.P. Burdy, *Le Soleil noir. Un quartier de Saint-Étienne 1840–1940* (Lyons: Presses Universitaires de Lyon, 1989), p. 180.

42. Horne, *Labour at War*, p. 195.

43. P. Bernard and H. Dubief, *Decline of the Third Republic 1914–1938* (Cambridge, Cambridge University Press, 1985). L.A. Tilly and J.W. Scott, *Women, Work and Family,* 2nd ed. (New York: Rinehart, Holt and Winston, 1987).

44. J.L. Robert, "Women and Work in France during the First World War," in *The Upheaval of War. Family, Work and Welfare in Europe, 1914–1918,* ed. R. Wall and J.M. Winter (Cambridge: Cambridge University Press, 1988), p. 257. For a general view, J. McMillan, *Housewife or Harlot: The Place of Women in French Society, 1870–1940* (Brighton: Harvester Press, 1981). F. Thébaud, *La France au temps de la guerre de 14* (Paris: Stock, 1986). L.L. Downs, "Women in Industry 1914–1939: The Employers' Perspective" (Ph.D. diss., Columbia University, 1987).

45. S. Zener, "De l'ouvrière à l'employée," *Le Mouvement Social* (July-September 1987). Burdy, *Le Soleil noir,* pp. 33–34.

Introduction

46. G. Cross, *Immigrant Workers in Industrial France* (Philadelphia: Temple University Press, 1983). G. Noiriel, *Le creuset français* (Paris: Le Seuil, 1988). Burdy, *Le Soleil noir*, pp. 179–201. T. Stovall, *The Rise of the Paris Red Belt* (Berkeley: University of California Press, 1990), pp. 68–70, 82. H. Morsel and J.F. Parent, *Les industries de la région grenobloise* (Grenoble: Presses Universitaires, 1991), p. 140.

47. Noiriel, *La tyrannie du national. Le droit d'asile en Europe (1793–1993)* (Paris: Calmann-Lévy, 1991), pp. 92 and 178–180.

48. J. Siwek-Pouydesseau, *Le syndicalisme des fonctionnaires jusqu'à la guerre froide* (Lille: Presses Universitaires de Lille, 1989). Wishnia, *The Proletarianizing*, pp. 181–182, 188–189, 191–192, 198–200, 223–274. F. McCollum Feeley, *Rebels with Causes: A Study of Revolutionary Syndicalist Culture among the French Primary School Teachers between 1880 and 1919* (New York: Peter Lang, 1990).

49. Horne, *Labour at War*, pp. 203, 267. Wishnia, *The Proletarianizing*, pp. 194–195, 198–199.

50. Archives of the late Pierre Waline, letter from Albert Thomas to Alfred Lambert-Ribot, 13 June 1926.

51. L.H. Haimson and C. Tilly, eds., *Strikes, Wars and Revolutions in an International Perspective. Strike Waves in the Late Nineteenth and Early Twentieth Centuries* (Cambridge: Cambridge University Press, 1989).

52. P. Fridenson, "The Impact of the First World War on French Workers," in *The Upheaval of War*, ed. R. Wall and J.M. Winter, pp. 243–245. J. Girault, *Benoît Frachon, communiste et syndicaliste* (Paris: Presses de la Fondation nationale des sciences politiques, 1989). J.L. Robert, "Ouvriers et mouvement ouvrier parisiens pendant la grande guerre et l'immediat après-guerre" (thèse de doctorat d'État, University Paris I, 1989). L. Mairry, "La vie politique dans le département du Doubs sous la Troisième République" (thèse de doctorat d'Etat, University Paris IV, 1990). J. Girault and J.L. Robert, *1920: le Congrès de Tours* (Paris: Messidor, 1990).

53. Kuisel, *Capitalism and the State*, pp. 51–58, 62–65. J.J. Becker and S. Berstein, *Victoire et frustrations 1914–1929* (Paris: Le Seuil, 1990), pp. 179, 181, 327, 395. G. Cross, *A Quest for Time* (Berkeley: University of California Press, 1989), pp. 147–151.

54. P. Fridenson, "Note de lecture" (on M. Fine's Ph.D.), *Le Mouvement Social* (April-June 1974).

55. Horne, *Labour at War*, p. 394.

56. Rossiter, "Experiments," pp. 12–13.

57. *Ibid*, pp. 73–129.

58. G. Hardach, *The First World War* (London: Allen Lane, 1977), p. 293. L. Murard and P. Zylberman, eds., "Le soldat du travail," special issue of *Recherches* (September 1978). Daviet, *Un destin*, pp. 494–504, 510–526. F. Sugier, "La Première Guerre mondiale et le déclin du contrôle social dans les mines du Gard (1914–1922)," *Annales du Midi* (April-June 1991). J. Eisenberg Vichniac, *The Management of Labor: The British and French Iron and Steel Industries, 1860–1918*, (Greenwich, C:, JAI Press, 1990), pp. 165–187 and 193–196.

L'UNION SACRÉE

1

"That's The Death Knell Of Our Boys..."

Jean-Jacques Becker

On Saturday, 1 August 1914, at five o'clock in the afternoon, a police-man of the Plancoët detachment drove his automobile into the com-mune of Saint-Lormel, in the Côtes-du-Nord department of France. A few moments later, the bells began to peal, proclaiming general mobi-lization. "That's the death knell of our boys," murmured an old lady. "Berlin, here we come; long live France!" cried a young man, "we'll nail those Prussians, you'll see, lady." This is a story told by Mrs. Le Mée, a teacher in the little Breton village of Saint-Lormel, about the late after-noon of the day when France resolved to go to war.[1]

What was the temper of the French people at the time? Was it sor-row or was there really an outpouring of enthusiasm for the war, as tra-dition would have it? Several years ago, we came across an article which the vice-chancellor of the Académie de Grenoble, the historian Charles Petit-Dutaillis,[2] had written in 1915, based on notes gathered by the teachers in his district at the time of mobilization. We gained the impression, however, that the records he had collected could be seen in a different light: that the population often seemed surprised or even stunned by the turn of events rather than rising enthusiastically to seek revenge.[3]

Shortly thereafter, Yves Lequin analyzed somewhat similar records from Haute-Savoie and concluded that "the countryside of Haute-Savoie before the coming of the war had nothing in common with the Golden Legend so frequently propagated."[4] So far as the people of Toulouse are concerned, Pierre Bouyoux, a few years later, noted more

Notes for Chapter 1 can be found on page 35.

agitation and nervousness than enthusiasm in the dying days of July 1914.[5]

Is it possible to draw conclusions based on firm historical evidence rather than mere impressions? Can the people's real state of mind at the moment when war broke out be established with some confidence? Such an undertaking requires, in our view, a combination of quantitative and qualitative analysis of public opinion. One must ascertain both the various emotions experienced by Frenchmen at the outbreak of the war and the proportion of the population that shared each of these feelings.

How is this to be done? Obviously, there were no public opinion polls at the time and we have no way of discovering the opinions of a representative sample of the population. At best, retrospective surveys could be undertaken, such as Jacques Ozouf has done to some extent for teachers[6] or as Georges Castellan has done in Poitiers.[7]

However, this type of public opinion survey has several drawbacks. It can only be carried out within a limited category or geographical area. Moreover, it necessarily relies on very old people who lived through a particular period many years ago, who witnessed in the meantime many other events, both momentous and trivial, and whose memories could very well be seriously distorted, especially when they are asked about such a brief span of time.

However, we do have access to eyewitness accounts turned in by primary school teachers in certain departments. The Minister of Public Education, Albert Sarraut, asked all the teachers under his aegis to participate in the task originally initiated by the vice-chancellor of the Académie de Grenoble.[8] Though such an undertaking could have provided a gold mine of information, it turned out in the end to be less valuable than expected, either because the instructions were not carried out or because the accounts drawn up by the teachers were not collected. However, despite all the gaps, the documentation still proved very informative. The only question was how to put it to best use.

A questionnaire had been sent out to the teachers to help them make their notes. One of the queries ran as follows: "Mobilization. How was it done? Public mood, typical phrases one could hear repeated."

For every commune, in principle at least, a file was created describing the response to the mobilization order when it first arrived and as it was being carried out. When we examined these files, it became apparent that the reactions varied considerably. It therefore seemed worthwhile to analyze the words that the teachers typically employed, their frequency of use, and the consequences that flowed from them.

The observations of teachers in the Department of Charente can serve as an example of this procedure. Of all the departments in France, this was where the instructions of the Ministry were followed with the greatest zeal, or at least where the school inspectors and the academic inspector took the greatest care to ensure that the information gathered by the teachers was forwarded to the departmental archives. As a result, the files now contain information on 316 of the total 424 communes in the department.[9]

Some of these files are rather skimpy, for example, only containing details about the sums collected by teachers for war relief. However, in most cases they provide detailed responses. The teachers in some villages even filled several thick notebooks with their comments, which are informative enough to provide material for veritable monographs on the war era.

Notes on the mobilization in particular also vary greatly in size depending on the author. Not many mention the mood of the people on the eve of the Great War, but when they do, there is little sign of an expectation of war. The following sketch, for example, originates from Feuillade, a little village in the east of the department:

> Today is Saturday, 1 August 1914.
> We have the ceremonial awarding of prizes offered every year by a man of property in the commune.
> It is three o'clock. The courtyard is covered by an immense awning, the tables and benches have been taken out by the pupils and tomorrow's guests. The class goes outside and practices the little selections and the playlet.[10]

This mood was so widespread that a teacher in Mansle, one of the larger towns, could comment:

> As elsewhere across France, we did not believe any more that war would break out. Everybody said that no one would be so insane or criminal as to inflict such a scourge. Therefore, even after Austria's ultimatum to Serbia, we still hoped everything could be settled through a compromise, for which the diplomats would find the appropriate words.[11]

Under the circumstances, it is not unexpected that the mobilization order caused considerable surprise, as can be seen in a table of key terms taken from the teachers' notes (Table 1.1).

We should not deduce from this table that feelings of surprise predominated in Charente. This appears to have been the case in around sixty communes, or eighteen percent of the total, while there were few feelings of surprise or astonishment in only fourteen communes.

However, in the vast majority of communes nothing at all was mentioned in this regard. Moreover, in many cases the context indicates that people rather expected war to break out, even though this was not expressed in any specific words. However, a feeling of surprise did exist, although it was a minority sentiment.

Table 1.1

Words Expressing Surprise or Lack of Surprise
When Mobilization was First Announced in the Department of Charente
Teachers' Notes from 316 of 428 communes

Stupefaction	33 times
Surprise	20 times
Astonishment	3 times
Thunderstruck	twice
Partial Surprise	twice
Amazement	once
Shock	once
Not Surprising	13 times
Not Astonishing	once

What sort of surprise was it? In some instances, it was total: "a lightning bolt out of the blue,"[12] "the news of mobilization is like a lightning bolt. . . . Tools are dropped and all work ceases."[13] These evidently were small communes where people were more concerned with their agrarian labors than international politics.

Surprise at the outbreak of war was, however, less widespread than a feeling of stupefaction, that is to say, a refusal of the mind to admit the unthinkable. People could not believe that war was still possible. These feelings found expression in notes taken by a teacher in Becheresse:

> Even though the news on the last few days of July was alarming, the pacifist-minded rural population did not believe that war would break out. The order to mobilize was therefore greeted with a real feeling of stupefaction.[14]

How did the people of Charente react once the order to mobilize had arrived? It seems to us that a distinction has to be drawn between the precise moment when the news arrived (i.e., the late afternoon of 1 August) and the following days. In other words, reactions to the first announcement of mobilization have to be distinguished from reactions as the troops actually set about their departure.

The First Announcement of Mobilization

In the notes taken by the teachers of Charente, we were able to pick out 330 phrases referring directly to the reception accorded the first announcement of mobilization. This surpasses the total number of communes for which files are available because a single file could contain several pertinent terms, especially as some teachers were careful enough to report various contradictory responses that they observed in the face of such a momentous event. The figures therefore refer to the responses observed and are not related to the total number of communes.

We divided the reactions to the mobilization order into three categories. The first includes negative reactions, the second includes calm, composed reactions and the third indicates a surge of patriotic fervor. As a result, three graphs (Figures 1.1, 1.2, and 1.3) were drawn up.

Of the 330 reactions that were distinguished, 188 were negative, 66 indicated a calm, composed response and 76 indicated patriotic fervor, or in percentage terms, 57 percent, 20 percent and 23 percent respectively. This quantitative analysis produces a clear result: negative reactions were most frequently expressed, so it therefore seems reasonable to conclude that the mobilization order was received without enthusiasm in the Department of Charente.

Further nuances can be added to this conclusion. Among the unfavorable reactions, five appear most frequently: *consternation* (thirty times), *tears* (forty-six times, primarily among women), *sadness* (seventeen times), *resignation* (seventeen times), and *agitation* (thirty-six times). *Consternation* seems to have been the strongest response. A teacher in Benest wrote:

> This sad news was made known to the public to the accompaniment of pealing bells and the beating of drums. In less than an hour, all the inhabitants of the commune had gathered before the town hall. What consternation![15]

We should however examine more closely the significance of this reaction. It marks the extreme limit of reactions unfavorable to mobilization, and indeed there were no reports anywhere of any inclination to resist the mobilization order. The news of mobilization was met with a feeling of consternation, that is to say, anxiety and dismay, but it did not provoke any inclination to resist that was likely to result in a refusal of the order. Feelings of consternation seem to have been rooted in a profound pacifism, a horror of war, and were not motivated by ideolo-

Figure 1.1
The First Announcement of Mobilization,
Sentiments of the Population of Charente:
Negative Reactions

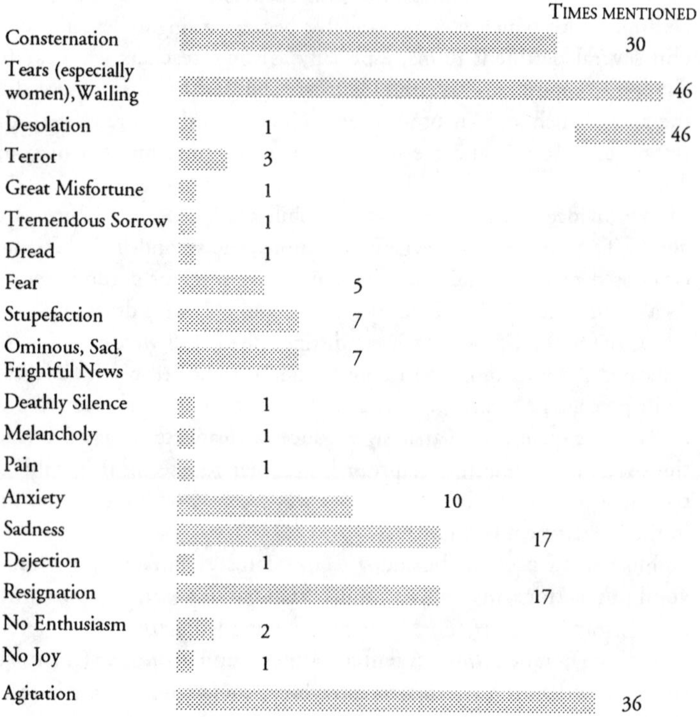

	TIMES MENTIONED
Consternation	30
Tears (especially women), Wailing	46
Desolation	1 / 46
Terror	3
Great Misfortune	1
Tremendous Sorrow	1
Dread	1
Fear	5
Stupefaction	7
Ominous, Sad, Frightful News	7
Deathly Silence	1
Melancholy	1
Pain	1
Anxiety	10
Sadness	17
Dejection	1
Resignation	17
No Enthusiasm	2
No Joy	1
Agitation	36

Figure 1.2
The First Announcement of Mobilization
Sentiments of the Population of Charente:
Composed Reactions

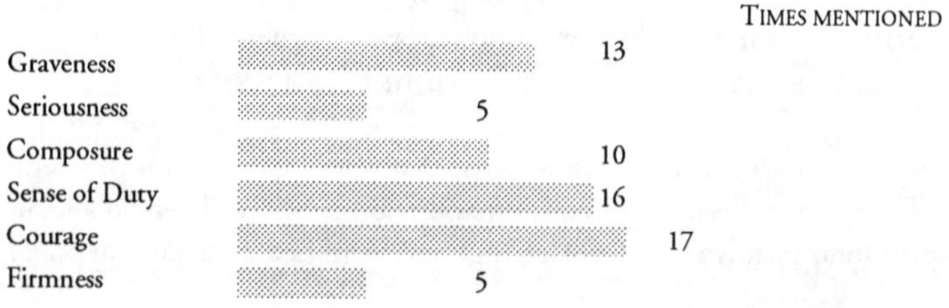

	TIMES MENTIONED
Graveness	13
Seriousness	5
Composure	10
Sense of Duty	16
Courage	17
Firmness	5

Figure 1.3
The First Announcement of Mobilization
Sentiments of the Population of Charente:
Favorable Reactions

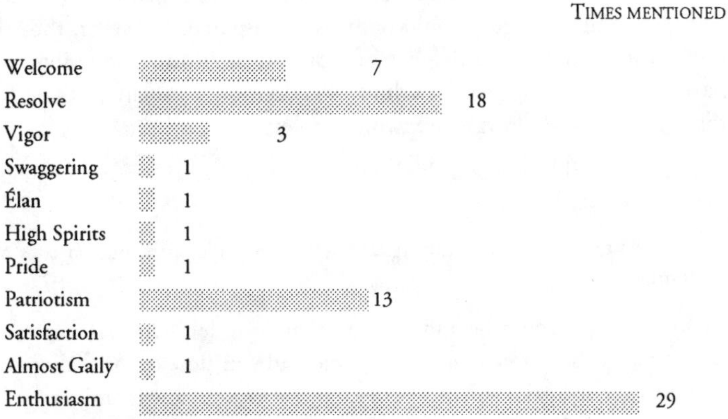

TIMES MENTIONED

Welcome	7
Resolve	18
Vigor	3
Swaggering	1
Élan	1
High Spirits	1
Pride	1
Patriotism	13
Satisfaction	1
Almost Gaily	1
Enthusiasm	29

gy. Moreover, only a minority responded in this way: among the feelings expressed in the first category, consternation represented only 15 percent.

The second unfavorable reaction, *tears* (usually on the part of women), was more frequent than *consternation*, accounting for 24 percent of the entire group. Even though tears occupy a large place in the first category, their significance could none the less be called into question. It is perhaps normal for mothers and wives to weep when their sons and husbands leave for war. However, the fact that large numbers of teachers felt compelled to note this reaction would seem to indicate that they saw more in it than a routine expression of the feminine sensibility. In addition, though only women tended to sob in public, it is likely men would also have done so were it not for their sense of propriety. The women's tears cannot therefore be treated as a routine reaction to the approaching separation from their menfolk, especially at a moment such as this, but rather should be seen as an expression of the profound sense of sadness that mobilization prompted in many cases.

The term *sadness* is also generally used in a very strong sense: "An immense sadness can be seen on the faces."[16] The sadness appears to have been deeply felt, the sentiment of an entire population rather than just a few individuals.

The interpretation we have given to the term *consternation* explains why it often goes hand-in-hand with *resignation*. People resigned themselves to the war in the same way they did to natural disasters or calamities about which they could do nothing.

Agitation represents a high proportion of the feelings included in the first category of negative reactions – 19 percent. The inclusion of agitation in the first category could perhaps be disputed. However, though there is inevitably some element of arbitrariness in the distinctions we have made, which we readily admit, this decision is usually justified by the context. The following are two examples:

> An agitated look appeared in all the faces. However, there were no public disturbances. . . .[17]

> At first, there was certainly agitation, but no panic: grief, but no cries or tumult.[18]

Many examples could be adduced. The emotion felt here was not exuberant patriotism. It caught in the throat and was close to the feelings of sadness, anxiety, grief and consternation that we are now examining.

In spite of the prevalence of the negative feelings that we have just analyzed, they were not the only reactions. We have therefore drawn up a second category of calm, composed responses, that is to say, less impulsive, more objective, to a certain extent "middle of the road" responses. The spectrum of terms assigned to this second category is narrower than for the previous category. Three of them seemed most characteristic: *composure, sense of duty* and *courage.* These terms are actually very close to one another and should not be identified in any way with *resignation* because they excluded the passivity inherent in the latter term. This second category represents the response of people who neither sought nor wanted war but who willingly accepted the need to do their duty. As a teacher in Foussignac wrote, "in spite of everything, all intend to do their duty"[19] – in spite of everything, or in other words, in spite of the feelings of anxiety triggered by mobilization.

Composure is often related to calmness, serene behavior derived from serene feelings. It indicates a rational acceptance of events that cannot be prevented.

The third term in the composed category, *courage*, confirms the two preceding terms. One meets a difficult situation with courage, even though those reporting this response are sometimes a little startled by it.

So far we have seen consternation, resignation and courage in the face of the mobilization order. However, the people of Charente also reacted more favorably. From resolve to patriotism to genuine enthusiasm, a certain proportion responded with greater ardor, although these reactions were more infrequent, according to the teachers' reports, representing only 24 percent of the total in Charente.

The word *resolve* seemed to have a quality that carried it beyond mere firmness, thus indicating the transition to a new category. Responding to the mobilization order with *resolve* seemed to imply more enthusiasm than did *composure* or *courage*. In Chantrezac, mobilization "was greeted by most with calm resolve."[20]

It seemed particularly important to emphasize the element of *enthusiasm* because it accounted for a large portion of the feelings assigned to the third category (38 percent), even though representing only 11 percent of all the terms we analyzed. Expressions of enthusiasm may have been confined to a small portion of the population, young people for example, and may have largely surfaced somewhat after the original news of mobilization had arrived. In Boisbreteau, for example, "some pessimists see everything in shades of black. But most quickly get a hold of themselves and the original daze gives way to an extraordinary calm, soon followed by widespread enthusisam."[21] In other cases, enthusiasm was expressed spontaneously and without reservations. A teacher in Douzat noted that "the mobilization was greeted enthusiastically."[22]

The Departure of the Troops

The same methodology was then applied to the sentiments that were expressed at the time when the troops were actually setting off, which occurred over a two-week period beginning on 2 August. Once again we picked out terms expressing the feelings of the mobilized troops and their families as recorded by the teachers of Charente. We collected a total of 288 terms and divided them into three categories: those reflecting feelings of resignation, those reflecting a sense of duty, and those reflecting a surge of patriotic fervor. Fifty-four terms fell into the first category, 103 into the second, and 131 into the third. If the percentage accounted for by each of the three categories is compared, one is struck by the profound shift in opinion that occurred in the space of just a few days, or even a few hours. Sentiments ascribed to the first category tumbled from 57 to 20 percent of the whole, while second category feelings rose from 20 to 37 percent, and third category feelings rose from 23 to 43 percent.

How is this shift in sentiments to be explained? Before attempting to do so, we should explain in greater detail the figures that we have drawn up (Figures 1.4, 1.5 and 1.6).

We have included quite a variety of reactions under the general

Figure 1.4
The Departure of the Troops.
Sentiments of the Population of Charente: Resignation

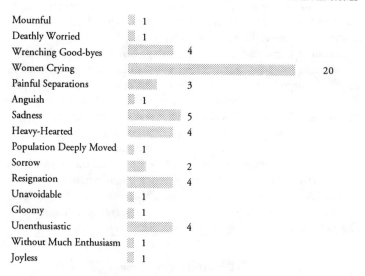

TIMES MENTIONED

Mournful	1
Deathly Worried	1
Wrenching Good-byes	4
Women Crying	20
Painful Separations	3
Anguish	1
Sadness	5
Heavy-Hearted	4
Population Deeply Moved	1
Sorrow	2
Resignation	4
Unavoidable	1
Gloomy	1
Unenthusiastic	4
Without Much Enthusiasm	1
Joyless	1

Figure 1.5
The Departure of the Troops
Sentiments of the Population of Charente: A Sense of Duty

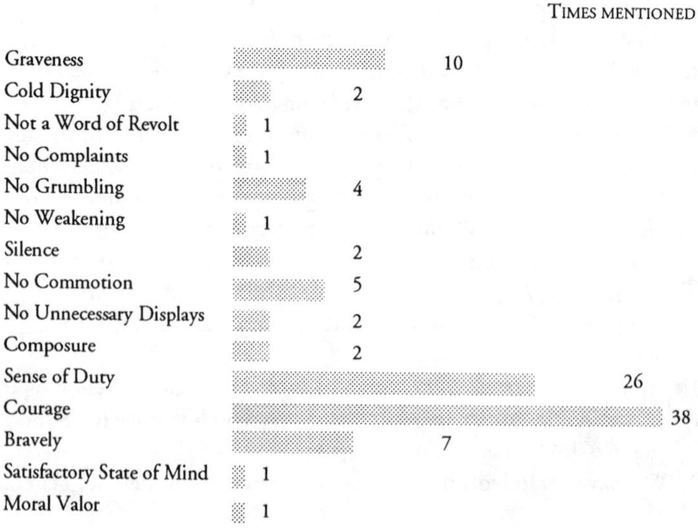

TIMES MENTIONED

Graveness	10
Cold Dignity	2
Not a Word of Revolt	1
No Complaints	1
No Grumbling	4
No Weakening	1
Silence	2
No Commotion	5
No Unnecessary Displays	2
Composure	2
Sense of Duty	26
Courage	38
Bravely	7
Satisfactory State of Mind	1
Moral Valor	1

26

Figure 1.6
The Departure of the Troops
Sentiments of the Population of Charente: Favorable Reactions

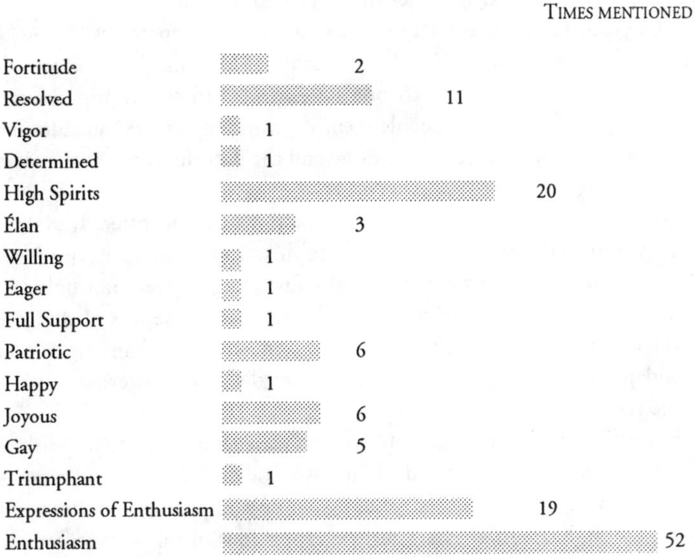

TIMES MENTIONED

Fortitude		2
Resolved		11
Vigor		1
Determined		1
High Spirits		20
Élan		3
Willing		1
Eager		1
Full Support		1
Patriotic		6
Happy		1
Joyous		6
Gay		5
Triumphant		1
Expressions of Enthusiasm		19
Enthusiasm		52

heading of *resignation* because none of these reactions goes so far as to indicate any desire to resist the mobilization order. The reaction that most often reappeared at the time of departure, accounting for 37 percent of the responses in the first category, was tears – once again usually those of women. *Wrenching good-byes* and *painful separations* can be considered very similar reactions.

That many would feel grief at such a time is hardly surprising, even though it was widely believed that the war would be of short duration and the separations correspondingly brief. Caution is therefore advised in interpreting this response. In some cases, the tears may have expressed a negative response to the war, but in general they merely expressed the pain of parting from loved ones as they set out on a perilous adventure. Nonetheless, the frequent reports of tears (though less widespread than at the time when mobilization was first announced) seem to discredit the notion that there was a general air of enthusiasm for the war.

In some records, the word *sadness* or such similar terms as *heavy-hearted* or *anguished* appear. Sometimes, though not often, it is the soldiers who are alluded to: in Alloue, "they departed with heavy hearts."[23]

27

In other cases, no distinction is drawn between the sentiments of those who departed and those who remained behind. However, in general, feelings of sadness were primarily confined to those who remained behind: "the people sadly watched their loved ones depart."[24]

The records speak as well of "resignation," and departures that were "joyless," "unenthusiastic" or "unavoidable": "Mobilization was regarded as an obligation to which one necessarily had to submit, though without joy."[25] For other people seemed primarily to regret abandoning work at home that needed to be done and the peaceful life that they had been leading.

In any case, the feelings of consternation that had often accompanied the initial announcement of mobilization seem to have disappeared. The expressions ascribed to the first category were not only less numerous but also generally less deeply felt than those recorded at the time when mobilization was first announced. The changing mood could perhaps be captured in the phrase: the less consternation, the more resignation.

The first category mood of "we can't avoid it" was distinguished from a second category mood of "it has to be done." These sentiments were often expressed in negative terms – "no complaints," "no weakening" – though the most characteristic expressions of this second category were "the departure accepted with courage," "bravely," with "a sense of duty." The number of times these three expressions appeared were added together, producing the considerable total of 68 percent of the reactions ascribed to the second category. More significant yet is the fact that they represented 18 percent of all reactions in all the categories. This cluster of expressions therefore occupied a place of prime importance among all those reported.

Within the second category, there was no shift in mood comparable to the one we saw in the first category. The mobilization order was received with composure and the soldiers departed with a sense of duty. However, the frequent and growing use of these moderate expressions, devoid of great emphasis, indicates that a considerable proportion of the people of Charente were not swept up by great patriotic fervor. They left for war simply and quietly, as courageously as they went about their daily lives.

Terms that conveyed considerable patriotic zeal were included in a third category that covered almost half of all the terms mentioned. Four of them seemed to epitomize the category: *resolved, high spirited, patriotic* and *enthusiastic*.

We shall confine ourselves here to examining the place of the term *enthusiastic* in the reports of the Charente teachers because the response to mobilization has traditionally been seen as strongly enthusiastic. It accounts for 54 percent of the expressions in the third category – which is very high – and 24 percent of all expressions in all three categories. It therefore slightly surpasses the cluster of phrases around "sense of duty" (23 percent).

In light of this evidence, it would be a vast exaggeration to claim that the Department of Charente was wildly enthusiastic about the war, though it would be equally misguided to underplay the frequency of this sentiment and not to appreciate fully its increased frequency compared to the period when mobilization was first announced. Suffice it to say that we came across "enthusiasm" 29 times in the responses to the first announcement of mobilization and 71 times in the responses to the actual departure.

However, there is reason to ponder the deeper significance of this enthusiasm. Was it superficial or deep-seated? In many cases, nothing would indicate that the enthusiasm was contrived, though it should be noted that most demonstrations of enthusiasm took place at train stations where the passage of decorated trains, decked out with flowers and bellicose inscriptions, and the swirling crowds of departing soldiers and their families tended to stimulate patriotic pride. Some teachers, however, thought that appearances were deceptive. A teacher from Aubeterre commented: "The songs of those who were blustering and boasting rang false to me and it seemed that they had drunk in order to screw up their courage and hide their fear."[26] A teacher from Mansle wrote:

> The cars of the train are decorated with flowers. Vulgar drawings and inscriptions, usually poorly written, indicate hatred of the Hun and hopes for quick revenge. . . . The soldiers sing, joke, call back and forth and attempt most of all to work themselves into a daze. The affectedness of this clamorous gaiety is easy to grasp.[27]

Can the conclusions of our study of Charente be extended to the rest of France? Even if the truth about this department has been discovered, or at least approximated, the same sentiments cannot simply be presumed to have prevailed elsewhere.

Fortunately, less abundant though still substantial records were available elsewhere, enabling us to undertake much the same study in five other departments: Côtes-du-Nord, Gard, Haute-Savoie, Isère, and Hautes-Alpes. The results are very informative and indicate that even though the frequency of the key terms in each category varies somewhat from one department to another, the basic conclusions are the same.

In all six departments, negative reactions formed the largest category of responses when mobilization was first announced, surpassing 70 percent of all reactions in Côtes-du-Nord and 50 percent in Haute-Savoie, with the other departments somewhere between these extremes. On the other hand, while the favorable responses to mobilization surpassed the composed responses in Charente, the favorable category was the least frequent in four of the other six departments (see Figure 1.7). The word *enthusiastic* failed to appear at all in the reports from Isère, Haute-Savoie, and Hautes-Alpes.

However, in these six telltale departments, sentiments falling into the third category – that of *patriotic fervor* – also became most frequent during actual mobilization, representing between 42 and 57 percent of the feelings expressed, for an average of 50 percent. First category sentiments became least frequent in five departments out of six, with percentages fluctuating between 10 and 28 percent on average.

The sudden, profound shift in public opinion was therefore not limited to Charente and occurred in much the same way in the six other departments for which sufficient records are available. In view of the fact that these departments were distributed across France and were of varying political and religious traditions, it seems very likely that conclusions drawn from them can be generalized to the rest of France, even though some departments – especially perhaps those in the East, though no proof is available – may have been more enthusiastic about mobilization.

It could be objected that our historical evidence stems largely from rural areas and is not representative of urban views. Urban opinion is, paradoxically, more difficult to establish because noisy demonstrations by a minority of people can easily leave a false impression. However, an analysis of the prefects' reports and of the news appearing in the rural press about events in the larger cities leads us to conclude that, although the range of opinion was equally broad, city people generally demonstrated more enthusiasm for the war than rural people, especially at the time when mobilization was first announced. There was not a sufficient difference, however, to require a modification of our basic conclusions, which are as follows:

1. The traditional view of French public opinion at the time when the mobilization order was first received is considerably distorted by the failure to account for the consternation felt by a substantial proportion of the population. The frequency and variety of expressions indicating a

negative reaction to the mobilization order – helpless grief or somber resignation – would indicate that it represented a large portion of public opinion in France.

2. At the time the mobilization order was first received, enthusiastic responses were rare, though not entirely absent.

3. By the time the soldiers departed, those who responded negatively to mobilization had become a minority, though they still existed. A certain portion of the population, while accepting the necessity of mobilization, submitted without the slightest enthusiasm.

Figure 1.7

(a) Sentiments of the Population in Six Departments
At the Time When Mobilization was First Announced

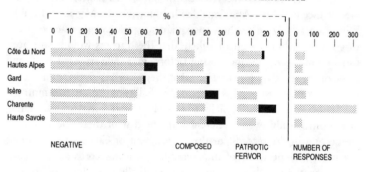

(b) Sentiments of the Population in Six Departments
(mobilized or not)
During Actual Departure

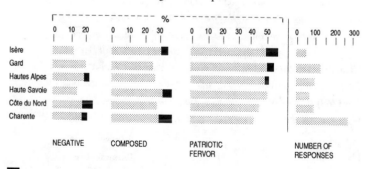

31

Ultimately then, it can be said that the French left for war sadly in some cases, but without grumbling, that they often left quite willingly, and that there was a very widespread feeling that they simply had a duty to perform. Though some of the population waxed enthusiastic, this was not typical of the entire population nor even a majority of it.

One final point remains to be clarified. What accounted for the shift in public opinion, as detected by our quantitative analysis, between the time when mobilization was first announced and the eventual departure of the troops? In other words, why did a population that did not wish for war willingly submit to such a wrenching disruption of its daily life? Obedience to the law of the land would not seem to be a sufficient explanation, as is readily apparent in other circumstances.

Could the teachers' records help to clarify this matter? Neither the vice-chancellor of the Académie de Grenoble nor the Minister of Public Education asked the teachers to explain why the people readily agreed to go to war, but it seems unlikely that the teachers would have been unaware of the various motivating factors and would have failed to echo some of the standard justifications that they heard.

Noteworthy first of all is the paucity of allusions to the two motivating factors that are traditionally advanced: revenge and Alsace-Lorraine. We counted only twenty references to the first of these and eleven to the second in the records for the Department of Charente, in 6.3 and 3.4 percent respectively of the communes whose records are available. Moreover, the people of Charente were actually more inclined to refer to these questions than people in the other telltale departments, as the following table indicates:

Table 1.2 Frequency of Reference to "Revenge" and "Alsace-Lorraine" in Schoolteachers Reports of Popular Sentiment in 1914

DEPARTMENT	REVENGE MENTIONED	ALSACE-LORRAINE MENTIONED
Charente (316 communes)	20 times—6.3%	11 times—3.4%
Côtes-du-Nord (68)	2 times—2.9%	3 times—4.4%
Gard (63)	1 time—1.5%	1 time—1.5%
Hautes-Alpes (80)	5 times—6.2%	1 time—1.2%
Isère (44)	2 times—4.5%	1 time—2.2%
Haute-Savoie (36)	0 times—0%	0 times—0%

These results are astounding. Much of what is often alleged is invalidated by this evidence that the subjects of revenge and Alsace-Lorraine actually played a very small part in shaping public opinion.

The scarcity of references to revenge and Alsace-Lorraine is all the more striking in that those comments that do exist are not always bellicose by any means, as can be seen for instance in the following: "For a long time in our dear land of France, we hoped that never again would there be war. . . . Alsace and Lorraine, to be sure, were not forgotten, but utopians and dreamers hoped that these beloved provinces could be returned to us by a means other than arms."[28]

A second noteworthy fact is that the primary school teachers of Charente, like those in the other departments, reported in great detail on the real motivations of the departing soldiers. They were simple and can be reduced to three complementary propositions: "France did not want war; she was attacked; we will do our duty."[29]

There are virtually no differences of opinion about where the responsibility for the war lay. All references in this regard are to the effect that France was not to blame: "France cannot be blamed"[30]; "Not a word of reproach against the Republic"[31]; or "They know that France did everything it could to preserve the peace with its neighbors, it only asked to be left to live in peace."[32] One teacher notes the extreme importance of this conviction: "You can feel how different the attitude would have been if France had initiated a war of provocation and conquest."[33] The belief in France's peaceful intent was so profound that substantial numbers of people continued to think that an amicable settlement could be found, even after mobilization had begun. We found such sentiments expressed ten times in only five files covering ninety communes in Charente.[34]

Equally unanimously, the French blamed Germany and its emperor for the war: "No one doubts that Germany is the aggressor."[35] From the firm conviction that Germany was responsible for the war, it was easy to go one step further and embrace the notion of "permanent provocation": "Germany has been arrogant for too long a time"[36]; "The Germans have been trying to pick a fight with us for a long time."[37] The result was a surge of anger ripening into hatred of those responsible for the war: "We'll teach those dirty Prussians a lesson."[38]

The third proposition was derived naturally from the second: there was no other possibility but to do one's duty: "The motherland needed them. They would bravely make the sacrifices she asked of them."[39]

These fundamental sentiments were found in virtually all the communes of Charente, while the records from the other departments confirm their basic thrust: France had been attacked and had to defend itself. It is easy to understand that such a view could inspire enthusiasm or determination or resignation but that it was not likely to incite Frenchmen to resist.

This, we believe, is the key to the shift in public opinion between the first announcement of mobilization and actual departure. It expressed the indignation of a people firmly convinced of their own pacifism and of the provocations to which they had been subjected. The result was a negative reaction to the surprise announcement of mobilization, soon followed by a surging desire to defend oneself.

Is there not however a certain contradiction between the initial negative reaction to mobilization and the conviction that so quickly took root that Germany had been seeking a quarrel with France for a long time? If the public had really been convinced that war was inevitable sooner or later, would the outcome of the final crisis not have appeared natural and fully expected? At first, at least, this was hardly the case.

We believe that the contradiction is more apparent than real, because the impression of incessant German provocations was grafted onto the conviction that France had been the innocent victim of attack. This helped to explain an event that, by its suddenness, seemed to defy all logic. It was because the public believed that France had been the victim of attack that it was prepared to believe subsequently that France had long been subjected to German threats. This was a natural outcome of collective and individual psychology. An unforeseen event causes impressions that had been vague and haphazard to coalesce, creating the impression that one had long been aware of what had just been discovered. It was all the easier for French public opinion to adopt this view because belief in a German threat had long existed, and not only in nationalist circles. Even though nationalist views had little effect on broad public opinion, as we believe was the case, they were in the wind to provide the necessary explanations once a moment of crisis arrived. In this sense, nationalism can be said to have played a role in the public response to the war. In the main, however, it was the conviction of unprovoked aggression that determined the attitudes of the French and that explains why the war was accepted by almost the entire population. This conviction also explains why the French departed without the enthusiasm of conquering heroes but with the resolve of those who feel they have a duty to perform. "The men for the most part were not in a joyous mood; they were determined, which is much better."[40]

At the outset of this chapter, we posed the question of whether public opinion in France was epitomized by sadness or a belligerent élan at the time of mobilization. Though the methodology we have employed can perhaps be criticized and improved, several points have been demonstrated beyond, we think, any reasonable doubt:

1. A clear distinction needs to be drawn between the moment when

the mobilization order first arrived and the actual departure of the troops. The traditional failure to do this has prevented scholars from understanding the true state of public opinion. As a general rule and especially in times of crisis, studies of public opinion should be confined to as short and as homogenous a period of time as the sources will allow.

2. It is no longer possible to claim that France was swept by a wave of enthusiasm for the war as the troops mobilized.[41] Some outward signs of this have been unduly emphasized, leading people to draw false conclusions. A certain portion of the French population did respond enthusiastically, but this portion was a small minority.

3. In any case, the sentiments of Frenchmen at the time of mobilization were diverse, contradictory, and far from unanimous. This conclusion may appear banal and obvious, but it needs to be stated.

Notes to Chapter 1

1. Departmental archives, Côtes-du-Nord, series R.

2. Ch. Petit-Dutaillis, "L'Appel de guerre en Dauphiné," *Annales de l'Université de Grenoble* 27, no. 1 (1915).

3. J.-J. Becker, "L'Appel de guerre en Dauphiné," *Le Mouvement social* 49 (October-November 1964), pp. 33–44.

4. Y. Lequin, "1914-1916. L'opinion publique en Haute-Savoie devant la guerre," *Revue savoisienne* (1967), pp. 11–18.

5. P. Bouyoux, *L'Opinion publique à Toulouse pendant la Première Guerre mondiale* (Toulouse, 1970), Microfiches Hachette, p. 60.

6. J. Ozouf, "L'Instituteur 1900–1914," *Le Mouvement social* (July-September 1963).

7. G. Castellan, "Histoire et mentalité collective," *Bulletin de la Société d'Histoire moderne* (1964), no. 2.

8. Circular of 18 September 1914.

9. Departmental archives of Charente, J 76 to J 95.

10. *Ibid.* J 82.

11. *Ibid.* J 85.

12. *Ibid.* J 93, commune of Saint-Projet.

13. *Ibid.* J 85, commune of La Magdelaine.

14. *Ibid.* J 77.

15. *Ibid.* J 78.

16. *Ibid.* J 79, Commune of Champniers.

17. *Ibid.* J 77, Commune of Baignes-Sainte-Radegonde.

18. *Ibid.* J 78, Commune of Brettes.

19. *Ibid.* J 82.

20. *Ibid.* J 79.

21. *Ibid.* J 78.

22. *Ibid.* J 81.

23. *Ibid.* J 76.

24. *Ibid.* J 77, Commune of Bazac

25. *Ibid.* J 81, Commune of Curac.

26. *Ibid.* J 77.

27. *Ibid.* J 86.

28. *Ibid.* J 82, Commune of Fontclaireau

29. *Ibid.* J 92, Commune of Saint-Gervais.

30. *Ibid.* J 93, Commune of Saint-Quentin-en-Chalais.

31. *Ibid.* J 93, Communes of Saint-Médard et Auge.

32. *Ibid.* J 90, Commune of Rivières.

33. *Ibid.* J 92, Commune of Saint-Christophe-de-Chalais.

34. *Ibid.* J 87 to 91.

35. *Ibid.* J 80, Commune of Chassors.

36. *Ibid.* J 93, Commune of Saint-Maurice.

37. *Ibid.* J 89, Commune of Rancogne.

38. *Ibid.* J 90, Commune of Reparsac.

39. *Ibid.* J 85, Commune of Lonnes.

40. Marc Bloch, *Souvenirs de guerre (1914–1918)*, (Paris: A. Colin, 1969), p. 10.

41. This is shown in greater detail in the third part of our work entitled *1914: Comment les Français sont entrés dans la guerre. Contribution à l'étude de l'opinion publique, printemps-été 1914* (Paris: Presses de la Fondation nationale des Sciences Politiques, 1977), which inspired this article. For another example, see P.J. Flood, *France 1914–18. Public Opinion and the War Effort* (London: Macmillan, 1990).

Also see Y. Pourcher, "Un quotidien des années de guerre: Les signes d'une rupture du temps, des habitudes et des normes dans *Le Journal* de l'Indre et Loire (1914–1918)," *Sociétés* 33 (September 1991), pp. 277 and 280.

2

The Radical Socialist Party During the First World War

Serge Berstein

It is certainly a challenge to undertake a study of the Radical Socialist Party during the First World War. How could this party, belatedly and incompletely organized, without a recognized leader, and embodying a very vague ideology, withstand the tempests of war and preserve the minimal amount of cohesion necessary to shape the opinions and actions of its members during the war? In many respects, the substance of the party – its members, committees, and federations – evaporated after the declaration of war, leaving very little behind to constitute a party. However, this objective view of reality does not conform to the general feeling as expressed by public opinion, politicians, and even historians. In their view, Radical parliamentarians, ministers, and newspapers continued to speak for the party, as they drowned what was distinctive about Radical Party convictions in the broad consensus of the *union sacrée*.

The views expressed by Radical parliamentarians, ministers and newspapers during the war certainly carried some weight, especially as they were not without influence among ordinary party members (even though party ties were very loose), and they attempted after the war to have the attitudes they had adopted during the war accepted as peacetime Radical policy. In this, however, they met with little success. Deprived of all contacts with party members during the war and cut off from their roots, they ended up representing no one but themselves. The history of the Radical Party during the First World War is first and foremost the tragic somnolescence of a formidable political organization. Only this enabled its rudderless leadership to allow its image to be

Notes for Chapter 2 can be found on page 52.

totally deformed through participation in the *union sacrée,* an experience that inflicted wounds that took many years to heal.

A Disorganized and Apathetic Party

On the eve of the Great War, Radicalism was a power to be reckoned with in French politics. In the elections of 1914, Radical candidates garnered 13.38 percent of the votes cast, which put them in second place slightly ahead of the United Socialists at 12.60 percent and slightly behind the Democratic Republican Party at 13.99 percent (although the latter party had very little real organization in the country).[1] The strength of the Radical Party was based in particular on the support it received in four regions: southwestern France, where it dominated a compact series of departments stretching from Landes to Hérault; central France, with a core area in Lot, Cantal and Corrèze and outcroppings in Creuse, Puy-de-Dôme, Lozère, and Ardèche; east central France, in the departments of Jura, Saône-et-Loire, Côte-d'Or, and Ain; and finally, the departments of the Paris region, with the exception of Seine.[2] This support for the Radical Party produced 165 parliamentarians elected under the banner of the United Radicals. Although this implied clear allegiance to the Radical Party, only 136 of these candidates actually became members of the Radical parliamentary group once the election was over.[3]

There were two main reasons for supporting the Radicals. First was the party's image as a descendant of the French Revolution, embodying its ideals of liberty, fraternity, and social progress and thereby appealing to large numbers of rural and middle-class voters and even some workers. Most of all, though, support for the party was based on the existence in France of a series of Radical committees, often quite old, which had been strongholds of "Republican" ideals during the heroic struggles surrounding the Dreyfus affair and the policies identified with Combes. It is claimed there were about a thousand committees with a total of 200,000 members, which would have made the Radical Party the largest political formation in the prewar era, indeed the only real "mass party" in France at the time.[4]

Although there was considerable grassroots support for the Radical philosophy in France, the party failed to translate it into commensurate political influence. This was largely due to the weak, fragmented nature of the party organization. The Radical Republican and Radical Socialist Party was weighed down throughout its history by the terms of its creation. The party's central organs, which supposedly established its official views and policies, consisted of little more than a superstructure appended to pre-existing grassroots committees that had come together in 1901 and whose activities it struggled to coordinate with only limited success. The continual insistence before 1914 on the "autonomy of the committees" was a reminder of the non-binding nature of the deal that the founding fathers – Léon Bourgeois, Brisson and Goblet – had offered the "Republicans" in order to induce them to join the new party: "No sacrifices will be demanded of anyone. It is a free, perfectly free understanding at which they have arrived."[5]

The situation changed somewhat after 1901 to be sure. The formation of the United Socialist Party eliminated the hope of uniting all "republicans" and forced the Radicals to make further efforts to define their ideology and organize themselves. However, the development of central institutions was resisted by the committees and parliamentarians who did not want to have their freedom of action curtailed. Similarly, the attempt to join committees together in department-wide federations failed, with only twenty such federations formed by the time the war broke out.[6]

Under these conditions, the party's central organs were only able to formulate very broad, vague policies and did not have any genuine decision-making abilities. In addition, the Executive Committee, which included elected representatives from the departments as well as members by virtue of the offices they held in the party, failed to develop into the type of standing Radical parliament with monthly meetings envisaged by the party statutes. Instead it became a club dominated by Parisians and parliamentarians, who were the only people able to attend the meetings.[7] Furthermore, the party president was not so much the leader of French Radicalism as its symbol. The job of party president tended to be an honorific position that did not imbue the incumbent with any additional powers. As a result, the Radical Party had no real leader. This failing made it impossible for the party to wield power and reduced it to awarding its votes to Prime Ministers from other parties. Neither Combes, who was only a symbol now, nor Pelletan, a popular orator at party conventions, nor *a fortiori* Delpech, Lafferre, or Vallé, who were successive party presidents, actually led the Radical Party at any time. The only president of the prewar period who made a serious attempt at organization and coordination was Joseph Caillaux, a recent party member who became its president in 1913. He attempted for instance to gain control over the party by forcing the deputies to form a single group answerable to the Executive Committee.[8] However, these efforts were torpedoed by the scandal in the president's private life that exploded in March 1914, and when war broke out shortly afterwards, the Radicals still did not have a strong party organization. The slow and patient effort to restrict the parliamentarians' freedom of action and to force them to respect decisions made at party conventions failed in a similar manner.

Although the Radicals did not succeed in endowing their party with a strong internal organization, they did manage to develop a coherent platform. While the party convention of 1901 had produced an intentionally vague and imprecise program, with the express intent of not alienating anyone who considered himself a Republican, the pressure of events forced the party, convening in Nancy in 1907, to adopt a much more definitive program, which was then further refined by successive party assemblies. The disintegration of the *bloc des gauches* (left organizations' alliance) eliminated the advantages of extremely vague party programs, while the emergence of the Socialist Party (1905) increased the pressure to draw a clear distinction between Radicals and "collectivists," lest the former appear to be just another variety of "reds," albeit somewhat lighter in hue. The end of the great era of militant anti-clericalism and the assumption of power by governments that were nominally Radical, although they spent most of their time attempting to suppress working-class agitation, made it essential to set forth a definite program that would define the social goals of the Radical Party and inspire government action.

Reduced to its two basic features, the Radical Party program can be quickly summarized: the defense of traditional French institutions and social reform. The Radicals were fully integrated into the republican regime with which they identified fully and whose forms they considered unalterable because already politically perfect. No longer did they demand the elimination of quasi-monarchical institutions that had emerged at the time of the Moral Order, for instance the Senate (where Radicals were now solidly ensconced). At most, the Radicals wanted to democratize the Senate through the election of Senate delegates by universal suffrage.[9] Even changing such a contingent factor as the type of electoral system could strike the Radicals as an attempt to subvert the Republic that they were sworn to defend: when some Radicals decided to claim that proportional elections represented the republican ideal, a few realists reminded them that voting by *arrondissement* had proved its value by producing left-oriented majorities in the Chamber of Deputies. Meanwhile, some ideologues denounced proportional elections as a disruptive element in the *bloc des gauches*.[10]

Solidly entrenched as the ever-vigilant champion of the very institutions it used to decry, the Radical Party was left to deliberate upon its social program, which would be the key to its relations with both the moderates and the socialists. It came out in favor of gradual reform, placing the party halfway between the liberals and the socialists. The Radicals rejected the socialist notion of class struggle and even any notion of class at all, which they saw as a source of division, hatred and violence.[11] They confirmed their role as defenders of private property, "which they did not wish to begin or even prepare to begin to eliminate."[12] On the other hand, the Radicals denounced the "indifference" of the liberals who were allegedly prepared to sacrifice little people to the greed and egotism of the powerful.[13] In place of each extreme, the Radicals offered a reform program that took as its theoretical basis the "solidarism" advocated by Léon Bourgeois and that saw the state as the master architect. The Radicals wanted to limit the power of capitalism by returning to the nation "*de facto* monopolies."[14] The social structures would be changed to eliminate the wage earning class and constitute a society of equals in which everybody owned his own tools or land, possibly through the establishment of cooperatives.[15] These social reforms became very important to the Radical Party because they constituted its key difference from other political parties.

The party's foreign affairs policy was inspired by the same sense of the golden mean. In contrast to the attitudes inspired by Hervé, which induced many socialists to spurn any display of patriotism, the Radicals took pride in their loyalty to the Jacobin tradition and were eager to proclaim their love of the motherland and devotion to the army.[16] Unlike the extreme nationalists, however, they sought inspiration in the ideas of Léon Bourgeois, who applied the same principle of solidarity to foreign affairs. Rejecting the "might is right" ideology of the great powers at the turn of the twentieth century, the Radicals advocated the development of an international code based on the right of peoples to self-determination. This would be carried out through plebiscites and guaranteed by a "Society of Civilized Nations" equipped with an international police.[17]

The popularity of the Radicals in the early part of the century was largely based on this republican program featuring social reform (which was the essence of Radicalism and not a deviation from basic principles as in the case of the socialists) and a noble idealism in international relations (preceding in fact that of Woodrow Wilson). These policies placed the Radicals firmly on the left of the political spectrum, as could be seen in the results of the 1914 legislative elections, when 51 percent of the Radical deputies were elected at the second round of votes, with

40 percent of them owing their success to left-wing voters.

What, however, remained of this left-wing party – powerful and influential, though poorly organized, and incarnating the France of the golden mean with a program for slow, gradual reform – after the declaration of war?

The first effect of the war was to destroy whatever structure the Radical Party did have. The fragile party organization, painstakingly constructed after 1901, simply vanished. At the grassroots level, mobilization disrupted the local committees, thus cutting off the party hierarchy from the ordinary members. The suspension of political activity therefore devastated the foundations on which the party rested. The few departmental federations that had been painstakingly formed became hollow shells, degenerating in the best of cases to a few local notables or elected members holding occasional meetings. However, political developments during the war alienated ever more of these local notables from the Radical Party, and by 1919 – one year after the conflict ended – fewer than fifteen departments still had a party organization.[18]

The central party hierarchy, deprived of any impulses from the grassroots, grew apathetic. The lack of any political life during the first few years of the war meant that no party conventions were held and that no official Radical Party activities took place at all before October 1917. Similarly, the Executive Committee ceased to meet. Joseph Caillaux, elected party president at the Pau convention in 1913, remained remarkably discreet, less because he was still smarting from the events of March 1914 than because he neither could nor wanted to claim the effective leadership of the party. No party convention could be held to confirm him in his position, and in any case, not many Radical deputies would have endorsed his leadership when he appeared to be the leading advocate of peace without victory, which was not a popular option among the Radicals in the *union sacrée*.[19] Caillaux also tended to attract many "pacifist" supporters, among whom the members of his own party would not even have formed a majority. Under the circumstances, Caillaux could only be hindered and embarrassed by his position in the Radical Party, whose functions he carried out only in a theoretical sense.[20]

After the war, party members were bitter about the consequences of a poor party structure and their apparent elimination from the French political scene. According to Secretary-General Bouffandeau, these years "were marked by a morbid discouragement, or rather political indifference. The old committees no longer met, and no new ones were formed. The youth seemed indifferent to politics and to us. We had been victimized by the self-denial which we had practiced for the sake of the motherland – for while the Radical Party was quiet in the trenches and behind the lines, you know what religious proselytizing was going on at the front and in the medical units, and you know how quickly the other parties began to propagandize again."[21]

As a result of the paralysis of the party's institutions, its members in parliament became its exclusive spokesmen. However, by subordinating Radical Party beliefs to the *union sacrée*, they robbed the party of its essence and severely damaged its image as a left-wing group.

The Radical Party's Loss of Identity in the Union Sacrée

A patriotic heir to the Jacobin tradition and a confirmed champion of a strong national defense, the Radical Party leapt into the *union sacrée* without any self-examination or internal debate. Did the *union sacrée* not embody the domestic truce, the fraternal union of all patriotic Frenchmen against the aggressor? It would be criminal not to lend one's full support.[22] Throughout the war, Radical parliamentarians therefore supported this common front without hesitation. Radicals participated in the Viviani government of 26 August 1914 (Malvy at Interior, A. Sarraut at Public Education, Doumergue at Colonies, and Bienvenu-Martin at Labor), while three other party members served as undersecretaries of state.[23] Even more telling was the Radical Party participation in the Briand government, since the Prime Minister sought to gain the party's support by including among the four ministers of state the two most symbolic representatives of Radicalism: Léon Bourgeois, the theorist of solidarism and the most moderate of Radical ministers, and Emile Combes, the old leader of militant anti-clericalism.[24] All in all Briand, like his successors Ribot, Painlevé, and Clemenceau, found at least half his ministers among Radical parliamentarians.[25] During the entire four years of war, some ministries such as Interior, Colonies, and Public Education were virtual Radical Party preserves. In return, Radical parliamentarians maintained their loyalty to the various governments through thick and thin, constituting the core of their majorities and ensuring their survival through difficult situations.[26]

But was this unstinting devotion to the *union sacrée* exclusively the product of patriotic self-abnegation and the party's willingness to sacrifice its political convictions for the greater good of the nation at war? In fact, there was a much more profound reason for such unflinching loyalty: the party simply lost touch with the essence of Radicalism when it plunged into an alliance saturated with rightist values and points of reference. There should be no illusions about the nature of the internal truce wrought by the *union sacrée*. The champions of the social status quo greatly reinforced their position by contrasting divisive politics with unifying nationhood and demanding that internal political disagreements be foresworn for the sake of national salvation. Proponents of social change were urged to mute their demands and check their desire for reform or revolution for the sake of France. This tended as well to cast their former political activism in a very negative light. "Politics" was discredited during the war years, and no party was more closely identified with the intense politicking of the prewar era than the Radical Party.[27] Feeling the need to vindicate themselves, the Radicals did all they could to remove any stigma by zealously affirming their "national" credentials.

Meanwhile, the lack of political debate during the war masked the reality of what had happened under the *union sacrée*. Only in 1919 did it become clear that the Radical Party had been almost totally co-opted by the right in the areas of economic policy, social policy, and domestic policy. Participation in the *union sacrée* led straight to participation in the *Bloc national*, which explains the plan to form an alliance between the Radical Party and the Democratic Alliance.[28]

There was at least one area, international relations, where the Radical Party clearly sacrificed much of its substance as soon as the war began through its participation in an *union sacrée* dominated by the views of the right. This was virtually the only area, moreover, where issues could be handled in full public view. Under the *union sacrée*, the party soon jettisoned all the noble ideals set forth by Léon Bourgeois and acclaimed by the prewar party conventions concerning the right of peoples to self-determination and the creation of a new international order in which right and justice would triumph and from which military conquest would be banned.

Two examples will serve to illustrate the chasm between the Radicals' theoretical program and their actual policies under the *union sacrée*. The first is related to France's war aims, which were only explicitly stated in June 1917 by the Ribot government. They included, besides the restitution of Alsace-Lorraine, a return to the borders of 1790 in northeastern France and the detachment from the German *Reich* of the territories on the left bank of the Rhine not already annexed by France in order to form a neutral, autonomous buffer state temporarily occupied by French troops.[29] The Radical Party would obviously approve the restitution of Alsace-Lorraine, annexed by Germany in violation of the right of peoples to self-determination, but what about the violation of the same principle inherent in the French government's intentions to annex German territory on the left bank of the Rhine and to create a Rhenish state, independent and no doubt under heavy French influence? Not only did the Radicals vote massively in favor of the government's war aims, in contrast to the socialists, but through Charles Dumont, deputy for Jura, Le Bail-Maignan, deputy for Finistère, and René Renoult, deputy for Haute-Saône, they even proposed the parliamentary agenda approving these war aims. In the agenda, the Radicals' sweeping statement of confidence in the government clashes curiously with a reiteration of the idealistic principles which they claimed still to support, even though there was very little evidence of them in the stated war aims:

> Far from any thoughts of conquest or subjugation of foreign populations, [the Chamber] expects that the efforts of the armies of the French Republic and the Allied armies will make it possible, once Prussian militarism has been defeated, to obtain lasting guarantees of peace and independence for all peoples, whether small or large, through an organization, now being prepared, called the League of Nations.[30]

This attitude on the part of Radical deputies accurately reflected feelings in the party hierarchy, thus illustrating the extent to which the war had distorted prewar Radical principles. There were accordingly many Radicals among the leaders and members of the Committee for the Left Bank of the Rhine, which rallied many members of parliament, intellectuals, businessmen, and journalists around a program based on the creation of a buffer state on the left bank of the Rhine.[31] Founded by Tréfeu, a former secretary of the Radical Party leader Lockroy, the Committee was led from its creation by an eminent member of the Radical Party, Jean-Louis Bonnet, president of the Federation of the Seine and an outstanding activist of the prewar period.[32] When the Radical Party was reconstituted in October 1917, it adopted the Committee's views without a moment's hesitation. A Radical deputy named Franklin-Bouillon, who led the Federation of Seine-et-Oise, became the Committee's spokesman on the party's Executive Committee. At the same time in the official *Bulletin du parti*, Albert Milhaud, who would later become the party's secretary-general, outlined the status which the Rhenish state would have, namely a neutral territory whose independence would be guaranteed by France, Great Britain, and Belgium. Since it would not be large enough to assure its own defense, this would be provided by the three protecting powers, whose armies would also guard "the avenues of their capitals and the keys to their great cities." Finally, the economic prosperity of the

Rhenish state would be assured, "without detriment to our own," through a customs union or commercial treaties with the peoples of western Europe.[33] It was not only the nationalistic passions of a people at war which pushed the Radicals to embrace French chauvinism, but also, as we have seen, the economic advantages which victory could confer and of which they were well aware. For instance Edouard Herriot, the future prophet of collective security and the spirit of Geneva, was happy to accept in the summer of 1917 the presidency of the Support Committee for the Federation of Anti-Germanic Leagues of the East and South-East, composed of a group of industrialists eager to gain every advantage they could after the war was over in the competition with Austrian and German products.[34]

A similar distortion of prewar Radical principles can be seen in attitudes to the Bolshevik revolution in Russia. There was of course no ideological affinity between Lenin and the Radical Party, and it is not surprising that the Radicals were hostile to a revolution which smothered all the hopes raised in February for the emergence of a liberal democratic regime.[35] However, as was amply demonstrated during the interwar period, belief in the right of peoples to self-determination implies abstention from ideological struggles in foreign countries. Under wartime conditions, though, the Radicals adopted a very different position. In the summer of 1918 Kerensky, the former head of the provisional government in Russia, visited the Radical Party offices in France in order to request the party to do what it could to pressure the French government into intervening militarily against the Soviet regime. The party's Executive Committee examined the matter, and their discussions reveal the attitude which French Radicals adopted toward Russian Bolshevism: it was a German creation intended to divide the Allied camp by weakening Russia and making it easy prey for the German armies. Under such circumstances, intervention was justified in order to prevent Germany from seizing a decisive advantage. Bolshevism had to be crushed – not, of course, out of self-interest, but "in order to save the Russian Republic from the mortal disease implanted by Prussian militarism." In a typical gesture for the time, the Executive Committee dismissed as inopportune and wrong-headed the timid objection raised by one of its members: "Won't we raise the entire Russian people against us and infringe on the right of democracies to self-determination?"[36]

Radical Party participation in the *union sacrée* therefore eventuated in a loss of identity. The ideas and principles which constituted the essence of Radicalism were thrown overboard in favor of policies that were rooted in and ultimately served the political interests of the right, although they certainly also reflected the wartime national consensus.

What was the difference between a nationalist such as Barrès and a Radical who shared his party's views on France's war aims or armed intervention in Russia? In so far as social and political policy were concerned, the distinctions became so slight that upstanding Radicals appeared together on a common list with Barrès in the 1919 elections. The only major issue still separating large numbers of Radicals from the right was secularism.

How can this disintegration of Radicalism within the *union sacrée* be explained? It cannot be seriously claimed that the policies which the Radical Party had adopted ever since the turn of the century prove that it was already drifting to the right, i.e., that its base of support was in the bourgeoisie and that the war only served to accentuate this trend. This is to ignore the decisive influence of Radicalism's political traditions which firmly anchored it on the left and which proved solid enough in the postwar period to drag the party out of the alliance with the right undertaken during the war. It was the war which was the crucial factor, a traumatic enough experience in itself to blot out for a time the party's political heritage. The consciousness of the danger facing France and the utmost priority that had to be attached to saving the nation certainly played a large role, although wartime propaganda, censorship, and slanted information also had an effect. The war caused a political upheaval affecting all parties. The right adapted easily because its political touchstones remained largely unchanged and its outlook served as the basis of the *union sacrée*. French socialism, on the other hand, underwent a severe crisis, but its well-articulated beliefs and strong organization helped to preserve a minimal amount of party unity, even though it was always on shaky ground. Radicalism suffered the most and disintegrated almost totally because of its weak party structures, lack of centralization, and a program which had been developed only recently and remained a vague and nebulous collection of ideas which allowed each group to emphasize whatever it wished. As a result the Radicals were engulfed by the *union sacrée*, forced to abandon many of their convictions, and soon identified with the right, whose policies dominated. The Radical Party's plight was all the more desperate because Frenchmen did not feel inclined to reward it for its unstinting devotion to the *union sacrée*; instead, it emerged from the war totally discredited.

The Radical Party Discredited

Until 1917, the Radical Party still appeared to be a major pillar of the *union sacrée* and could seriously claim to be making a pivotal contribution to the French war effort. With censorship hiding the disagreements among the country's leaders from public view and with Caillaux acting very prudently in his role as virtual leader of a *revolving* majority,[37] there was little to tarnish the image of a great patriotic party doing its utmost for the national cause. Radicals certainly had to overcome some misgivings based on the fact that it was largely they who had kept the political debate boiling before the war, but they seemed to have done everything possible during the war to redeem themselves.

The situation changed, however, during the summer of 1917, when a series of "affairs" became public, severely staining the image of the Radical Party at a time when it was trying to reconstitute itself. First in August 1917 came the forced resignation of Malvy, the solidly entrenched Minister of the Interior since 1914, who had become a leading figure in the party. The spark that ignited the uproar was the revelation of Malvy's relations with Almereyda, the editor of the newspaper *Le Bonnet rouge* who had been convicted of carrying on secret communications with the enemy,[38] although the fundamental reason was that Malvy was generally suspected of sympathizing with pacifist-minded socialists and labor unionists. On various occasions, pressure had been exerted on Briand and Ribot when they were Prime Ministers to rid themselves of their Minister of the Interior.[39] In both cases, Radical Socialist solidarity had saved the deputy from Lot, but in August 1917 his colleagues ceased to protect him out of fear that they themselves might be implicated in treason. Clemenceau played a major role in this change of attitude and in the evolution of the entire Malvy affair by accusing the Minister of the Interior during a debate in the Senate of having betrayed the national interest by protecting the pacifist agitation of leftist minorities and by tolerating the anti-militarist activities of journalists allegedly in the pay of Germany.[40] In this way, the view gained currency that pacifism was treasonous, a notion which became a firm government policy when Clemenceau became Premier.[41] In August 1917, however, such charges were still hurled only at particular individuals and not at the entire party to which they belonged. Thus another Radical named Steeg was able to replace Malvy as Minister of the Interior.

The situation changed for the worse in September 1917 with the revelation of further "affairs," in which the accusors blithely equated pacifism with treason. Treason was certainly involved in the case of the Radical deputy Turmel, accused of having been paid by the Germans. However, when an adventurer named Bolo was accused of acting as a middleman for the Germans in their attempts to purchase the *Journal,* did the fact that Joseph Caillaux knew him make the Radical Party leader suspect as well?

The entire situation had less to do with the actual facts than with the political purposes to which they could be put, proving once again how illusory was the domestic truce under the *union sacrée*. Any incriminating evidence was very tenuous. The only real reproach that could be made against Malvy is that he had some sympathy for left-wing activists and shielded them from prosecution for their opinions. In other words, he upheld the spirit of the *union sacrée*. He certainly cannot be held responsible for the fact that some individuals acting on Germany's behalf succeeded in penetrating pacifist circles. In so far as Caillaux is concerned, he was guilty only of the carelessness which he so often displayed during his career, allowing people of doubtful reputation who later ran afoul of the law to penetrate his circle. Bolo in 1917 was in the same tradition as the crook Rochette before the war and the shady journalist Dubarry in the 1920s.

For the rest, what can be said about the action which led to Caillaux's arrest, namely sequestering in a safe in Rome files imprudently named "Rubicon" which contained plans for an authoritarian reorganization of the state and the laying of criminal charges against those political leaders who had declared war, headed by the President of the Republic?[42] These files are not so much evidence of an organized plot against the Republican form of government as of a lack of political sense and of foolishness in treating hastily written notes based on an impetuous analysis of the facts as if they were valuable documents. The charges laid against the two Radical leaders were flimsy, and the High Court of Justice found them both innocent of treason. It bent over backwards however to find them guilty of other charges. Malvy was banished for five years in August 1918 for "breach of duty,"[43] and Caillaux was sentenced in April 1920 for imprudent acts serving enemy interests to three years in prison, five years of banishment from Paris and other large cities, and ten years of withdrawal of civil rights.[44] These were eminently political judgements which only underline the eagerness of the senators to uphold the right-wing interpretation of the *union sacrée* which predominated after 1917.

The basically political nature of the Malvy and Caillaux affairs is not in doubt. It was Clemenceau who blew the Malvy affair up to its full proportions and had Caillaux arrested in January 1918. He intentionally discredited the two most compelling Radical Party leaders as much as possible, thus eliminating the possibility that they might induce Radical deputies to join a majority of the left and sign a conciliatory peace with

Germany. Lucien Le Foyer, a former Radical deputy from Paris, wrote the following about Clemenceau, who had become Prime Minister in November 1917: "He arrests him because public opinion, whether rightly or wrongly, has made the name Caillaux synonymous with peace."[45] By thus destroying through an accusation of treason and imprisonment a man who could have offered a credible political alternative, Clemenceau eliminated all possibility of it. Well aware, however, of the weakness of the legal case, Clemenceau avoided a trial and awaited the eve of victory before sending Caillaux before the High Court of Justice.[46]

The blow struck at the two Radical leaders devastated their party as well, whether intentionally or not. Some Radicals saw Clemenceau's political exploitation of the affairs of late 1917 as an attempt to settle an old score dating back to his days as a Prime Minister in 1906-1909, when he had very poor relations with the Radical Party, which constantly denounced his policy of social repression and delaying reform and finally succeeded in overthrowing him.[47] According to Lucien Le Foyer, for example, "It is the Radical Party that is being targeted through Malvy and Caillaux."[48] The operation mounted by Clemenceau – whatever the reasons for it – was greatly facilitated by the reaction, or lack of it, on the part of Radical Party members. The Radicals' loss of identity in the *union sacrée* had gone so far that they observed the political maneuvering against their party leaders without so much as raising a complaint. Very few Radical parliamentarians dared to break with the majority and vote against Clemenceau.[49] Most clutched the *union sacrée* all the more closely to their breasts and forgot that they had ever been party colleagues of Caillaux and Malvy.

In October 1917, at the time when the campaign against the two leaders was reaching its height, a decision was suddenly made to hold a Radical Party convention, the first since the Pau convention of 1913 that had made Caillaux party president.[50] The purpose of the new convention was clear: to demonstrate that the party had an independent existence and was not identical with its former leader, against whom such grave charges had been laid. The convention brought together those Radical officials from before the war who still wished to associate with the party's parliamentarians and had as its highlight, of course, the selection of a new party president. This first plenary assembly of Radical Party leaders since the outbreak of war quickly revealed the discomfort of some old Radicals with the openly conservative slant of the *union sacrée*, which was dragging the party toward the right. Some voices rose to denounce censorship and to demand a "social democratic government." The election for party president saw the victory of Charles Debierre, a senator for the Nord and one of the party leaders from the Combes era who was the candidate of the party's left wing, over Couyba, a senator for Haute-Saône who was backed by René Renoult, a personal friend of Clemenceau.[51]

This swing to the left had few consequences however. The right-wing current within the *union sacrée* was simply too strong for the Radical Party to resist. Without really canvassing the views of the party members, the new leaders elected at the Paris convention immediately fell in line with the party parliamentarians who wished to continue working closely with the majority. Despite the inclination of some deputies to ally themselves with the socialists and attempt to form a left-wing government, the Radical-Socialist parliamentarians together with the party office (the first Cadillac Committee) agreed on 16 November in a vote of fifty-nine to twenty-six to authorize those deputies who had been asked to enter the Clemenceau government to do so.[52] The newly reconstituted party was accordingly very reluctant to intervene in defense of its former leaders who had been accused of treason and carted off to prison. Indeed several Radical senators, and by no means the least prominent, voted in August 1918 to condemn Malvy for breach of duty.[53] Alfred Dominique, a member of the left wing of the party and the secretary-general of the Federation of the Seine, demanded in a letter sent to the Executive Committee on 25 August 1918 that these senators be expelled from the party,[54] but procedural maneuvers lasting until March 1919 deferred the question so long that the party's Discipline Commission declared that it could not take action.[55] All this shillyshallying is clear evidence of the Radical Party's strong desire to avoid appearing as "the party of Caillaux and Malvy" and to eschew all association with men whose patriotism was in question. The party's participation in the *union sacrée* therefore induced it not only to adopt a rightist political program, which it had previously decried, but also to deny those of its leaders who remained faithful to the spirit of prewar Radicalism.

In the immediate aftermath of the war, the Radical Party remained deeply shaken by the consequences of its participation in the *union sacrée*. Thrown into disarray by mobilization, without strong leadership, its identity submerged, the Radical Party had been practically assimilated by the right, which took advantage of the wartime situation to rally the nation around its own agenda. Even the party's strong participation in the government of national salvation could not protect it against profound moral discredit. The brunt of this opprobrium was not directed at the faction that had eagerly participated in the *union sacrée* but rather at those loyal to the prewar party who defended its political, social, and international principles. The resulting bifurcation of the Radical Party's image among the people was greatly reinforced by Clemenceau's success in labeling as ignominious traitors those party leaders like Malvy and Caillaux who attempted to generate original ideas distinct from the consensus which the right attempted to impose through the *union sacrée.*

The wounds left by this experience did not heal for many years. Immediately after the war, the right attempted to take advantage of the success of its wartime strategy and invited the Radical Party to integrate into a vast national, anti-Bolshevik formation which would take the form either of a new party focused around the Democratic Alliance or of an electoral coalition known as the *Bloc national.* Only after several years of struggle did the Radical Party finally recover its soul. It is symptomatic to note that this outcome was only achieved when the party had been thoroughly reorganized and the grassroots, whose voices had been silenced throughout the war to the benefit of the party parliamentarians, regained control and led Radicalism back to its left-wing heritage.[56]

Notes to Chapter 2

1. G. Lachapelle, *Les Elections législatives des 26 avril et 10 mai 1914* (Paris: G. Roustan, 1914).

2. Results of our calculations, using the previous source.

3. G. Bonnefous, *Histoire politique de la IIIe République,* vol. 1: *L'avant-guerre* (Paris: P.U.F., 1965), p. 405.

4. *10e Congrès du Parti radical et radical-socialiste* (Rouen, 1910), p. 88. *Bulletin du Parti radical et radical-socialiste* (15 July 1919). For the popularity of the Radical Party in France on the eve of the First World War see S. Berstein, *Histoire du Parti radical,* vol. 1: *La recherche de l'âge d'or* (Paris: Presses de la Fondation nationale des Sciences Politiques, 1980), chap. 1: "L'héritage."

5. *Premier congrès du Parti républicain radical et radical- socialiste* (Paris, 1901), p. 45.

6. *8e Congrès* (Dijon, 1908), pp. 267–271; *11e Congrès* (Nîmes, 1911), pp. 30–32; *12e Congrès* (Tours, 1912), p. 22; S. Berstein, *op. cit.*

7. *4e Congrès* (Toulouse, 1904), p. 110; *6e Congrès* (Lille, 1906), p. 129.

8. *13e Congrès* (Pau, 1913), pp. 13 and 29–30. For Caillaux see J.C. Allain, *Joseph Caillaux,* vol. 1: *Le défi victorieux, 1863–1914* (Paris: Imprimerie nationale, 1978).

9. *Congrès 1907,* p. 54.

10. *Ibid.,* pp. 54 and 107–109; *Congrès 1909,* pp. 82 and 95; *Congrès 1910,* pp. 177–180; *Congrès 1911,* pp. 215–219; *Congrès 1912,* pp. 11–13 and 27–62.

11. *Congrès 1907*, p. 54 and *Congrès 1908*, p. 112.

12. *Congrès 1907*, p. 57.

13. *Ibid.*

14. *Congrès 1907*, pp. 57–59.

15. *Ibid.* Also J. Stone, *The Search for Social Peace* (Albany: SUNY Press, 1985).

16. *Congrès 1907*, pp. 6 and 60.

17. *Congrès 1913*, pp. 99–102 and 115–119; *Congrès 1906*, p. 141.

18. This is taken from a list of candidates in the 1919 elections in *Recueil des textes authentiques des professions de foi et des programmes électoraux des députés proclamés élus* (Barodet), 1919.

19. E. Bonnefous, *op. cit.*, vol. 2, pp. 347–348 and 354.

20. For Caillaux's projects see P. Miquel, *La Paix de Versailles et l'opinion publique française* (Paris: Flammarion, 1972), pp. 15–16.

21. *Congrès 1925*, p. 32.

22. For the origins of the *union sacrée* see J.J. Becker, *1914: Comment les Français sont entrés dans la guerre* (Paris: Presses de la Fondation nationale des Sciences Politiques, 1977), and for the significance of this phenomenon see J.J. Becker and S. Berstein, *Victoire et frustrations 1914–1929* (Paris: Editions du Seuil, 1990).

23. E. Bonnefous, *op. cit.*, vol. 2, p. 41.

24. *Ibid.*, p. 94. For political and governmental life during the First World War see J.J. Becker and S. Berstein, *Victoire et frustrations, op. cit.* and S. Berstein and P. Milza, *Histoire de la France au XXe siècle*, vol. 1: *1900–1930* (Brussels: Editions Complexe, 1990).

25. *Ibid.*, pp. 448–451.

26. For example, one could point to the 7 December 1916 vote of confidence in Briand's diplomatic and military policies (Bonnefous, *op. cit.*, vol. 2, p. 203) or the vote of June 1917 approving Ribot's war aims (*ibid.*, pp. 265–267).

27. The development of the political implications of the *union sacrée* from a simple internal political truce to a firm affirmation of the rightist agenda has been studied by J.J. Becker, *La France en guerre, 1914–1918* (Brussels: Editions Complexe, 1988).

28. For these projects see S. Berstein, *Histoire du parti radical, op. cit.*

29. J.J. Becker and S. Berstein, *Victoire et frustrations, op. cit.*, and E. Bonnefous, *op. cit.*, vol. 2, pp. 259–260; G. Soutou, *L'or et le sang* (Paris: Fayard, 1989).

30. E. Bonnefous, *op. cit.*, p. 265.

31. P. Miquel, *op. cit.*, p. 222, n. 2.

32. *Bulletin du Parti républicain radical et radical-socialiste,* 14 December 1918.

33. *Ibid.*

34. Rhône departmental archives 4 M 4 529, reports from the Rhône prefect to the Ministry of Commerce, Industry, Post and Telegraph (2 August 1917) and to the Ministry of War (16 April 1918).

35. In this regard, see H. Lerner, *La Dépêche, Journal de la démocratie. Contribution à l'Histoire du radicalisme en France sous la Troisième République*, 2 vol. (Toulouse: Publications de l'Université de Toulouse-Le Mirail, 1978).

36. *Bulletin du parti*, 17 August 1918. For the Radical Party and the Russian Revolution, see S. Berstein, "Le parti radical-socialiste et l'U.R.S.S. (1917–1939)" in Comité Français des Sciences Historiques, *Actes du XIe colloque des historiens français et soviétiques (Paris 18–21 septembre 1989), vol. 2: La France de 1919 à 1939 vue d'Union Soviétique; L'Union Soviétique de 1919 à 1939 vue de France* (Paris: Imprimerie Nationale, 1990).

37. P. Miquel, *op. cit.*, p. 15 and most of all, J.C. Allain, *Joseph Caillaux*, vol. 2: *L'Oracle 1914–1944* (Paris: Imprimerie nationale, 1981).

38. E. Bonnefous, *op. cit.*, vol. 2, pp. 300–303.

39. *Ibid.*, pp. 95–96, 231, 236–237.

40. *Ibid.*, pp. 370–371.

41. For Clemenceau, see the highly favorable and even somewhat hagiographic work by J.B. Duroselle, *Clemenceau* (Paris: Fayard, 1988).

42. *Ibid.*, p. 409 and J.C. Allain, *op. cit.*

43. Duroselle, *op. cit.*, pp. 400–401.

44. *Le Radical*, February-April 1920; *Le Progrès de l'Allier*, 25 April 1920; *La Tribune ariégeoise*, 1 May 1920.

45. L. Le Foyer, *Défense des persécutés*, 18 January 1918 (Paris, 1923), p. 37.

46. E. Bonnefous, *op. cit.*, vol. 2, p. 409.

47. This episode illustrates how incorrect is the frequently expressed view that Clemenceau was a quintessential Radical. Between 1880 and 1890 he was indeed one of the early theoreticians of Radicalism at a time when it was still an extremely diffuse intellectual movement. However, he never participated in the party created in 1901, with the exception of a few months, and his relations with it were strained. Nevertheless, public opinion (including many Radicals themselves) often considered him a Radical and even one of the founding fathers of the party.

48. *Défense des persécutés*, 6 December 1917, *op. cit.*, pp. 20–21.

49. In the vote of 8 March 1918 approving the government policy of repressing pacifism, only fourteen Radical deputies joined the socialists in opposition (E. Bonnefous, *op. cit.*, vol. 2, p. 382).

50. Characteristic of the spirit of the *union sacrée* at the time was the reaction of the *Dépêche de Toulouse*, which condemned the holding of a political convention as inopportune and likely to damage the war effort (H. Lerner, *op. cit.*, chap. 16).

51. *Bulletin du parti*, November 1917; Kayser Archives, file E.

52. E. Bonnefous, *op. cit.*, vol. 2, pp. 343–345.

53. Kayser Archives, file E. Among the Radicals who refused to vote in favor of condemning Malvy was Edouard Herriot, who, after the verdict, publicly embraced him. See S. Berstein, *Edouard Herriot ou la République en personne* (Paris: Presses de la Fondation nationale des Sciences Politiques, 1985).

54. *Bulletin du parti*, 21 September 1918.

55. *Ibid.*, 21 September 1918 and 8 March 1919; Kayser Archives, file E.

56. S. Berstein, *Histoire du parti radical, op. cit.*

MOBILIZING
THE NATION

3

Industrial Mobilization in 1914–1918: Production, Planning, and Ideology

Gerd Hardach

The nations that went to war in 1914 controlled a major part of the world's economic resources, and as the conflict dragged on, industrial might was increasingly seen as the factor that would eventually decide the outcome of the struggle – not the grand fleets frozen in position or the armies ensconced in their trenches. The emerging primacy of industrial production over military strategy was not at all foreseen before the war, let alone planned.

In August 1914, both the Central powers and the Allies expected a quick war that would be waged and won with a limited amount of war *materiel.* This blind spot in military planning presents a problem not only for the history of military strategy but also for social history. The armed forces had been only partly "modernized" as industrialization progressed. The military had taken part of course in the general modernization and industrialization, and in the developed industrial societies of continental Europe the military retained much of its influence, although this was less so in Great Britain and the United States. While technical progress was absorbed into the armed forces in the perverted form of new and improved means of destruction, strategic planners remained amazingly traditional in their outlook and failed to take industrial developments into account. The general staffs planned their campaigns much as they always had, making allowance for new arms and means of transportation but not for the mighty economic potential of industrial societies in the imperialist era.

Only after the Battle of the Marne and the "race to the sea" was mil-

Notes to Chapter 3 can be found on page 84.

itary mobilization followed by four years of systematic industrial mobilization. The belligerents converted much of their industrial base from peacetime production to war production. The market and profit mechanisms made way for some elements of industrial planning, and a new ideology of cooperation and organization began to replace liberalism as the perceived foundation of economic growth. This then is the subject of the following essay.

Production and Resources

The history of industrial mobilization is one of an enormous economic transformation entailing a shift in industrial priorities toward armament production. On the most general level, the goal of industrial mobilization was the same in all the belligerent countries: "maximum slaughter at minimum expense,"[1] as Bertrand Russell bitterly commented, or in the more socially acceptable formulation of the time, to allow industry to make the greatest possible contribution to national defense. This was the fundamental aim of industrial mobilization in all the warring countries, although the practical problems this posed for the various governments and the industries themselves differed according to the particular situation in which each country found itself. At the very least, the practical problems of industrial mobilization were more or less severe and more or less pressing in the various countries. In Germany during the first years of the war, access to sources of raw materials was a major difficulty because of the Allied blockade. In Great Britain, industrial mobilization caused considerable friction between the unions on the one hand and the government and industry on the other regarding the organization of work in the new armaments industries. The most pressing problem in Russia was the discrepancy between an enormous army encompassing millions of men and relatively low industrial capacity. In France, the first bottlenecks in munitions production appeared as early as 1915 because of the extreme shortage of labor and the loss of the coal and steel producing areas in the north and north-east.[2] The history of industrial mobilization includes both aspects: the general problems caused by the transition from a peacetime to a wartime economy and the particular situation in which each country found itself insofar as munitions production was concerned.

The French mobilization plan of 1912 ("Plan 17") makes no mention of industrial mobilization. Munitions manufactured and stockpiled in peacetime were expected to cover all needs. Current production would only replace material that was consumed. The state yards and factories and the few private companies that specialized in arms production were expected to suffice; no one even considered trimming the entire industrial sector for military production. Most war material was still produced by the state, even in France, a surprising fact given that arms production at the time was usually associated with such large private companies as Le Creusot, Krupp, and Vickers. However, most of the arms and munitions manufactured before 1914 by Le Creusot, for example, were intended for export.[3] The state munitions plants in Bourges, Puteaux, and Tarbes produced shells and artillery pieces, while the factories in Saint-Etienne, Châtellerault, and Tarbes produced arms for the infantry. Private companies such as Le Creusot, Saint-Chamond, and Firminy produced some cannons, and in the months preceding the war, Le Creusot began production of 105-mm cannons for the French army, although they were not delivered until after the declaration of war.[4]

The lack of attention to the arms industry is well illustrated by the course of mobilization during the first days of August. Only 11,000 skilled workers who were subject to the military draft were exempted, and 7,600 of them worked in state-owned munitions plants. While state and private munitions manufacturers in France employed some 45,000 to 50,000 workers at the outbreak of war,[5] these numbers fell drastically as a result of mobilization. The work force at Le Creusot, for example, fell from about 12,000 to 6,600.[6] Although the Battle of the Marne (6 to 9 September 1914) was fought and won using the limited prewar arms program, it was soon evident even during the early war of movement that munitions were being consumed at a far faster pace than peacetime planners had assumed. Artillery shells are often taken as an example. At a time when the production plan still called for the manufacture of 10,000 75-mm shells per day, individual batteries were firing off as many as 1,000 per day, and the High Command was demanding an increase in production to 100,000 per day.[7]

Industrial mobilization began on 20 September 1914 with the Bordeaux Conference, to which Minister of War Millerand invited the major French industrialists.[8] The most important subject was the reorganization of shell manufacturing in order to increase daily production to 100,000 75-mm shells.[9] All metal-working companies, whether large or small, which could be employed to this end were enrolled, and huge government orders were handed out. For instance, Commentry-Fourchambault-Decazeville received its first order for more than 80,000 semi-steel shells at 12.50 francs per shell, and then another for 40,000 shells at 11.50 francs per shell.[10] In January 1915, André Citroën signed a contract to produce more than one million 75-mm shrapnel shells at 24 francs each to be "manufactured in a factory yet to be built." This order was followed by others. The government agreed to pay Citroën in advance 1.2 million francs in cash. Advances of up to 4.8 million francs were also offered for new machinery.[11] By the summer of 1915, the High Command's demand of September 1914 for 100,000 shells per day was practically fulfilled.[12]

The private arms manufacturers who had been customary sources of supply received new artillery orders. As early as September 1914, eighty artillery pieces were ordered from Schneider et Cie, and discussions with Saint-Chamond were beginning. By May 1915, 512 75-mm cannons had been ordered from Schneider and 200 from Saint-Chamond. Unlike shells, most artillery pieces were still manufactured in state-owned facilities even after the first year of industrial mobilization. In August 1915 these factories were producing 300 pieces a month and by December 600 a month.[13] State-owned factories also produced most of the arms used by the infantry, although private industry did receive orders for parts.[14] Daily production in January 1915 was 300 rifles and 10 machine-guns, which rose by December 1915 to 1,500 rifles and 36 machine-guns.[15] Gunpowder was produced exclusively by the state, although private industry did manufacture explosives and also supplied the chemical raw materials. Production of gunpowder and explosives soared from 41 tons a day in August 1914 to 255 tons a day in July 1915.[16]

Production increased considerably during the first year of industrial mobilization, but still could not keep pace with demand. When the war of position, with its vast consumption of munitions, began in the winter of 1914-15, demand soared once again. Each increase in production by one side stimulated output by the other. The mounting arms production was limited only by shortages of labor and raw materials.

In the first two weeks of August 1914, 2.9 million men were mobilized in France. Another 2.7 million followed in their footsteps during the following ten months to replace losses and boost the strength of the armed forces. The total active male population was some 12.6 million. From the outset, there were many service releases so that draftees could return to the public service and the railroads; industry, however, was not originally considered essential to the war effort, and the 3.4 million men working in this sector were mobilized at an above-average rate.[17] Even in sectors as vital to the war effort as metallurgy and chemicals, the work forces were sharply cut back as soon as hostilities broke out. By August 1914, "base metal-working" (ninth occupational category in the industrial statistics) employed only 33 percent of the work force employed in July, and the "chemical industries" (second category) employed only 42 percent. The average for all branches of industry was 34 percent.[18]

Immediately when industrial mobilization was declared, industrialists demanded the return of workers who had been inducted into the army. The government now accorded munitions production a higher priority than military service, and industrialists were given the right to recall workers who had been mobilized at the outset of the war, from recruit depots and even from units at the front. In place of workers whom the army considered essential (for example those specialized in artillery or military engineering) and those who had disappeared or been killed, wounded, or taken prisoner, companies received a consignment of an equal number of men. By the end of 1915, about 500,000 former soldiers had been returned to the munitions industry.[19] Through service releases, the arms industry work force slowly returned to its prewar levels, at least insofar as the unoccupied area of France is concerned. By July 1915, the work force in metallurgy had returned to 82 percent of its prewar level and in the chemical industry to 66 percent of its prewar level. By January 1916, metallurgy had reached 100 percent and the chemical industry 93 percent of their prewar levels.[20]

After numerous service releases in the summer of 1915, the army began refusing to release more workers. This compelled Albert Thomas, the Undersecretary of State for Artillery and Munitions, to deny the industrialists' requests for more service releases: "General Headquarters asks that no more men be released from service at the front, because the efforts of the commander in chief and the Ministry of War to provide the army with all men capable of military service would be compromised if the ranks of our combatants were further thinned by new requests for industrial labor. Accordingly, men will only be released from the front in cases of urgent need."[21] The number of munitions workers who had been mobilized remained much the same thereafter. In August 1917, a total of 518,000 soldiers had been released to war industries and another 300,000 to agriculture, in comparison with a total of 5.2 million still serving in the military (at the front, within France and in North Africa).[22] Since the munitions industries were no longer working at full capacity in any case because of the shortage of raw materials, the army wanted to reduce further the number of soldiers who had been released. One of Thomas's remarks shows the competition for scarce personnel between the military and industry: "I defended our position of course, as I always have, by pointing to both the shortage of labor and the artificiality of the view that there is an inevitable relationship in every factory between the quality of the materials and the number of specialists who work on them. But it is obvious that our position in this regard is becoming more and more difficult."[23] Since only limited numbers of skilled workers could be released from the army, the Undersecretary of State for Artillery recommended two solutions to the arms industry in late 1915. One was to employ auxiliary workers: first women and then foreigners, people from the colonies, and prisoners of war. Indeed, by the time the armistice was signed, the arms industry employed a total of 1.7 million workers, including 497,000 soldiers, 430,000 women, 425,000 civilian workers, 133,000 children of less than eighteen years of age, 13,000 crippled people, 108,000 foreigners, 61,000 colonials, and 40,000 prisoners of war.[24] The second solution was to improve the organization of work in order to increase the productivity of the workers already employed. According to a government report, productivity in metallurgy was increased by up to 50 percent by applying Taylorism.[25]

The war industries also experienced great difficulties obtaining sufficient supplies of raw materials. When the front stabilized after the Battle of the Marne, a large part of the industrial regions in northern and north-eastern France were in German hands. In comparison with 1913, this resulted in production losses of 49 percent for coal, 64 percent for pig iron, and 58 percent for steel. The productive capacity situated along the front also could not be used.[26] Table 3.1 shows production and imports throughout the war. Production fell to a very low level in 1915, and then rose gradually until 1917. The mobilization of all reserves in 1918 caused production to fall once again. Coal imports also fell considerably, but increased imports of iron and steel partially offset the shortfall in domestic production. Imports declined again in 1918 because of a shortage of available shipping that resulted from submarine warfare and the needs of the American expeditionary corps.

On the whole, the French war economy was more an illustration of the new view that emphasizes the tremendous potential for economic growth in early twentieth century France than of the traditional view of "a France grown old before its time, cautious, fully matured, even tinged with Malthusianism."[27] French industry, which has often been criticized for its heavy, cumbersome structure, adapted quickly to arms production. Under the very difficult conditions of sweeping mobilization and enemy occupation of the industrial regions of the north and north-east, enormous quantities of arms and airplanes were produced in very little time. Until the end of the war, France remained the largest

Allied producer of arms, although much of this production was based on increased imports of coal, coke, iron and steel.

Table 3.1: French Heavy Industry 1913–18
(in millions of tons)

	COAL		PIG IRON		STEEL	
	PRODUC- TION	IMPORTS	PRODUC- TION	IMPORTS	PRODUC- TION	IMPORTS
1913	40.8	23.9	5.2	—	4.7	-0.4
1914	27.5	17.2	2.7	—	2.7	-0.2
1915	19.5	19.6	0.6	0.2	1.1	1.0
1916	21.3	20.3	1.5	0.6	2.0	2.6
1917	28.9	17.3	1.7	0.7	2.2	2.6
1918	26.3	15.0	1.3	0.4	1.8	1.8

Source: A. Fontaine, *L'industrie française pendant la guerre*, Carnegie Series (Paris, 1925), pp. 194, 374ff. Imports are net.

Negative figures denote a surplus of exports. Dashes indicate amounts less than 50,000 tons.

Table 3.2: Allied Munitions Programs 1918

	FRANCE	BRITAIN	ITALY
1. Artillery Pieces (per month)			
Production Jan.-Feb. 1918	971	689	444
1918 Plan	1,106	?	503
2. Shells (per day)			
Production March 1917-March 1918	261,200	229,400	42,600
1918 Plan	278,000	218,700	102,000
3. Rifles (per day)			
Production Mar. 1917-Mar. 1918	3,200	3,200	3,600
1918 Plan	3,000	3,000	3,500
4. Machine Guns (per day)			
Production Mar. 1917-Mar. 1918	90	204	25
1918 Plan	70	386	60
5. Infantry Munitions (millions per day)			
Production Mar. 1917-Mar. 1918	6.0	4.7	2.7
1918 Plan	3.4	6.8	4.2

Source: Ministry of Munitions of War, *Review of Allied Munitions Programmes*, 1918, SHA, 10 N 146.

Wartime Planning

Some writers have drawn on Marxist political economy in order to place wartime developments in the long-term history of capitalism: free-market capitalism, according to this view, gave way to "simple" monopoly capitalism, which in turn yielded to the state monopoly capitalism of today. The First World War is thought to mark the transition between the second and third stages:

> The earliest forms of state monopoly capitalism appeared with the beginning of the imperialist phase. Not until the First World War, however, did it really set its stamp on the entire economy of the warring nations. The merciless struggle between capitalist groups required an enormous increase in production within the framework of the wartime economy, a mobilization of the forces of production such as monopoly capitalism could not achieve without state assistance. The role of the state therefore increased and its power mounted.[28]

The Marxist-Leninist analysis of the stages of capitalist development is indeed controversial, but the wartime economy of 1914–18 can be characterized in any case on a purely empirical basis as a system in which the market principle and the planning principle intermixed on a fundamentally capitalist base. Industrial mobilization led to the creation of new interventionist economic institutions, both public and private, in all the warring countries. The old "invisible hand" was replaced by a new "interventionism" that strengthened the connections between the government and the economy.[29]

The planning structures in France were more clearly separated into the public and private spheres than in other countries. Industrial mobilization prompted both the state and industry to create their own mechanisms for planning and coordinating arms production. It is true that these mechanisms were interconnected, but their organization was separate and they pursued, in part at least, different goals.

At the heart of the public-sector organization of the munitions industry was the Artillery Branch (the "Third Branch"). It was the most important authority in questions of munitions, but not the only authority. At the outbreak of the war, special sections already existed in charge of gunpowder and explosives, infantry armament, engineering materials, and airplanes. Orders from these sections to various manufacturers often overlapped.

The Artillery Branch became an Undersecretariat of State in the Ministry of War in May 1915 and was then transformed again in July 1915 into the Undersecretariat of State for Artillery and Munitions.

The new Secretariat of State was responsible for artillery, military equipment, gunpowder and explosives, special munitions for engineering, and aeronautics.[30] In the political system prevailing at the time, a Secretariat of State had virtually the same power in its area of competence as a Ministry,[31] and the Minister of War's responsibility for arms production was henceforth merely formal. The Undersecretariat of State for Artillery and Munitions can therefore be compared with the Ministry of Munitions created in Britain at about the same time.[32]

As in Britain as well, political responsibility for arms production was assigned to a man who was not a civil servant, or a soldier, or an industrialist, but simply a politician. From his appointment to the position of Secretary of State in May 1915 until his resignation as a Minister in September 1917, Albert Thomas, a deputy and eminent member of the Socialist Party (SFIO), combined two roles: socialist politician and organizer of arms production.[33] We have now become accustomed to socialist ministers of armaments and war, but the combination was still novel and astonishing in 1915. *The Times* of London carried an interview with Thomas in November 1915 under the banner heading: "Pacifist Becomes Producer of Guns."[34] As Secretary of State and then Minister in December 1916, the socialist Thomas commanded generals and senior civil servants and ran a quasi-military organization. This did not exempt him however as a socialist from surveillance by the political police;[35] regardless of the *union sacrée*, the French elite had not lost its distrust of socialists, whether they were right-wing socialists or not.

Thomas did his best to separate his two roles, and historians would do well to go along with this and not seek a "socialist arms policy." By his assigned duties as well as his own conception of them, Thomas was first and foremost an organizer of arms production as Secretary of State and then Minister – just like his colleagues abroad, Lloyd George in Great Britain, the financier Bernard Baruch in the United States, and the industrialist Walter Rathenau together with the conservative military men Koeth and Groener in Germany.

Thomas installed himself along with the leading lights of his own general staff and an ever-expanding administrative staff in the old Claridge Hotel on the Champs-Élysées. Their frenetic activity was all-encompassing, covering the co-ordination and production of arms, the distribution of labor and raw materials, the development of new arms, the technical aspects of arms production, and even the mounting social tensions in the munitions industry.

When the Undersecretariat of State for Artillery and Munitions became the Ministry of Armaments in December 1916, new tasks were added. A decree of 31 December set forth the area of competence of the new Ministry of Armaments *vis-à-vis* both the army and private industry: it would establish armament production programs in cooperation with the Ministry of War, requisition what it needed with the assistance of the latter, provide advice on the technical use of arms by the army in order to prevent "waste and deterioration," and help to organize artillery units, particularly in regard to a new piece of "assault artillery," or more familiarly, tanks. Its responsibilities thus extended to the very doorstep of the military command. Insofar as the private sector was concerned, the Ministry of Armaments became the ultimate co-ordinating authority: "When, in regard to military production, competition breaks out or threatens to break out between two or more rival orders, whether originating from the various services of the Ministry of War or of Armaments or from other public services or even private industry, the Ministry of Armaments shall decide, after consultations with the appropriate interministerial committees, the sequence in which the purchases, work, and manufacturing will be carried out as well as arrange for the necessary transportation."[36] The Ministry of Armaments' coordinating function in regard to private industry was exercised through the labor, raw material, and price controls introduced in 1915.[37]

To the Ministry of Armaments' military and economic responsibilities was added another large domain: social policy. The importance of this responsibility grew enormously as the social conflict intensified in the war industries. In 1917 the government introduced mandatory arbitration of labor conflicts. When the workers and owners involved in a labor dispute were unable to reach a settlement, the Ministry of Armaments acted as the ultimate arbiter.[38] As a logical extension of this arbitration function, the Ministry found itself passing decrees on minimum wages, first for the Paris region and then for the rest of France. In this way, the Ministry of Armaments ended up playing an important role in conflicts between labor and capital.

When the Painlevé cabinet was formed in September 1917, Thomas stepped down and was replaced by the industrialist Loucheur, who had been Undersecretary of State in the Ministry of Armaments since December 1916.[39] The responsibilities of the Ministry of Armaments were again more strongly focused on arms production itself, while most of the sociopolitical problems were assigned to the Ministry of Labor. Despite Loucheur's protests, program development, control over the use of war material by the army, and command of the "automobile service" and the "assault artillery" were transferred to the Ministry of War.[40]

While the state organized the war economy, industry created associations of its own, controlled by large companies and completely independent of the government. The core of this private organization of munitions production was the division of industry into production groups, each led by a large company called the "group leader." This group leader received the total order for the group and subcontracted parts of it to the other members.

The first production groups, Le Creusot and Saint-Chamond, were formed immediately following the Bordeaux arms conference of 20 September 1914.[41] Other groups followed, formed by large companies in iron and steel, the distribution industry, and the railroads: Firminy, Loire, Montluçon, Penhoët, Belfort, Marine, Renault, Société de l'Eclairage électrique, and the railway companies Paris-Lyon-Marseille, d'Orléans, and du Midi, plus the state railways.[42] Group leaders responsible for the production of a particular product regularly attended conferences held by the Undersecretariat of State for Artillery and then the Ministry of Armaments. While only three groups were involved in artillery production, namely Le Creusot, Marine-Homécourt, and Artillerie,[43] fifteen groups were involved in shell production. Because the technology was simpler for shell production, numerous new companies had entered the field.[44]

Thanks to the production group system, the number of industrialists directly involved in planning munitions production remained relatively small, despite the large number of different factories involved. For instance, 375 different companies were involved in shell manufacturing by the end of the war.[45] The Renault group can be used as an example of the system. It included les Automobiles Brasier, les Ets Chenard et Walcker, les Ets Clément-Bavard, Delage et Cie, les Automobiles Delahaye, la Société des Ets Delaunay-Belleville, les Ets de Dion-Bouton, la Société de l'Eclairage électrique, la Société lorraine des Anciens Ets de Dietrich et Cie, la Société des Anciens Ets Panhard et Levassor, les Automobiles Renault, les Automobiles Unic, and the members of the Syndicat des Mécaniciens, Chaudronniers et Fondeurs.[46] In the Paris region, however, which was vital to the munitions industry because of the automobile and mechanical industries concentrated there, industrialists also dealt directly with the government, outside the production group system.[47]

The common interests of the various munitions industries were represented by the Comité des Forges and the Chambre syndicale des fabrications de matériel de guerre, which were both dominated by heavy industry. For example, Léon-Lévy, an executive manager of the Cie des

Forges de Châtillon-Commentry et Neuves-Maisons, was the chairman of the Chambre syndicale des fabrications de matériel de guerre and one of the vice-chairmen of the Comité des Forges.[48]

The private war economy was composed basically of a cartel of large munitions manufacturers, similar to the cartels formed before the war but larger. The various manufacturers were linked by the powerful *Comité des Forges.* The cartel provided the technical and organizational advantages of centralized and coordinated production; however, from an overall economic and social perspective, it also exemplified all the disadvantages of economic concentration.

In France, there was no institutional merger between the trusts and the government to compare with the War Industries Board in the United States or the organizations that were developed in Germany. The government considered private munitions manufacturers more as partners and at times even as competitors with an undesirable rival claim to power. The Undersecretariat of State for Artillery and then Ministry of Armaments therefore attempted to maintain direct contact with individual industrialists so that the government would not be entirely dependent on the Comité des Forges. Characteristic in this regard was Thomas's insistence that a "circular to industrialists," in which he provided information on basic questions of arms policy, should be sent directly to the "group leaders" without passing through the Comité des Forges: "We must not become entirely subordinate to the Comité des Forges when transmitting information. It is quite capable of forwarding only that information which conforms to its own views."[49]

The institutions of industrial mobilization did not include Labor. As Undersecretary of State and then Minister, the socialist Thomas was certainly considered a personal symbol of the *union sacrée,* but he did not directly represent the workers or their unions. Beginning in early 1917, the Ministry of Armaments organized consultative committees in which workers participated, and a little later the "shop steward" system enabled workers to participate in discussions on the factory level. However, neither of these institutions provided co-determination or even any real influence. Instead of affording workers a real say in planning, these innovations were intended more as a ploy to forestall demands for worker control.[50]

In its official propaganda, the government claimed the right to oversee arms production and presented industrial mobilization as a kind of reorganization of the hierarchy to ensure through government direction that industry produced first and foremost for National Defense with no concern for private interests. In practice, however, the government was never able to implement this and indeed did not even seriously try. When industrial mobilization was instituted, a fundamental decision was made to retain private means of production even under wartime conditions, rather than requisitioning industry as some wished to do.

However, the requisitioning of private companies as part of industrial mobilization seemed to many, and not just socialists, to be an essential ingredient in Republican virtue – just as the male population was conscripted as part of military mobilization. In July 1915, the Chamber of Deputies' subcommittee on armaments debated three procedures for controlling the arms industry: the "German system" of taxing war profits; the "British system" of limiting war profits; and a third system that would "place industries that produce for the war effort under military command." A majority of the committee preferred the third approach, i.e., requisitioning.[51] Not only would industrialists be personally subject to mobilization just like workers, but their factories would be as well: "It is impossible to succeed with the industrialists unless you proceed with the requisitioning pure and simple of their companies."[52]

However, neither the government as a whole nor Albert Thomas personally agreed with this approach. The government considered its right to requisition, which had been legally established before the war,[53] as an exceptional measure.[54] This view placed Thomas at odds with the socialist deputies in the Chamber. A resolution on war policy which Auriol presented to the socialist deputies in November 1916 featured the demand that munitions industries be requisitioned:

> The government is urged to take all necessary measures, in particular: 1. the requisitioning of all companies; 2. the mobilization of all managers, engineers, etc.; 3. the imposition of war taxes on wealth, the revision of contracts, and the implementation of economy measures; 4. the mobilization of all eligible, young, able-bodied men for active service in the army, while calling upon older people to work in the national interest; 5. the assumption of effective control over the entire war effort.[55]

Socialists continued until the end of the war to demand that the arms industry be requisitioned, but without succeeding in changing the government's attitude.[56]

Since industrial mobilization therefore did not change the private status of the means of production, industry continued to consider the manufacture of munitions to be a business like any other; that is to say, the primary object was profit, not sacrifice for one's country. This could be seen in the effect of industrial mobilization on individual companies, for example the *Société anonyme de Commentry-Fourchambault-Decazeville*. In August 1914, management advised the board that operations had been completely shut down as a result of the war.[57] Three months later in November, war production had begun: the company provided the state with rails and armor plating and was looking forward to a large order for shells.[58] By December 1914, mines and steel manufacturers were beehives of activity. Steel production was almost all destined for the state.[59] In January 1915, French mines extended the working day from eight to nine hours and raised prices: "The increase in our costs and the continual rise in the demand for energy have caused our collieries to follow the example of similar French companies and to raise their prices by two to three francs per ton, an increase which was received without any protest on the part of our clients."[60]

The war also increased the demand for steel, and manufacturers increased capacity: "After passing through a difficult period caused by an interruption in orders for the war effort, the Decazeville plant is now assured of several months of work. We are preparing to start up a second blast furnace as soon as the third bank of coke ovens is lit."[61] The Montluçon steel works received another large order for shells in March 1915: "The plant also foresees other orders for various kinds of projectiles which will likely provide work for a long period to come."[62] Montluçon was in a position easily to increase production if it could only increase its work force. It therefore requested that its work force be returned to its full prewar level when the Ministry of War began to release skilled workers from the army to the factories.[63] By the end of the first year of war, management had grounds for satisfaction, because the war had proved to be a permanent source of work. Although the company attempted to undersell its competitors, prices were still "highly remunerative" because of the large volume of sales.[64] Gross profits increased from 4.6 million francs in 1913–14 to 7 million francs in 1914–15.[65] From the viewpoint of the Undersecretariat for the Artillery, however, Montluçon prices were relatively low, as Thomas agreed in a letter to management. At the same time, he criticized other industrialists who profited from the wartime situation by raising their prices to excessive levels: "There are, alas, too many industrialists with whom we have to argue about prices, and too many as well – though still relatively few – who threaten not to construct any new facilities unless we pay prices that sometimes seem rather high to us."[66]

The Montluçon case was selected at random, not at all as an example of the infamous "war-profit scandals" but rather as an illustration of the basic principle underlying industrial mobilization. Industry was very willing to convert from peacetime to wartime production, not for patriotic reasons only as the contemporary official propaganda would have it, but also because of the prospects for huge orders and fat profits. Industry in fact demanded these profits as its just reward. When, after the first year of industrial mobilization, the government expressed its desire to reduce the excessive prices it had paid in previous contracts, some industrialists threatened to cease arms production. Thomas appealed to the patriotism of these industrialists, but at the same time did not forget their business acumen and agreed not to reduce prices after all.[67]

Industrialists even gave their profits priority over military needs, as could be seen when the army occasionally requested changes in munitions programs. In September 1914, the sole concern of the Ministry of War had been to boost production to the maximum. Everything that industry could possibly produce was purchased. However, by the summer of 1915 the production of light artillery and ammunition had reached the required level, and the Ministry of War wished to scale back production in these areas in order to free up labor and primary materials for a new heavy artillery program which the army wanted. Industrialists opposed this plan, though, because they were reluctant to abandon a well-established and profitable line of production. In the industrialists' opinion, the government should simply have purchased any arms that were produced.

This view was based on firm precedents. During the period of extreme shortages at the beginning of the war, the Ministry of War had signed contracts which established only a "minimum amount" which manufacturers promised to deliver and which obligated it to purchase any additional amounts which manufacturers could produce during the term of the contract. By the summer of 1915, however, the Ministry of War wished to abandon this principle, and in a "circular to industrialists" in August 1915 Thomas announced that the state would reserve the right to determine the quantity of munitions it wished to purchase from industry: "It would be unworthy of them [the industrialists], unacceptable to the government, and contrary to the needs of National Defense for industry to foist on the state products for which it has only a limited need."[68]

Thomas did not confine himself in this circular to stating the obvious fact that the state could not purchase products which it had not ordered, but went on to claim for the state the right to intervene in the type of products which an industry chose to produce in accordance with the higher interests of the war economy. "The government for its part will have the duty to regulate and organize production. If, some day, we reach the limits of the country's strength and the government is compelled to distribute orders and labor in order of priority, we may have to place some heavy burdens on industrialists. But the government knows that it does not appeal in vain to their devotion to the Motherland and that it will not be necessary to resort to authoritarian measures."[69] In actual fact, the state never resorted to these measures and continued to satisfy the demands of industry. The industrialists for their part finally agreed to the new program, though they insisted on long-term contracts at high prices.[70] Indeed, work on the new program was delayed for several months because industry wanted to ensure before commencing production that all its price demands were satisfied.[71]

Thereafter, planning and profit were not mutually exclusive but rather complementary principles of industrial mobilization. The military High Command established production schedules in cooperation with the Undersecretariat for Artillery, soon to become the Ministry of Armaments. The Undersecretariat and then the Ministry assigned the production programs partly to state-owned factories and partly to private industry in the form of normal commercial orders. The Undersecretariat and the production group leaders met regularly to distribute the orders among the various factories on the basis of their capacity. These meetings also made it possible to keep an eye on the progress that was being made and to discuss in detail problems that arose, such as the shortage of manpower and raw materials. The normal procedure is illustrated by the following extract from the minutes of such a meeting:

> M. Albert Thomas asked the Société de Saint-Chamond how things stood with its production of rough shells. M. Laurent replied that the factory would soon be ready and could produce about 10,000 rough shells a day in January. The Undersecretary of State made a note of this figure and requested that everything be done to fulfill the program that had been decided upon.[72]

The relations between government and industry therefore involved a considerable amount of planning. However, industry retained the right to contract freely, that is, to accept or refuse orders for munitions, thereby maintaining its ability to demand high prices because of the military emergency.

As was the case with the placing of orders, labor and primary materials were also distributed on the basis of a combination of central planning and market forces. The widespread unemployment that existed during the first few weeks of the war quickly turned into a general labor shortage once industrial mobilization commenced. In the first year of industrial mobilization, the army released some 500,000 workers to munitions factories. At first industrialists were given the exclusive right to decide who would be released. The government had no control over the distribution and use of labor in factories until the summer of 1915. Workers had no clearly defined right to be released or to decide for themselves whether they preferred to serve the cause of National Defense in the army or in the munitions industry.[73] This disparity in rights between industrialists and workers produced some dissatisfaction in the general population because the industrialists evidently preferred to have relatively young, strong, productive workers released, while skilled workers who were fathers of families and beginning to show their age remained at the front. Not until a year later did the government and Parliament yield to public pressure and decide to disregard the protests of the industrialists and release older skilled workers to industry instead of the younger workers who had previously been released.[74]

When this wave of releases finished in late 1915, the Undersecretariat of State for Artillery and later Ministry of Armaments attempted to find other labor sources for industry, in particular women, foreigners, colonials, and prisoners of war.

The fact that the state was assigning workers to industries under the industrial mobilization program meant that it became directly involved in wage conflicts. At first this was only true of munitions workers who had been mobilized before being released to industry and who were therefore still subject to military regulations. They were bound to the factory that had requested their services and had neither the right of free association nor the right to go on strike.[75] This was justified by drawing an analogy between soldiers at the front and workers who had been mobilized and then released to the armaments industry. Both, it was felt, should be treated in the same way. However, this meant that the state was significantly modifying the relations between capital and labor in the case of mobilized workers. Manufacturers had in fact free rein to impose wages and working conditions on mobilized workers, who were forbidden to strike and could be returned to the front for the slightest protest. Despite the officially sanctioned *union sacrée*, numerous industrialists took advantage of this situation and reduced the wages of mobilized workers. In May 1915 the Metal-Workers' Federation provided evidence that despite the surge in military production and the increased prices, the wages received by many mobilized workers were lower than prewar levels. A long list of arms manufacturers had claims made against them, including such well-known companies as Renault, Le Creusot, Eclairage électrique, Firminy, Moteurs "Rhône," and numerous others.[76] It is therefore not surprising that industry obstinately insisted on the maintenance of military status, and concomitant low wages, for all workers released from the army, and that in the summer of 1915, industry demanded obligatory assignments for civilian workers as well, so that they could not leave their jobs for better paid positions elsewhere. As compensation for reduced wages, the Comité des Forges proposed that many more Medals of Labor be awarded to especially hard-working individuals.[77]

The government rejected the idea of obligatory assignments for all workers, but retained special status for previously mobilized workers. The latter comprised a large portion of the work force in the munitions industry: Le Creusot for example employed 20,000 people in June 1917, of whom 55 percent had been mobilized, 31 percent were civilians, foreigners, or prisoners of war, and 14 percent were women or adolescents.[78]

In order to prevent extreme exploitation of mobilized workers, the Undersecretariat of State for the Artillery began to review wages in the arms industry in the summer of 1915, and in some cases the work force Inspection Service suggested increases.[79] Thomas justified this interference in private industry by evoking the state's special duty to mobilized workers: "The military work force, in fact, is a special case. The right of free association and the right to refuse to work are denied to mobilized workers; the State therefore is morally their guardian, so to speak, and its intervention is not only legitimate but often helpful. The high cost of living is making itself felt, some demands may be justified, and the decisions of arbitrators, expressed with tact and moderation, may be very useful."[80] State intervention was therefore seen as compensation for the fact that mobilized workers were denied the right to defend themselves by organizing or going on strike. This trade-off continued, however, to work to the disadvantage of workers. Government studies showed that in the summer of 1916 many industrialists were still paying mobilized workers less than civilians, even though they were legally entitled to equal pay.[81]

As a result of mounting agitation within the working class and the increasing number of strikes, the government's wage policy was expanded from mobilized workers to all munitions workers, and its applications were broadened. The decree of 17 January 1917 established compulsory arbitration of wage disputes, which would be brought before standing conciliation and arbitration committees composed of an equal number of managers and workers and chaired by a representative of the Ministry of Armaments. If the two parties failed to reach an agreement, the government mediator made a final decision which could be mandatory. The government set the wage rates to which the arbitrators referred before making individual decisions. In early 1917 these government rates per hour in the Paris region were as follows: skilled workers up to 1.50 francs, male laborers 1 franc, women 0.75 francs, and young girls under 16 years of age 0.35 francs.[82] The Labor Branch in the Ministry of Armaments claimed to be very encouraged by this system, which, it declared, effected a compromise between capital and labor. "As the negotiations proceeded, both the industrialists and the trade unions displayed a genuinely conciliatory attitude and a desire to reach an agreement. The settling of the wage rates was generally a time of reconciliation between industrialists and labor organizations. Lasting relationships were established which will make it possible to avoid incidents and will be the surest guarantee of the success of the conciliation procedure."[83] However, an independent report by Halbwachs on compulsory arbitration was much more skeptical in tone: "The decree of 17 January 1917 instituting a compulsory arbitration and conciliation procedure in case of labor conflicts between management and non-mobilized workers in companies and factories contributing to the war effort was received with concern and prompted serious objections on the part of representatives of the workers' interests. They believe that the workers will derive very few benefits from these measures aimed at ensuring industrial peace. The most visible and immediate result of these methods is to suspend all strikes, that is, to deprive the workers of their most effective weapon."[84] In the end, the workers did not allow themselves to be intimidated by such government tactics, and the number of strikes actually rose from 314 in 1916 to 696 in 1917, while the number of strikers rose from 41,409 to 293,810.[85] The discrepancy between enormous wartime profits on the one side and declining real wages on the other gave rise to a justified outcry.

In the first year of industrial mobilization, primary materials did not seem to be in particularly short supply, even though a large amount of France's coal, iron, and steel producing capacity had been overrun by the Germans. Central planning of iron and steel supplies did not begin until November 1915, and the impulse to do so came much more from abroad than from within France itself. The British government in fact began controlling iron and steel exports from Great Britain and insisted that the hitherto unregulated purchases in France be brought under a central authority.[86]

Table 3.3: Wages and Prices

	WAGE INDEX IN MUNITIONS INDUSTRY	GENERAL WAGE INDEX	COST OF LIVING IN PARIS	COST OF LIVING IN PROVINCES
1913–14	100	100	100	100
1916	125	125	134	138
1917	150	130	160	173
1918	240	175	211	235

Source: L. March, *Le Mouvement des prix et des salaires pendant la guerre*, Carnegie Series (Paris, 1925), pp. 244, 297.

In May 1916 the Comité des Forges, which was already making purchases for its members, obtained a monopoly on the importation of crude iron and steel from Britain. Gradually all imports of iron and steel as well as the output of some newly constructed metal factories were distributed by the Comité des Forges. In July 1918, shortly before the end of the war, a decision was made to turn all French production of crude iron and steel over to the Comité for distribution. This status as sole distributor endowed the Comité, which was already an extremely powerful organization, with an unprecedented pivotal role in munitions production and even in French industry in general. However, the favorable treatment accorded big industry did not go unchallenged. Protests from the processing industry during the war prompted the establishment of an inquiry into the practices of the Comité des Forges, an inquiry which was continued after the war in the full glare of publicity.[87]

Industrial mobilization, at least insofar as the distribution of iron and steel is concerned, resulted much more in further privileges for monopolies, which were already extremely influential, than in increased government control over the economy. State financing of the building of new factories for private industry had the same effect. Under the influence of the lengthy war of position, the Secretariat of State for Artillery made plans to increase the capacity of heavy industry beginning in May 1916 in order to lessen French dependence on imports for armaments production.[88] This program called for the construction of several blast furnaces, steel mills, and banks of coke ovens by the largest producers of iron and steel. When the industry hesitated because of its doubts about the long-term viability and profitability of the new installations, the government agreed to provide direct funding. In early 1916 an agreement had already been signed with Schneider et Cie providing for a state investment of 7 million francs in a new metallurgical plant at Caen. This advance was to be paid back through a permanent 10 percent reduction in prices and five installment payments beginning one year after the conclusion of a peace treaty.[89] The new agreement bestowed an even richer deal on the industry, with the state providing 50 percent of the financing as a straight subsidy without any need for reimbursement or profit-sharing. At the same time, the chemical industry persuaded the state to finance some of its new factories and to transfer to it the operations of some state-owned plants.[90]

It was industrial mobilization that transformed arms production, which had been predominantly state-operated, into a huge private industry. In August 1914, 75 percent of the workers in the arms industry were employed in state-owned factories, while 25 percent were employed in private industry; by May 1915 these proportions had been reversed, and the state share continued to decline throughout the war. The bourgeois policies which the government pursued with the support of the right wing of the Socialist Party allowed National Defense to become another great fountain of wealth for industry.

Table 3.4: Workers in the Munitions Industry

	WORKERS IN STATE OWNED INDUSTRY		WORKERS IN PRIVATE INDUSTRY		TOTAL
	NUMBER	PERCENTAGE	NUMBER	PERCENTAGE	NUMBER
Aug. 1914	38,000	75	12,000	25	50,000
May 1915	71,000	23	242,000	77	313,000
1918	295,000	18	1,280,000	82	1,675,000

Source: Oualid-Picquenard, op. cit., pp. 45–47.

The tax on war profits affected only a small part of the profits actually earned.[91] Although he always defended the munitions industry in public, Thomas was fully aware of this: "I am also informed by very reliable sources, both accounting experts and engineers who do financial studies, that the concealment of war profits is a common practice."[92] There were some spectacular examples. Hotchkiss & Co., with share capital of 4 million francs and real working capital of 6.2 million francs at the beginning of the war, generated profits by 1916 of between 37 and 51 million francs.[93] Citroën's profits rose between 1914 and 1917 to 6.1 million francs, on which, after the deduction of depreciation, 60,000 francs were paid in war profit taxes.[94] The government justified large profits by pointing to the particular efforts of industrialists: "to preserve the stimulative effect of industrial profits"[95] was the general idea behind industrial mobilization, in contrast to wages, which were increasingly brought under state control.

Planning as developed in the course of industrial mobilization meant that production targets were increasingly set during direct talks between government and industry and that the armaments industry received as much as possible of the available resources in manpower and raw materials. However, industrial mobilization did not mean that the government gained any control over industry. In fact, the great monopolies grew even stronger as a result of industrial mobilization because arms production was concentrated in the heavy industries gathered together in the Comité des Forges and in some companies belonging to "new" industries such as Renault. Industry accepted planning as a part of industrial mobilization, but it rejected any state control over the economy. After the armistice, the Ministry of Armaments – now renamed the Ministry of Industrial Reconstruction – attempted to cooperate with other government agencies in order "to produce general national production programs"[96] for the reconstruction of the previously occupied territories and for supplying the civilian population with consumer goods such as shoes and clothing. However, the proposed plans for the reconstruction of the peacetime economy were thwarted by resistance from industry, which was only too eager to rid itself of any controls imposed during the war.[97]

The Ideology of Industrial Mobilization

Industrial mobilization did not resolve the conflict between capital and labor. As we saw in the previous section, it failed to break down the traditional economic structures. In fact, massive government intervention on behalf of the great munitions manufacturers tended to reinforce the conflicts that already existed within the industry. The social reality of industrial mobilization was totally at odds with its ideology, as propagated above all by Albert Thomas in numerous speeches and articles, first in his role as Undersecretary of State and then as Minister of Armaments.

The ideology behind industrial mobilization, as imagined by Thomas, was a direct continuation of the "organized economy" which he had advocated before the war. According to the theory of the organized economy, the progressive concentration and centralization of capital represented a step forward in overcoming the inherent anarchy in capitalism. The state should encourage and complete this trend in the capitalist economy through a policy of partial nationalization (the Bank of France, railroads, insurance companies, the oil industry, and alcohol monopoly) and by extending the cooperatives. Private initiative and public control would be combined to produce a better organization of the forces of production.[98] "Albert Thomas," wrote one observer, "has big plans. Under the influence of Professor Milhaud, he intends to set production on a new foundation. He hopes to precipitate a great social movement toward a collective economy."[99] Thomas's vision combined the socialist principle of organization and the capitalist principles of profit and private forces of production. There was an evident parallel here with German reformism and revisionism, which Thomas explicitly praised.[100]

As a result, Thomas was prepared not only to implement industrial mobilization but also to defend it on an ideological level. He spoke of it as the first step in the emergence of a new economy in which organization would replace anarchy and class cooperation would replace class conflict: "The industrial war, which is making enormous demands on France, can be a springboard for genuine renewal."[10] In April 1916, Thomas elaborated on his ideas in a speech to the management and workers of Le Creusot. His theme was the new spirit of cooperation between the state and industry which industrial mobilization had brought:

> Yesterday, in peacetime, industrialists were always complaining about the government. Yesterday, they were isolated, pushed, and pulled this way or that at the whim of the competition. Today their efforts are disciplined. They have responded to the appeal from the nation and have allowed this basic level of organization, which even the most audacious of us would never have dreamed possible. An overarching government organization has emerged within industry, coordinating all initiatives but not suffocating any. Yesterday, industrialists competed, or at least were not united and sometimes fought with one another. All that has been overcome by a common will in time of war.[102]

The working class was to find its place as well in this merging of industry and the state:

> Workers – my fellow workers – I have forgotten nothing of my past. Tomorrow when you – friends in the struggle, friends in hope – have to

assert once again your legitimate rights because the victorious outcome of the war has not eliminated all social conflict, you will find me with you struggling to achieve the ideals of justice and liberty which were and remain ours. But you – or we – will only develop genuine strength, only be genuinely capable of asserting our rights, to the extent that you are prepared to give of yourselves without stint for the glory and salvation of the nation.[103]

Again, Thomas pointed to industrial mobilization as the model for the future peacetime economy: "The industrial union must be maintained in peacetime so that the industries grouped together in a great national organization lend one another mutual support beyond all petty and harmful rivalries. For the sake of the country and even for the sake of individual interests, we must take a brave, frank look at some very basic questions and abstain from random, simplistic solutions."[104]

Thomas's speech at Le Creusot was no isolated event. Indefatigably he propagated the same ideology of organized production in speeches at Citroën,[105] at Schneider in Caen[106] and at Renault.[107] Even the political police, who kept Thomas under surveillance, made note of the fact that the Undersecretary of State seemed to have adjourned the class struggle and was exhorting workers to produce more and refrain from strikes:

Insofar as the class struggle is concerned, we have not forgotten it and will take it up again. But at the present time, under the union sacrée, there is a quiet, hypocritical campaign being waged by the old parties. For this reason, workers in our munitions factories must know how to work hard for the present without abandoning their long-term goals. If they make an outstanding contribution to National Defense during the war, their voice will be all the stronger and more legitimate after the war. In conclusion, after the victory it is the Socialist Party that will organize the society of tomorrow.[108]

In November 1917, after his resignation as Minister, Thomas returned the praise of "the industrial society of tomorrow" before the shop stewards from Renault.[109] After the armistice, Thomas made another statement, suggesting that the institutions of the wartime economy should provide the underpinnings of an organized peacetime economy. He reminded the French deputies of the useful role, in his view, played by cartels and agreements signed before the war, which ensured regular increases in production, and he referred once again to the speech he had delivered at Le Creusot.[110] Several years later, the idea of an organized economy re-emerged in a letter which Thomas – now the director of the International Labor Office – wrote in 1930 to Paul Faure, the secretary general of the Socialist Party. In this letter Thomas offered his view that the Socialists should make the organized economy a major plank in the their next election platform. Thomas no longer emphasized the concentration and centralization of capital as the essence of the organized economy but rather, as he had before the war, the nationalization of such branches as mining, electricity, railroads, and insurance.[111]

The interpretation which Thomas gave to industrial mobilization is rather troubling. His views certainly represented a logical stage in his long-term political and intellectual development, and were not the result of a sudden conversion. This is clearly visible in documents produced before 1914 or after 1918. However, Thomas's attitude was also opportunistic to the extent that it legitimized and considerably reinforced the political and economic status quo during a time of crisis. It was of course very possible to take a totally different view of the concentration of capital. The 1914 election manifesto of the Socialist Party, signed by Thomas himself, stated: "Under increasingly heavy oppression by capitalism, which is growing more and more powerful and extending concentration throughout all areas of life who does not feel along with us the urgent need for indispensable social change?"[112] Despite all of Thomas' rhetoric, his appeals to the working class to postpone its demands until after the victory suited the dominant classes perfectly. Such appeals to the workers to renounce their hopes, sublimated in the contemporaneous euphemism *esprit de travail* (spirit of hard work), appeared once again in an editorial which the Undersecretary of State for Artillery wrote in November 1916: "Labor has been magnanimous enough to stifle for the duration of the conflict its demands for workers' rights, to refrain from laying down tools out of hatred for capitalist profits, at a time when everything which the workers do serves to strengthen the ramparts of fire and steel protecting our brothers at the front."[113]

On the other hand, Thomas considered the various demands made by industrialists to be quite legitimate. In a speech delivered before British workers in February 1918, he defended French armaments makers and therefore his own policies: "It is said that they are raking in scandalous profits and that I placed fewer controls on them than you. Was I wrong? Or was I right? Despite much criticism from within my own party, I still believe that I was right and that if I had not left a good profit margin for new, unfamiliar products, I would not have developed a taste for enterprise and risk among our industrialists."[114]

Thomas lauded the positive results of the truce between capital and labor, particularly the canteen and dwelling units installed by manufacturers in the new armament factories. At the inauguration of a factory canteen at Citroën in July 1917, Thomas proclaimed: "As I dare say before this assembly of workers, French employers are showing themselves here to be equal to the grandeur of our entire war effort."[115] But the conservative army officers in the Prussian War Ministry thought nothing of implementing much the same kind of social policy. It is therefore not surprising to discover that Thomas's speeches were received with greater enthusiasm by the nationalist right than by his own party friends, who spoke ironically of the "Creusot socialism" which he evidently wished to introduce in collaboration with Messrs. Schneider and Renault.[116]

The type of industrial mobilization ideology which Thomas implemented undeniably had a conservative political effect, despite all the socialist rhetoric that accompanied it. This conservative effect is underscored by Thomas's political views, which placed him in the right wing of the Socialist Party as a man who always gave his unconditional support to the government's war policy. Thomas' entry into the Ministry of War in May 1915 had been very controversial. The fact that a third socialist was entering the government – and in such an important position – seemed to indicate that the Socialist Party had gained confidence and political influence, but on the other hand, a minority within the party and the trade unions were upset to see the Socialist Party confirming in such visible fashion its support for the government's war policy at a time when the one-sidedness of the *union sacrée* was already apparent and the opposition was beginning to gather strength.[117] According to a police report written in February 1915, "There is a strong current of discontent among the Socialist rank-and-file concerning the general attitude of the party leadership."[118]

At the time of the cabinet change in December 1916, Guesde and Sembat resigned, although Briand kept Thomas on as a concession to the left, even increasing his responsibilities. The former Secretariat of State became a full-fledged Ministry of Armaments. The Socialist members in parliament approved this participation in the government by a vote of 44 to 15 and the party congress held in December 1916 approved it by 1,637 to 1,282. The majority view was holding, but the opposition was clearly gaining ground.[119] In 1917 came the "great refusal" in the army and industry, and with it the end of the *union sacrée*. After the rapid spread of revolutionary fervor in the summer of 1917 and its defeat that autumn, the majority in the party and the unions retired to a "centrist position," i.e., not revolutionary but still critical of the government's war policy.[120] Thomas himself withdrew from the government when a new cabinet was formed in September 1917, although he did so reluctantly.[121] After December 1917,

Clemenceau's government prosecuted the war to its conclusion without Socialist participation and with an uncompromisingly right-wing attitude.

The reformist wing of the Socialist Party continued, however, to laud industrial mobilization as a great success for socialist policy-makers. A motion put before the National Congress in October 1918 stated: "The Congress, asked to censure Citizen Thomas, takes advantage of the opportunity thus presented to express its gratitude to the aforementioned for the service he rendered at the Undersecretariat for War Production and then at the Ministry of Armaments to the causes of National Defense and socialism, which cannot be separated. It is proud that the nation saw fit at one of the most critical junctures in the war to call upon a socialist to organize and increase the production of arms essential to the defense of French soil."[122] The left, on the other hand, precisely pointed to industrial mobilization as an example of the inherent contradictions in reformist policy and of its ultimate failure. By the end of the war, Thomas was politically isolated within his own party.

Various ideological currents of the era converged in the philosophy of industrial mobilization. First, of course, was the ideology of reformism. Second was the *union sacrée*, according to which the experience of the war would overcome all class antagonisms. Thomas never abandoned this view, despite the worsening social conflicts during the war, and he participated in reactionary attempts toward the end of the hostilities to breathe new life into the *union sacrée* when it began to fail. On the occasion of the "National Demonstration of the *Union Sacrée*" in February 1918, Thomas again repeated his credo of national harmony.[123]

The third current was productivism, the technocratic ideology according to which class antagonisms had been superseded by organization and production.[124] The connections between productivism and industrial mobilization are not surprising. In fact, Thomas advocated Taylorism not only during the 1920s as director of the International Labor Office[125] but already during industrial mobilization. Just like industrial mobilization, Taylorism encountered stiff resistance from the working class. A resolution of the Socialist Federation of the Seine expressed the fear that managers might use Taylorism to exploit workers:

Having noted the circular issued by Comrade Albert Thomas on 27 April 1916, and convinced that when advocating Taylorism Comrade Thomas in no way intended to recommend a system of work against which the working class has already protested, but nevertheless fearful that the business leaders see the implementation of Taylorism as an excuse for exploiting the workers, we wish to express our desire that Comrade Thomas clarify his intentions in order to avoid any erroneous interpretations on the part of the owners.[126]

The interpretation which Charles Maier has given to the productivism of the 1920s applies equally as well to industrial mobilization: "Those who by invoking industrial utopias sought to deny the relevance of power subordinated themselves to those who really had power, political or economic. But perhaps that was what they actually desired."[127]

Conclusion

Historians have a tendency to be anachronistic and partial, even when trying not to be. It is therefore not surprising that we would seek out in the industrial mobilization of 1914 to 1918 those elements which have a direct relationship to the present: mass production, the beginnings of industrial planning, and the rise of a militantly productivist ideology. However, it is important to understand that there are really no direct links between this period and the present. Technical progress, planning, and even the ideological justification of industrial mobilization, a justification which occasionally seems very modern, were instead all rooted in the wartime situation. The postwar period was more a period of reaction than progressive change. Socialism faltered and bourgeois politicians sought primarily to return to the institutions and ideologies of the prewar era. The industrial mobilization of 1914–18 can be viewed only as a great historical experience which cast an illuminating light on the true potential of the forces of production and on the crisis in the conditions under which production was carried out.

Notes to Chapter 3

1. Cited by W. K. Hancock, *Four Studies of War and Peace in this Century* (Cambridge, 1961), p. 18.
2. See G. Hardach, *The First World War* (Harmondsworth, 1977).
3. E. Schneider to the armaments subcommittee, PV of 16 April 1915. Archives nationales AN C 7509.
4. "Les fabrications de guerre et l'industrie française," memorandum by M. Halbwachs, June 1917. AN 94 AP 343.
5. See F. Reboul, *Mobilisation industrielle*, vol. 1 (Nancy, 1925).
6. Le Creusot file AN 94 AP 80. According to M. Schneider, his company employed a

total of 31,000 people before mobilization, of whom 13,000 were at Le Creusot. See armaments subcommittee, PV of 16 April 1915, AN C 7509.

7. See Reboul, *op. cit.*

8. See R. Pinot, *Le Comité des Forges de France au service de la Nation (août 1914–novembre 1918)* (Paris, 1919).

9. *Ibid.*, p. 186. There were no minutes taken at the conference. De Wendel, who was present, noted only half as much, or 50,000 shells, as the production objective. However, the number 100,000 was continually reported. The latter number must therefore have been set at this time or shortly afterward. For De Wendel's role see J.-N. Jeanneney, *François de Wendel en République. L'argent et le pouvoir, 1914–1940* (Paris, 1976).

10. Letter from Commentry-Fourchambault-Decazeville to the Heavy Industry Branch, 25 October 1915, copy in AN 94 AP 73.

11. Notes on the balance sheets of the Société des engrenages Citroën and the Société des automobiles Mors. Service historique de l'Armée, Vincennes, 10 N 180 (henceforth the abbreviation SHA will be used).

12. 75-mm shell program, 18 August 1915. SHA 10 N 11.

13. *Ibid.*; and in addition, see Compagnie des Forges et Aciéries de la Marine et d'Homécourt, "Artillerie de Campagne (Modèle Saint-Chamond)," 15 June 1915, AN 94 AP 80.

14. Ministry of Armaments, 22 January 1918, SHA 10 N 17. R. Pinot, *op. cit.*, pp. 192ff.

15. War Production: statistics AN 94 AP 349.

16. "Les fabrications de guerre et l'industrie française," memorandum by M. Halbwachs, June 1917, AN 94 AP 343.

17. See A. Fontaine, *L'Industrie française pendant la guerre*, Carnegie Series (Paris, 1925).

18. *Ibid.*, p. 96.

19. Reboul, *op. cit.*

20. Fontaine, *op. cit.*, p. 96.

21. Meeting of shell manufacturers, PV of 28 January 1916, AN 94 AP 72.

22. Size of the French armies, 1 August 1917. AN 94 AP 54.

23. War Committee, 7 September 1917, AN 94 AP 54.

24. Reboul, *op. cit.*, pp. 170–171.

25. Ministère du Commerce, ed., *Rapport général sur l'industrie française* (Paris, 1919), vol. 2, p. 928.

26. Fontaine, *op. cit.*, pp. 40–41.

27. P. Fridenson, *Histoire des usines Renault.*Vol. 1: *Naissance de la grande entreprise, 1898–1939* (Paris, 1972), p. 9.

28. *Traité d'économie politique. Le capitalisme monopoliste d'Etat* (Paris, 1971), vol. 1, p. 22.

29. J. F. Godfrey, *Capitalism at War. Industrial Policy and Bureaucracy in France 1914–1918* (Leamington Spa, 1987).

30. *Bulletin officiel du ministère de la Guerre,* 2 August 1915.

31. See P. Renouvin, *Les Formes du gouvernement de guerre*, Carnegie Series (Paris, 1925).

32. See David Lloyd George, *War Memoirs*, 6 vols. (London, 1933–36). *History of the Ministry of Munitions*, 12 vols. (1921–22).

33. A biography of Thomas does exist, though it could not draw on all the archival material that is now available: B.W. Schaper, *Albert Thomas. Trente ans de réformisme social* (Paris, 1959). See in addition: G. de Lusignan, D. Mayer, B. Gille, "Albert Thomas," *L'Actualité de l'Histoire* 24 (1958); M. Rebérioux and P. Fridenson, "Albert Thomas, pivot du réformisme français," *Le Mouvement social* 87 (April–June 1974); M. Fine, "Guerre et réformisme en France, 1914–1918," *Recherches* 32/33 (September 1978); Godfrey, *op. cit.*, pp. 186–194.

34. *The Times*, 30 November 1915.

35. See, for example, the report on Albert Thomas of 3 April 1916 about a meeting of the Federal Socialist Committee of the Seine held on 2 April 1916, AN F7 13074.

36. Decree of 31 December 1916, article 5.

37. *Bulletin des usines de guerre*, 8 January 1917.

38. Decree of 17 January 1917. Cf. *Bulletin des usines de guerre*, 22 January 1917 and 11 June 1917. W. Oualid and C. Picquenard, *Salaires et tarifs. Conventions collectives et grèves*, Carnegie Series (Paris, 1928).

39. Godfrey, *op. cit.*, pp. 194–199.

40. Letter from Loucheur to the Prime Minister, 22 September 1917, SHA 10 N 1.

41. Sous-secrétariat d'État à l'Artillerie, "Notes sur l'organisation en France de la fabrication des munitions," SHA 10 N 1.

42. This list (with the exception of Renault) is cited in Oualid-Picquenard, *op. cit.*, p. 48. See also R. Pinot, *op. cit.*, p. 186.

43. Meeting of heavy industrialists, PV of 28 June 1916, SHA 10 N 29.

44. Meeting of the group leaders for the manufacture of 75 cm shells, PV of 30 December 1915, AN 94 AP 72.

45. Ministére du Commerce, *Rapport général*, vol. 2, p. 929.

46. Pinot, *op. cit.*, pp. 186–87.

47. Sous-secrétariat d'État à l'Artillerie et aux Munitions, Cabinet, Service technique, "Note sur l'organisation en France de la fabrication des munitions," SHA 10 N 1.

48. *Comité des Forges de France*, regular general assembly of 16 May 1916. Report of the Board of Directors (Paris, 1918).

49. Undersecretariat of State for Artillery, Memorandum to Industrialists, 24 August 1915, AN 94 AP 72.

50. Cf. R. Picard, *Le Mouvement syndical pendant la guerre*, Carnegie Series (Paris, 1927). See as well below the chapter by G. Hatry.

51. Armaments subcommission, PV of 5 July 1915, AN C 7557.

52. *Ibid.*

53. Act of 3 July 1877; Act of 3 July 1911, art. 58, 59.

54. *BUG*, 11 September 1916. See below the chapter by A. Hennebicque.

55. Chamber, Socialist group, 28 November 1916, AN 94 AP 247.

56. See Oualid-Picquenard, *op. cit.*, pp. 112–120.

57. PV of the Administrative Council, 27 August 1914 (first meeting after the declaration of war), AN 59 AQ 13.

58. *Ibid.*, PV of 19 November 1914.

59. *Ibid.*, PV of 17 December 1914.

60. *Ibid.*, PV of 21 January 1915.

61. *Ibid.*, PV of 9 March 1915.

62. *Ibid.*, PV of 22 April 1915.

63. *Ibid.*, PV of 9 March and 17 June 1915.

64. *Ibid.*, PV of 16 December 1915.

65. *Ibid.*, PV of 18 November 1915.

66. *Ibid.*, PV of 18 November 1915 (extract from a letter by Albert Thomas).

67. Meeting of shell manufacturers , PV of 1 October 1915, SHA 10 N 29 (these minutes can also be found, though not in their entirety, in both the Thomas holdings in the *Archives Nationales* and the army's *Service historique*).

68. Undersecretariat for Artillery and Munitions, circular to industrialists of 24 August 1915, AN 94 AP 72.

69. *Ibid.*

70. Meeting of industrialists, PV of 28 August 1915, SHA 10 N 29.

71. *Ibid.*, PV of 26 November 1915, SHA 10 N 29.

72. *Ibid.*, PV of 30 December 1915, AN 94 AP 72.

73. *Ibid.*, PV of 25 June 1915, SHA 10 N 29.

74. *Ibid.*, PV of 3 June 1916, SHA 10 N 29.

75. See A. Rosmer, *Le Mouvement ouvrier pendant la guerre*, vol. 1: *De l'union sacrée à Zimmerwald* (Paris, 1936), pp. 429ff.

76. *Ibid.*

77. Industrialists' meeting, PV of 25 June 1915, SHA 10 N 29.

78. Committee on the use and distribution of military labor. Report on visits to Schneider et Cie at Le Creusot on 10 to 27 June 1917, AN 94 AP 80.

79. Industrialists' meeting, PV of 30 October 1915, AN 94 AP 72.

80. *Ibid.*

81. Undersecretariat of State for Artillery, circular of 25 August 1916, AN 94 AP 51.

82. Ministère de l'Armement et des Fabrications de guerre, *Tarifs et réglementation des salaires, applicables pour les fabrications de guerre de la région parisienne – Décision du 16 janvier 1917*, AN 94 AP 348.

83. Ministère de l'Armement et des Fabrications de guerre, Direction de la main-d'oeuvre, Note sur l'établissement des tarifs de salaires, 29 August 1917, AN 94 AP 348.

84. Strikes and obligatory arbitration in the munitions industry. Halbwachs report on views among workers, 30 March 1917, AN 94 AP 348.

85. R. Picard, *op. cit.*, p. 105. The number of workers on strike for 1917 in these statistics is underestimated.

86. "Note sur les opérations du *Comité des Forges* dans les approvisionnements en fontes brutes des usines travaillant pour la défense nationale," n.d.; "Note au sujet du rôle du *Comité des Forges* dans la vente des aciers pendant la guerre," 13 February 1919; "Note au sujet de la centralisation des aciers," 19 January 1918: all these notes in AN 94 AP 233.

87. Chamber of Deputies, Customs Commission, PV of 27 December 1917, M. Marc Réville, chairman, AN 94 AP 233.

88. Budget Commission, PV of 7 February 1917, AN C 7559, file 2251.

89. Contract of 16 February 1916, AN 94 AP 80.

90. Budget Commission and Contracts Commission, PV of 16 February 1917, AN C 7559, file 2252.

91. See in the Carnegie Series: G. Jèze, *Les Dépenses de guerre de la France* (Paris, 1926); H. Truchy, *Les Finances de guerre de la France* (Paris, 1926).

92. A. Thomas, note of 14 February 1918, AN 94 AP 366.

93. Note on the Hotchkiss contracts, SHA 10 N 181.

94. Note on the balance sheets of the Société des engrenages Citroën and the Société des automobiles Mors, SHA 10 N 180.

95. *BUG* (*Bulletin des usines de guerre*), 12 March 1917.

96. *BUG*, 2 December 1918, p. 249.

97. See for the anti-government atmosphere after the war the pamphlet of A. Delemer, *Le Bilan de l'étatisme* (Paris, 1922).

98. A. Thomas, *La Politique sociale* (Paris, 1913).

99. G. de Lusignan, "Albert Thomas et la justice sociale," *L'Actualité de l'Histoire* 24 (1958), p. 8.

100. A. Thomas, *Politique sociale, op. cit.*, p. 65.

101. Undersecretariat of State for Artillery and Munitions. Note of Albert Thomas, undated but approximately November 1915, AN 94 AP 51.

102. *BUG*, 1 May 1916, pp. 2–3.

103. *Ibid.*

104. *Ibid.*

105. Speech of 12 July 1917, *BUG*, 16 July 1917.

106. Speech of 19 August 1917, *BUG*, 27 August 1917.

107. Speech of 1 September 1917; extracts in Rebérioux-Fridenson, *op. cit.*, pp. 90–91.

108. Meeting of the Federal Socialist Committee of the Seine, held on 2 April 1916. Report of 3 April 1916, AN F 13074.

109. Speech of 25 November 1917, AN 94 AP 238, cf. Rebérioux-Fridenson, *op. cit.*, pp. 92–93.

110. Chamber of Deputies, sitting of 21 February 1919, *Journal officiel*, 22 February 1919.

111. Reproduced in *L'Actualité de l'Histoire* 24 (1958).

112. "Aux travailleurs de France." Socialist Party (SFIO), legislative elections of 1914, AN C 7767.

113. "L'Esprit de travail," *BUG*, 13 November 1916.

114. A. Thomas, "L'Effort industriel de la France," address delivered in Cardiff on 25 February 1918, AN 94 AP 343.

115. *BUG*, 16 June 1917.

116. Schaper, *Albert Thomas, op. cit.*, p.110.

117. See A. Kriegel, *Aux origines du communisme français, 1914–1920* (Paris, 1964), vol. 1, p.101. Jules Guesde and Marcel Sembat had entered the government on 26 August 1914.

118. "Chez les unifiés," report of 5 February 1915, AN F7 13074.

119. See A. Rosmer, *Le Mouvement ouvrier, op. cit.*, vol. 2, *De Zimmerwald à la révolution russe* (Paris, 1959), pp. 207, 211–12.

120. See Kriegel, *op. cit.*, vol. 1, p. 169–170, and R. Wohl, *French Communism in the Making, 1914–1924* (Stanford, 1966).

121. See A. Thomas, "Relation des événements qui se sont succédé du 2 au 12 Septembre 1917," AN 94 AP 356.

122. Socialist Party (SFIO), National Congress of 6–10 October 1918, motion 4 (Thomas, Dubreuilh, Grenier, Renaudel, Soutif).

123. Text of the speech in AN 94 AP 356.

124. See C. S. Maier, "Between Taylorism and Technocracy: European Ideologies and the Vision of Industrial Productivity in the 1920s," *Journal of Contemporary History* (1970); reprinted in his *In Search of Stability* (Cambridge, 1987), chap 1.

125. Maier, *op. cit.*, pp. 37–38.

126. Socialist Federation of the Seine, Section 15, AN 94 AP 348.

127. Maier, *op. cit.*, pp. 53–54.

4

Albert Thomas and the War Industries

Alain Hennebicque

Some time ago, Madeleine Rebérioux and Patrick Fridenson drew attention to Albert Thomas, who was a central but still little-known figure in the reform movement in France.[1] The lack of thoroughgoing studies of the relationship between the French government and industry during the First World War, as pointed out by Patrick Fridenson,[2] together with Martin Fine's thesis[3] have induced me to investigate Albert Thomas's industrial policies and, more particularly, his guiding principles. He was, as he himself recognized, more a man of action than of thought. In a letter to Gaston Jèze in January 1916, he remarked about himself: "In the haste of our daily activities, we don't have time to stop and reflect as much as we would like about the basic philosophy behind our actions."[4] Thomas did not reflect often enough about the overall effect of his wartime policies, as a later Socialist minister, Paul Ramadier, has noted,[5] and he also failed to turn over to the Carnegie Foundation the volumes he promised about his munitions policies. There are very few studies of the relationship between his public pronouncements and actual practices, and an examination of all his activities would require more research than I am able to provide for this chapter.

This study is based for the most part on the materials on Thomas in the French National Archives, especially his office records,[6] the records under "War Manufacturing,"[7] and the records of the Gunpowder Service.[8] The first part of this study is also based on the records of Buat, who was Minister Millerand's chief of cabinet,[9] on the archives of the Budget Commission of the Chamber of Deputies,[10] and on the appearances before the Budget Commission of Viviani, Millerand, and

Notes to Chapter 4 can be found on page 125.

Thomas in June 1915 and of Galliéni and Thomas in November 1915 available in the National Archives.[11] I also used freely Gilbert Hatry's book on the Renault works during the war, published in 1978.

The desire to find a guiding principle in Thomas' life led us in particular to the files on "social taxes" in the Thomas collection.[12] Although these records hardly extend beyond the spring of 1917 and concentration on this aspect tends to highlight Thomas's legislative activities, such an approach illuminates the importance of the turning point of 1916 and provides a chronological framework for our study.[13]

When Albert Thomas became undersecretary of state in the War Ministry on 18 May 1915,[14] hostilities had been under way for almost ten months and production had been increasing for eight months. Although Thomas was more or less involved in this process, he had not had a free hand and had to deal with the situation as it existed. He entered a ministry which had been functioning since September 1914 according to Millerand's principles and methods of organization. War production was ensured in large part through the efforts of private industry, and orders for supplies were contracted out in the usual way. Insofar as general organization of production was concerned, Millerand had established regular cooperation between the government services and industry representatives, or their leading organizations, and had delegated part of his authority to large companies which made group leaders responsible for organizing similar types of manufacturing. However, this system was far from universal, as perhaps has not been sufficiently noted.[15] Insofar as the tools at the government's disposal are concerned, the various services had been reinforced to increase their effectiveness. However, their general organization was still far from perfect, although their deficiencies were less glaring, it seems, than one might infer from the violent attacks to which the minister of war was subjected in parliament.[16] Finally, these eight months of war production had demonstrated to the government services how much the real efficiency and the latitude the government had in applying the requisition acts of 1877 and 1911 had been overestimated, and what little power the state really held *vis-à-vis* French industrialists.[17]

When Thomas assumed his duties, he also had to take into account the views of the industrialists, whose attitude toward war production and its constraints was less clear cut than appearances might suggest. As Gerd Hardach reminds us, military orders certainly provided work in industries that had been hard hit by mobilization,[18] but this pertains primarily to industrial sectors which could produce military goods either immediately or without significant retooling. The discussions conducted in the winter of 1914 and the summer of 1915 demonstrated that other manufacturers – and they were in the majority – were not always very eager to contribute to the war effort, as can be seen in the difficulties Millerand experienced in trying to persuade French industry to produce light arms.[19] The huge orders of the summer of 1915 once again brought this issue to the fore. Some "established" arms manufacturers with an international clientele or even some subcontractors could not always resist the temptation to sell to the highest bidder and certainly did not rush to meet the needs of the war effort. The services and Schneider, for example, failed to see eye to eye on the first contract awarded to Citroën, on some Russian orders, and on the modification of artillery pieces originally intended for Denmark.[20] In respect to the conditions attached to military contracts, war material manufacturers sought to defend what they saw as their right "to remain the sole masters of their own manufacturing." In July 1915 they reminded the government, through their association president, Léon-Lévy, that "the contract system, as it now exists, clearly leaves to the contract signatory the right to manufacture in the way in which he sees fit, apart from deliveries to the control service, as set forth in the contract itself, and the right of the state to control the employment of mobilized workers."[21]

However, this rejection of any state interference in company management did not preclude demands for state intervention when it would be helpful. Industrialists accordingly besieged the government with requests for more workers, more primary materials, and even demonstrations of state authority in order to straighten out recalcitrant subcontractors. Renault, for instance, asked Millerand to intervene in December 1914 in order to force small rocket manufacturers in the Paris group to specialize,[22] and again in May 1915 asked Thomas to create a "centralization and distribution section" in order to supply aircraft and automobile manufacturers with the specialized steels which they were having difficulty procuring for themselves.[23]

Insofar as prices were concerned, industrialists followed the issue attentively after the uncertainties of September and October 1914. Legitimate demands based on costs or the amortization of equipment should not be confused with other demands which can only be explained by a lust for maximum profit. Despite the tacit silence that surrounded the company managers' greed, this greed was apparent from the outset on both an individual and collective basis. Thomas referred to it as early as the autumn of 1914 in the notes he made about a visit to factories in central France.[24] A year later, when Deputy Clémentel was expressing his outrage at the pressures exerted by manufacturers,

Thomas reminded him that the manufacturers had begun eliminating the competition even before the war by controlling prices and orders for arms. He noted that "this organization, going back to peacetime, has succeeded in increasing its strength relative to the State to the extent that the State's needs have outstripped the possible supply."[25]

The attitude which industrialists took was all the more crucial because Thomas arrived at the undersecretariat within a few weeks of the failure of the Artois offensive and the resulting heavy demands for munitions and war material. The demand for heavy artillery munitions had remained constant since December 1914, when suddenly it doubled without any warning in June 1915 for 120-mm shells and doubled twice in thirteen days for 155-mm shells. At the end of the month, Joffre asked for the first time since the beginning of the war that the production of rapid-fire heavy artillery pieces be resumed.[26]

In parliament, the munitions industry question was finally on the agenda. When the chambers were recalled in January 1915, industry profits, efficiency, and the use of mobilized soldiers in the factories had become burning issues. The majority in the Chamber of Deputies worked particularly diligently at producing a spate of proposed bills and position papers by various commissions or their presidents, a burst of activity which reflects the extreme sensitivity of the issues surrounding war production. Some of these proposals were narrow attempts to deal with one aspect of the problem, usually the use of mobilized labor or the financial issue, while others were more general and sought to provide a comprehensive solution.[27] Among the latter proposals, two are of particular interest because they were advanced when Thomas was responsible for arms production and because they reflect the two main tendencies among the majority in the Chamber of Deputies.

The first proposal was tabled on 6 August 1915 by Mistral and numerous Socialist deputies. It demanded, first, the requisitioning of mines and industries in order to maximize production and minimize costs, and second, the placing of mobilized workers under military regulations.[28] The second proposal reflected the views of the Chamber's Army Commission about Mistral's bill and set forth in a report written by Lucien Voilin. This document, which quickly became known as the Mistral-Voilin proposal,[29] was submitted to the government on 12 November 1915. In contrast to the first proposal, it rejected requisitioning in favor of the establishment of state technical control over the war industries and a dual legal status for mobilized workers. In particular, they would be considered civilians when on the job, including for pay purposes, and soldiers insofar as assignment to factories and discipline outside working hours were concerned. In addition, war industries would be subjected to strict financial controls. Separate standard book-keeping procedures would be required for all work performed on behalf of the government, and profits would be restricted to 10 percent of the capital invested or to the average profits earned over the two financial years prior to the outbreak of war plus 20 percent. All excess profits would be returned to the government, and contracts concluded before the adoption of the law would become retroactively subject to it.

1. A Nexus of Treaties

Thomas's own approach was based on a conviction which was largely shared by the authors of the parliamentary proposals: economic conditions had returned to a semblance of peacetime stability and it was therefore possible to establish a sound, comprehensive plan.[30] However, Thomas drew quite different conclusions from those of the parliamentarians. In his view, war production was hostage to a supreme imperative: maximum output of maximum quality. This was an industrial problem that was only amenable to industrial solutions. Thomas therefore began pointing out as early as July 1915 the danger of drawing superficial analogies between military mobilization and industrial mobilization. They were different problems requiring different solutions.[31]

Thomas was very aware that his industrialist's approach to arms manufacturing placed him at odds with the majority opinion in parliament as well as with the general public, which was very sensitive to the enormous discrepancies in the living conditions of mobilized soldiers and mobilized workers in factories and to the profits of the war industries. This can be seen in the Dalbiez proposal on labor,[32] which emphasized the extent to which "the presence, far from the front, of young, vigorous men, whether mobilized or not, greatly troubles families who know that their family members face great suffering and danger." A proposal put forward by Mistral[33] sought to "put an immediate end . . . to the scandals that have been denounced" in regard to the pricing of military supplies.

Thomas was fully aware of these criticisms and acknowledged their basis in fact in a letter to Clémentel on 29 July 1915. However, he remained adamantly opposed to proposals which, "even if based on an ideal of justice, which is admirable and perfectly legitimate in itself, ignore another important objective to which all others must be subordinated: maximum production."[34] This conviction induced Thomas, like Millerand and the armed services before him,[35] to reject the widespread belief in parliament that industrial capacity, especially in small business, was not fully utilized. The latter view was expounded by Treignier, president of the Army Commission's subcommittee on armaments, at a hearing held in June 1915.[36] It was also at the heart of the Mistral proposal and was taken up again by Viollette in 1916. On 28 November 1916, Thomas was required to explain himself at length in this regard before a secret committee.[37] He was convinced and could only reiterate that capacity was fully utilized and that increased production could only come from new factories or expanded facilities which would take time to construct. Insofar as the 155-mm steel shells so much in demand after July 1915 were concerned, Thomas could only point out that there were only five manufacturers who had just begun to deliver the order for 180,000 such shells placed in December 1914-January 1915. In August, 2,250,000 additional shells were ordered from the five established manufacturers and fifteen new manufacturers, whose deliveries were to start over the following six months. However, by January 1916 only one of the new manufacturers was actually able to deliver, and its production accounted for only 20 percent of the total.[38]

Thomas also realized that if all small business capacity was not fully utilized, it was not because of contempt for the armed services or greed on the part of the business leaders, but because of the quality and quantity of production that was needed. As he noted in the margin of the Mistral proposal, "small businesses could not do this quickly and by themselves."[39] The best solution in Thomas's view was not to set all of France to work manufacturing shells but to obtain maximum output from those companies able to satisfy minimum requirements. However, Thomas refused to accept the radical proposals of his industry service head, Hugoniot, who suggested in August 1915 that the production of large steel shells be encouraged by a bonus system which, he acknowledged, would favor big industry.[40] Thomas' grand plans were much more focused on new approaches, as can be seen in the support he was providing Hugoniot at the same time for pressing shells by direct use of falling water or for construction of the Saint-Pierre des Corps pressed shell factory.[41]

The problems in the war industry were therefore open to various types of solutions. Some in the Chamber of Deputies favored requisitioning while others, undoubtedly a majority, like the Army Commission preferred massive intervention on the part of the state, especially in the financial area. Thomas's fundamental conviction, which he repeated in identical terms in his July 1915 letter to Clémentel and in his speech of February 1917, was that an arrangement should be developed which had "undergone practical testing in industry and which appeals to all sorts of private initiative, asking it to make a greater effort but of the same sort in which it is already engaged."[42]

Thomas believed that company managers should be left in charge of their firms and should retain responsibility for managing them, because they were the pivotal cog in the production process.[43] Thomas often repeated this view, which was reformulated more crudely by his adviser Simiand in a note on the Voilin report, where he said that one should state "straight-out" that any plan to operate industries with only workers and technicians on the one hand and loaners of capital on the other was "simply to forget the key to production, that is management and the captains of industry. . . . Can the entrepreneurial spirit be requisitioned, the taste for risk, if the *sine qua non* of risk-taking has been eliminated, namely the reward?"[44] In Thomas's view, entrepreneurs had to be allowed a fair return for their efforts. It would be foolish to admire and encourage genuine initiative, while discarding "what in the industrial world constitutes the reward for initiative and risk-taking."[45] Furthermore, and in contrast with Voilin and Clémentel,[46] Thomas often repeated his October 1915 reply to the latter[47] that "in many cases war production, far from posing fewer difficulties than normal production, has posed greater difficulties."[48] War profits therefore could not be considered a risk-free bonus.[49] Thomas and the government under his influence consequently rejected all proposals based on requisitioning or on the British example of "controlled factories," such as that of Voilin, which made explicit references to British practice. They refused to "impose on all companies in the arms industry a new system based on theories developed independently of the lessons of experience,"[50] and which would tend "to eliminate or at least reduce and equalize at a fairly low level the profits earned by these companies."[51] Far from believing that the income gap between especially dynamic industrialists and laggards should be reduced, Thomas and Simiand believed that it should be increased.[52]

This does not mean, however, that Thomas turned a deaf ear to the criticisms of the existing system. As early as the summer of 1915 he was very aware of the huge disparity in the living conditions of men at the front and those allowed to work in industry, and between industries that were still operating and those that had been forced to shut down,[53] and he was extremely concerned about the risk of a split with public opinion.[54] Until July 1916, he maintained that these inequities could only be attenuated by asserting "through an innovation with a high moral and social standing the solidarity which must continue to bind together those parts of the nation which are most favored in some respects with those which have been called upon to play a role which is considerably less advantageous."[55] This moral and social innovation was a double social tax on manufacturers' profits and on the wages of mobilized workers. The moral rectitude of this innovation would be demonstrated by the fact that the money thus raised would be directed to industries that had suffered because of the war or to the families of casualties of the war, and would not become part of the government's general revenues as in the Mistral-Voilin proposal. The funds would be jointly administered by the state, representatives of manufacturers and mobilized workers, and representatives of the beneficiaries.[56] Thomas appears therefore to have consciously advocated and carried on the industrial policies established by Millerand at a time when both chambers of parliament would have liked to strike out in other directions. In July 1915, eight weeks after his arrival in the Undersecretariat, Thomas expressed to Clémentel the view he would continue to hold for another year. While recognizing that the system he was defending had to be judged comprehensively, he responded to Clémentel's criticisms by asking whether "as of now, one could not say that, on the whole and most particularly in regard to the manufacturing with which I have been involved, the development of production and increases in performance that have been achieved so far do not constitute a strong argument in favor of the system that has been adopted."[57]

There was nevertheless another aspect to Thomas' policies which his defense of the *union sacrée* or of the initiative shown by the captains of industry should not obscure: he was a man in a powerful position who was eager to defend the interests of the state and for whom wartime manufacturing could never be compared to peacetime manufacturing. He often expressed the view that the state, which defended the higher interests of national defense, was "the guiding principle which focuses all efforts on a single goal."[58] This concern is illustrated by several firm warnings to industrialists who seemed more preoccupied with increasing their sales than satisfying the needs of the army. In the summer of 1915, Thomas reduced production of fuse covers for 75-mm shells and assigned it exclusively to small companies. When the large companies protested, Thomas responded: "It is impossible for the industrialists to whom we have assigned these reduced orders to impose higher quantities upon us, which is precisely what we wished to avoid. It would be unworthy of industry, unacceptable for the government, and contrary to the interests of National Defense for industry to impose on the state products for which it has only a limited need." In regard to 75-mm shells, the production of which eventually surpassed the amounts which even Joffre wanted, and which had to be curtailed for a while because of a lack of steel, Thomas reminded the manufacturers that "in accordance with the terms of the contracts, production could only be increased if authorized by the Heavy Industry Service. No industrialist has sought this authorization, and none has even informed the service in advance of the increase in its production."[59] At the same time, Thomas wrote a note to Major-General Pellé castigating certain "industrialist parliamentarians" who tried to exploit the appeal for "cannons and munitions" in order to "obtain orders for which I have no use."[60]

These concerns of Thomas are even more apparent in the service reorganization undertaken between June and November 1915. This reorganization had three parts: first, the gradual expansion of the authority of the undersecretary of state for war, from simple civilian director of artillery in May to head of all arms manufacturing for the army and related material procurement in November;[61] second, the creation of new services such as the Labor Service and the Industrial Service,[62] and then the Raw Materials Service, the Transportation Service and the Power Service;[63] and third, the internal reorganization of the old and new services, based on a division between the "Central Administration," in charge of "management, coordination, and decision making,"[64] and "External Services," which were themselves further divided into study and experimentation units and manufacturing services. The DGFA for example comprised the old services of the Board of Artillery Manufacturing Inspectors and the Heavy Industry Branch and the new industrial, transportation, power, and raw material services.[65]

This reorganization and expansion of the powers of the office of the undersecretary of state should not be interpreted as reflecting a desire for more state intervention or for nationalization of all war production. This would have contradicted Thomas's basic principles. What happened was that industrialists were experiencing mounting difficulties and were themselves often demanding government intervention, as could be seen for instance in regard to steel. The industrialists who signed contracts in July and August 1915 to deliver large steel shells did so without first securing adequate sources of raw materials. They then turned either to the government or to Schneider, in Le Creusot, a manufacturer and importer of American steel. In order to avoid such incidents, Thomas decided to organize a steel service "which would hold all orders effective after . . . from all factories in France. From this date on, it would centralize all the needs of industrialists and of the services of the Ministry of War and distribute them among the various mills depending on the proximity of the user and the urgency of the order."[66]

Insofar as coal was concerned, it was Léon-Lévy, president of the union of manufacturers of war material, who requested that the state railroads build up stocks in the Loire area. Though Thomas did not reject this out of hand, he preferred that the industrialists make their own arrangements.[67] In addition, some of the new services were still simple research or informational units in 1915.[68]

The creation of the new services did not free Thomas from his heavy reliance on industrial organizations, which he considered superior to simple military missions. In the autumn of 1915, he persuaded the Comité des Forges (the heavy industry association) to create an office for the purchase of hematite ovens from foreign countries.[69] At the same time, he wrote in a personal letter to Félix Binder, who had been sent to the United States: "in so far as our representatives in America are concerned, it is the industrialists themselves who should do the talking. Unfortunately French administrative rules, and even more, the habits of parliament and common predilections in our unhappy country prevent us from following, as I would like, the example set by Lloyd George."[70] Thomas returned to this theme again one year later with Dharvernaz, who also was on a mission in the United States.[71] However, the service reorganization also should not be reduced to simply a pragmatic reaction to certain situations. Thomas was anxious to provide the government with the means he thought it needed in order to intervene actively. The reorganization was intended first and foremost to provide the government with greater autonomy *vis-à-vis* the large industrial associations. Reminding the Chamber of Deputies on 27 February 1917 of the foundations of his policies, Thomas proclaimed: "Does this mean that in appealing to industry through the contract system . . . we would necessarily be happy with the form of organization it was beginning to adopt with its trusts and marketing cartels?"[72] It seems significant in this regard that the first two services created by Thomas were the Labor Service and the Industrial Service, which assumed certain tasks previously performed by the Comité des Forges.

The Labor Service recovered for the government the right to recall workers. This was an area where abuses had been both numerous and highly criticized, as Thomas himself recognized as early as June 1915 in his comments before committees of the Chamber. In regard to "shirkers," he commented: "We are aware of several hundred. I don't quite dare say there are thousands, but there are certainly large numbers in most companies. . . . When we begin asking industrialists for names, we must ensure that it is not taken as an opportunity to call up false workers. There must be effective controls."[73]

According to the departmental order of 12 June 1915, the Industrial Service was to receive and study proposals from industrialists and to organize and categorize production capacities, especially in regard to small business.[74] Formerly this had been the responsibility of group leaders, and as was seen previously in regard to labor, their performance had been heavily criticized.[75] The role of the Industrial Service was further expanded in November 1915, when it was charged with "carrying out systematic studies in order to ensure that industrial production of arms and munitions is at a maximum across the entire country" and with centralizing the available relevant information.[76]

The reorganization of the various services ultimately was intended to provide the state with the tools it needed to perform a task which Thomas considered essential and urgent: to foresee through medium-term planning all that would be needed to fulfill the programs presented by the supreme command and to coordinate the efforts to fulfill these programs. He stated his intentions clearly before the commissions of the Chamber of Deputies in June 1915 when he said that he wanted not only "to respond to the utmost of our ability to the needs and wants of the army" but also "to reach beyond the immediate program, which varies according to circumstances . . . and beyond the requests of men who, because of the position in which they find themselves, cannot always foresee what will be needed for tomorrow's campaign."[77]

In December Thomas announced that the June shell-production plan had been spread over six months and that the shell contracts signed in July had served as a rule of thumb for the Powders Service over the same period. Thomas recognized that he had assumed a heavy responsibility in undertaking a six-month general program, but declared that "if we have established a program in cooperation with the government, with the Technical Service, and with parliament, which meets the expressed needs of the supreme command, it is in order to have an ideal, a stimulus. We don't want to experience any more periods of crisis and difficulty such as we previously witnessed."[78] However, such an approach did not immediately convince the various services. General Gossot, the inspector of studies and experimentation, pointed out to Thomas in August that the Gunpowder Service responded to the semiannual program established by the Artillery Service only through production forecasts established in the normal way one month in advance.[79]

Insofar as the war industries were concerned, the role of the state was reaffirmed in various ways between 1915 and the speech of February 1917, all of which implied basically that industry was no longer free.[80] The special treatment of these industrialists and their work forces came with "very tight controls and strict compliance, which require of these industries and their work forces the singular effort which is both the reason for and the justification of their special treatment."[81]

The reorganization of the services therefore did not end the controls instituted by Millerand but actually reinforced them.[82] Thomas quickly demonstrated that he did not intend to limit the controls exercised by the state to checking the use of military labor or the delivery of products "by the deadlines established in the contracts and in accordance with the regulations," as Léon-Lévy suggested in July 1915 on behalf of the War Material Manufacturers.[83] Thomas's intent was particularly apparent in the war industry bills which the services began preparing in the summer of 1915, bills that were all the more significant in that they aimed only to legalize standard practices. They included a clear statement of the principle (already implicit in the letter to Clémentel in July 1915) of the right of the state to control, through its agents, military production and manpower.[84]

This control was to be of two types. One somewhat "ordinary" type carried out by the heavy industry officer, detachment leader, and labor controller was defined in a later report in the following terms: the state oversees orders, the receipt of manufactured goods, and the rational use of labor; ensures that facilities are fully used and that the night work performed is compatible with the work force; and establishes priorities for the manufacture of various goods.[85] In addition to these ordinary controls, Thomas claimed for the state the right to have representatives continually checking the arms industries. At first the industrialists opposed the presence of such people. In his response to Léon-Lévy, Thomas promised to define clearly their role, but at the same time defended the principle of "unexpected spot checks" which provided "direct information on particular matters of interest to National Defense." He continued that "the patriotism of industrialists enables them to understand that their shops and factories, which they have placed at the service of National Defense, could not continue to enjoy all the liberties and independence of purely private companies."[86] When the issue was apparently raised again by Léon-Lévy and the industrialists, Thomas responded clearly in October that "no one will deny the minister his right and duty to keep an eye on all factories."[87]

The plans established in 1915 revealed further determination to take measures when a company's performance was judged inadequate. They attempted to develop a legal basis for what Thomas had been attempting to do through a combination of threat and persuasion: if management proved inadequate, the state had the right to impose a services representative "invested with control over the technical, industrial or commercial management of the company insofar as manufacturing related to contracts signed with the state is concerned."[88] This was done at Marrel, for instance, where Thomas appointed a military director.[89] In case of a disagreement with the manufacturer, the decisions of the state representative would be enforced until the conflict was settled by an arbitration committee including one representative of the service involved, an industrialist working in the same sector, and a chairman appointed by the Council of Ministers who could award damages.[90] Finally, in cases "of notorious incompetence or bad faith,"[91] the services asked that the requirements for requisitioning set forth in the 1877 act be eased, particularly the contradictory types of inventories which limited its effectiveness. In case of incompetence on the part of the industrialist, the bill allowed the state to requisition property, totally or in part, in the form of buildings or equipment and to take immediate possession of supplies and stocks after a summary inventory had been taken and signed by the owner.[92] By the summer of 1915, Thomas was therefore eager to impose service control over the war industry by attempting to "gain a hold over industrialists without having to actually requisition their property."[93]

The same kind of determination was also apparent very early in regard to all conditions contained in contracts signed with the government. In a letter to a deputy in July 1915, Thomas wrote that his services were attempting "to squeeze the cost of contracts as much as product quality will allow,"[94] and in a note on the price committee written toward the end of August he wrote that this was a "crucial" issue.[95] In the summer of 1915, he ordered the services to prepare studies on the cost price of certain products such as large steel or semi-steel shells.[96] The turning point came in early September with the creation of a Contracts Commission directly under the Undersecretariat of State. Ten people sat on the commission: the president (Claveille), four "members" (including Cordier, the chairman of the Chambre syndicale des forces hydrauliques, de l'électro-métallurgie et de l'électro-chimie, General Mourret, and Résal, the honorary engineer in chief of locomotives for the Chemins de Fer de l'Est), and five "secretary reporters" who studied businesses and reported on them orally (including one finance department inspector, an artillery officer, an assistant controller in the Undersecretariat of State, and a lawyer from the Court of Appeal in Paris). It had to be consulted "in regard to contracts signed with this administration, the prices and conditions contained in the contracts, and participation in supply companies for its services."[97] Thomas wished it to be a "technical council" whose members were "totally reliable, both in regard to the technical aspect and to their independence from any private interests which may be involved."[98] The commission played a dual role: it supervised contracts, to be sure, but in addition and although it denied it,[99] it acted as a think tank which played a key role in developing "an overall organization in accordance with certain fixed rules regarding both the financial interests of the state and the higher interests of National Defense."[100] The commission had an abiding influence in two areas: general contract policies (which it followed closely, often pointing out basic principles to be followed in regard to particular cases) and prices (after the initial September rates, which it periodically modified either as a result of its own investigations or investigations it asked the services to carry out).[101] The correspondence between its president, Claveille, and Thomas in the autumn of 1915 illuminates the contracts policy pursued by the Undersecretariat of State and underlines the pivotal role played by the former director of the Chemins de Fer de l'Etat in defining contract policy.[102]

These policies aimed first and foremost at ensuring that the interests of the state were upheld in the contracts which it signed. Responding to a letter from Claveille, Thomas summarized the objective as follows: assess the financial and moral worth of bidders to ensure that the state runs a minimum risk in signing contracts with them, systematically eliminate intermediaries and subcontractors not associated in advance with a job, reestablish penalty clauses for delays (a point to which Thomas was particularly attached),[103] insert cancellation clauses for the state during the life of the contract or in case of a cessation of hostilities, and require definite guarantees, the payment of interest on advances provided by the state, and a detailed accounting of expected investments.[104] Ultimately this meant a return to the General Clauses and Conditions Books of 1903 and 1907 – adapted to wartime by Claveille. In addition, since the state was not able to call on fully equipped industrialists and often had to help them build plants and even provide equipment and start-up and operating capital,[105] "new forms of cooperation with industry or of state participation in industry" had to be developed.[106] The principles proposed by Claveille and approved by Thomas were the following: the state would have the right to take over in their entirety (if not fully written off) new, amortized installations created to supply wartime markets, and to require in such cases production at reduced prices or participation in the management and profits of plants which were built with its help and which could be used after the war.[107] Thomas also insisted that the director general of Gunpowder insert these clauses into contracts for increasing hydraulic power and for the construction of chemical plants.[108]

Finally, Thomas was particularly concerned about doing more to uphold the interests of the state in prices negotiated with munitions manufacturers. Like Clémentel, Thomas believed that industrialists should be rewarded for their efforts but only to a "fair and equitable extent."[109] This could be done in two ways: either by carefully examining prices at the time contracts were signed or by confiscating part of the profits afterwards. Thomas's letter of 15 October to Clémentel indicates that he was considering both approaches, and it seems that at least until July 1916 he was leaning toward the first approach. The tax he proposed in his letter to Clémentel in July 1915 was primarily social in nature.[110] When it was refused by the government in early 1916, however, it became simply a possibility.[111] The services therefore attempted to gain a better understanding of cost prices. On 15 January 1916, Thomas wrote to the president of the general union of iron smelters "that in the absence of an extensive, competitive market, as in peacetime, we have the right and the duty to look into the manufacturing process and the genuine factors in the cost price of the various products for which we place orders."[112] The DGFA demanded that suppliers of shells break down prices into three components: metal, depreciation and labor costs.[113] This information was checked on the spot by the local Heavy Industry Services. The services also made use of studies carried out in state-operated factories and information provided by sympathetic private manufacturers[114] or taken from parliamentary investigations, such as that conducted by Deputy Couesnon in 1915 into brass manufacturing, partially at the request of Thomas. The services subsequently consulted Couesnon about brass contracts.[115] Contracts signed under the mixed management system after the autumn of 1915 made it possible, thanks to the financial controls they contained, to check the prices furnished by industrialists. The first contract of this type seems to have been the one signed on 5 October 1915 with the Société de l'Eclairage Electrique, managed by Loucheur, for 300,000 75-mm shells and an equal number of fuse covers. A study carried out at the end of the contract showed that, thanks to the normalization of production, the cost price had declined by 16 per cent in eight months, maintaining the margin per shell at about the same level, despite the increased cost of materials and successive reductions in the final price.[116] In this way, the proportion attributable to depreciation and manufacturing costs could be distinguished and prices could be set, first for semisteel shells and then in the autumn of 1915 for steel shells.[117] In addition, supplementary sources of profit could be identified, such as those realized by shell manufacturers and even more so by brass manufacturers on scrap and turnings. Insofar as brass is concerned, Couesnon showed that the contracts signed at the time of mobilization overestimated the cost of producing brass from copper and zinc and overlooked the fact that almost all scrap could be reutilized.[118] Thanks to Couesnon's efforts and to the studies carried out by the services and the Contracts Commission, these errors were set right, and mixed committees of officers and manufacturers set new prices in November 1915.[119] In the view of Thomas and his collaborators, these efforts would make it possible to lower prices when contracts were renewed by eliminating double amortization, reducing some excessive prices, taking advantage of the increasing habitualness of this type of production, and resisting demands for increased prices as a result of the mounting cost of materials and labor.[120]

Though eager to control, coordinate, and discipline, Thomas denied exercising the same type of meddlesome control over industry of which Clémentel had accused the previous administration in June 1915, asking Thomas "to call off this unspoken battle, of which everyone is aware, between your Artillery Branch and industrialists."[121] Beginning in the summer of 1915, Thomas insisted (even twice on the same day in his speech at Le Creusot[122] and then in a circular[123]) on the need for "mutual confidence" between the government and manufacturers. He returned to this theme one year later in a letter to the manager of Firminy in which he wrote: "[Y]ou know the complete confidence I showed in working with you. . . . My great strength consists now in being able to work flat out for the defense of the country with some industrialists like you, whom I know well and in whom I have full confidence."[124] When the first results of the work performed by the Contracts Commission raised the ire of some industrialists in the autumn of 1915, Thomas clearly affirmed before the shell manufacturers that "the state has never gone back on its signature."[125] His solutions to some thorny issues about which industrialists were particularly concerned, such as the amortization problem, illustrate his constant desire to demonstrate that the government was more understanding of the needs of industrialists than the former services had been.

The basic principles behind amortization policies were defined in

November 1915 during the discussions about an order for 400,000 270-mm steel shells with Brunon and Valette.[126] The contract provided for three-quarters of the plant created for this purpose to be amortized over the course of one order. The Control Branch suggested only 25 percent per year, with the government taking control of the amortized equipment and only allowing the manufacturer an option to buy it back after the war at the purchase price less the amount that had been written off. In its analysis of the market, the Contracts Commission concluded that the vast majority of shell manufacturers had had to acquire all new equipment at wartime prices. Furthermore, this equipment would be useless for the most part after the war because it could not be adapted to peaceful purposes or would be worn out through intensive use. In response to the reservations expressed by the Control Branch, the Commission stated that it was "realistic and equitable" to take all this into account in setting amortization periods. In addition, the Commission added a significant remark that returned to the conclusions of an earlier report on the supervision of normal factory operations: One should avoid adding to the general rules established by the state "irritating conditions likely to destroy the good will shown by our industry."[127]

In a similar vein and as can also be seen in the report on normal operations cited above, Thomas very quickly resorted to indirect methods of inducement, financial in particular, in order to have his policies accepted. The arms factory projects developed in September 1915 provide an excellent illustration. Alongside the articles establishing the government's technical control were financial articles concerning social taxes designed to encourage production or, in the end, to economize on mobilized labor.[128] All these regulations provided for 10 percent reductions in employers' contributions for industrialists who added equipment, built new plants without state assistance, modified or created companies for the production of munitions, or provided reliable production in quality and quantity without surpassing the mobilized labor rates established by the services. By the same token, 10 percent increases were applicable to companies which received financial assistance from the state, utilized subcontractors, or whose production was unreliable or late.[129] All this was the ultimate result of a conviction often stated by Thomas and some of his collaborators that there should be a premium for initiative and risk as well as a penalty for companies which "passively took advantage of conditions that were already very favorable or were created by others."[130]

Thus, contrary to the opinion of the Army Commission and also, certainly, the opinion of some of his close collaborators such as Simiand[131] or even Claveille, who apparently favored a more coercive approach to industry, Thomas refused to institute an entirely new system, trying instead simply "to put into law what practice has wrought over the years and shown to be efficient."[132] He sought to reconcile all the pressures on him while maintaining the contract system. However, the system had to be somewhat readjusted in the government's favor, since the controls it imposed were the only defense against the much more invasive controls favored by the Chamber of Deputies. Contracts were accordingly freely arrived at, as Thomas reminded the Chamber on 27 February 1917,[133] and signed in the usual manner, but the parties were no longer in the unequal bargaining positions of the beginning of the war. Thomas believed that the government, responsible for the higher interests of national defense, competent, mindful of the needs of industry but also strengthened by its knowledge of costs and the threat of requisitioning, should be able to obtain through a mixture of firmness and suasion the maximum production it sought at conditions that were acceptable to all contractors.

The outcome of the brass affair provides a good illustration of this approach, which Thomas outlined to Claveille in his response of September 1915.[134] In order to review the contracts concluded at the time of mobilization, three meetings were held involving Mourret, the representative of the Contracts Commission, the director of the Heavy Industry Service, the president of the Chambre syndicale and several industrialists. On 30 November, Mourret summarized the position of the services as follows: "We pay different prices, but we don't want to ruin anyone. Each receives his fair share. We don't want to pay someone more who is able to produce at a lower cost." The answer of Vésier, the president of the Chambre syndicale, showed that industry could understand this: "Under normal circumstances, both large and small survive. Why should anything change now? The state attempts to establish a price that will not pose undue difficulties. That is what counts."[135] However, Thomas refused to accept new formulas for calculating prices developed by these conferences. Instead he proposed a different model and told Claveille that if industrialists would not accept it, a different method would have to be used, possibly requisitioning, although "the latter measure would only be taken as a last resort." Thomas concluded by offering his opinion that it would be easy to persuade industrialists to accept the "equitable" formula which he was proposing — and which indeed they did accept.[136]

In this attempt to reach a delicate balance, what part was played by circumstance and personal preference? First, it is clear that Thomas's policy reflected, at least to some extent, a balance of forces rather crudely described by François de Wendel in the Chamber of Deputies in June 1916: "In general, the government cannot possibly take over from private industry at the present time. Under these conditions, it is necessary to use the methods it has at its disposal and, as I just said, to exploit self-interest."[137] As Thomas himself wrote to Clémentel a few months later, it was necessary to "pay a large bonus" in order to launch new production lines.[138] Thomas and his services also knew that it was not so much materials as manpower that was in short supply. As a result, "the present system could not possibly be replaced by any other system ... because of the lack of management personnel to replace the personnel now running the companies."[139] Considering after the war the dilemma posed at the time, Thomas said that he was blamed for not having created state-operated companies, but that there would have been two risks in this: if he had put army officers in charge, "people would have said, as they did, that I was putting incompetent people in charge who didn't understand anything about business," and if he had drawn on "reserve officers, that is industrialists . . . we would have been blamed for having an interest in the contracts."[140]

Nevertheless, without going into the views expressed by Thomas after the war about what he had done, it seems likely for various reasons that the contract system which he defended corresponded quite closely to what he would have wished. This is apparent in the telling notes he made during the first debate on the Mistral-Voilin proposal in the Chamber of Deputies in June 1916 and more especially in the notes in which he expressed his reaction to the speech by François de Wendel. De Wendel had continued the remarks cited above as follows:

> It is because some industrialists, some merchants, and I would even say some middlemen saw an opportunity in risking everything to earn a lot of money that we were able, in the critical period of the autumn of 1914 and frequently since then, to surmount difficulties which at first seemed insurmountable. Are we the day after such a test going to renounce a method which has served us so well? That seems totally inconceivable to me.

While admitting the existence of "considerable, even excessive" profits and the need to get at them, de Wendel concluded by saying that it would be "a serious mistake to deny industrialists the hope of additional profits. Greater efforts must be rewarded with greater profits, without which the mainspring of progress would disappear." In a note to Simiand, Thomas summarized his reaction as follows: "He speaks the truth, but in a very capitalist form. It is necessary to point out in what ways those truths accord with our socialist doctrine and in what ways we will be forced to revise it."[141] In the view of both Thomas and de Wendel, the contract system ensured the best performance, despite the fact that it had been originally instituted as a result of the particular circumstances prevailing at the outbreak of the war.

The reasons for this conviction become clear if we consider two policies which appear in the records from late 1915 and early 1916 and which shed light on the foundations of Thomas's policy. At the same time that the Contracts Commission was established, the first project on the munitions industry called for the services to "establish a fixed, unitary price for each element of production, periodically reviewed by the interministerial Contracts Commission."[142] The second policy was to encourage new industrialists to appear through the large bonuses paid for launching new types of production, thus modifying the supply-demand ratio in the government's favor and making it possible for the government to conclude contracts under more favorable conditions. It was this hope which the first draft of the bill addressed, indicating that the fixed prices for each element could only be revised by the Commission "with no increase possible except that justified by the increased price of raw materials, duly noted by the same Commission."[143] This policy did not seem unreasonable in view of the fact that solely in the month of August 1915 fifteen new manufacturers of large steel shells emerged and were awarded contracts. It was not by chance that Thomas asked Simiand to create a file on his zinc policy,[144] an area in which, after the initial upsurge in prices, new factories in France and abroad had begun to stabilize the market, making the contracts signed in the first half of 1916 much less expensive for the government.[145] It therefore seems certain that Thomas hoped to use the contract system combined with appropriate controls in order to make industry as efficient an industry as possible in the service of the French war effort.

2. The Change of Course in 1916

When the Mistral proposal, as modified by the Army Commission, came before the Chamber of Deputies on 8 June 1916, no agreement could be reached with the government.[146] The next day, Thomas had the debate adjourned by announcing the introduction of a new proposal called the "Transactional Bill."[147] However, it merely repeated the same principles which Thomas had been championing for a year, and the discord only deepened when the Army Commission examined it.[148] Reporting to Thomas on the Army Commission discussions, Voilin noted that the two proposals were "based on entirely different principles." He informed Thomas that the Commission, if it could not requisition, wanted at least a share in management, and that it would call for this if necessary before the Chamber of Deputies. Voilin therefore asked the government to reexamine its position in order to reach an agreement before the proposal returned to the Chamber.[149] At the end of July, Thomas officially presented the Commission with a new policy which came much closer to its own views, providing for a share in management and an equal split between the government and the manufacturer of profits exceeding 10 percent of the value of the contract, with retroactive effect. This would require all contracts concluded since the outbreak of the war to be reviewed.[150] Discussions between Thomas and the Commission continued on this basis in a climate of close cooperation. Noting the work that had been done, Oualid, a collaborator of Thomas, indicated in August that "in order to proceed in harmony with us and to present his report by the beginning of autumn, Voilin would like to have . . . the document which the Undersecretary of State told him could be drawn up. In this way, there would be no apparent difficulties. Voilin would ask purely and simply for the adoption of the text proposed by the Undersecretary of State."[151]

In October, Voilin published the new text of the Mistral-Voilin proposal in a "supplementary report" which, although it was simply a proposed law, represented the "text which we studied together concerning the profits of arms manufacturers," about which Thomas had spoken in a letter to Voilin written in October 1916.[152] This provoked serious differences of opinion within the government, whose official position remained the June Transactional Bill. Thomas gave the new text his official blessing, saying that he approved its principles and making no attempt to hide the fact that he had helped to draft its main provisions.[153] Ribot, on the other hand, maintained his former objections: to revise contracts was to renege on solemn undertakings, solely to the disadvantage of government suppliers and with the risk that serious industrialists would be discouraged. The tax prescribed by the new text would be smaller than that instituted by the law of 1 July 1916 and could only be implemented slowly and after many procedures. After the war, Ribot still believed that the right given to the government to appoint an assistant manager would only have increased costs.[154] Despite repeated requests from the Budget Commission to move forward,[155] the entire bill was delayed until the middle of February. It was only during the debates in the Chamber of Deputies and, according to Voilin, thanks to President Poincaré's personal intervention that the government adopted the bill as its own.[156] In February then, Thomas became a proponent of this proposal which he said he supported "for significant political reasons . . . for national reasons."[157] By July, this support had led to a virtual rupture in ministerial solidarity. Nevertheless, Thomas continued to affirm that the system of arms production in effect at the time needed no fundamental change.[158] Speaking for the government before the Chamber on 27 February 1917, Thomas insisted that "most of the articles reinforce the system that already exists, a system that we built up, piece by piece, through the policies we pursued day after day."[159] Thomas's approach was therefore not without its ambiguities, as was pointed out by some members of the Chamber, particularly those on the left, who believed that Thomas did not support the bill wholeheartedly.[160] It is therefore essential to point out what was innovative about this new approach and what was a continuation of previous methods and to attempt to explain the reasons for this new approach adopted in mid-1916, of which the agreement with the Army Commission was only the most visible aspect.

First of all, the new text certainly included many of the ideas that Thomas had been advocating since 1915. The bill was not composed on the spot out of whole cloth, but was responsive to Thomas's traditional concern about building an industrial mobilization system "flexible enough to respond as quickly as possible to any need which may arise."[161] All articles in the bill dealing with technical controls and mobilized labor were taken from previous plans designed by the services.[162] In these areas, there was complete continuity and agreement with the Commission. The financial part of the proposal eliminated the coercive aspects of Voilin's original suggestions, especially controls over accounting and cash flow related to government contracts and the need to keep separate, standardized books. Instead, a double accounting system was adopted: the first covering operations between 1 August 1914 and 1 January 1917, and the second from 1 January 1917 until the cessation of hostilities.[163] Furthermore, government confiscation of profits in excess of 10 percent of the value of a contract was replaced by a share in management. As a result, manufacturers continued to be eligible for additional profits,[164] and the amortization and reduction plans were preserved, which Thomas had championed and which benefited those industrialists who had thrown themselves into the manufacture of munitions right from the start. In conformity with the practices adopted by the Contracts Commission, the new text proposed under "exceptional amortization" that installations which had been specially built for the war effort and were of no use or market value after the war could be fully written off unless the state wished to take them over. In addition, the extra costs of "reusable" equipment incurred because of the war effort could also be fully written off, if that equipment was located in France.[165]

However, the new law did more than simply consecrate established practices, as can be seen in particular in the financial area, which Thomas touched upon in his speech of 27 February 1917. In this respect, the minister and with him the government, defended policies which they formerly had opposed. The new proposal was aimed explicitly at munitions manufacturers who, it was now admitted, had profited directly from the war, "sometimes without any particular effort on their part."[166] War profits were therefore no longer seen exclusively as legitimate remuneration for the effort expended, as Thomas and the services had maintained as late as June 1916, but also as a "phenomenon of surplus social value, only part of whose increase can be explained by activity and individual initiative."[167] This was breaking the conspiracy of silence which the government had maintained by consistently denying that any problem existed in regard to profit levels in the arms industry. When questioned about this matter when provisional credits were being voted for the third quarter of 1915, Ribot had spoken only of the savings to be made: "It is the general attitude which has to change; the Quartermaster General's staff have to be persuaded that there are limits to what they can spend."[168] When questioned in the same regard by the Socialist Deputy Bedouce, Millerand had explained that the shortfalls that were discovered were simply the result of "the nature of things and inherent difficulties in so complex an operation. . . . One should not lose sight of the forest for the trees," he continued.[169] Similarly, Briand had responded at the end of the year to questions from Symian, Colliard, and several of their colleagues by confining the problem to a few inevitable disparities.[170] In January 1916, Ribot presented the bill addressing this problem as "an extraordinary contribution in regard to the exceptional profits realized during the war."[171] During the debates in parliament and with the support of the Budget Commission,[172] he firmly refused to distinguish between "profits realized on contracts with the government and those realized on general commerce," claiming that "the government cannot treat those which have contracted with it more harshly than others," and "it is unacceptable to focus general suspicion on those who have worked and are working for the war effort."[173]

Thomas himself in his various plans had only envisaged a "social" tax explicitly intended to help industries damaged by the war. The new proposal therefore broke with prior policy in an area in which industrialists had always proved extremely touchy, as can be seen in their responses in parliament during the debate on the special contribution and the Mistral-Voilin proposal,[174] as well as in Thomas's files on various matters. For instance, the arguments used by the services in financial discussions surrounding the use of equipment belonging to Schneider for the war effort were very poorly received. The company retorted that it was "surprised to find for the second time among the arguments you make the view that 'the state of war has undoubtedly benefited your industry,' when in reality it has taken risks which have been recognized by the minister himself." This grievance went all the way to Thomas himself, who wrote in a note to Ronneaux, "I saw the people from Le Creusot, who complained quite bitterly about the war benefiting their industries. Fournier appeared extremely annoyed." Thomas continued: "It is a view which we should not express in our letters, lest we ourselves repeat in fact what we find excessive about the law on war profits and about the limitations placed on these profits."[175] In a letter to Dumuis, Thomas wrote at the same time, "I was moved by our conversation yesterday and am worried about the state of mind in which I found you. . . . You can tell me exactly what is worrying you, whether in regard to the law on war profits, certain technical incidents, or work force problems." This response even implies that the issue had damaged their previously trusting relationship.[176] Not surprisingly, the issue was raised once again in the general discussions held in the Chamber of Deputies in February 1917. De Wendel emphasized that the new text "intends to create in our legislation a new category of taxpayer: munitions manufacturers, or more generally, government suppliers."[177] De Dion was even more extreme, speaking of a plundering law which reneged on signatures, and he provoked a serious incident with the Socialists during the session by declaring that the text was creating a situation "which will undermine, when the time comes again to borrow, the confidence which the entire country must feel."[178]

The new text also shows that Thomas decided in July 1916 to support the principle of a general limitation on profits in future contracts and a review of previous contracts. He therefore accepted henceforth the "general measures" demanded by the Army Commission, some of which certainly reflected his wishes, such as participation in management, although none of the armed services' previous plans had included such measures. Thomas therefore sacrificed one aspect of his policies to which he was particularly attached, that of a solidarity tax and accounts in which the receipts would be placed. The tax on the wages of mobilized workers was removed in the autumn as a result of pressure from the Army Commission, and the receipts from participation in management or the special contribution on previous contracts went into the Treasury's general revenues.[179]

It is possible that this change of course was motivated by political expediency. By 1915 Thomas was very aware of the difficulties which might arise from the disparities in the treatment of various categories of mobilized men. Public opinion became increasingly sensitive to this issue in 1916. Thomas may therefore have felt, as he wrote in a letter to Japy in March 1916, that the "martial spirit" was endangered,[180] which he had so praised in his speech at Le Creusot.[181]

Most of all, Thomas was coming under increased pressure from the majority in the Chamber of Deputies, especially the Socialists, who criticized his pricing and contract policies while advocating more stringent measures. One of them, a second lieutenant in the Gunpowder Service (and a professor at the Collège de France in civilian life), wrote to him in late 1916: "At the present time, you no longer have, whether in the country, parliament, or your services, the vast supply of confidence and good will which previously made it possible for you to hesitate or even be wrong. If you fail now, what a defeat for our ideas, what a misfortune for our party!"[182] As Thomas wrote to Poincaré in February 1917, "two ideas have become extremely popular and strong and are a focal point for the leftist opposition: a review of war profits (and for that matter an investigation of all the industrialists' transactions), and second a government share in management."[183] Pressure from parliament in this direction had already become apparent in early 1916 in the additional articles presented at the end of the discussion on "special contributions" by Merlin and Couesnon, and which were voted for by the Socialists despite the opposition of the government and of Voilin himself.[184] The pressure became even more apparent in July, when the Army Commission refused the Transactional Bill prepared by the government and threatened to introduce itself Voilin's text before the Chamber.[185] The mounting difficulty which the Budget Commission was experiencing in attempting to block requisitioning also reveals this pressure.[186] Its president reacted by pushing the government to provide an opinion on Voilin's text.[187] Thomas was very sensitive to these criticisms and to the reasons behind them. Already at the time of the debates on the Mistral-Voilin proposal, he had asked Simiand to put together the gist of a response to the criticism of his pricing policy.[188]

In August, Thomas asked the services to prepare studies on contracts cancelled for nonfulfillment or renunciation in order to "respond to the widespread idea that you only need to receive war contracts in order to make profits."[189] In his letter to Poincaré in February 1917 he invoked "grave political reasons" for defending the Mistral-Voilin proposal.[190] It therefore seems likely, as the *Bulletin des usines de guerre* suggests, that Thomas attempted to reach a compromise that would "reconcile both approaches, that of freedom and that of requisitioning, by taking from each of them what seems to be most reasonable about it," while attempting to avoid, no doubt, a total triumph for the second approach.[191]

There was more involved here, it seems, than political opportunism. In the records compiled for his use in February 1917, Thomas found notes showing, by the calculations of the very services that worked most closely with him on policy, that the eighteen months of effort spent on reducing prices had not produced adequate results. This pertained first of all to the government's knowledge of cost prices. The instructions issued in September 1915 on Claveille's advice had failed to have the expected results. Officers of the Heavy Industry Service were "highly embarrassed" and usually simply asked industrialists for information which they should have obtained for themselves. Many industrialists invoked business confidentiality and refused to respond, and most provided only approximate answers "which revealed only thin profit margins."[192] The instructions were reissued in April 1916,[193] and reemphasized once again in July, but all apparently to no avail.[193] The Heavy Industry Service was overworked, the task was complicated, and there were not enough experts on hand to conduct the necessary investigations, according to a note of the Contracts Commission in early 1917.[194] A study carried out by the services in 1917 in order to respond to a report of the Senate Commission on Contracts indicates that this was the case in regard to rockets and fuse covers. The author advised opposing the report with "observations of fact," but allowed that the facts were still not available for these products. He added: "This case shows that it is not easy, even for us, to have actual statistics, even after several years." He points out in passing how difficult it was to determine the individual costs of production for each company and therefore to use the results seen in shared management, since cost prices fluctuated considerably, and differences between companies were quite large. A later report attached to the file indicates that in March 1917 cost prices varied by about 56 percent for companies with a daily production of between one and one hundred.[195] To these difficulties must be added what were surely the most serious obstacles: those placed by industrialists in the way of the contractual system.

Prices certainly declined on the whole, as Thomas pointed out in his speech of 27 February 1917.[196] A comparison of prices in the first contracts for shells at the outset of the war and those provided by Raiberti in his report of December 1916[197] shows the following decreases: 27.5 percent for 90-mm steel shells, 22.5 percent for 105-mm steel shells, 25.5 percent for 155-mm steel shells, 20 percent for 220-mm steel shells, 20 percent for 270-mm steel shells, 33 percent for 90-mm semi-steel shells, and 39 percent for 155-mm semi-steel shells. However, the services never succeeded in reaching the "fair" levels which Thomas had hoped to obtain in October 1915.[198] In a very tough note which he asked Simiand to make into a letter to Poincaré, Thomas outlined the reasons: the demand outran the industrialists' capacity, and "they choose the most profitable among several orders." Thus Thomas acknowledged the demise of his hopes for a better balance between supply and demand. The consequences, he wrote, were:

> the need to raise all prices and to offer equally high profits for all calibers of shells. They build the equipment, but here too they do not build it unless the profits are large. In both cases, the consequences are that we are forced to pay the prices they demand if we do not want to suffer a reduction in industrial output. Despite all our negotiations, despite our delays and our warnings, we cannot obtain anything. . . . We have to yield, yield as quickly as possible, so that there are not any delays and so that industry feels a certain indispensable enthusiasm.[199]

Finally, little came of the desire to establish a new relationship between industry and government through profit-sharing and participation in management. Thomas admitted before the Chamber of Deputies in February 1917 that apart from contracts with Eclairage Electrique, shared management had only been achieved in four or five cases.[200] It therefore seems likely that Thomas – as he implicitly said before the Chamber by declaring that the financial aspect of the bill "aims above all to ensure that excessive profits are no longer possible in future"[201] – was able to draw the consequences of the failure of his contract policy in the area of pricing. Unlike the Socialists, Thomas did not want to make this a public issue and openly denounce munitions manufacturers, as he remarked to Simiand in a "personal note."[202] It therefore seems very likely that he decided to support the plan for shared management in order to make it possible to remedy the failings of his pricing policy, satisfy the Army Commission without endangering most of the principles he espoused, and, he hoped, avoid any harm to the pace of production. There is no clear connection between Thomas's musings on his contracts policy and Voilin's new text, but the direction is clear. After remarking that it was necessary to acquiesce rapidly in order to preserve what was essential, namely high levels of production, Thomas added at the conclusion of his "personal note":

> [H]owever we must be aware right away, this situation will give rise to a price review, to a renewed public outcry about the excessive profits that are allegedly being extracted by industry [now they will have to produce], but then the people's innate sense of justice will emerge. However, we have to show immediately that we have not been duped.[203]

The new policy was evident as well in the desire to expand the government-controlled sector. As Thomas pointed out in February 1917,[204] the government had certainly not neglected to use the industrial capacity under its control, though it had simply continued its basic prewar policies on a larger scale. New installations were constructed mainly "for products that are too difficult, too uncertain, or too dangerous for private industry,"[205] primarily light arms, cartridges, powders, and explosives, of which the state produced from 62 to 97 percent of the total.[206] The state therefore did not expand its area of direct involvement between 1914 and 1916, except for the pressing of shells, which could be considered to fall under the categories mentioned above.

The situation changed, however, in 1916. The artillery program presented by Joffre in May of that year required a considerable increase in output.[207] After his great success at Saint Pierre-des Corps, Hugoniot apparently became one of Thomas's closest collaborators, and during the discussions they held during the summer, Hugoniot suggested the construction of a huge, highly efficient state-run factory. Hugoniot refused, however, to become the general manager of this factory, because he "cannot adapt industry to army regulations."[208] As an alternative, a private group would be called upon, particularly Citroën, which Hugoniot had consulted, and which could build in eight months a factory producing 50,000 shells a day, and which would revert to the state after one year.[209] In September, however, Hugoniot finally did agree to assume responsibility for such a factory,[210] and Thomas decided to create a huge arsenal costing 150 million francs which was able to produce cannons and shells of various calibers.[211] The reasons which were advanced illustrate the continuing preoccupation with the proposals on war industries. In addition to the technical arguments developed at length by Hugoniot,[212] Thomas advanced three main reasons, while seeking to provide assurances that he had no preconceived ideas[213] and was not trying to replace private industry with state-controlled plants.[214] The Roanne arsenal would serve to "moderate" the high prices demanded by industrialists, who were increasingly concerned about how much longer the war would last and whether they would be able to amortize their costs.[215] New investments were needed, but industrialists hesitated to make them because of these concerns, or else they demanded that the government provide most of the money. Thomas felt as a result that it was preferable for the state to make the investments and retain ownership of the plant and equipment.[216] The services estimated real savings solely for the manufacture of 75- and 155- mm shells at 474,800 francs a day, a rate which would amortize the plant in 315 production days.[217] Finally, Thomas considered it beneficial for the state in the long run, in the face of an industry that had been considerably strengthened during the war, to possess the plant and equipment for the construction of heavy guns, which it had lacked before the war and which would prevent the creation of what Thomas called a "veritable monopoly."[218] The arsenal appeared from many points of view to be a model state-run institution of the kind which Thomas hoped would replace the state's existing factories. It would put into practice the principles which Hugoniot had advocated since 1915 and which Thomas had defended before the Senate in March 1917:[219] extensive mechanization and rationalization of work, complete independence for the manager, especially in the choice and the remuneration of his coworkers, and an employee interest in the operating results.[220]

Thomas's high hopes for the war industry in the autumn of 1915 had therefore been shattered by the escalating demand and the mounting uncertainty about the duration of the war, which seemed increasingly to condition the attitude of industrialists, as the Socialist Deputy Bedouce pointed out in regard to the Roanne situation. All the while reaffirming the principles to which he remained attached, Thomas mounted a frontal assault on profits, which he never did succeed in controlling totally, and threatened French industrialists on their own turf. Was he aware that he was making even more difficult the operations of "this productive but unstable system" which he alluded to together with Dumuis in October 1916?[221] It is impossible to say, but certainly many people around him immediately perceived the stakes and the risks involved. In June 1916 Hugoniot concluded that the plan for a huge, state-run industry would encounter opposition from the Artillery Service, industry, and the entire parliament.[222] Once the project was launched, Thomas sounded out the Socialists in the Chamber of Deputies. They said they realized that this project surpassed anything which the state had undertaken since 1914 and that it was a crucial experiment for their plans for a state-run industrial system; however, they were also aware of the obstacles it would encounter, particularly reluctance on the part of the administration, "petty impediments" in parliament, and "surreptitious resistance" from industrialists.[223] Bedouce was even more forthright: precautions needed to be taken, they had not been taken, and "you have thrown yourself into this project in order to finish it quickly, without worrying about all the necessary formalities." Bedouce also noted that "industrialists will realize that this is a telltale project and that if it succeeds, it will disprove their claims." He closed with a remark that deserves more discussion: "Why not have a place in the administration for worker representatives?"[224]

3. An Assessment of Thomas's Policies

Albert Thomas therefore found himself in a highly unusual situation for almost three years: first because he was, in the words of John F. Godfrey, "a Socialist while performing the functions of a capitalist as director of the nation's wartime industrial program";[225] second, as Martin Fine notes, because he found himself at "one of the major focal points of interaction between business and labor,"[226] and third, as Gerd Hardach points out, because the development of industrial production, which seems in retrospect so obviously necessary, was approached in France in a very hesitant, gradual fashion.[227] After the failure of the Artois offensive and with the enormous orders for war material that ensued, it fell to Thomas to really mobilize industry, that is, to utilize fully the existing capacity and to create new capacity in order to fulfill programs whose results would not be felt for six months at the earliest.

There are several views of Thomas's efforts. Gerd Hardach, basing his argument on the experience of industrial mobilization in Germany and in other Allied countries, emphasizes the contrast between the rhetoric of government planning and control and the paltry actual results. He attributes this outcome to timidity and weakness on the part of planners who "did not want to risk a direct confrontation with the interests of capital."[228] Godfrey, in his more recent book, and with reference to Thomas in particular, takes a very similar view, pointing to a lack of will in the government, which abdicated its authority to the benefit of the Comité des Forges insofar as metal supplies are concerned. Godfrey recalls the attacks on the "Duke of Roanne" after his departure and contrasts his weakness with Loucheur or Clémentel. While insisting on the pragmatism of the latter men, Godfrey still finds in Clémentel a desire to pave the way for the world of the future which was missing in Thomas.[229]

Thomas's policies do seem to be dominated by his great concern about reconciling liberty and authority and by the need to defend the interests of national defense, of the government, of manufacturers, and of workers. He was always searching for that point of productive though unstable equilibrium of which he spoke in 1916. This preoccupation was certainly a product of the circumstances and in particular of his eagerness to preserve the *union sacrée,* to which he was particularly attached, like Jouhaux, to whom he was very close, as Martin Fine has shown.[230] The virulent personal attacks on him, which Godfrey recalls,[231] must have impressed upon him the extreme sensitivity of public opinion in this regard. This is probably what explains his caution in regard to "war profits." However, Thomas's conciliatory approach also reflects an appreciation of the needs of industry and an attempt to come to grips with production problems, which is not surprising in view of the eclectic personal relationships of his youth or his friendship before the war with Louis Renault, a fact which has been pointed out by Martin Fine.[232] Thomas's approach cannot be reduced to opportunism or personal weakness. The internal documents that are available provide clear evidence that his hostility to requisitioning, his affirmation of the role of business leaders, and his insistence on the need to encourage and reward initiative sprang from an unbroken set of convictions, which his plans to renew the state-run factories only confirm.

These convictions found expression, in theory, in Thomas's attachment to the contract system and, in practice, in his formation of a military-industrial complex, in Patrick Fridenson's words.[233] This complex included – in addition to academics, pointed out first by B.-W. Schaper[234] – technicians with very important roles such as Claveille, who came from what would now be called the nationalized sector and became Minister of Transport in December 1916, or Hugoniot, an adventurous self-made man, a telephone operator at age fourteen and an entrepreneur at eighteen, the chief technical services engineer with the Paris subway at age twenty-nine, and when working with Thomas, a leading champion of industrial rationalization.[235] Loucheur was another technician whose precocious appointment as an unofficial adviser has been noted.[236] Thomas's inclination toward conciliation, the emergence of the military-industrial complex, and his friendly relations with some industrialists[237] should not obscure the fact that he believed that there was an essential balance between liberty and control, and that the latter was justified in the face of the former only by evidence that it would be used wisely. We are therefore inclined to put more emphasis than other researchers on the role which Thomas wanted the state to play. Unlike Gerd Hardach in general and John F. Godfrey in respect to Thomas himself, we do not think that the government aimed only to establish the general framework of production and eliminate any difficulties which industrialists might encounter, while allowing big industry to take charge of organizing the economy. Furthermore, we do not think that Thomas was less firm in his attitude toward industrialists than Clémentel or Loucheur.[238] Thomas seems in fact to have decided immediately that the state should orientate, coordinate, and even draw up plans – the term stems from 1916 – even though these plans were still sectorial in nature.[239] The state's appeal for services was always associated with some controls, whether in regard to individual companies or broader organizations. Returning to this topic several months after the war, Thomas decried the reputation of the Comité des Forges for "carrying on in the public realm culpable, uncontrolled activities." He pointed out that the full support of the Comité was essential to the war effort. There had been some problems, he said, as at Caen or Roanne, but "I knew about these things on the day they happened, and I resisted these efforts in order to remain master of my services."[240] Thomas exercised an enlightened, effective control – effective both in regard to immediate needs and to safeguarding the nation's future interests when it subsidized the construction of plants and equipment. Industrialists themselves were well aware of this control, and de Wendel based his arguments on it when he declared before the Chamber of Deputies in June 1916 that "this technical control is already functioning. . . . The Undersecretary of State has been perfecting it for almost eighteen months now. What more could be done? What could be done better?"[241] Thomas seemed to echo these sentiments seven months later, when he noted in preparation for a debate in the Chamber in February 1917 that the munitions plants "cannot do anything without the state. . . . In fact the state has controlled private factories as much or more than in any Allied country."[242]

Furthermore, if the stages in the development of this "exuberance of the State," of which Fabienne Bock speaks,[243] are examined, it was in 1915 and around Thomas that it first became apparent. Thomas appears therefore as the pioneer whose trail-blazing work Loucheur used to good advantage.[244] Thomas's political background made him better able than many others "to conceive of the phenomenon on his own and to accept the logic of state expansion," just as it inured him against the widespread "repression of the wartime experience" after the conflict was finished.[245] When Thomas established his brand of state control, in theory and in practice, he can easily be understood to have been carrying on the ideas he had espoused as a deputy, for instance defending in 1911 the economic sovereignty of the nation against private interest groups,[246] recommending in 1913 "new forms" of association between the state and industry, and demonstrating a stronger inclination, like the French and German reformers who advocated an "organized economy,"[247] to guidance and control than to actual property transfers.

The war was therefore not only a "laboratory" for him, in the words of Martin Fine,[248] but also an opportunity to test in the real world his prewar theories in the social and industrial realms. He changed under the experience, adding to his reputation as a union leader, advocate of Creusot socialism, and apostle of class collaboration a new dimension as a manager and a statesman.

There is only time to mention in passing a topic that has not yet been broached, namely the limits which Thomas placed on state intervention in the material organization of production. Did he attempt to impose on industry the program suggested by Hugoniot in his note to Thomas of August 1916,[249] that is, to prescribe outputs and the methods for achieving them? The answer may seem clear in the light of the very informative sources cited by Madeleine Rebérioux and Patrick Fridenson and in particular Thomas's speech at Renault on 1 September 1917.[250] However, the issue is complicated. In August 1916, in a note on the proposals of La Fournaise company, Hugoniot wrote to Thomas that "France does not yet produce half of what she is capable of producing."[251] Furthermore, in his contracts policy of 1915–16, Thomas appeared very much as the champion of subcontractors against the ambitions of the group leaders. In the summer of 1916, following the advice of the Contracts Commission, he changed course on the question of a single price for all shell contracts, thus helping small manufacturers.[252] While well aware of industrial imperatives, Thomas therefore hesitated to draw all the consequences in terms of concentration, mass production and work organization. He apparently changed his mind at the time of the Roanne affair. The decision to go ahead with Roanne marked Thomas's shift to the intensive methods of production advocated by Hugoniot, as Thomas himself stated explicitly in his appearance before the Senate in March 1917.[253] Thomas's interest in productivism seems therefore more acquired than innate, a result of the imperatives of the time and certainly his contact with such men as Hugoniot.

Despite J. F. Godfrey's assertions to the contrary,[254] Thomas never wanted to limit his influence to wartime production. From very early on, he was concerned about the repercussions of present actions on the future. In 1915 he asked the women of Saint-Chamond to continue working in industry now that they had become accustomed to it, because "tomorrow when the hour of victory arrives . . . a new challenge will face us: French industry must henceforth dominate the world in all markets and score new victories."[255] As Martin Fine and Jean-Michel Chevrier have noted,[256] Thomas shared with many others – Socialists, reform union leaders, industrialists in the most dynamic sectors such as Loucheur, and centrist politicians such as Clémentel[257] – two convictions which he attempted to advance while serving in government. First was the conviction that the war could be a force for renewal, the mainspring of an economic revitalization of France which would enable it to emerge triumphant from the economic struggles of the approaching peace. He stated this explicitly in a debate in the Chamber of Deputies in February 1917 when, in a response to Jean Bon, he declared that now, just as in the days when he was a deputy, "in all the analyses that I make, in all the bills that I present, I am constantly concerned about the future of the country – a country which, on the eve of the war, had insufficient industry, and which, if it wants to survive the economic struggle that will follow the military struggle, will need a solid, powerful industry."[258] As he said at Le Creusot in 1916, the "wartime spirit" and new forms of organization and production should not disappear with the arrival of peace, but become the foundations of the new France.[259]

To what extent was it possible, however, to lay the groundwork for the future under the pressures of present needs? Martin Fine points to Thomas's work in the social area, which he carried out together with Jouhaux, and shows that the shop steward system and mixed commissions were intended to pave the way for the future "technical organization of work" and advance the cause of reformism.[260] The wartime period also saw the forging of close, ongoing relations with industrialists, which went so far as a friendship of mutual esteem with some leaders of industry.[261] Thomas very frequently expressed the hope, as did Jouhaux and some industrialists, that the new conditions imposed on French industry by force of circumstance would have a lasting effect on habits and attitudes.

A distinction should certainly be drawn between intentions and actual industrial development. Insofar as intentions are concerned, all the recent research shows that Thomas hoped that the war would lead to an intensification of production, in particular through the spreading of Taylorism.[262] Concerning actual industrial development, Thomas's ambitions were only very partially achieved, and he was soon able to perceive the limits. In a letter to Senator Bérard in 1916, Thomas wrote that "even though it is undeniable that the development of French industry would be extremely advantageous, various measures, unfortunately, have not enabled us to achieve this result." As a result, it was not possible "at the present time to attempt to develop industry and we may even be forced to reduce the proportion of factories not working directly for National Defense."[263] Thomas was accordingly only able to take or encourage those legislative measures that did not have any immediate negative repercussions on production, such as Section 9 of the Mistral-Voilin proposal, which according to Voilin was intended to provide a satisfactory amortization period so that "capitalists" would be encouraged to invest their money in French industry and not abroad, as they had done before the war,[264] or those measures made possible by a fortuitous convergence of immediate and future needs, as can be seen in the Caen[265] and Roanne examples. In these cases the confluence of various factors is clear, making it possible to consider broader issues such as the transformation of state-operated factories into regular corporations, all of whose shares were owned by the state, which were controlled through general meetings and boards of directors involving a broad variety of people, and which freely recruited their managers and contracted with the state in the usual commercial manner.[266]

This convergence of present and future needs was even clearer in the chemical industry. By the end of 1915 Thomas was attempting to ensure that the considerable progress which French industry had made since 1914 in a field in which it had previously depended on Germany was maintained. A report submitted by Exbrayat in January 1916 proposed maintaining the sulphuric acid factories constructed after 1914 in order to create a large chemical industry able to hold its own alongside German industry. Saint-Gobain had expanded considerably, and steps needed to be taken to ensure that it did not destroy its competitors through a price war, thus lowering production to prewar levels.[267] As a result of the efforts of Thomas and Clémentel, the National Dyes Syndicate was established. The state urged the companies to come together and provided part of the capital in the form of equipment that would not be needed after the war. The new Syndicate pledged to use the capital that was provided in such a way as to "effectively fulfill its role in regard to the national interest in the chemical industry," and accepted state control over prices, type of production, the appointment of general managers, and the distribution of profits which were to be shared with the state.[268]

Finally, which aspects of his wartime policies did Thomas hope to carry forward into the France of the future? Two speeches in the Chamber of Deputies provide the basis of a more precise response than the general texts we have already seen. The first speech was delivered on 27 February 1917. The notes for it are of particular interest because Thomas underlined everything which should be preserved in the future. The system under discussion, he clearly stated, could provide a "new method" for the future. He expressed the hope which we have previously seen that the state, "now equipped with a better understanding of industrial imperatives . . . will continue to guide the efforts of industry. It will assist in grand national projects just as it assisted in the great war effort."[269] In early 1919, Thomas stated further that the state should agree with industry on new forms of collaboration, bearing in mind the experiences of the war years, and encourage and possibly even impose the organization of cartels. The most original aspect of Thomas's new policy was that he wished to go beyond state guidance and the formation of cartels in industry in order to establish in the peacetime economy the system of controls developed during the war. Thomas outlined this point rapidly in the conclusion to his speech in 1917: industry would become accustomed to revealing everything and cost prices would be publicly established. These ideas were repeated in 1919, with Thomas insisting on three types of controls: control of the cartels by the state, controls exercised by organized bodies of consumers, and finally controls exercised indirectly through a broad expansion of the role of the public sector in all areas.[270]

Thomas's wartime experience thus carried him far beyond organized capitalism, or what he called the "organized economy" in his speech before the Chamber of Deputies on 21 February 1919. The agreement with the National Dyes Syndicate provides a fairly convincing example of what he had in mind. Thomas was moving in fact in the direction of a type of controlled capitalism, a descendant in many ways of the system introduced by the Mistral-Voilin proposal. The reasons why the "avant-garde of French industrialists," with whose ambitions he had much in common, refused to follow him need to be reevaluated. Certainly, as Patrick Fridenson and Madeleine Rebérioux have suggested, trade unions played such a large role in Thomas's vision of the future that even the most open-minded industrialists refused to support it.[271] Is it not likely that this type of capitalism, not only organized but controlled, went much further than they were prepared to accept?

Notes to Chapter 4

1. M. Rebérioux and P. Fridenson, "Albert Thomas, pivot du réformisme français," *Le Mouvement Social* (April–June 1974), pp. 85–97.

2. P. Fridenson, *Histoire des Usines Renault* vol. 1: *Naissance de la grande entreprise, 1898–1939* (Paris, 1972), p. 90, note 2.

3. M. Fine, "Toward Corporatism: the Movement for Capital-Labor Collaboration in France, 1914–1936," (Ph.D. diss., University of Wisconsin-Madison, 1971).

4. Archives Nationales (AN), 94 AP 36, letter from Thomas to Gaston Jèze, 20 January 1916.

5. P. Ramadier, "La pensée politique d'Albert Thomas," in *Albert Thomas vivant* (Geneva, 1957), pp. 65, 76.

6. AN, 94 AP 28 to 44.

7. AN, 94 AP 63 to 83.

8. AN, 94 AP 102 to 105.

9. Archives of the Service Historique des Armées, in Vincennes, 6N6 to 6N19.

10. AN, C 7543–4, minutes of the sessions from 10 December 1914 to 25 August 1915.

11. AN, C 7558. For debates in the Chamber of Deputies and the Senate the abbreviations *JODC* (Chamber) and *JOAC* (Chamber appendices), and *JODS* and *JOAS* for Senate debates and appendices were used.

12. AN, 94 AP 62.

13. We were able to see two master's theses at the Université de Paris X, that of J. Bitchakdjian, "Les débuts des industries françaises d'aéronautique: la société des moteurs Salmson, 1913–1917," 1969, and that of J.-M. Chevrier, "Le rôle de Loucheur dans l'économie de guerre, 1914–1918," 1972.

14. AN, 94 AP 51, documents related to the organization of the Undersecretariat of State for Artillery and Munitions, n.d.

15. A. Hennebicque, "Les débuts des fabrications de guerre, août 1914-printemps 1915," forthcoming.

16. *Ibid.*

17. *Ibid.* This fact was noted as early as January 1915, according to Bacquet, the director of artillery, and confirmed by L. Renault.

18. G. Hardach, "Französische Rüstungspolitik, 1914–1918," *Organisierter Kapitalismus*, ed. H.-A. Winkler (Göttingen, 1974), p. 102.

19. A. Hennebicque, *op. cit.* and G. Hatry, *Renault usine de guerre 1914–1918* (Paris, 1978).

20. A. Hennebicque, *op. cit.*

21. AN, 94 AP 37, the president of the *Chambre syndicale des Fabricants et Constructeurs de matériel de guerre* to the War Ministry, 9 July 1915.

22. A. Hennebicque, *op. cit.* For the labor force and raw materials see R. Pinot, *Les industries métallurgiques et la guerre* (Paris, 1916), p. 200ff.

23. AN, 94 AP 47, memorandum with handwritten note by Thomas, "Renault, May 1915."

24. A. Hennebicque, *op. cit.*

25. AN, 94 AP 31, letter to Clémentel, president of the Budget Commission, 15 October 1915.

26. A. Hennebicque, *op. cit.*

27. *Ibid.* Thomas reminded the Chamber of these parliamentary initiatives on 27 February 1917 (*JODC*, 27 February 1917, p. 497, col. 1).

28. *JOAC* no. 1187, 6 August 1915.

29. AN, 94 AP 62. Typewritten copy of the Voilin report sent by Pédoya, president of the Chamber's Army Commission, on 12 November 1915.

30. AN, 94 AP 71, Thomas to the president of the Contracts Commission on 25 September 1915, although the idea was already apparent in a letter to Clémentel on 29 July (AN, 94 AP 62).

31. AN, 94 AP 63, letter to Clémentel on 29 July 1915.

32. *JOAC,* 1 April 1915, no. 835, p. 335.

33. *JOAC,* no. 1187, 6 August 1915.

34. AN, 94 AP 62, rough draft on labor in the war industries, statement of grounds, September 1915.

35. SHA, 6 N 16, memorandum in response to the Doumer report in April 1915.

36. AN, C 7558, appearance of Viviani, Millerand and Thomas before the joint Budget and Army Commissions, fourth session, 9 June 1915.

37. *JODC,* Secret Committee, session of 3 December 1916, p. 247, col. 2.

38. AN, 94 AP 72, industrialists' meeting and statements of monthly production.

39. AN, 94 AP 62, handwritten note from Thomas.

40. AN, 94 AP 72, memorandum on the general increase in shell production, 28 August 1915.

41. AN, 94 AP 71, memoranda of 24 October and 5 November 1915 on Fully and Le Cernon. For Saint-Pierre des Corps, AN, C 7558, appearance of Galliéni and Thomas before the Budget Commission on 2 December 1915.

42. AN, 94 AP 62, bill on the war production system, called the "Transactional Bill," part I, statement of grounds. The letter to Clémentel has already been cited. For the 1917 speech, see *JODC,* 27 February 1917, p. 496, col. 3.

43. Ibid.

44. AN, 94 AP 62, memorandum from Simiand, no date but probably February 1916.

45. AN, 94 AP 62, "Transactional" bill, second part, social deductions, statement of grounds.

46. AN, 94 AP 62, Voilin Report, no. 1173 of 10 February 1916 and AN, 94 AP 31, letter from Clémentel to Thomas, 1 October 1915.

47. AN, 94 AP 31, answer to Clémentel, 15 October 1915.

48. AN, 94 AP 62, memorandum from Simiand cited above, the main outline of which appeared already in the answer to Clémentel in October 1915, cited above.

49. *Ibid.,* Simiand's memorandum.

50. AN, 94 AP 62, "Transactional" bill, first part, statement of grounds.

51. *Ibid.,* second part, social deductions, statement of grounds. See as well the note AN, 94 AP 62 of 17 September 1915 analyzing the bills in progress and which reads in part: "no limitation on profits as in England. The economic forces are allowed free reign, within the legal limits."

52. *Ibid.,* Simiand's note.

53. *Ibid.,* letter to Clémentel, cited above.

54. *Ibid.,* letter from Thomas to Japy, 7 March 1916.

55. *Ibid.,* letter to Clémentel, cited above.

56. *Ibid.,* "rough draft" on the war industries, dated 23 September 1915.

57. *Ibid.,* letter to Clémentel, cited above.

58. *Bulletin des Usines de Guerre,* first series, no. 11, (10 July 1916), report on "Questions économiques."

59. AN, 94 AP 72, Circular to Industrialists, 24 August 1915.

60. AN, 94 AP 51, 27 August 1915.

61. AN, 94 AP 51, note on the organization of the Undersecretariat of State, n.d. (probably the end of 1915).

62. *Ibid.*, departmental order of 12 June 1915.

63. *Ibid.*, note cited above.

64. *Ibid.*, instructions of 25 November 1915 on the organization of the Direction Générale des Fabrications d'Artillerie (DGFA).

65. *Ibid.*, instructions cited above.

66. AN, 94 AP 71, note from Thomas to Claveille, 17 October 1915.

67. AN, 94 AP 72, general meeting of steel shell manufacturers on 28 August 1915.

68. AN, 94 AP 51, instructions of 25 November, cited above, and ibid., note to be sent to signatories of old contracts with the DGFA, n.d., end of 1915.

69. AN, 94 AP 72, general meeting of shell manufacturers on 30 October 1915.

70. AN, 94 AP 30, personal letter to Binder, 20 October 1915.

71. AN, 94 AP 33, 19 September 1916.

72. AN, 94 AP 62, handwritten notes from the speech.

73. AN, C 7558, hearing cited above, 9 June 1915, pp. 478–93 and 540–50.

74. AN, 94 AP 51, departmental order of 12 June 1915.

75. A. Hennebicque, *op. cit.*, especially in regard to the criticisms made at Le Creusot and Saint-Chamond in the spring of 1915.

76. AN, 94 AP 51, order of 25 November, cited above.

77. AN, C 7558, appearance of Viviani, session of 15 June 1915.

78. AN, C 7558, appearance of Galliéni, session of 2 December 1915.

79. AN, 94 AP 104, Gossot's note of 7 August 1915.

80. *JODC,* 27 February 1917, p. 500, col. 1.

81. AN, 94 AP 62, letter to Clémentel, 29 July 1915.

82. *Ibid.*; and AN, C 7558, appearance of Vivani, fifth session, 15 June 1915, in regard to the delivery of shells.

83. AN, 94 AP 37, letter to the minister of war, 9 July 1915.

84. AN, 94 AP 62, war industry bill, first version September 1915, Art. 2; Second version, October 1915, Art. 1.

85. AN, 94 AP 43, Report on controlling factories and coordinating orders, n. d. but prior to December 1916.

86. AN, 94 AP 43, Thomas's response to a letter from Léon-Lévy, 23 July 1915.

87. AN, 94 AP 72, general meeting of shell manufacturers, 30 October 1915.

88. AN, 94 AP 62, bill cited above, second version, Art. 2.

89. AN, C 7558, appearance of Galliéni, session of 2 December 1915.

90. *Ibid.*

91. AN, 94 AP 62, undated note from the services on a requisition bill presented by Deputy Couesnon on 15 February 1916.

92. *Ibid.*, bill, Art. 3.

93. *Ibid.*, Simiand's note on the Voilin report, cited above.

94. AN, 94 AP 408, letter to Cruppi, 10 July 1915.

95. AN, 94 AP 71, 31 August 1915.

96. AN, 94 AP 71, Sarrazin report, 10 August 1915 (large steel shells), report of 21 August 1915 (the role played by the increase in the price of primary materials in the increasing price of large steel shells); note AN, 94 AP 62 of 23 January 1917, the Contracts Commission reports on an inquiry carried out in August 1915 into large semi-steel shells.

97. AN, 94 AP 51, departmental decree of 3 September 1915.

98. AN, 94 AP 69, Simiand, report to the minister and proposed decree for creation, n.d.

99. In a note of 8 February 1917, AN, 94 AP 62.

100. AN, 94 AP 51, letter from Thomas to the president of the Commission, 25 September 1915.

101. AN, 94 AP 62, note of 8 February 1917, cited above, which provides a summary of his activities.

102. AN, 94 AP 71, letter from Claveille on 23 September 1915, notes of 14 October and 18 November; responses from Thomas on 25 September and 28 October 1915.

103. AN, 94 AP 61, note of 28 October 1915.

104. AN, 94 AP 71, Thomas's response to Claveille's program, 25 September 1915.

105. AN, 94 AP 69, Simiand report, cited above.

106. *Ibid.*

107. AN, 94 AP 71, Claveille to Thomas and Thomas's response, 23 and 25 September 1915, cited above.

108. AN, 94 AP 103, reports from the Gunpowder Branch, 24 and 30 September 1915.

109. AN, 94 AP 31, letter to Clémentel, 15 October 1915.

110. AN, 94 AP 62, letter to Clémentel, 29 July 1915.

111. AN, 94 AP 31, gist of a response to Deputy Brousse, 22 February 1916.

112. *Ibid.* and AN, 94 AP 43, 15 January 1916.

113. *Ibid.* AN, 94 AP 62, note from the Contracts Commission, 8 February 1917.

114. *Ibid.*

115. *JOAC,* Couesnon Report, no. 3267, 5 April 1917.

116. AN, 94 AP 69, note from the Contracts Commission on the price of 75-mm shells, 13 July 1916.

117. AN, 94 AP 71, note of the Contracts Commission, 21 September 1916 and *ibid.,* note from the Chambre syndicale des Fabricants, 20 October 1915.

118. *JOAC,* report 3267, cited above.

119. AN, 94 AP 33, Thomas to Couesnon, 4 November 1915 and *ibid.* AP 36, minutes of the mixed commissions, 9, 13, 20 November 1915.

120. AN, 94 AP 62, undated note on contracts concluded by the Undersecretariat of State, probably June 1916.

121. AN, C 7558, Viviani's appearance, cited above, first session, 8 June 1915.

122. AN, 94 AP 238, speech at Le Creusot, 25 August 1915.

123. AN, 94 AP 72, 25 August 1915.

124. AN, 94 AP 408, letter to Dumuis, manager of Firminy, 10 October 1916.

125. AN, 94 AP 72, general meeting of shell manufacturers, 30 October 1915.

126. AN, 94 AP 71, view of the Contracts Commission, 18 November 1915.

127. AN, 94 AP 43, cited above.

128. AN, 94 AP 62, "Transactional" bill, second part, social deductions, Article 2.

129. *Ibid.,* Bills, versions one and two, September-October 1915.

130. *Ibid.,* note from Simiand, cited above.

131. *Ibid.,* conclusion of the note cited above.

132. *Ibid.,* "Transactional" bill, first part, statement of grounds.

133. *JODC,* 27 February 1917, p. 498, col. 1.

134. AN, 94 AP 51, letter to Claveille, cited above.

135. AN, 94 AP 36, minutes of meetings, November 1915.

136. AN, 94 AP 36, note to Claveille, 22 December 1915.

137. *JODC,* 9 June 1916, p. 1312, col. 2. See also J. N. Jeanneney, *François de Wendel en République* (Paris, 1976).

138. AN, 94 AP 31, 15 October 1915.

139. AN, 94 AP 62, answer to Couesnon's note, cited above, 15 February 1916.

140. *JODC,* second session of 21 February 1919, p. 799, col. 1.

141. AN, 94 AP 62, note to Simiand, 11 June 1916.

142. *Ibid.,* Bill, first version, September 1915.

143. *Ibid.*

144. *Ibid.,* note to Simiand, cited above.

145. AN, 94 AP 69, Contracts Commission, notices no. 7001 and 7002, n.d. but probably spring 1916, on extra-pure zinc contracts.

146. *JODC,* 8 June 1916, p. 1283.

147. *Ibid.,* 9 June 1916, p. 1312, col. 1.

148. The government bill can be found in AN, 94 AP 62, Transactional Bill, June 1916.

149. *Ibid.,* letter from Voilin to Thomas, 5 July 1916.

150. *Ibid.,* "text unofficially presented by the Undersecretary of State for the Army Commission, 21/27 July."

151. *Ibid.,* note from Oualid to Thomas on 12 August 1916.

152. *Ibid.,* letter to Voilin on 17 October 1916.

153. *Ibid.,* Thomas to Klotz, president of the Budget Commission, 6 December 1916.

154. *Ibid.,* Klotz to Thomas on 26 December 1916, to which he attached a copy of Ribot's letter to the Commission on 28 November 1916. See as well *ibid.,* Ribot's letter to the Budget Commission on 4 February 1917.

155. *Ibid.,* Klotz to Thomas on 28 November 1916, 9 and 23 January 1917.

156. Voilin's second supplementary report, *JOAC* no. 3047, 23 February 1917, pp. 167–168.

157. AN, 94 AP 62, letter to Poincaré on 16 February 1917.

158. *Ibid.,* letter to Klotz on the Jobert Amendment, 18 September 1916.

159. *JODC,* 27 February 1917, p. 498, col. 2.

160. Cf. the speech of J. Bon, the Socialist deputy for Saint-Denis, *JODC,* 27 February 1917, p. 503, col. 2.

161. AN, 94 AP 62, note to Simiand, 12 June 1916 and Voilin, second supplementary report, cited above, Art. 1.

162. Voilin, ibid., Arts. 2 to 4 for technical control, 5 to 7 for labor.

163. *Ibid.,* Art. 9.

164. *Ibid.,* Art. 10.

165. *Ibid.,* Art. 9.

166. "La loi sur les usines de guerre," *Bulletin des usines de guerre,* second series, no. 46, 12 March 1917.

167. *Ibid.*

168. *JODC,* 28 June 1915, p. 963.

169. *Ibid.,* p. 325, col. 1.

170. *JODC,* 17 December 1915, p. 2188, col. 2.

171. *JOAC,* no. 1655, 13 January 1916, pp. 8ff.

172. Cf. Péret's report, ibid., no. 1724, pp. 99–107.

173. *JODC,* 17 February 1916, p. 329, col. 2.

174. Lazare Weiller, *JODC,* 10 February 1916, p. 830, col. 1; Lairolle, *ibid.,* 11

February, p. 844; de Dion, *ibid.,* p. 858; Touron, in the Senate, *JODS,* 25 May 1916, p. 453, col. 1; and de Wendel, cited above.

175. AN, 94 AP 41, letter from Schneider on 7 October 1916; *ibid.,* note from Thomas to Ronneaux, 9 October.

176. AN, 94 AP 408, 10 October 1916.

177. *JODC,* 22 February 1917, p. 455, col. 1.

178. *Ibid.,* 27 February 1917, p. 501, col. 2.

179. AN, 94 AP 62, letter from Voilin, 25 October 1916.

180. AN, 94 AP 104, letter to Japy, 7 March 1916.

181. Reproduced in *Bulletin des usines de guerre* 1 (1 May 1916), pp. 2–3.

182. AN, 94 AP 104, letter from Landrieu to Thomas, 13 December 1916.

183. AN, 94 AP 62, letter to Poincaré, 16 February 1917.

184. *JODC,* 22 February 1916, p. 350, col. 3.

185. AN, 94 AP 62, letter from Voilin, 5 July 1916, cited above.

186. *Ibid.,* cf. the Jobert proposal, no. 2687, of 15 November 1916 and the subamendments of Compère-Morel, Sixte-Quenin, Turmel and Jean Bon.

187. *Ibid.,* Klotz to Thomas, 28 December 1916.

188. *Ibid.,* note to Simiand, 12 June 1916.

189. *Ibid.,* note of 8 August 1916.

190. *Ibid.,* 16 February 1917, cited above.

191. "La loi sur les usines de guerre," *Bulletin des usines de guerre* 46 (12 March 1917), p. 362.

192. AN, 94 AP 62, note from the Contracts Commission, 8 February 1917.

193. AN, 94 AP 72, note from the DGFA, 19 July 1916.

194. AN, 94 AP 62, note of 8 February 1917, cited above.

195. AN, 94 AP 69, Report on Metals, n.d. (1917).

196. *JODC,* 27 February 1917, p. 499, col. 2.

197. AN, C 7621, December 1916.

198. AN, 94 AP 31, letter to Clémentel, cited above.

199. AN, 94 AP 69, personal note to Simiand, n.d. (late 1916).

200. *JODC,* 27 February 1917, p. 499, col. 3.

201. *Ibid.,* p. 501, col. 1.

202. AN, 94 AP 69, note to Simiand, cited above.

203. *Ibid.*

204. *JODC,* 27 February 1917, p. 497, col. 2.

205. *Ibid.*

206. *Ibid.*

207. AN, 94 AP 77, note from Thomas to Colonel Ronneaux, 23 September 1916.

208. *Ibid.,* Hugoniot to Roques, 26 June 1916.

209. *Ibid.,* note on the organization of large plants producing 75-mm explosive shells, 28 August 1916.

210. AN, 94 AP 78, handwritten notes from Thomas's appearance before the Senate, March 1917.

211. AN, 94 AP 77, note to Ronneaux, cited above and "decision" of 13 October 1916.

212. *Ibid.,* letter to Roques and note, cited above.

213. AN, 94 AP 78, handwritten notes, cited above.

214. AN, 94 AP 77, letter to Lebrun, general reporter on the war budget, 22 February 1917.

215. AN, 94 AP 78, handwritten notes, cited above.

216. AN, 94 AP 77, note to Ronneaux, cited above.

217. *Ibid.,* gist of a response to Lebrun, 21 February 1917.

218. *Ibid.,* note to Ronneaux and letter to Lebrun, cited above.

219. AN, 94 AP 78, handwritten notes, cited above.

220. AN, 94 AP 77, note from Hugoniot to Thomas, 1 October 1916.

221. AN, 94 AP 408, letter of 10 October 1916, cited above.

222. AN, 94 AP 77, Hugoniot to Roques, 28 June 1916, cited above.

223. AN, 94 AP 77, note for the minister, 2 February 1917.

224. *Ibid.,* note from Bedouce, 7 February 1917.

225. J. F. Godfrey, *Capitalism at War* (Leamington Spa, 1987), p. 191.

226. M. Fine, "Guerre et réformisme en France," *Recherches* 32–33 (September 1978), p. 315.

227. G. Hardach, "Guerre, Etat et main d'oeuvre," *ibid.,* p. 290.

228. G. Hardach, *ibid.,* p. 302.

229. J. F. Godfrey, *op. cit.,* pp. 224, 292.

230. M. Fine, *op. cit.,* p. 310.

231. J. F. Godfrey, *op. cit.,* p. 193.

232. M. Fine, op. cit., p. 309.

233. P. Fridenson, *Histoire des usines Renault, op. cit.,* p. 92.

234. B.-W. Schaper, *Albert Thomas. Trente ans de réformisme social* (Paris-Assen, 1959), p. 108.

235. According to his biography, AN, 94 AP 51, June 1915.

236. J.-M. Chevrier, p. 34.

237. Pointed out by Fridenson, *op. cit.,* p. 92 and note 4, p. 92.

238. G. Hardach, "Französische Rüstungspolitik," op. cit., p. 108; J. F. Godfrey, *op. cit.,* conclusion.

239. AN, 94 AP 104, note to the Gunpowder Branch, March 1916.

240. *JODC,* 21 February 1919, second session, p. 799–800.

241. *JODC,* 9 June 1916, p. 1312, col. 1.

242. AN, 94 AP 62, handwritten notes, cited above, February 1917.

243. F. Bock, "L'exubérance de l'Etat en France," *Vingtième siècle. Revue d'Histoire* 3 (July 1984), pp. 41–51.

244. J.-M. Chevrier, *op. cit.,* p. 60.

245. F. Bock, *op. cit.,* pp. 44 and 51.

246. B.-W. Schaper, *Albert Thomas, op. cit.,* p. 87.

247. In "La Politique socialiste," cited by P. Ramadier, "La pensée politique," *op. cit.,* p. 74.

248. M. Fine, "Toward Corporatism," *op. cit.,* p. 24.

249. AN, 94 AP 77, cited above.

250. M. Rebérioux and P. Fridenson, "Albert Thomas," *op. cit.,* pp. 90–92.

251. AN, 94 AP 77, note of 28 August 1916.

252. AN, 94 AP 62, note from the Contracts Commission, 13 July 1916.

253. AN, 94 AP 78, handwritten notes, cited above.

254. J. F. Godfrey, *op. cit.,* p. 187.

255. AN, 94 AP 238, September 1915.

256. M. Fine, "Toward Corporatism," *op. cit.,* pp. 20–22 and J.-M. Chevrier, *op. cit.,* p. 46.

257. For Clémentel, see Ph. Bernard and H. Dubief, *Decline of the Third Republic* (Cambridge, 1985); J. F. Godfrey, *op. cit.*; R. F. Kuisel, *Capitalism and the State in*

Modern France (Cambridge, 1981), pp. 38–43.

258. *JODC*, 6 March 1917, p. 585, col. 2.

259. *Bulletin des usines de guerre* 1 (1 May 1916), pp. 2–3.

260. M. Fine, *op. cit.*, p. 310.

261. M. Fine, *op.cit.*, p. 312.

262. G. Hardach, "Guerre, Etat et main d'oeuvre," *op. cit.*, p. 293; M. Fine, "Guerre et réformisme," op. cit., p. 311; G. C. Humphreys, *Taylorism in France, 1904–1920* (New York and London, 1986), pp. 145–224.

263. AN, 94 AP 30, June 1916.

264. *JODC*, 6 March 1917, p. 584, col. 1.

265. AN, 94 AP 79, letter to Laurent, manager of Marine-Homécourt, 19 January 1916.

266. AN, 94 AP 77, draft transformation bill.

267. AN, 94 AP 105, February 1916. See also J.-P. Daviet, *Une multinationale à la française* (Paris, 1989), pp. 189 and 193–194.

268. *JOAC*, bill for the ratification of the contract concluded on 11 September 1916 with the National Dyes Syndicate no. 3247, 3 April 1917, p. 592ff.

269. AN, 94 AP 62, notes, cited above, 27 February 1917.

270. *JODC*, 21 February 1919, second session, pp. 799–800.

271. M. Rebérioux and P. Fridenson, "Albert Thomas," *op. cit.*, p. 97.

EMPLOYERS AT WAR

5

Gnôme et Rhône – An Aviation Engine Firm in the First World War

James M. Laux

The enormous production of aircraft engines must be considered as one of the major manufacturing achievements in France during the 1914–18 War. The Société Gnôme et Rhône led all other French firms in output, and the demand for its engines was so great that they also were made in Britain, Italy, Russia, the United States, Sweden, and even Germany. Gnôme et Rhône owed its national and even world predominance to the rotary design of its engines, which made them extremely lightweight and relatively reliable.

The Origin of the Firm

Louis Seguin, a twenty-six-year-old graduate of the Ecole Centrale (1892), founded the Gnôme firm in 1895. Seguin was the grandson of the famous Marc Seguin, the inventor-engineer from the Lyonnais who had helped introduce the cable suspension bridge to Continental Europe and had developed the tubular boiler for locomotives in the 1820s, and who, with his bothers, had built some railways and many dozen suspension bridges. Marc Seguin's fourteenth son, Augustin Seguin, in 1866 joined the Chantiers de La Buire, a railway equipment manufacturer in Lyon, as associate manager and then managing director. He remained with this firm until its failure in 1894.[1] Augustin's son Louis followed the family tradition of engineering. He was born and grew up in the Lyon region but went to Paris for his higher educa-

Notes to Chapter 5 can be found on page 150.

tion. Like many young French engineers of the 1890s, especially those of the Ecole Centrale, he was attracted to a new industry just beginning in Paris and Lyon – automobiles and, more particularly, internal combustion engines. The Gnôme firm that he established in 1895 in the Paris suburb of Argenteuil with forty workers manufactured these engines first for industrial purposes and later for automobiles. Almost from the beginning Henry Luquet de Saint-Germain, an automobile dealer, helped finance the firm. In 1898 Louis Seguin merged his young enterprise with an old Lyonnais hardware maker that dated back to 1818. He became the dominant figure in this firm, now called the Société des Fonderies de Cuivre de Lyon, Mâcon et Paris Thévenin Frères, L. Seguin et Cie. When Maurice Thévenin died in 1909, Louis Seguin became the sole manager of the company.[2]

Meanwhile, Seguin separated the engine manufacturing operations from the rest of the firm, establishing the Société Anonyme des Moteurs Gnôme in June 1905 with a capital of 600,000 francs and a lease on the factory in Gennevilliers where the Paris activities then were carried on. Louis Seguin became president, with René Luquet de Saint-Germain (the son or nephew of Henry) as managing director. At first Gnôme thrived by selling engines for automobiles and trucks. It bought the factory in Gennevilliers from its sister firm, and in 1907 it issued more shares to increase its capital to 1.2 million francs. But at this point the automobile business turned bad, as sales suddenly diminished in the recession of 1907–08. The Gnôme company looked for other markets, offering small gasoline engines for agricultural purposes and small gas engines as well. It struck gold, however, in another new industry, aviation.

Laurent Seguin, a younger brother of Louis Seguin, at this time was a student at the Ecole Centrale. About 1906 or 1907, assigned to make an original project, he designed a new aircraft engine. Legend has it that the young student received a zero mark for his effort, but Laurent Seguin convinced his brother Louis to make a prototype at the Gnôme factory. He had tried to solve a basic problem in early aviation: provide a means of traction that furnished great power for very little weight. Early aviators had tried both electric motors and steam engines without much success. In America the Wright brothers used small water-cooled internal combustion engines of their own design and manufacture for their flights from 1903 on. These engines were a considerable accomplishment for self-taught mechanics, but from 1903 to 1905 they weighed from 8.6 to 3.5 kg per hp. This relatively heavy weight usually required the Wrights to launch their craft from rails assisted by a weight dropped from a pylon behind the plane. But once in the air, the Wright engines were quite reliable.[3]

In France, the best of the early engines mounted on aircraft came from the atelier of Léon Levavasseur in the Paris suburb of Puteaux. His Antoinette engine was a small V-8 with water cooling, first used on motor launches in 1904–06. Pioneer aviators such as Ferber, Santos-Dumont, and Blériot then adopted it for their aircraft from 1905 on, and it was widely used during 1908–10. Levavasseur reduced the weight by using aluminum where possible and injecting gasoline directly into the cylinders. His engines, rated at 24 hp and 50 hp, weighed approximately 1.5 kg per hp, but they showed no essential difference from conventional automobile engines. Nor did the first Renault aviation engine, an air-cooled V-8, supplying 50 hp, which appeared in 1907. This model was rather heavy and a disappointment, but in a few years Renault would develop its air-cooled V-8 engines to an outstanding level of quality.[4]

The Anzani and REP (Robert Esnault-Pelterie) aviation engines of this period followed less conventional designs. The former, derived from a motorcycle engine, was air-cooled with three cylinders arranged in the shape of a Y, and the REP, also air-cooled, had seven cylinders in a fan configuration. These types appeared in 1906–07 but overheated even more quickly than the Antoinette.

It was the Gnôme engine that dethroned the Antoinette. Laurent Seguin's design derived from the REP and the Anzani, for it had seven air-cooled cylinders in a radial arrangement; but to provide further cooling, the cylinders and crankcase rotated about the stationary crankshaft at 1200 rpm, and the propellor was attached to them. The concept of using a system with rotating cylinders for an internal combustion engine was not original with Seguin. In France, Millet experimented with the idea in the late 1880s, but the later claims of Fernand Forest, shamelessly promoted by the journalist Charles Faroux, cannot be taken seriously.

In the United States, at least two automobiles used rotary engines: the Balzer of New York around 1900 and the more important Adams-Farwell of Dubuque, Iowa, from 1898 to 1913. Adams-Farwell built some fifty cars whose engines of three or five cylinders rotated in a horizontal plane. This company probably never exported a car to Europe, but the two leading American automobile magazines thoroughly described its system in October 1904,[5] and it is possible that Seguin may have seen these articles. His nickel-steel cylinders were not cast but machined from a solid forging with very thin cooling fins turned in the cylinder itself. The fuel mixture entered the cylinder from the crankcase through a valve in the steel piston-head. The engine required an unusually large amount of lubricating oil (castor oil was used), for it escaped through the exhaust valves due to centrifugal force. The high consumption of oil and gasoline was not a serious fault in these early days of short flights, but the rotary had other disadvantages: some of the engine's power – about 15 percent – was wasted in turning it, and it lacked flexibility in speed because of the automatic operation of its valves and its primitive carburetor. Centrifugal force acting on the cylinders limited its rpm to 1,200, and the gyroscopic effects of the rapidly rotating cylinders affected the maneuverability of the aircraft.[6]

The Gnôme company displayed its first rotary engine – seven cylinders, 50 hp, weighing between 1.3 and 1.5 kg per hp – at the November 1908 Salon de l'Auto.[7] A few aviators experimented with this new type in the following months, but the flights by Henry Farman and others using Gnôme engines at the Reims aviation meeting in August 1909 demonstrated before 250,000 spectators the reliability and superiority of this engine.

Early Success

The Gnôme company lost money from 1907 through 1909 as its automobile business declined, and it developed the rotary engine, rather expensive to manufacture because of the considerable machining of its parts and the close precision necessary. But after the Reims meeting, orders flooded in. Gnôme expanded its factory, and by March 1911 it had bought 1,150,000 francs of machine tools, mostly from Alfred Herbert in England.[8] In 1910 Gnôme made several hundred of its engines and a net profit of nearly 2.3 million francs. In the following years it did even better, as production and profits continued to mount. In 1911 the 100 franc per value of its shares was reimbursed to its owners.

Outstanding performances gained for the Gnôme engine a wide and loyal following. In the French military aviation trials of October-November 1911, the four top-ranked aircraft all used Gnômes: the Deperdussin, winner of the Gordon Bennett airplane race in 1912, mounted a Gnôme engine; in September 1913 Roland Garros was first to fly across the Mediterranean Sea from France to Tunisia, using a Morane-Saulnier monoplane with a Gnôme engine; and the winner of the Schneider Trophy race for seaplanes held at Monaco in April 1914 was an English Sopwith powered by a Gnôme 100 hp monosoupape engine.[9]

Table 5.1: Société des Moteurs Gnôme, 1905–1913
(money values in francs)

	CAPITAL 000	SALES 000	EARNINGS 000	AMORT'N & RESERVES 000	NET PROFIT 000	DIVIDEND
1905	600	820	167	84	83	10
1906	800	1,200	261	129	132	15
1907	1,200	—	429*	328	101	0
1908	"	—	(69)	171	(240)	0
1909	"	—	(30)	112	(142)	0
1910	"	—	2,297	1,416	881	26
1911	"	5,800	3,723	220	3,503	26
1912	"	9,000	5,258	312	4,946	150
1913	"	16,500	8,640	598	8,042	200

*Inflated by premium charged for new issue of 4,000 shares.
( ) Indicates a financial loss.
Sources: Arch. Nat., 65AQ M224; Service Hist. de l'Armée de l'Air, Archives, A 94; E. Chadeau, *L'Industrie Aéronautique en France* (Paris, 1987), 58, 64.

Table 5.2: Two French engines and an American engine: Specifications

	GNÔME 100 HP	RENAULT 70 HP	CURTISS OX
Net delivered hp	85	72	85
Weight	140.1 kg	210.2 kg	198.8 kg
Weight per hp	1.65 kg	2.92 kg	2.34 kg
Gasoline per hour	46.1 lit.	35 l	30.3 l
Oil per hour	10.2 l	3 l	1.9 l
Fuel weight, 4 hours	171.5 kg	111.7 kg	94.4 kg
Total weight, 4 hours	311.6 kg	321.9 kg	293.2 kg
Weight per hp, 4 hours	3.67 kg	4.47 kg	3.45 kg

Source: Adapted from *The Aeroplane* (London), 22 Jan. 1914, p. 89.

Table 5.3: Société des Moteurs Gnôme, 1914—1918
(money values in francs)

	CAPITAL 000	ASSETS 000	SALES 000	NET PROFIT 000	DIVIDEND	ENGINES PRODUCED
1914	1,475	25,365	*22,100*	9,602	200	*1,800*
1915	"	40,516	*41,000*	13,138 *	250	2,917
1916	"	84,289	*75,750*	14,284 *	300	4,864
1917	"	99,752	97,000	7,887 *	300	*7,000*
1918	"		93,000	6,805	250	*5,000*

*These figures are those announced by the company. Real net profits for 1915–1917 must have been at least double the total for these years.

Figures in italics are author's estimates.

Sources: "Rapport . . . Flandin." 6 March 1918, 306–308; Service Historique de l'Armée de l'Air, Archives, A 94; Arch. Nat., 65AQ M224.

The Gnôme's overwhelming dominance in France was echoed beyond the frontier. In 1910 Sir George White obtained the British sales agency for his British and Colonial Aeroplane Company. Then in 1912 another pioneer British promoter of aircraft manufacturing, George Holt Thomas, got the British sales and manufacturing rights for his Aircraft Manufacturing Company. In the following year Thomas organized the Gnôme Engine Company and contracted with Peter Hooker, Ltd. of Walthamstow in North London to manufacture a few of the 100 hp monosoupape models for him because the British military authorities preferred to buy engines made at home. Thomas soon bought the Hooker firm, which was making only one engine per week by August 1914.[10] To supply the Russian market, primarily military, Gnôme decided to open a factory in Moscow. It produced its first engines in October 1913, but this operation was probably limited to assembly of imported parts. An Italian branch in Turin had begun operations in May of the same year. In America, Gnôme engines were sold, but not manufactured, by the Sloane Aeroplane Company of New York City.[11]

While expanding its manufacturing operations, the Gnôme company also followed a natural evolution and raised the power of its engines, first by increasing the size of its seven cylinders to supply 80 hp, a very successful type, and then by placing two engines in tandem on the same crankshaft. This resulted in a small 14-cylinder engine of 100 hp and a large 14-cylinder type of 160 hp. The tandems turned out to be disappointing in practice, but late in 1913 Gnôme introduced the single valve (monosoupape) engine that abandoned the valve in the piston and replaced it with ports uncovered by the piston as it moved down the cylinder. Rated at 100 hp, for a short time it seemed to answer the need for a more powerful engine. Table 5.2 shows a comparison of two of the best French aircraft engines of the period with the best American. The Gnôme's clear weight advantage became less significant when it became a question of flights for an extended time.

Merger with Rhône

Gnôme's technical and financial success brought imitators. In France several firms began manufacturing rotary engines from 1910 on, among them Clerget-Blin, Rossel-Peugeot, Esselbé, D'Henain, and Burlat (from Lyons). In addition, the "Rhône" rotary engine had a particularly good design and offered a serious competitive threat to Gnôme. The Société des Moteurs "Le Rhône" was founded in September 1912 by Edouard Martin, an aviator from Neuilly, and Paul Decourtis, an engineer living in Paris, with a capital of 2.1 million francs. A prominent machine tool manufacturer in Paris, Henri Ernault, became president of the Rhône company, but the key figure in the firm was an engineer from Lyon, Louis Verdet, a graduate of one of the Ecoles des Arts et Métiers (a technical school on the secondary level). Verdet had designed an air-cooled rotary engine that was somewhat more conventional than the Gnôme. Cast iron sleeves were inserted in the steel cylinders, and the fuel mixture moved from the crankcase to the cylinder head by an exterior copper pipe. As the valves could be controlled, unlike the automatic system in the Gnôme, the speed of the Rhône engine could be varied. It burned less gasoline and its oil consumption was barely more than half that of the Gnôme, a considerable advantage for long-distance flying. The Rhône company offered engines of 60 hp with seven cylinders and 80 hp with nine cylinders of the same size. It also mounted each of these in tandem pairs to supply 120 hp and 160 hp, but as with the Gnôme, this arrangement lacked reliability. As sales of Rhône engines rose, the company moved in 1913 from its small shop in Montreuil, an eastern suburb of Paris, to a factory on the Boulevard Kellermann in the 13th arrondissement, where it employed some 150 workers in 1914.[12]

The Gnôme company acted quickly to get control of this dangerous rival and offered its owners very attractive terms to sell out. Rhône agreed to a merger under the name Gnôme et Rhône, and the two firms began operating together in June 1914, although the legal technicalities were concluded only in March 1915. Rhône stockholders received a total of about 7.7 million francs in the form of 2,750 newly issued shares of Gnôme et Rhône with a par value of 100 francs each but currently selling at about 2,800 francs. Each share would pay a 250 franc dividend for the year 1915, and the 100 franc par value was reimbursed. The share capital of Gnôme et Rhône amounted to 1.475 million francs. It was a good bargain, then, for the Rhône shareholders, whose investment rose in value from 2.1 million to 7.7 million in less than three years. The sources are silent as to how generously the key figure, Louis Verdet, shared in this bonanza.[13]

Just before the war, Gnôme et Rhône operated two factories in the Paris region. The larger, at Gennevilliers, employed between 650 and 800 workers in the 1913–14 period. In September 1913 its equipment included 512 machine tools, among them 25 automatic turret lathes operated by unskilled workers. The firm apparently believed it needed more skilled workers, however, for it had its own school for apprentice metalworkers. The major parts of the engines were machined from forgings rather than castings, as, for example, the crankcase weighing 6 kg was cut in three hours from a block of steel weighing 49 kg, and a cylinder beginning as a piece of 37 kg, eight hours later weighed only 2.8 kg. Employees probably worked a ten-hour day six days a week, standard in Paris metalworking at this period, and they received an average daily wage of 9 francs. The factory had a capacity of five engines per day in 1913. Gnôme et Rhône made about 1,400 in that year, and 1,800 in 1914, probably including some 250 made in the former Rhône factory.[14]

Gnôme et Rhône in the War

When the war broke out, the French aerial services mobilized twenty-three squadrons of aircraft, comprising 132 planes, along with 136 in reserve, a total of 268. The front-line squadrons used machines made by nine different manufacturers.[15] Gnôme 80 hp engines powered a large majority of these aircraft, along with small numbers of Renault 70 hp, Salmson (Canton-Unné) 85 hp (a seven-cylinder water-cooled radial engine), and Rhône 80 hp.[16] This situation quickly changed. The types of military aircraft were cut to five to simplify maintenance and reduce the cost of production, and the different types of engines were increased as the Service Aéronautique searched for more power and reliability. It ordered large numbers of engines whose prototypes promised these qualities. Renault received orders for its air-cooled 80 hp V-8 and 130 hp V-12 engines. Before the end of 1914, Salmson obtained orders for 731 of its nine-cylinder water-cooled radial rated at 130 hp and 100 of a 200 hp radial for a total price of 12,764,910 francs.[17] The government ordered nine-cylinder rotary engines of 130 hp from Clerget,[18] and the Anzani company began supplying considerable numbers of low-powered radial engines for training planes.[19] Gnôme et Rhône, surprisingly, received orders for only 315 engines by the end of 1914, just 3.4 million francs worth, including spare parts.[20] The large orders for Salmson engines may be explained by the higher power supplied by these engines and by the fact that an important stockholder in that company was Senator Charles Humbert, an influential Paris journalist and a powerful figure on the Army Committee of the Senate.

The Gnôme engines were somewhat out of favor with the Army. General Hirschauer, Director of Military Aeronautics from October 1914 to September 1915, when testifying in a secret session of the Aeronautical Sub-Committee of the Army Committee of the Chamber on 3 April 1915, revealed that he was not ordering any Gnôme engines at all at this time, preferring the Rhône type, currently made in both the Kellermann and the Gennevilliers factories. As a reason, he cited the Rhône's mechanically operated valves, allowing flexibility in the speed of the engines. In fact, it appears that from 1915 through the rest of the war, few Gnôme engines were purchased for French combat aircraft; the company's best sellers were Rhône 80 hp and 110 hp types. In light of this, the decision Gnôme made to buy out Rhône turned out to be crucial.

The mobilization of reservists in August 1914 may have reduced production at the Gnôme et Rhône factories by taking an important part of the labor force, but the lack of orders may have been more important. Recovery came swiftly, however, as the output of engines rose from only 15 in September to 149 in November and 215 in December,[21] both later figures well above the prewar monthly average of 125. In 1915 output rose to 2,917 engines, or 243 per month. The rising production came from factory expansion and an increased labor force. At the Kellermann plant, 340 workers were employed by September-October 1915, at Gennevilliers 870, and at an additional factory in Lyon, leased from a small automobile producer in the fall of 1914 when the German Army remained uncomfortably close to Paris, 200 were at work in October 1915.[22] It is not clear if the output of the Moscow factory is included in the production total for 1915. A high proportion of the Gnôme et Rhône output in that year was sold to

France's allies – 1,300 engines, or 45 percent, to Britain, Italy, and Russia.[23]

In France during 1915–16 Rhône 80 hp engines powered the smaller combat aircraft such as the Caudron G3 and the twin-engined G4, the Morane-Saulnier Parasol, and especially the thousands of small Nieuport observation and fighter aircraft. At the end of 1914, the company offered a Rhône 110 hp type similar to the 80 hp but with larger cylinders. Government orders followed and the 110 hp began to appear at the front in the spring of 1916. During the entire war 9,650 Rhône 110 engines were produced in France, slightly more than the 8,700 Rhône 80 hp type[24] (Tables 5.4, 5.5). In 1917 the Nieuport fighters using the Rhône 110 gave way to the Spad 7 and then the Spad 13 aircraft. By the middle of 1917 almost all the Rhône engines still being manufactured (7,188 of the 110 hp were delivered in that year[25]) were destined for replacement or for training aircraft. In an effort to keep up with the race for more power, the company developed a new Gnôme 150/160 hp monosoupape. It tested well and raised high hopes. By August 1917 the army had 4,100 on order. But in flight it proved unreliable, and most of the orders had to be cancelled. Eighty-six of these engines were delivered in 1917 and probably very few thereafter.[26]

In 1916 Gnôme et Rhône employed some 3,000 workers, who made 4,684 engines (1,720 or 35 percent for export to allies), and the company may have manufactured about 7,000 with some 5,000 workers in 1917.[27] But 1918 was a bad year, symbolized at its beginning by the death of Louis Seguin at forty-nine years of age on 7 January. Louis Javey, who had sat on the board of directors for several years, replaced Seguin as president; René Luquet de Saint-Germain continued as managing director. Rotary engine production, mostly of the Rhône 110 hp type, reached no more than 3,000.[28] A prototype Rhône 170 hp rotary was tested and won a government order for 100, but little came of this. A new Gnôme radial engine with twenty cylinders did not find favor,[29] but shows that the company was finally willing to consider abandoning the rotary design. It was obvious by 1916 that the future demand would call for engines of 200-300 hp or more. The company's inability to prepare and produce such types threatened it with serious decline.

Foreign Manufacture of Gnôme et Rhône Engines

Already we have mentioned that in 1914 in England the Peter Hooker firm began making a small number of Gnôme monosoupape engines. Three days after the war began, George Holt Thomas of the Gnôme

Engine Company persuaded the Daimler automobile company of Coventry to make 80 hp Gnôme engines. Working from a sample engine, as no drawings or specifications were available, Daimler had a prototype ready for test in eight weeks. But production of these and other aircraft engines was not as rapid, partly because of a lack of magnetos in Britain. Of the 1,720 engines built there in 1915, 350 were rotaries, mostly Gnôme et Rhône types, along with some Clerget models made by Gwynnes Ltd. In 1916 the French Gnôme et Rhône company's revenue from license fees paid by foreign manufacturers of its engines reached nearly 4.4 million francs, up from 1 million in 1915. At least 3 million of the 1916 figure came from England, indicating a sizeable increase there. Early in 1917 the Hooker company was producing the two standard Rhône engines, 80 hp and 110 hp, as well as the Gnôme 80 hp and 100 hp, and in that year the French company's license fees from Britain and Italy more than doubled over that of 1916.[30] The total output of Gnôme et Rhône engines in Britain during the war has not been discovered, but it must have reached several thousand.

In 1915 Gnôme et Rhône sold its Italian branch to a Turin group that continued to make or assemble engines there. The company also lost control of its Russian factory when its workers seized it in the 1917 Revolution. Valued at one point at 4.7 million francs, it was written off as a total loss in February 1918.

The Germans used some Rhône engines during the war. Some of these may have come from the Swedish licensee, Thulin. The Oberusel company, purchased by Anthony Fokker, manufactured some also, perhaps copied from captured French engines.[31] But the number of German rotaries was small, as the military authorities there preferred the classic six-cylinder in-line engine, made by Daimler-Mercedes, Benz, Argus, NAG, and Maybach. Somewhat heavier than French types, these engines had much more durability. By 1918, however, French fighter aircraft using Hispano-Suiza engines could outrun and outclimb their German antagonists.

American manufacturing of Gnôme et Rhône engines began when, early in 1916, the British licensee, George Holt Thomas, placed an order with the General Vehicle Company of Long Island City, New York, to make the 100 hp Gnôme monosoupape. Although it required some time for this company to find raw materials of the requisite quality and to set up production facilities, by early 1917, 250 engines had been shipped to Great Britain. After the United States entered the war in April 1917, American representatives in Europe urged that 5,000

Gnôme 150 hp and 2,500 Rhône 80 hp engines be built in the United States for the American Army. The American government persuaded the General Motors Corporation to take over the General Vehicle Company and make 150 hp engines. Preparations had begun on this order when word came from France that the 150 hp model was unsatisfactory, and the order was cancelled. General Vehicle went back to the 100 hp model and made 280 more by the end of the war. To make the 2,500 Rhône 80 hp, the American authorities had to search diligently to find a willing manufacturer. They finally convinced a Westinghouse subsidiary, the Union Switch and Signal Company of Swissvale, Pennsylvania, to undertake the job. At first troubled by erroneous specifications sent from Paris, it finally delivered its first engine in May 1918 and a total of 1,057 by the war's end. All of those Rhône engines were used in training aircraft. The total number of aviation engines produced in the United States from April 1917 through October 1918 was 32,420, of which 15,572 were the 400 hp Liberty, 8,458 the Curtiss OX, and 4,100 the Hispano-Suiza.[32]

One can make a general estimate of Gnôme et Rhône engines produced outside of France during the war as between 6,500 and 8,000; up to 4,500 in Britain, 1,600 in the United States, perhaps 1,500 in Italy, and 300 in Germany. We assume that those produced in Russia were simply assembled from French-made components.

Financial Results

Along with other war contractors, Gnôme et Rhône experienced rising sales and expanded profits through much of the war. Before long, such profits and the resulting very high dividends aroused questions, complaints, and outrage. Government officials, both of the executive and the legislative branches, inquired into the earnings made by aviation companies, including Gnôme et Rhône. They found high profits, indeed, as well as much confusion and sloppy work throughout the process of military procurement.[33] The investigators rarely seem to have gone beyond an examination of annual balance sheets of the military suppliers, but by their publicity and the possibility of government requisition of the factories they did manage to keep the prices for aircraft engines from rising as fast as the cost of living and sometimes even won a modest reduction in price. Gnôme et Rhône received about 10,000 francs for its Rhône 80 hp engine, plus about 2,000 francs for spare parts. For the Rhône 110 hp, the government originally paid 15,535 francs, a figure reduced to 14,000 in 1917.[34] The latter figures probably include spare parts also.

There can be no doubt that Gnôme et Rhône made large profits, but their size is difficult to calculate. Certainly the company arranged its published accounts to show as modest a profit as possible. Some of the earnings spent on land, buildings, and equipment did not appear in the balance sheets. A parliamentary investigation headed by P.E. Flandin, no socialist he, and based on the company's published annual reports, calculated a net profit of 33.6 million in 1916 compared to the company's figure of 14.3 million. Flandin based his figure on the reserves the company set aside for possible war profits taxes due under the law of 1 July 1916.[35] Flandin's results would show a net profit of 6,918 francs per engine in 1916, and the company's, 2,937 francs. Dividends reflected the company's prosperity, rising from 200 francs per 100 franc share in 1913 and 1914 to 250 francs in 1915 and 300 francs in 1916 and 1917. These payments required only a small part of the profits. Some of the rest went into a new plant and equipment, but most was placed in various reserve accounts. Reserves reached 54.6 million francs by the end of 1916, of which 30 million were held in French government securities. Some of these were earmarked for whatever the company owed in war profits tax. The assets claimed by Gnôme et Rhône quadrupled from 25.4 million francs at the end of 1914 to 99.8 million three years later.

In April 1917 the company had its stockholders approve a special distribution of 22,125,000 francs in reserves through a payment of three 500-franc shares for each 100-franc share held. This would have raised the Gnôme et Rhône capital to 23.6 million francs. At the end of the year, however, the management abandoned this plan and instead won stockholder approval in December 1917 to distribute to each Gnôme et Rhône share one 500-franc share of a new company, Société des Forges et Fonderies de l'Aviation, a total of 7,375,000 francs. The new firm actually was a section of the Gennevilliers factory, built in 1916 and comprising an iron, aluminum, and bronze foundry and a forge. The motivation for this step was not announced, but one may assume that fiscal reasons were not irrelevant to it. A few years later, it looked like a bad, or perhaps a very clever, idea; a financial group apparently outside the sway of Gnôme et Rhône management obtained control of the Forges et Fonderies and charged Gnôme et Rhône very high prices for products that the company said it could not obtain elsewhere. The only way for Gnôme et Rhône to regain control of its supplies was to buy back a controlling interest in the Forges et Fonderies at a high price.[36] The company used some of its wartime profits in this transaction, and the money ended in the hands of its wartime stockholders without being taxed. One may wonder about this curious episode.

The End of the War

In 1918, as orders for its own rotary engine slackened, Gnôme et Rhône began making some Salmson 240 hp radial engines; but several interruptions occurred. In February 1918 the growing effervescence of labor in Paris was reflected in a brief strike in which unskilled workers at the company asked for a daily wage rather than piece rates.[37] A few weeks later, the anti-war strike of May 1918 that involved most of the Paris metalworking and aviation firms closed the Kellermann factory, which employed 1,340 workers, about one quarter of whom were women.[38] It, too, was brief, but immediately thereafter most of the Gnôme et Rhône activities were transferred to Lyon and Tours. German shelling and possible aerial bombardment of Paris recommended this move to the Ministry of Armament, as did the threat of additional political strikes in Paris.[39] When the Germans started to retreat, the return to Paris began, but some of the equipment in Lyon went to Tours, where Gnôme et Rhône had bought control of a small automobile manufacturing company, Rolland et Emile Pilain, which had been doing some subcontracting for it. The management of Gnôme et Rhône was thinking about what it could do with its capital and skill in the postwar world when demand for aviation engines surely would shrink. It did not expect to abandon the engine business entirely, but it decided to plunge into a wide variety of other activities. In the automotive area, it would use its Rolland et Emile Pilain connection to reenter the automobile business, and it also arranged to make chassis for the Pic-Pic (Piccard-Pictet) firm of Geneva. It planned to manufacture an agricultural tractor and a motorcycle. It obtained a license from Fiat-Ansaldo to produce diesel engines on that firm's system, and it was prepared to construct a variety of other internal combustion engines. Further afield, it arranged to make woolen textile machinery and sewing machines; it planned to manufacture marine equipment – pumps, compressors, and refrigerators.[40]

Although a common thread of precision machinery ran through all of these proposed activities, the company was unrealistic in trying to enter so many different markets at the same time. Did it have design engineers skilled in all these areas? Were its ties with consumers close enough so that it knew what they wanted? These problems, together with the recession of 1920–21, brought failure to all of these ventures except for motorcycles and aviation engines. The latter revived only on the basis of the Jupiter engine, a radial type licensed from the Bristol Company (formerly the British and Colonial) of England, which Gnôme et Rhône began to manufacture in the early 1920s. The many failures were expensive and cost the company the large reserves built up during the war. However, they may have reduced the ultimate sums due for the war profits tax, for in September 1926 the final decision asked for only 8 million francs,[41] which of course were considerably depreciated from their purchasing power of ten years earlier.

The misjudgments made in 1918 and 1919 were followed by changes in Gnôme et Rhône top management. In 1922 the Seguin family and their associates left the firm and a new group centered on the bankers Henry Bauer and Charles Marchal took over. Soon Paul Louis Weiller emerged as the dominant figure in the new group. He was the son of the industrialist, financier, and politician Lazare Weiller and himself had been an aviator during the war. Under P.L. Weiller's leadership, Gnôme et Rhône remained a leading French aviation manufacturer through good years and bad until it was nationalized in 1945 under the title SNECMA.

Conclusion

The history of Gnôme et Rhône and the French aviation industry as a whole to 1918 demonstrates two points clearly. First, it shows the initiative and skill of French mechanical engineering in the generation ending in 1918. French technology not only led the early automobile industry but aviation as well. Second, and this is less widely recognized, it illustrates the massive production effort involved in manufacturing large numbers of complex machines almost from the beginning of the war. The quantity of output should be underlined in particular, as it contradicts the conventional wisdom that in this period the French often had brilliant ideas but never managed to get them into production. France produced between 88,850 and 92,386 aircraft engines during the war. Britain made about half as many (reliable sources give figures ranging from 41,034 to 52,598), and Germany 40,449.[42] Of the French production, Gnôme et Rhône turned out an estimated 20,500 engines, of which about 19,000 were rotary types. This output exceeded that of any other French engine producer, as Renault made somewhat under 14,000, Salmson about 8,000, and a very large proportion of the 35,000 Hispano-Suiza engines were produced by over a dozen different French manufacturers on license from the Hispano-Suiza company. Gnôme et Rhône not only led French firms in production, but its wartime output was unsurpassed by any other firm in the world.[43] The war demonstrated that quantity production of complex machines was not an American monopoly, that once French industrialists were persuaded that the market was unlimited, or almost, they knew how to produce *en grande série* also. At the time, most Frenchmen somehow missed this fact. Was it because few, if any, postwar journalists celebrated the remarkable French wartime production achievement, or that consciousness of this achievement was swept aside by quarrels over war profits or by the outrage expressed over the destruction caused by trench warfare and by the retreating Germans?

The Gnôme et Rhône story began with a very successful innovation, the early rotary engine, but the company's designers had great difficulty raising the power of these engines over 150 hp. The firm failed to devote enough resources at the right time to experiments with alternative engine designs, either using aluminum as Bentley did in England[44] or moving to the radial type. Then, after Louis Seguin's death, the company did begin to explore other industrial activities, but rather wildly, without enough reflection and calculation. The pendulum swung from stubborn caution to overoptimistic euphoria. The tale is fascinating. What a pity that none of those who acted a part in it have left an account of the rise and descent of Gnôme et Rhône.[45]

Notes to Chapter 5

1. M. Laferrère, *Lyon: Ville Industrielle* (Paris, 1960), p. 278; P.E. Marchal and L. Seguin, *Marc Seguin* (Lyon, 1957).

2. *Cours de la Banque et de la Bourse* (Paris), 18 and 21 February 1907, found in Archives Nationales, Paris, 65 AQ M224; Laferrère, *op. cit.*, pp. 409–410.

3. See Leonard S. Hobbes, *The Wright Brothers' Engines and their Design* (Washington: Smithsonian Institution, Annals of Flight 5, 1971), p. 62 and passim.

4. For the Antoinette, *L'Aérophile*, 15 February 1908, pp. 59–61; and G. Voisin and C. Dollfus in *Pionneers*, October 1965, pp. 9–16. For Renault, *L'Aérophile*, 1 December 1919, p. 361; and G. Hatry, *Renault et L'Aviation* (Paris: JCM, 1988).

5. *Horseless Age*, 26 October 1904, pp. 417–21; *Automobile*, 29 October 1904, pp. 496–98. See B.R. Kimes, "Adams-Farwell," *Automobile Quarterly*, Fall 1969, pp. 144–51.

6. On these points I have received generous assistance from Robert Meyer of the Smithsonian Institution and from Neil Armstrong, sometime Professor at the University of Cincinnati, who has flown a 1912 English Avro with a rotary engine.

7. L. Marchais et al., *Vingt-cinq ans d'aéronautique française* (Paris, 1934), vol. 1, p. 64.

8. AN 65AQ M224; *Automobile Engineer* (London) 2 (August 1912), p. 242.

9. J.M. Laux, "The Rise and Fall of Armand Deperdussin," *French Historical Studies* 8 (Spring 1973), p. 99; Harald Penrose, *British Aviation: The Pioneer Years* (London, 1967), pp. 513–14.

10. Penrose, *op. cit.*, pp. 255, 455, 497–98, 536.

11. AN 65AQ M224; Robert A. Kilmarx, *A History of Soviet Air Power* (New York, 1962), p. 8.

12. AN 65AQ M224; a few pages about the firm by one of its workers in this period can be found in R. Francotte, *Une Vie de Militant Communiste* (Paris, 1973), pp. 65, 79–80.

13. AN 65AQ M224.

14. AN F 22 531; Service Historique de l'Armée de l'Air, Vincennes, Archives, A 94; P. James, "Une Usine Modèle," *L'Aérophile*, 15 September 1913, pp. 412–13.

15. Albert Etévé, *La Victoire des Cocardes* (Paris, 1970), pp. 130–31.

16. *Ibid.*, Fig. 10–18.

17. The Salmson firm was organized early in 1913 with a factory in Billancourt near Paris making engines designed by G. Canton and G. Unné. It specialized in water-cooled radial engines of high power. See J. Bitchakdjian, "Les Débuts des Industries françaises d'aéronautique: la Société des moteurs Salmson" (Mémoire de Maîtrise, University of Paris-Nanterre, 1969); for the 1914 orders see p. 42.

18. Pierre Clerget, a self-taught automotive engineer from Dijon, designed an aviation engine for the auto maker Clément-Bayard in 1907. He then formed his own firm with financial support from Eugène Blin in 1909 and made a wide variety of engines, none of which sold very well until the war.

19. A Milanese, Alexandre Anzani learned machine work in his uncle's shop and moved to the auto industry after a successful career as a bicycle racer. He came to Paris around 1900 and worked for the Buchet auto engine company. About 1905 he began his own firm making motorcycle engines.

20. Service Historique de l'Armée de l'Air, Archives, A 94.

21. AN C 7509.

22. AN F 22 531.

23. "Rapport . . . Flandin," *Journal officiel, Documents parlementaires, Chambre*, 6 March 1918, Annexe 4411, pp. 606–09.

24. Etévé, *op. cit.*, p. 254.

25. J.L. Dumesnil papers, AN 130AP 9.

26. AN 130AP 8 and 9; Etévé, *op. cit.*, p. 249.

27. "Rapport . . . Flandin," pp. 608–09; AN 130AP 8 and 9. In August 1917 the Darracq company had an order for 630 Rhône 110 hp engines and Caffort Frères of Marseille and Lyon was working on 550 of the same type. We assume that these firms produced about 600 of the 7,603 Gnôme et Rhône engines delivered in 1917.

28. Of the total of 6,349 rotary engines made in France during the first eleven months of 1918, at least 3,300 were the Clerget type, leaving some 3,000 Gnôme et Rhône, but not all of these were made by Gnôme et Rhône. See Direction des Etudes techniques, *Rapport général sur l'industrie française* (Paris, 1919), vol. 1, p. 387; and Etévé, *op. cit.*, p. 254.

29. Etévé, *op. cit.*, p. 277.

30. AN 65AQ M224; *Flight* (London), 27 November 1914, pp. 1159–61; H. Penrose, *British Aviation: The Great War and Armistice* (London, 1969), pp. 93, 227.

31. P. Gray and O. Thetford, *German Aircraft of the First World War* (London, 1962), p. 99.

32. B. Crowell and R.F. Wilson, *The Armies of Industry* (New Haven, 1921), vol. 2, pp. 383–97.

33. See "Considerations générales sur les marchés de l'aéronautique," *Journal officiel, Documents parlementaires, Chambre*, Annexe 3271, 5 April 1917, pp. 629–31, by P.E. Flandin, and the same deputy's "Moteurs le Rhône," Annexe 3270, 5 April 1917, pp. 628–29, where he found that at least 400 Rhône 80 hp engines had been lost somewhere after they left the factory. On the government's difficulties in obtaining lower prices see "Rapport Lelong," in Service Historique de l'Armée de l'Air, Archives, A97.

34. Letter from D. Vincent, Undersecretary for Aeronautics, quoted in *Journal officiel, Débats, Chambre*, 24 September 1917, p. 2414.

35. "Rapport . . . Flandin," pp. 307–08.

36. Crédit Lyonnais, Paris, Archives financières, Dossier Gnôme et Rhône; AN 65AQ M224.

37. AN F7 13 367.

38. *Ibid.*; M. Dubesset et al., "Quand les femmes entrent à l'usine: les ouvrières des usines de guerre de la Seine, 1914–1918" (Mémoire de Maîtrise, University of Paris VII, 1974), p. 71bis.

39. Philippe Bernard, "A propos de la stratégie aérienne pendant la première guerre mondiale: mythes et réalités," *Revue d'histoire moderne et contemporaine* 16 (1969), pp. 371–72.

40. Crédit Lyonnais, Dossier Gnôme et Rhône; *Journée industrielle*, 16 July and 22 August 1918, 22 June 1919.

41. AN 65AQ M224.

42. Etévé, op. cit., p. 254; Direction des Etudes Techniques, *Rapport général*, vol. 1, p. 387. Great Britain, Air Ministry, *Synopsis of British Air Effort during the War* (Parliament, Papers by Command, cmd 100), p. 16; Penrose, *British Aviation: The Great War*, p. 606.

43. For the output of French firms see G. Hatry, *Renault usine de guerre* (Paris: Lafourcade, 1978), p. 68; AN 130AP 8; Service Historique de l'Armée de l'air, Archives, A 94; Marchais, op. cit. vol. 2, p. 795. The production listed for the important British firm, Aircraft Manufacturing Company, in Penrose, *British Aviation: The Great War*, p. 471, is erroneous, as the figures are for total national production. In Germany, Daimler's wartime deliveries reached 19,876 and Benz 11,360, according to J.A. Gilles, *Flugmotoren 1910 bis 1918* (Frankfurt/Main, 1971), p. 123.

44. W.O. Bentley in 1916 designed the B.R.1 and B.R.2 rotary engines, based on the Clerget design, but more powerful. The B.R.1 produced 150 hp and the B.R.2 reportedly reached 250 hp, but few of these engines could be delivered before the war ended. See Penrose, *British Aviation: The Great War*, pp. 229–30, 303, 377; and Glen D. Angle, *Airplane Engine Encyclopedia* (Dayton, 1921), pp. 79–81.

45. E. Chadeau, *L'Industrie aéronautique en France, 1900–1950: De Blériot à Dassault* (Paris, 1987), has much information on the later history of Gnôme et Rhône.

6

The Calcium Carbide Case and the Decriminalization of Industrial Ententes in France, 1915–26

Robert O. Paxton

Like other European states, the French Third Republic had no laws that specifically limited or controlled the industrial and commercial cartels that were proliferating at the end of the 19th century.[1] Article 419 of the French Penal Code, however, made it illegal to influence prices, either upward or downward, by various procedures including "meeting or assembly among the principal holders of a single merchandise or foodstuff tending not to sell or to sell only at a certain price." Article 419 was the principal legal obstacle to the formation of cartels in 19th century France. Occasional prosecutions in terms of Article 419 were insufficient, however, to prevent the growth of an elaborate network of industrial and commercial ententes there after the 1880s, less powerful than German cartels but probably second only to them in quantity.[2] What may have been the Third Republic's most ambitious anti-trust action was undertaken during the First World War against the sales office ("comptoir de vente") of the Calcium Carbide Consortium, the "Société commerciale de carbure et de produits chimiques." The calcium carbide manufacturers were acquitted at the end of a trial which involved eminent personalities, and, in its aftermath, the French Parliament amended Article 419 so as to delete the crime of coalition from the Penal Code.[3] By testing Article 419 against an influential industrial cartel, in an atmosphere influenced by wartime productivism and of anticipated postwar economic competition with Germany and the United States, the enemies of the calcium carbide manufacturers

Notes to Chapter 6 can be found on page 174.

(hereafter "carburiers") unwittingly precipitated a decision favoring greater industrial and commercial concentration in France.[4]

Article 419: From Law to Practice

When Article 419 was drafted as part of the French Penal Code in 1810, modern industrial and commercial concentration was unimaginable. Article 419 was originally aimed at the hoarding of grain and other essential consumer goods that had troubled social peace during the 18th century and Revolution.[5] Subsequently, as industrial and commercial enterprises attained larger scale and greater market power in the 19th century, Article 419 was turned against monopolistic practices among them. In 1836, in the principal monopoly case of the July Monarchy, the court decided that Article 419 could apply in the prosecution (unsuccessful) of stagecoach companies for rate-fixing, and in 1852 Article 419 was used as "a veritable anti-trust law" against the Compagnie des Mines de la Loire.[6] Article 419 continuted to be used against large manufacturers after 1871, but most anti-coalition cases involved local monopolies in brewing, fertilizer, quarries, and the like.[7]

The evolution of French jurisprudence weakened the impact of Article 419 on large firms in the decades before 1914. The law of 22 March 1884, better known for authorizing labor unions and agricultural associations, also permitted industrial and commercial interests to organize in self-defense. Thereafter courts in France, as in other industrial nations, tended to distinguish between "good" and "bad" trusts. In French political economy, "good" trusts were defensive coalitions against ruinous competition, intended to stabilize the market and to avoid overproduction. Thanks to "good" trusts, whole branches of industry or commerce could be managed so as to favor the survival of small French enterprises, to furnish regular employment to French workers, and to maintain price stability for French consumers. "Bad" trusts, in this view, were offensive coalitions, with a double goal of speculation and driving out competitors. Although their price wars might benefit consumers in the short term, in the long run they threatened to destroy whole industrial sectors by ruinous competition, to the detriment of small firms, workers, and consumers, and to the benefit of foreign trusts.[8] Before a judge, legal texts in hand, the attorneys for a coalition would have trouble finding these qualitative distinctions in the wording of Article 419. In the courtroom, the defense of coalitions rested on technical considerations. According to some jurists, only coalitions responsible for major changes in prices could be prosecuted under Article 419 and not those, however monopolistic, which kept prices stable.[9] Other jurists held that a coalition to modify prices, in itself, was insufficient cause for prosecution under Article 419, in the absence of some fraudulent means.[10] Some commentators went so far as to claim that Article 419 did not apply to manufactured goods.[11]

As a result of such conflicting and uncertain jurisprudence, no first-rank French industrial or commercial firm was condemned under Article 419 in the decades before 1914. In 1887–1889, Eugène Secrétan, who had attempted to corner the world copper supply, was acquitted of all criminal charges under Article 419 for a technical reason: not all the elements of the crime were present, because Secrétan had not agreed with all the producers to sell at only one price.[12] The Comptoir de Longwy, principal sales agent of Lorraine steel, was acquitted in 1902, in a civil case under Articles 1131 and 1133 of the Civil Code; Jules Méline himself was the defense lawyer.[13] After the 1890s, almost all condemnations under Article 419 seem to have concerned food and drink. By 1902, Edouard Dolléans believed that Article 419 had become inapplicable to monopolies of production. For example, no consumer ever charged the sales consortium of the Nord-Pas-de-Calais coal cartel (Comptoir de vente des charbonnages du Nord-Pas-de-Calais) with infraction of Article 419.[14] In 1918, Minister of Commerce Clémentel observed with satisfaction that France had wisely carried out a silent repeal ("abrogation à la muette") of the article in question.[15]

During the First World War, a double evolution took place. War production favored economic concentration to an unprecedented extent. From the beginning War Minister Millerand preferred to work with the largest enterprises and well-organized industrial associations where an administrative framework was already in place. Albert Thomas accentuated this tendency, first as Undersecretary of State for Artillery and then as Minister of Armament. On the other hand, prosecutions under Article 419 became more frequent. While shortages encouraged speculation and hoarding, wartime social solidarity required energetic action against such actions. As before, most of the cases concerned essential consumer goods. Indeed all the successful prosecutions involved foodstuffs.[16] One of the cases tried at this time clarified considerably the jurisprudence concerning Article 419. Condemning on 24 December 1916 an association of milk producers at Nogent-le-Rotrou, the court decided that a coalition intended to influence prices offered in itself sufficient grounds for prosecution, without the need for any fraudulent action.[17] At this point, a coalition could be prosecuted solely for price-fixing. In other words, a "good" trust could now be prosecuted.

The Calcium Carbide Consortium

Alongside the sales agencies ("comptoirs de vente") of Lorraine steel and of the coalfields of the Nord and Pas-de-Calais, the calcium carbide industry furnished a classic example of national and international industrial organization.[18] Calcium Carbide was a new industry, based on a process of chemical transformation in high-temperature electric ovens developed by the French chemist Moissan and patented in 1894 by the engineer Louis-Michel Bullier. In the decades before 1914, this industry seemed destined for a greater future than it actually attained. In addition to acetylene for welding, the producers expected calcium carbide to be important for heating, automobile headlamps and streetlights, and certain chemical by-products.

There were strong inducements to setting up a calcium carbide cartel. Electro-chemical production required a large initial investment in hydro-electric power. However, faced with competing technologies for heating and lighting, the market was soft. Since raw materials were abundant, the possibility of overproduction caused grave concern. The holders of the patent complained of meager revenues.[19] Even before the expiration of the fifteen-year patent, the carburiers began in 1901 to conclude price agreements among themselves. In 1904, after the acquittal of the Lorraine steel sales consortium ("Comptoir de Longwy"), they created a similar consortium, or "comptoir de vente," the "Société commerciale de carbure." The "Société commerciale" (hereafter we will call it simply "the consortium") held exclusive rights to sell calcium carbide in France at a price fixed jointly by the seven holders of the Bullier patent, each of whom received a percentage of the market. When in 1909 the carburiers failed to obtain the renewal of their patent, their organization prepared to face newcomers.

The French carburiers also protected themselves against foreign competition. The industry was growing rapidly in areas where hydro-electric power was cheap, such as Scandinavia, Switzerland, and Austria. The French carburiers found that a tariff of 85 francs per ton was insufficient. In 1910, an international agreement among European producers limited the Société commerciale's market to France and the French empire and guaranteed, in return, that foreign producers would stay out of the French market. Two other sales consortia, in London and Nuremberg, shared the rest of the European continent. Thus protected from outside competitors, the French carburiers surmounted the expiration of their patent in 1909 without great difficulty. They were able to increase the price from 250 to 290 francs per ton in 1910, and keep it stable thereafter, despite the arrival of several newcomers in the field.

One newcomer presented a serious threat in 1913, however. The Rochette brothers proposed to build a calcium carbide plant with a capacity of ten thousand tons (total French annual production was then forty thousand tons). Moreover, Rochette offered a price 25 to 30 francs below the consortium's price anywhere in Europe. This was an open assault on the cartels, both national and international. After Rochette rejected all the consortium's offers for entry into it, the director of the consortium, de Riva-Berni, announced a "great coup" against him. In February 1914, he cut the consortium's price to 210 francs. Then Rochette joined the consortium, with a share of 8000 tons.[20]

Eventually about a fifth of the market was given up to "outsiders." Most of them raised no objections to the cartel, for they sheltered behind the advantageous price set by it. In 1912, the consortium successfully sued for patent infringement J. Cartier, of the Société anonyme des forces motrices de la Garonne. When the war broke out it remained only to set the amount of the damages he owed to the consortium.[21] At that moment in history, neither public opinion nor jurisprudence gave the enemies of the consortium much hope for any political or legal remedy against it.

The war drew attention to the multinational character of the consortium. Not only were the French carburiers linked to foreign cartels by market-allocation plans, but German and Swiss capital dominated some of the largest members of the French consortium, and Germans, Swiss, and Austrians played a large role on the Board of Directors of the Société commerciale (which, in addition to commercializing calcium carbide, sold throughout Europe other chemical products such as cyanamide for French and Swiss firms). In August 1914, the carburiers made new arrangements for the war, which everyone thought would be short. Foreign members withdrew from the Board of Directors of the Société commerciale. The international market was redistributed. Norway, a neutral, took over the Austro-German market from its previous suppliers in Allied countries, and, in exchange, Britain took over the Russian market from Norway. In discreet contacts made through neutrals some French, German, and Austrian board members gave each other mutual assurances: after the war accounts would be settled and the international cartel would go on as before.[22] These transactions probably conformed to normal practices in multinational enterprises and were a rational adaptation to a short war, but in the very different perspective of a long war, they made the French carburiers vulnerable to charges of treason.

Within France, the war destabilized the market that the consortium had so carefully balanced. Production of war matériel drove the need for calcium carbide from 40,000 tons in 1913 to 69,000 tons in 1917, essentially for welding shell casings. As usual, Albert Thomas's services preferred to work with the largest and best organized producers. Anxious not to trouble its relations with the free-lancers, the consortium urged Thomas's services to exercise "prudence" and "equity," that is, to offer war contracts to independent producers.[23] The independents did not have any excess capacity, however.[24] Moreover, the consortium already possessed the administrative machinery that Thomas needed to regulate production, prices, and sales. When, therefore, in December 1915, the decision was taken to regulate the calcium carbide market, it seemed convenient to work with the Société commerciale. Thus calcium carbide users found themselves obliged to obtain a visa from the Ministry of Armament, which usually referred them to the consortium. Prices rose in stages from 210 francs per ton in August 1914 to 500 francs in 1918 and even higher in an emerging black market, because of increasing scarcity.

The civilian shortage of calcium carbide was exacerbated by the fact that the consortium preferred to reorient part of its productive capacity to other more remunerative electrochemical products such as iron silicate, and import enough calcium carbide from Switzerland and Spain ("au prix fort") to fulfill its contracts with the State. Albert Thomas's services acquiesced to this policy, as well as to the price increases, because they needed the other electrochemical products and because the consortium's structures were useful to them.[25] The civilian consumers of calcium carbide, however, denounced strongly what they considered a "malthusian" limitation of production designed to force prices up.[26] Even more damaging was their assertion that Germans had infiltrated the French calcium carbide industry, with the aid of French traitors, in order to slow down French war production.

The "Affaire"

The consortium's enemies began to attack it even before wartime tensions took on full force. In a March 1915 pamphlet, the Deputy of the Basses-Pyrénées, Baron Paul Lacave-Laplagne, a member of the Gauche Démocratique, denounced the Société commerciale de carbure as a "German-Swiss Syndicate" which had expelled French producers from an industry invented by French science. Lacave-Laplagne sent a copy of his pamphlet to the Budget Committee of the Chamber, to Deputy

Adolphe Landry, who was conducting a study of small business, and to the Minister of Justice, to whom he explained, tendentiously, that the consortium was an "international (German) of organization."[27] From the beginning, therefore, the case mixed patriotism with economics in a way that makes it hard to isolate attitudes toward industrial concentration.[28]

Lacave-Laplagne's accusations found ready ears. Deputy Maurice Long, of the Budget Committee, sent a report to Prime Minister Viviani. When the Budget Committee learned subsequently that Lacave-Laplagne was the son-in-law of J. Cartier and an important shareholder in the enterprise which in 1912 had lost its case against the consortium, however, it backed off with embarrassment and ordered the Long memorandum withdrawn.[29] Justice Minister Aristide Briand, however, took the matter seriously enough to order a preliminary enquiry. When he received confirmation of some of Lacave-Laplagne's allegations, he ordered *juge d'instruction* Paul Coutant to begin indictment hearings ("ouvrir une instruction"). René Viviani, who succeeded Briand as Garde des Sceaux, took the matter even more seriously. Despite a certain reticence among the high magistracy, he and Coutant pursued the case with fervent zeal. They are good examples of the milieux in which, in France of the early twentieth century, one encountered ideological opposition to industrial concentration.

In the absence of any substantial biography of Viviani,[30] one is left with the conventional image of one of those "independent" socialists of the pre-1914 generation who gravitated to the center in the interest of a political and legal career. However, unlike Millerand with whom he had begun in politics as an independent socialist, Viviani remained attached to certain reformist causes. In addition to working for legislation on pensions for the elderly and participating in the campaign for women's suffrage, he was responsible, as a lawyer, for vigorous opposition to trusts. In 1912 he defended (without success) a small business in the Midi sued for breach of contract by a consortium for the import of sulphur. In that case he submitted that the contract was illegal under Article 419.[31] Interpellated in the Chamber in 1917 on the calcium carbide case, Viviani affirmed that the recent acquittals in cases under Article 419, such as that of Secrétan, rested on an "interpétation vicieuse" of the law, and that he had "taken up again the old jurisprudence of fifteen years ago which held that Article 419 is applicable" to new forms of industrial coalition. In 1919 he reminded the Chambre that he had resisted pressures to dismiss the calcium carbide case, and regretted that the accusations of hoarding made against the consortium had still not gone to trial.[32] The records show that Viviani took charge of the case personally instead of assigning it to the Direction des Affaires Criminelles. Notes written in his own hand defend the idea that a coalition intended to modify prices (as in the price war between the carburiers' consortium and Rochette) was, even in the absence of "fraudulous means," sufficient grounds for conviction under Article 419.[33] When in October 1916 Procureur de la République (Attorney General) Lescouvé advised Viviani to dismiss the case, Viviani overrode the magistrate's advice.[34]

The examining magistrate (*juge d'instruction*) Paul Coutant had entered the magistracy in 1912, after having filled the offices of *greffier* and of *juge de paix* in Paris. A somewhat unconventional jurist, he had taught law at the Ecole Supérieure de Pharmacie in Paris.[35] His chief passion in life lay elsewhere. Under the pseudonym of Stéfane-Pol, he was a prolific author. His domains were history, social commentary, and fiction, emphasizing subjects such as pacifism, George Sand, and an ancestor of his wife, Le Bas, member of the Convention, and host and disciple of Robespierre.[36] Coutant seized upon the calcium carbide case with such a Jacobin passion, in order to protect the weak against powerful interests and France against foreign enemies, that his indictment was almost overturned on appeal, for procedural errors ("vice de forme"). He found not only grounds for charges of coalition under Article 419; he also found grounds for additional accusations of commerce with the enemy and aid to the enemy in time of war (Articles 76 and 77 of the Penal Code) in the mingling of French, Swiss, German, and Austrian capital and directors in the calcium carbide industry before as well as after August 1914. For example, he misinterpreted a contract concluded in 1912 between the consortium and Krupp – a contract which included clauses concerning dispositions to take in case of war – as proof of conscious aid to Krupp by the French carburiers to prepare for war against France.

These aspects of the case attracted the attention of the sensationalist press, since public opinion was already aroused by the espionage case of Bolo Pasha.[37] Some journalists and deputies concluded from details revealed in the trial and from the carburiers' efforts to mobilize powerful influences in business and politics in their favor that they were trying to cover up an important German conspiracy. It is, however, the question of industrial concentration on which we wish to focus here. For the calcium carbide affair was at the root of the successful effort to remove the crime of coalition from the French Penal Code.

Despite the zeal of Viviani and Coutant and public overexcitement, the carburiers were finally acquitted of all the charges brought against them. First came the accusations of treason.[38] The charge of coalition was abandoned by the Parquet (prosecutors' office) in 1919. Even when parliamentary pressure revived it in 1923, there was no doubt that the verdict would be acquittal because those principally responsible for the prosecution were no longer in power.[39] The Third Republic's last effort to prosecute an industrial coalition for price-fixing had failed.

There are many explanations for the failure. It was a difficult case, begun by business rivals with a personal stake in the outcome. Two groups of consumers of calcium carbide – manufacturers of carbide lamps and welding equipment, welding shops, and the like – organized themselves specifically for this case and became plaintiffs ("parties civiles") in the prosecution of the consortium. Documents in the file show that they received money from J. Cartier.[40] Judge Coutant let his ardor prevail over his legal responsibilities. His written judgments are studded with invective against this "coalition of suspicious foreigners and bad Frenchmen"; against de Riva-Berni, the director of the Société commerciale, of Italian origin, whom he described as "this cosmopolitan foreigner" who had not performed his military service; and against the carburier Giraud-Jordan, who displayed, according to Coutant, "an attachment to everything foreign."[41] Worse still, he retouched – and appparently sharpened – a report drafted by independent experts, an act that offered the carburiers a chance to appeal (without success) for dismissal of the case, in November 1916.[42] The charges of commerce with the enemy and aid to the enemy rested on acts carried out either before the war or before the decree of 4 April 1915, which forbade any business relationship with enemy enterprises. The best-founded charge was coalition, under Article 419. Although the consortium had corresponded to French conceptions of a "good" trust, by its policy of price stabilization, it had acted like a "bad" trust in its price war with Rochette. If the Société commerciale de carbure couldn't be found guilty of monopolistic price-fixing, under article 419, then no firm could be.

The Opponents of Industrial Concentration

The calcium carbide case allows us to follow the contours of French opinion with respect to industrial concentration, at the close of the First World War.

At the end of the war, the adversaries of industrial ententes were scattered, heterogeneous, and without a solid organizational base. They were also suspected of serving petty self-interest.

The revolutionary left, scornful of economic tinkering, showed little interest in the piecemeal prosecution of individual industrial coalitions within capitalism. The rare future members of the French Communist Party who took part in attacks on the carburiers, such as Ernest Lafont, used patriotic arguments more than economic ones. *Le Droit du peuple* found irony in the fact that it was not the party of Zimmerwald and Kienthal that was being accused of treason but "de bons et notables capitalistes." The newspaper took the opportunity to propose the nationalization of hydroelectric power, but ignored the issue of coalition.[43]

The reformist left was divided. *L'Humanité*, perhaps reluctant to embarrass Albert Thomas, limited itself to dry news accounts of the trials, without commentary, and expressed astonishment at the end that "so much noise had been made about this case."[44] However, Renaudel and Laval seem to have put pressure on Viviani not to abandon the case.[45]

The center of anti-coalition action was precisely that area of center-left individualists marked by the most diffuse party organization, the weakest ties with the worlds of administration and business, and the most essentially rhetorical political weapons. They included municipal socialists like Victor Augagneur, radicals like Julien Simyan, Maurice Bokanowski, and Maurice Long, and independent socialists like Paul Meunier, editor-in-chief of *La Vérité* and associate of Merrheim and Barbusse, or Victor Lesaché, of the Gauche républicaine démocratique. Son of a small merchant in Toulon, Lesaché was the most indefatigable denouncer among the deputies elected in 1919 of milk, sugar, and grain wholesalers. They also included neo-Jacobins like Judge Coutant himself and Vincent de Moro-Giafferi, the eloquent Corsican lawyer, elected deputy in 1919, and later an active member of the "Club des Jacobins" created in 1935 as well as the "Ligue pour la défense des libertés publiques."

These enemies on principle of industrial and commercial coalitions were separated by other principles from other adversaries of coalitions. Several social Catholics were also hostile on principle to business coalitions. As early as 1906, *La Croix* complained that calcium carbide cost thirty percent less abroad than in France because the French consortium sued every independent producer for patent infringement.[46] Some participants in the 1922 Semaine sociale expressed open hostility to industrial concentration.[47] These social Catholics held ideas about business influenced by Thomist political economy, paternalism, and anti-semitism. Their solutions were mainly of a moral nature. They were much too alienated from republicans of the center-left on other issues to make common cause against cartels with them.

The same was true of the handful of opponents of cartels on the far right. Léon Daudet was among the most virulent denouncers of the car-buriers. For him, the main problem was the penetration of the French economy by German capital, not a matter of scale or economic organi-zation. It was naturally impossible for him to join in any common anti-cartel front with the center-left.[48]

The institutions on which the enemies of coalitions based themselves were the Parliament and a part of the press. In January-February 1917, Bokanowski, Meunier, and Millevoye interpellated the government in the Chambre, affirming that powerful interests were working to obstruct the carburiers' trial. The Calcium Carbide case reappeared in Parliament in January 1919 when Edouard Barthe and Ernest Lafont denounced what they regarded as the government's favoritism toward big business.[49] Parliamentary committees, eager to reassert their powers against war government, were more effective weapons than interpella-tions. In January 1917, the Army Committee of the Chambre was the scene of pressures on Viviani by Renaudel, Laval, and Augagneur. Between 26 December 1916 and 23 May 1917, Julien Simyan, presi-dent of the Chambre's Committee for the Investigation of War Contracts, bombarded Albert Thomas with thirty-two increasingly detailed and sharply-worded demands for investigation of the Ministry of Armaments' relationship with the consortium.[50] The Commission's inquest exerted considerable pressure on the Ministry, forcing it to resist the price increases demanded by the Carburiers. During spring 1917, a large part of the Ministry's activities were devoted to this issue. But the Committee's pressure did nothing to change the close relations between the Ministry and the consortium. As rapporteur of this Committee, Paul Meunier spent months in 1919 trying to dig out why and thanks to what influences the carburiers had been acquitted,[51] before being sidetracked by personal legal problems.

The press was less effective. Only a small part of the press took an active part in the debates, mainly marginal newspapers avid for scan-dalous revelations and ready to accept prepared handouts in their eager-ness to cut costs (or even to attract subsidies). On 11 August 1916, the plaintiffs held a press conference in a bar on the Boulevard de Sébastopol. The documents that they handed out there (including some illegally extracted from the trial file) fed several newspapers for weeks. *L'Oeuvre*, expanded to a daily only a year before, made the calcium car-bide case its cause, and published something about it almost every day in August and September 1916.[52] *Le Petit Bleu*, whose director, Alfred Oulman, was a cousin of Lévy-Oulman, one of the plaintiffs' lawyers, published several articles demanding that the "rich" be prevented from covering up the "affaire" and wondering why the "guilty" were not already behind bars.[53] From early 1917 Gustave Hervé in *La Victoire* and Urbain Gohier in *L'Oeuvre française* denounced the carburiers as "traitors." As a whole, these newspapers treated the case as a matter of scandal rather than of economics. As for the four mass-circulation dailies (*Le Matin, Le Journal, Le Petit Parisien, Le Petit Journal*), they limited themselves to relatively neutral reports of the interpellation in Parliament in January-February 1917 and of the first trial in January 1918. *Le Temps, L'Echo de Paris,* and *La Revue parlementaire* published material favorable to the carburiers.[54] But the press was censored every time it touched on relations between the carburiers and the Ministry of Armament[55], and the anti-carburier papers fell too easily for the aura of scandal and secrecy that surrounded the case to offer anything more sophisticated than a ritual defense of the little man against powerful interests.

The adversaires of the carburiers for the most part had no coherent position against industrial and commercial coalitions. Most of them were more interested in "Boches" and "embochés"[56] than in a serious economic or social analysis. Insofar as they dealt with the political economy of cartels, they tended to see the case more often as a matter of individual misconduct than as a question of economic structure, or, at the most, as a question of "industrial morals" or "the patriotism of business."[57] Some clearly attacked the carburiers as a "bad" trust and not simply as a trust.

Both sides claimed ritually to be the defenders of small producers. No one argued that freer competition among independent producers would result in higher yield and productivity among these enterprises and more abundance for all. The case for small enterprises rested rather on social considerations. They were perceived as a "gathering of interests that makes up part of the national wealth"[58] or as something appropriate to the French egalitarian and individualist spirit. The only defense of small enterprises from an economic perspective in this debate came from the great economic historian Henri Hauser, one of the consortium's most ardent defenders. Hauser pointed out that small enterprises' "taste for high-quality work" could capture favorable positions in the market from big producers.[59] The defenders of the consortium submitted that competition (always portrayed as "ruineuse" or "brutale") was worse for small business than the benevolent protection of a consortium organized in the French fashion, as an association of free enterprises around a sales cartel ("comptoir de vente"), and not as an "American

164

trust" that swallows up all competitors, or as a "German cartel that dominates the weak." This, according to the carburiers' defenders, was the ideal formula for postwar France: one adapted to the dimensions of the modern market, yet remaining faithful to the "temperament of our nation."[60] Defenders of small business were sensitive to these arguments in favor of organization, because stability interested them more than either productivity or growth.

Consequently, the plaintiffs gained nothing much by accusing the consortium of "ruining the small carburiers."[61] No independent producer was involved in the suit, except for Cartier and Lacave-Laplagne, who in fact had only wanted to settle their 1912 suit out of court. Rochette, who could hardly be described as a small producer, quietly defended the consortium, to which he now belonged. In general the "small carburiers" worked happily under the protective wing of the consortium.

Prices – and defense of the consumer – could furnish more effective material for anti-cartel propaganda. If Rochette had the technical capacity to produce calcium carbide in his new plants more cheaply than the consortium, shouldn't he be encouraged? Didn't his productivity and output deserve recompense? Was not the new price of 210 francs per ton, brought about by his arrival in the market in 1913, advantageous for the national economy? These questions gained sharpness when, during the war, the price doubled and the consortium seemed to be accentuating the rise by limiting production. When the indefatigable deputy Julien Simyan pursued his investigations, even the Ministry of Armament had to admit that "the calcium carbide industry seems to be controlled by a limited number of persons," and that "price controls in effect since the end of 1915 have not been followed by an increase in production sufficient to satisfy needs."[62] French wartime production of calcium carbide fell below prewar figures, even as demand increased. While the French electrochemical industry turned to more lucrative products such as iron silicate, the consortium filled the calcium carbide deficit by imports from Switzerland and Spain.

At this point, the anti-cartel thesis began to conflict with the nationalism so conspicuous in anti-cartel circles. If enterprises like Rochette cut prices too much, claimed the defenders of organization, French industry would simply stop producing calcium carbide. Very few adversaries of cartels wanted to push the "free trade" argument to the point of opening the French market to cheaper foreign products. No enemy of the carburiers proposed the outright elimination of customs protection.[63] Judge Paul Coutant was practically alone in speaking in terms that recalled Adam Smith on the advantages of competition or Frédéric Bastiat's "harmonies." French consumers, he wrote, ought to buy calcium carbide wherever in the world it could be produced most cheaply. No one would suffer from that, he thought. Consumers would obtain calcium carbide at lower cost; the French electrochemical industry could turn to more lucrative products; and in case of war the French Army could always establish special production, as it had been obliged to do anyway.[64] As far as we know, Coutant's reasoning was unique during the debate about the calcium carbide consortium. Insofar as nationalist and moral reasons were as much responsible for public hostility to the carburiers as economic reasons, centered as much on their cosmopolitanism as on their grip on the market, the solutions proposed by the anti-carburiers could hardly envisage this kind of free world market from which the French consortium would quite likely have suffered and German and American giants benefited.

The Partisans of Industrial Concentration

The partisans of the consortium were better connected and better organized than their adversaries, and advanced a more coherent set of arguments.

Henry Gall, the best-connected of the defendants, was president of the Société des ingénieurs civils de France[65] and a member of the Chemical Arts Committee of the Société d'encouragement pour l'industrie nationale. His contacts related him, both personally and professionally, to influential people eager to defend the calcium carbide consortium and sales consortia in general. Henri Le Châtelier, very close to Gall as former president of the Société d'encouragement and president of its Chemical Arts Committee, was also the first Frenchman to have supported Frederick W. Taylor's techniques of industrial rationalization.[66] Not only did Le Châtelier testify in court for Gall; he led a delegation of French businessmen in October 1916 who warned Viviani that war production would be interrupted if the carburiers' prosecution were not suspended.[67]

Another pro-carburier network gathered around the disciples of Frédéric Le Play. Gall and another defendant, Giraud-Jordan, sent their sons to the Ecole des Roches, where disciples of Le Play taught the virtues of paternalism and British enterprise to the sons of French businessmen and high civil servants.[68] Paul de Rousiers, president of the Le Playist "Société internationale de science sociale," as well as a defender of "good" trusts and secretary-general of a business association, le

Syndicat des Armateurs de France, drafted for the court a "consulta-tion" in defense of the carburiers which had a large impact.[69]

Outside the circle of immediate friends and colleagues, French busi-ness and its associations generally came to the aid of the calcium carbide consortium, especially after the cloud of accusations of treason had been lifted in early 1918. Many industrialists worried about the threat of a revived Article 419. If one held to the strict letter of the law, wrote one of the carburiers to a British associate, one would have to prosecute nine-tenths of French industry.[70] Robert Pinot told the court that French industry could not live under the regime of Article 419. Pinot and other French business leaders worried about the competitive power of French industry in the postwar world. Pinot in particular had tried to spread sales consortia ("comptoirs de vente") on the Longwy model throughout French industry. "All of French industry," he told the court, "considers today that producers' associations are one of the essen-tial bases of its functioning."[71] When the prosecution of the carburiers began, Pinot installed a staff for their defense in his offices in the Rue de Madrid – where he served as secretary-general not only of the Comité des Forges but also of several other industrial associations, including the Chambre syndicale des forces hydrauliques, on which the carburiers depended.

Enthusiasm for industrial organization penetrated deep into certain milieux of the productivist left. Albert Thomas found himself danger-ously compromised when the carburiers' prosecution began. Not only had his services worked closely with the consortium, but they were implicated, through the consortium, in some rather complex and ambiguous contracts with Swiss hydro-electric chemical concerns that were provisioning both warring camps.[72] It is not surprising, therefore, that some members of Thomas's staff, such as Albert Claveille and Lt.-Col. Ernest Mercier, testified in court to the carburiers' patriotic ser-vices to war production.[73] When the prosecution began, Thomas dis-puted the charge of coalition in personal meetings with President Poincaré and War Minister Millerand, though he became more prudent when the accusations of treason were added.[74] But beyond personal considerations, Thomas believed that forces unleashed by war were steering society in directions promising for the future of socialism: more unified workers would have more influence in an industrial world that was more concentrated, organized, and productive, under closer State supervision.[75] The revival of Article 419 during the calcium carbide case worried him, for it seemed to threaten the efforts he had made to encourage armaments producers to set up powerful associations of pro-

ducers, under State supervision. It also worried some of those arms producers, who then asked Thomas whether his policy exposed them to
prosecution under Article 419. There is a very interesting correspondence on this subject between Thomas and Lucien Dior, president of
the Union des Fabricants d'acide sulfurique de France. Fernand Payen,
Thomas's legal counsel, thought that the State should have dealt with
independent producers. Thomas disagreed with this opinion, and
reminded Payen that he, Thomas, had taken the initiative to encourage
associations among armanents manufacturers. He conceded only one
point to Payen: the State ought to supervise the prices set by such associations: "That would go exactly in the direction of the organization I
would like to create."[76]

Etienne Clémentel was another supporter of industrial organization.
As a newly elected deputy of the "Gauche radicale" in 1901, Clémental
had encouraged government intervention against "the industrial dictatorship [which is] tending to develop."[77] As Minister of Commerce at
the end of World War I, however, Clémentel devised a plan to reorga-
nize the whole French economy from top to bottom in consortia
intended to reproduce in the postwar world the system of raw material
distribution developed in 1917-18 among the Allies. The revival of
Article 419 ran counter to this project. Clémentel did not intervene
personally in favor of the carburiers as Minister of Commerce, although
as President of the Budget Committee in 1915 he had ordered Briand
peremptorily to remove all Budget Commmittee documents from the
indictment dossier. However, he publicly criticized Article 419 on 20
March 1918 at the Musée social.[78] Moreover, his "alter ego and authorized spokesman," the economic historian Henri Hauser,[79] was a tireless advocate of the calcium carbide consortium. He saw in it a model
for all French industry after the war.[80]

The advocates of industrial organization defended a more coherent
position, on economic grounds, than their adversaries. The tendency to
overproduction within capitalism was already an almost universal
dogma in France, no less among capitalists than among Marxists. By
1914, Say's Law had very few believers in France. Many French industrialists expected a very severe crisis after the war due to excessive productive capacity combined with a collapse of demand. Words like
"overproduction" and "saturation of the market" recurred frequently in
the calcium carbide debate. Industrialists believed it would be impossible to keep the extra plants constructed during the war active.[81] The
return of Alsace-Lorraine, some feared, would create as many problems
as satisfactions, for it would double French steel-making capacity with-

in an uncertain export market.[82] On a world scale, the dangers of over-production would be further increased by the awakening of America and the recovery of Germany. It was widely agreed, within the reformist left as well as on the right, that the French economy could not meet its postwar challenges without stronger organization.

But while *L'Humanité* demanded economic reorganization for greater productivity,[83] the defenders of cartels wanted reorganization for market stability. "Good" cartels had traditionally been defined as legitimate defense against competition and market cycles. One group that tried to make industrial ententes legal after the war described a "lawful coalition" as one that "maintains the necessary harmony between production and consumption."[84] It is important to note that reorganization was perceived in terms of sales rather than production, and as an operation to stabilize the market for producers already in place, rather than in terms of a quest for cheaper, more efficient, or larger productive units. From this perspective, price cuts were as reprehensible as price raises, and the carburiers were perfectly justified in defending themselves forcefully against the "unacceptable imbalance" introduced into the market by Rochette in 1913.[85] The government prosecutor ("Procureur de la République") Lescouvé argued for a "non-lieu," i.e., against indinctment of the carburiers on the coalition charge, because their consortium, in his opinion, corresponded to the definition of a "good" trust: it balanced production and consumption in order to "avoid crises of overproduction, . . . prevent the ruinous collapse of prices, [and] . . . establish or maintain a reasonably remunerative market."[86]

While stability was the dominant note, the advocates of cartels tried to reassure the partisans of productivism that cartels were not automatically malthusian. As in the discussion of small business, those who promoted industrial ententes insisted that the French model of association, around sales consortia ("comptoirs de vente"), differed from bad foreign models. A sales consortium assigned shares of the market, not ceilings on production; it could help small dispersed enterprises to pool their research and market analysis costs and thus help French industry modernize.[87] Support for "infant industries" reinforced the appeal of ententes to productivists. Indeed how could a new technology such as the electrochemical industry develop in French enterprises in the face of American and German industrial giants except within a powerful organization? Albert Thomas was particularly sensitive to the problem of how to implant new productive technologies. He asked Maurice Halbwachs to examaine the carburiers' case with particular care to see "by what measures new industry could be shielded from prosecution or trouble."[88]

For those who favored cartels, world economic competition was the most effective argument of all. The carburiers' efforts had contributed to making their "infant industry" stronger in France, Switzerland, and Scandinavia than in Germany. The result "can bear comparison with German industry."[89] "Tomorrow's economic struggle," warned Henri Hauser, "will be a struggle between big battalions."[90] Even before 1914, patriotism had softened some old trust-busters like Francis Laur. At the end of the First World War, it persuaded many more that without industrial ententes French industry was bound to lose the world race: "To American trusts, Britain responded with trusts and Germany with Konzernen. To German Konzernen, France must respond with concentrated industry."[91]

The Abolition of the Crime of Coalition

There had been attempts to modify Article 419 for thirty years. Before the First World War, businessmen had not been unanimous on the question, however. In 1912, the Paris Chamber of Commerce had voted a resolution against modification, fearing "dangerous precisions" more than a bad statute fallen into disuse.[92] While metallurgists generally supported ententes before 1914, textile manufacturers opposed them, for they saw in them a danger to family enterprises and an invitation to parliamentary reprisals against tariff protection.[93] Wartime and postwar economic dislocation won the textile manufacturers over to the metallurgists' position. In 1924 they wanted to legalize ententes "intended to allocate orders, regularize production, centralize sales and purchases, and maintain balance."[94] To partisans of industrial organization, the calcium carbide case made the old statute seem more dangerous than before.

The postwar movement to amend Article 419 emerged directly out of the carburiers' defense. Henri Hauser, Paul de Rousiers, and Georges de Ségogne (author of another "consultation" on behalf of the carburiers) launched the campaign in 1916, within the Association nationale de l'expansion économique.[95] The ANEE drafted a text which legalized explicitly certain forms of industrial coalition, and limited prosecution to cases of fraud. On 29 October 1916, the Chamber of Commerce of Lyon – whose president, Jean Coignet, descendant of a long line of Lyons chemical manufacturers, had testified in favor of the carburiers – approved the ANEE text in order to permit French industry to adopt "the Germans' means of success." Even the Paris Chamber of Commerce, which had previously feared "perilous discussions" of complex texts, hoped to amend Article 419 by the most economical means possible, by simply eliminating the two lines that referred to coalition.[96] When the campaign was farther along, the Fédération des industriels et commerçants français sent delegations to the ministers and parliamentary commissions asking, first, for the abolition of this article, and, if that were not possible, its amendment to omit all reference to coalition and to permit condemnation only for fraud.[97] In 1923 the Société d'études et d'informations économiques, emanation of the Comité des Forges, published more thorough defenses by Paul de Rousiers of "good" ententes.

By that time several texts had already come before Parliament. By an extraordinary procedure, the Garde des Sceaux submitted the matter to a committee of extra-parliamentary experts in 1922, presided over by Senator Boivin-Champeaux and including such energetic defenders of the carburiers as Paul de Rousiers. Garde des Sceaux Maurice Colrat accepted their report and presented it to Parliament as a draft bill in 1923.[98] This remarkable text declared legal those industrial coalitions which preserved the necessary "harmony" between production and consumption, that is to say "good" trusts, defined in terms of their effect on market stability. So, in reaction to the Calcium Carbide Case, the "Chambre bleu horizon" seriously envisaged giving explicit legal sanction to industrial coalitions, in a way previously unknown in the juridical systems of most industrial nations.

When the bill came up for discussion, however, different postwar issues had made it less topical. The French business world was now more interested in dismantling wartime organizations than in legitimating them, and in reducing state intervention in economic affairs. Once more "liberty of commerce" had become a popular expression. At the same time inflation had given high priority to the cost of living issue, "la vie chère." Parliament was now working on widening the scope of Article 419, in order to prevent individual enterprises from hoarding; it even considered criminalizing mere attempts at hoarding not followed by any change in price.[99] On the eve of the elections of 1924, the accent was again on consumer goods.

The question of coalition was not forgotten, however. Although the paragraphs in the experts' report which openly legalized coalitions were withdrawn from the bill in committee, the text still granted "a kind of legal recognition" to ententes, as the rapporteur Raynaldy admitted.

The committee had simply cut from the old Article 419 the lines concerning coalition, in the kind of economical operation desired by the Paris Chamber of Commerce. According to Raynaldy, Parliament could resolve the problem of industrial and commercial coalitions "par préterition."[100]

For our subject, the decisive vote was not the final vote but the vote on an amendment proposed by Victor Lesaché, of the Gauche radicale démocratique et sociale. Lesaché wanted to put the crime of coalition back into the new text, in the very terms by which the old article 419 defined it. Ententes, he said, harmed French consumers, and despite its lack of use, article 419 had forced French cartels to act prudently, by defining themselves as devoted to ends other than price-fixing. Already "consortiums . . . are becoming a national danger." Without the penalties envisaged by the old article 419, the situation would be even worse. He summoned the Chamber to fufill its role as "guardian of the interests of millions of small shopkeepers" and of "38,000,000 consumers."[101]

The Lesaché amendment forced the Chamber to vote unambiguously on the issue of whether industrial coalitions in themselves, without the slightest fraudulent action, were contrary to French law. Once more we can follow rather precisely the main currents of opinion concerning cartels, but this time inside the Chamber of Deputies. It is striking to note that the amendment came from the individualist left. The revolutionary left, while voting for the Lesaché amendment, concentrated its fire on "exaggerated [war] profits" rather than on industrial concentration.[102] A curious minority supported Lesaché.[103] It included the Communists and the Socialists. The Radicals were divided: Daladier, Chautemps, Pierre Gheusi, and Justin Godart opposed cartels. Herriot and Albert Sarraut did not want to declare them illegal. Of course the majority opposed to the Lesaché amendment (391 deputies) was not composed only of businessman deputies such as the two de Wendels or Lucien Dior, himself president of an industrial syndicate. Most conservative and moderate deputies did not want to legislate against all forms of industrial organization, no more than certain Radicals, or even some members of the center-left like Paul Meunier, who had recommended energetic prosecution of the carburiers. Voting for the Lesaché amendment, along with the anti-cartel left, were several conservative paternalists such as General de Curières de Castelnau, Maurice de Rothschild and Count Jean de Leusse, as well as the social Catholic Robert Schuman and the dissident Action Française member Xavier de Magallon, thus illustrating the dispersal that we have already noted among the enemies of the calcium carbide consortium. In any event they were few in number. When on 3 December 1926 the Senate accepted the Chambre's text, Article 419 ceased to worry industrialists. "Coalition is lawful."[104]

Conclusion

We can draw only modest conclusions from our study of the calcium carbide case. No one could claim that industrial concentration grew significantly in France after 1926. That was always more a matter of economic conditions (and values) than of legislation. But we have been able to study the main lines of public opinion on this subject. Maurice Halbwachs observed one day to Albert Thomas that the debate about the calcium carbide consortium pitted jurists, who wanted to apply the letter of the law, against economists, who wanted to adapt the French economy to the postwar world.[105] This ingenious observation needs serious amendments. In the main, law faculties supported amending Article 419 and abolishing the crime of coalition.[106] The debate pitted the holders of anti-cartel opinions – dispersed, without coherence, extending from the individualist and neo-Jacobin left to a few social Catholics and a few paternalist conservatives – against a powerful coalition extending from productivists on the left, such as Albert Thomas and Herriot, to spokesmen for heavy industry, including a majority of moderates and conservatives who associated "liberty of commerce" with avoiding government regulation, even the regulation of cartels. It is hardly surprising that the judges acquitted the carburiers, and that Parliament, in reaction to this case, amended Article 419.

Robert O. Paxton

Notes to Chapter 6

1. In Germany, an important court decision in 1897 confirmed the right of cartels to penalize recalcitrant members. Despite frequent debate, the Reichstag never legistlated on industrial or commercial coalitions during the Empire. A law of 2 November 1923 gave the Minister of Economic Affairs of the Weimar Republic full power to annul contracts and dissolve cartels harmful to the national or public interest. See F. Blaich, *Kartell- und Monopolpolitik in Kaiserlichen Deutschland* (Düsseldorf, 1973); R. Liefmann, *Kartelle, Konzerne und Trusts* (Stuttgart, 1930), pp. 203–21; Erich Maschke, "Outline of the History of German Cartels from 1873 to 1914, in *Essays in European Economic History*, François Crouzet, W.H. Chaloner, and W.S. Stern, ed., (London, 1969), pp. 226–258.

Belgium had already abrogated articles 419 and 420 of its penal code.

British civil law, alone of all European juridical systems, formally forbade operations in restraint of trade, but no juridical sanction was taken against the rapid develeopment of cartels after 1900. See H. Levy, *Monopoly, Cartels, and Trusts in British Industry* (London, 1927), pp. 169–80.

2. Charles E. Freedeman, "Cartels and the Law in France Before 1914," *French Historical Studies* 15:3 (Spring 1983), pp. 462–78; François Caron, "Ententes et stratégies d'achat dans la France du XIXe siècle," *Revue française de gestion* (Sept-Oct. 1988), pp. 127–33. Jean-Pierre Daviet, "Trade Associations or Agreements and Controlled Competition in France, 1830-1939," in *Trade Associations in Business History*, Hirosaki Yamazaki and Matsuo Miyamoto, ed. (Tokyo: Tokyo University Press, 1988), pp. 269–98.

3. Law of 3 December 1926. *Journal Officiel, Débats, Chambre*, 4 December 1926, p. 12,722.

4. One must not conclude that this amendment was followed by an immediate increase in concentration. In fact, M. Didier and E. Malinvaud, "La concentration de l'industrie s'est-elle accentuée depuis le début du siècle?" *Economie et statistique* (June 1969), pp. 3–10, argue that the distribution by size of French firms remained substantially the same throughout this century, with the exception of a large decrease in the percentage of the smallest firms. They find some increase during the period 1906–1931, however. It must be underlined that they considered only the basic production unit, the firm, and not the sale or management unit, which might group several firms, or the financial unit, capable of setting policy for several firms. No doubt it was particularly at these higher levels that concentration took place, because French custom preferred the association of firms rather than their absorption in a single giant firm.

5. Article 420 increased the penalties envisaged by Article 419 in cases where foodstuffs were involved. It was also possible to annul contracts "for an illicit purpose" using a civil procedure under articles 1131 and 1133 of the Civil Code, the "illicit purpose" in the case of cartels being the violation of Article 419 of the Penal Code.

6. Caron, pp. 126–27.

7. L. Mazeaud, *Le Problème des unions de producteurs devant la loi française* (Paris, 1924), pp. 14–71.

8. For example, Paul de Rousiers, *Les Syndicats industriels* (Paris, 1911), p. 131, distinguishes trusts, whose goal was "success," from cartels, whose aim was "security." See also F. Laur, *De l'accaparement*, vol. 3: *La Concentration industrielle en France*, 2nd ed. (Paris: 1905), who praises the Comptoir de Longwy for its moderation and patriotism, but

demands prosecution against insurance groups. *Le Code pénal annoté par E. Garçon* (Paris, 1911), p. 182, urged judges to distinguish frankly between good and bad trusts in their decisions, by declaring defensive coalitions legal and speculative coalitions illegal.

For the introduction of similar distinctions in Germany and Austria, see F. Blaich, *Kartell, op. cit.*, p. 25 and T.F.Marburg, "Government and Business in Germany: Public Policy Toward Cartels," *Business History Review* 38 (1964).

In the United States, even that "trust-buster" Theodore Roosevelt made popular the distinction between good and bad trusts which affected the application of the Sherman Antitrust Act. Cf. G. Owen, *Industry in the USA* (Baltimore, 1966), p. 37.

9. The most important opinion on this point was that of Procureur-général Sarrut in the case of Secrétan's attempted corner of the world copper supply: Dalloz, *Recueil*, 1893, p. 51.

10. Opinion was far from unanimous on that point. The text of Article 419 clearly condemns those who modify prices by *any* of the enumerated techniques ("*or . . . by fraudulent means*") and not only those who use all these techniques. For a rather literal interpretation of this point, see *Le Code pénal annoté par E. Garçon, op. cit.*, p. 187.

11. F. Laur, *De l'accaparement*, vol. 3, *op. cit.*, p. 187.

12. Secrétan was found guilty personally on 28 May 1890 of distributing fictitious dividends, and the Cour de Paris annulled his contracts on 18 December 1890 without finding them criminal. See L. Mazeaud, *Le Problème, op. cit.*, pp. 32–34; *Gazette des tribunaux*, 24 October 1890.

13. P. Obrin, *Le Comptoir métallurgique de Longwy* (Paris, 1908), pp. 180–84.

14. M. Gillet, *Les charbonnages du Nord de la France au XIXe siècle* (Paris – The Hague, 1973), 298. This is the fullest study of a French cartel based on its archives. See also Michael J. Rust, "Business and Politics: the Comité des Forges and the French Steel Industry, 1869–1914," (Ann Arbor: University Microfilms, 1973), pp. 131–85, and Jean-Pierre Daviet, *Un Destin international: la Compagnie de Saint-Gobain de 1830 à 1939* (Paris, 1988).

15. E. Dolléans, *De l'accaparement* (Paris, 1902), pp. 10–11; *Revue d'économie politique*, 1918, p. 240.

16. Temporary supplementary decrees of 20 April 1916 and 23 October 1919 against "illicit speculation" were used more often than Article 419.

17. *Gazette des Tribunaux*, 5, 6, and 7 March 1917; L. Mazeaud, *Le problème, op. cit.*, pp. 228–29.

18. E. Troimaux, *L'Affaire des carbures* (Paris, 1918). Important files on the consortium and its prosecution may be found at the Archives nationales in Paris [hereafter "AN"] (Albert Thomas papers, 94 AP 109 and 94 AP 353, and Ministry of Justice-Chancellerie, BB18 76 BL 58, "Carbures" [provisional classification]), and at the Archives historiques de la guerre at the Château de Vincennes [hereafter "AHG"] (10 N 183, 10 N 186).

19. Ministry of Commerce, "Carbure de calcium: demande de prolongation du Brevet 236 160 pris par M. L.-M. Bullier le 9 février 1894," AN: F12 7451.

20. The fact that Louis Rochette later defended the consortium when it faced prosecution makes it likely that he was always more interested in joining the consortium than in overturning it.

21. Cour d'appel de Dijon, 31 December 1912.

22. Walter Rathenau had been one of the first Directors of Bozel, one of the members of the French consortium. Around October 1914, some French carburiers broke off contacts with the international cartel. Others continued to maintain discreet contact through Switzerland until 1915.

23. For example, Keller letter to Albert Claveille, 26 April 1916. Albert Thomas papers, AN: 94 AP 109, dossier "Entente avec les carburiers en avril 1916."

24. Questions to four independent producers and replies, 3 December [1916], Albert Thomas papers, *ibid.*, dossier "carbures."

25. Albert Thomas papers, *ibid.*, dossiers "Entente avec les carburiers en décembre 1915" et "Entente avec les carburiers en avril 1916."

26. AN: 94 AP 109, note by Maurice Halbwachs, 15 December 1916, which describes to Albert Thomas the grievances of the consumers against the consortium.

27. AN: BB18, Ministry of Justice, Chancellerie, 76 BL 58, dossier "Lacave-Laplagne." The pamphlet was reprinted in *Paris-Midi* for 27–28 April 1915 under the title "Sus au commerce allemand."

28. French attacks on industrial concentration traditionally had a xenophobic tone. Cf. Francis Laur's interpretation of Secrétan's copper corner as the work of the Rothschilds, in the Chamber of Deputies, 21 March 1889.

29. The President of the Budget Committee (Clémentel) to the Garde des Sceaux (Briand), 1 October 1915, AN: BB18, Chancellerie 76 BL 58. The carburiers explained to the Committee who Lacave-Laplagne was, and suggested unflatteringly that he had "succeeded in surprising the Committee's good faith." Later the enemies of the consortium accused the Committee of yielding to the carburiers' pressure.

30. The thesis of S.V. Gallup, "The Political Career of René Viviani," (Oxford, 1965), is still not published.

31. *Gazette du palais*, 2e semestre 1912, pp. 106–8: Cour d'appel d'Aix, 2e Chambre, Société française d'importation de soufre c/ Julien père et fils.

32. *Journal officiel*, Débats, Chambre, séance du 9 février 1917, p.356; séance du 24 janvier 1919, p. 210.

33. AN: BB18, Ministry of Justice, Chancellerie, 76 BL 58, Note, Direction Criminelle to Direction Civile, 14 February 1918, dossier "Instructions au procureur de la République."

34. *Ibid.*, Garde des Sceaux (Viviani) to Procureur de la République près le Tribunal de la Seine (Lescouvé), 21 November 1916.

35. C. E. Curinier, *Dictionnaire national des contemporains* (Paris, 1899–1905), vol. 5, p. 331.

36. "Stéfane-Pol," *Autour de Robespierre: le conventionnel Le Bas* (Paris, 1901); *ibid.*, *De Robespierre à Fouché* (Paris, 1906), among other titles. Coutant was also director of the Bibliothèque pacifiste internationale.

37. For a comparison with Bolo Pasha, cf. J. Labarthe, "La Haute Trahison des carburiers," *La Tribune de Paris*, 10 January 1918. The affair offered many details for public delectation. The two sides sent communiqués to the press, and probably paid for the insertion of certain articles. The Deputy Lucien Millevoie, whose great moment had been the revelation of the Panama scandal, leapt to the conclusion that the carburiers had furnished 300,000 tons of explosives to the Germans, whereas they had really sold 300 tons of cyanamide, treated to be used as fertilizer, to the Italians. Others somehow concluded that the carburiers had helped the Germans manufacture poison gas. Some private letters, leading to believe that Lacave-Laplagne only wanted to settle out of court in the trial that opposed his firm to the consortium, were made public during debates in the Chamber of Deputies (*Journal officiel*, séance du 13 février 1917, pp. 373–77). The Carburiers received anonymous threatening letters. AHG: 10 N 186, pièce 222.

38. Acquitted of aid to the enemy in time of war (Art. 77 of the Penal Code) by the Premier Conseil de Guerre, Paris, 11 February 1918; acquitted of commerce with the

enemy (Art. 76) by the Cour d'Assises de Paris, 28 May 1918.

39. 11e Chambre, Tribunal civil de première instance du département de la Seine, 12 February 1923. For parliamentary pressure for reopening the case in 1922, see Archives de la Chambre des Députés, XIe législature, Commission des marchés de guerre, AN: C 7737, C 7742.

40. L'Association française des consommateurs de carbure de calcium, d'oxygène et de produits électro-chimiques, président Jean Denoel; and Paul Jorat, manufacturer of acetylene equipment, 159 rue de la Roquette, Paris. For proof that Jorat was reimbursed by Cartier, AHG: 10 N 186, documents 170, 219, 223.

41. Paul Coutant, "Rapport d'ensemble," 16 December 1915 (AN: BB18 Chancellerie 76 BL 58); *ibid.*, "Ordonnance du 27 novembre 1916" (AN: 94 AP 109); rapport des experts, 31 March 1916 (*ibid.*).

42. AN: BB18, Chancellerie 76 BL 58, dossier "incident Lecaudey."

43. *Journal officiel, Débats, Chambre,* séance du 24 janvier 1919, p. 213; *Le Droit du peuple,* 10 September 1916, "Où nous conduit la phobie du socialisme. Le Scandale des Carbures."

44. 12 February 1918.

45. "Note pour le ministre sur l'Affaire des Carbures," 16 January 1917, in the hand of Maurice Halbwachs, Albert Thomas papers, AN: 94 AP 109.

46. 9 June 1916.

47. Cf. Abbé Danset, "Le mouvement de concentration de la grande industrie française depuis la guerre," *Semaines sociales de France,* XIVe session, Strasbourg, 1922, *Le Rôle économique de l'Etat* (Lyon, 1922), pp. 91–105.

48. *Action française,* 25 and 27 December 1916.

49. *Journal officiel, Débats, Chambre,* sessions of 16 January 1917, pp. 40–41, 9 February 1917, pp. 347–367, and 23 January 1919, pp. 203–220.

50. Albert Thomas papers, AN: 94 AP 109.

51. Paul Meunier's notes take up a large part of the files on the calcium carbide case in AHG: 10 N 183 and 10 N 186.

52. Almost daily 8 August–3 September; 22, 26 September; 29 November; 7 December 1916.

53. 18 June; 1, 6, 17, 20, 26, 31 August; 2, 4, 21 September 1916.

54. *Le Temps,* 22 January 1917; *L'Echo de Paris,* 14-15 March 1917; *La Revue Parlementaire,* 24 February, 31 March 1917. P. Albert, *Histoire générale de la presse française,* vol. 3 (Paris, 1972), p. 428 notes that the four mass-circulation dailies organized their own distribution and news-gathering cartel at this time.

55. Albert Thomas Papers, AN: 94 AP 353 includes a certain number of censored texts.

56. *Ibid.,* text of censored article for *l'Eveil,* 12 August 1916.

57. Experts' report (Albert Pfeiffer and Louis Bareiller-Fouché), pp. 2–3 (AN: 94 AP 109); *L'Oeuvre,* 29 November 1916.

58. Julien Simyan, letter no. 2216 M/C to Albert Thomas, 7 April 1917 (AN: 94 AP 109). Someone wrote "bafouillage" on the margin of Thomas' copy.

59. H. Hauser, "Modifications à faire subir aux articles 419 et 420 du Code Pénal," in Société des ingénieurs civils de France, *Travaux préparatoires du Congrès général du génie civil, Session nationale,* March 1918, Section VIII, p. 4. Hauser had no sympathy for the social argument in favor of small enterprises, and feared their tendency to throw themselves into "ruinous competition."

60. F. Laur, *De l'accaparement,* vol. 3, *op.cit.,* p. 210; H. Hauser, "Etude économique

sur l'industrie du carbure de calcium," Dijon, 13 January 1916 (Bibliothèque nationale: 4° V pièce 6763).

61. "Requête et mémoire à consulter pour P. Jorat, Denoël et consorts contre Hugo Koller, Henry Gall, Giraud-Jordan et consorts," 7 December 1917, p. 10 (AHG: 10 N 186).

62. Note no. 1 050 I/C, 7 May 1917 by Schweitzer, directeur du contrôle, Ministry of Armament, Albert Thomas papers, AN: 94 AP 109.

63. Frédéric Jenny, in *Le Temps* – normally pro-carburier – was the only one to make this suggestion (while defending the necessity for some forms of industrial entente in France). Cf. "La Protection du consommateur," *Le Temps*, 20 December 1922, p. 4. Around 1922, the cost of living – "la vie chère" – became more worrisome to public opinion than the legitimacy of industrial and commercial coalitions.

64. "Ordonnance du juge d'instruction, le 12 mars 1917," AN: BB18 76 BL 58. Coutant used this argument to counter the assertions of Paul Beauregard and of Paul de Rousiers, skillful witnesses for the defense, that the carburiers had acted "as wise businessmen and as good Frenchmen" in organizing a branch of French industry so as to shield it from foreign competition.

65. Cf. the triumphal return of Gall to his position in the Society after his acquittal of the treason charges, in Société des ingénieurs civils de France, *Mémoires et comptes rendus*, session of 22 February 1918.

66. H. Le Châtelier, *Le Taylorisme*, 2nd edition (Paris, 1934); A. Moutet, "L'Introduction du système Taylor en France," *Le Mouvement social*, October 1975. P. Fridenson, "Un tournant taylorien de la société française 1904–1918," *Annales E.S.C.*, September-October 1987.

67. Le Châtelier's version of his meeting with Viviani is in *Affaire des Carbures, 1er Conseil de guerre de Paris, Interrogatoire et dépositions* (Chambéry, 1918), pp. 101ff. For a darker version of Le Châtelier's words, see the document cited in note 61.

68. *Affaire des Carbures, op. cit.*, p. 289.

69. Consortium français des carbures. Société commerciale des carbures et produits chimiques, "Consultation de M. Paul Beauregard et M. Paul de Rousiers," AHG: 10 N 186, pièce 11. Cf. also P. de Rousiers, *Les Syndicats industriels, op.cit.*

70. Letter of J. Barut to Ernest Sawyer, 13 March 1917, AN: 94 AP 109. Sawyer sent the letter to François Simiand, Albert Thomas's chef de cabinet.

71. AN: BB18 76 BL 58, file entitled "Documents relatifs à l'ordonnance Coutant: Influences." (This file was assembled by the Deputy Abel, rapporteur of the Justice Ministry's budget, in the belief that "occult" influences had tried to prevent the carburiers' prosecution.)

72. Maurice Halbwachs prepared several files for Thomas in case he had to testify before a parliamentary commission. They explain in detail the Ministry of Armament's relations with the consortium and with Switzerland, and the transactions by which certain chemical products and electric power had been furnished to German enterprises. AN: 94 AP 109.

73. *Affaire des carbures. 1er Conseil de guerre de Paris. Interrogatoires et dépositions, op. cit.*, p. 284.

74. The Minister of Armament (Thomas) to the Garde des Sceaux (Viviani), 2 April 1917, AN: BB18 76 BL 58, dossier "Influences." Thomas denied to Viviani that his services had interfered with Coutant's indictment hearings ("instruction"), and explained that after Pinot had revealed the personal interest that Lacave-Laplagne had in the case, he had gone to see Millerand and Poincaré.

75. Cf. A. Thomas, "L'Esprit de guerre et l'avenir de la France," *Bulletin des usines de guerre*, No. 1, 1 March 1916.

76. Albert Thomas papers, secrétariat particulier. AN: 94 AP 33, dossier "Albert Thomas – Lucien Dior." Thomas observed to Dior that there was already a "de facto monopoly in the sulfuric acid industry (Saint Gobain)" and that excessive productive capacity would be a problem after the war.

77. *Journal officiel*, séance du 22 mars 1901, p. 883, cited in H. Prévost, *Les Ententes entre producteurs en France* (Paris, 1904), pp. 5, 244.

78. *Revue d'économie politique*, 1918, p. 240. For the exchange with Briand, see note 29 above.

79. *L'Europe nouvelle*, 14 December 1918, p. 2340. Hauser served as *directeur* of Clémentel's ministerial staff. See Pierre Chaunu, Introduction, *La Prépondérance espagnole* 3rd ed. by Henri Hauser (Paris, 1973), p. ix.

80. See notes 59 and 60.

81. Contracts for new factories subsidized by the Ministry of Armament usually contained a clause providing for their postwar dismantlement.

82. Cf. Camille Cavalier, *Après-guerre: La Métallurgie française (Rapport à la Ligue française)*, s.l.n.d., p. 22 (Bibliothèque nationale: 4° V. Pièce 6742).

83. For example, Coeylas, "La Réorganisation économique," *L'Humanité*, 30 January 1917, p. 2.

84. Draft bill ("proposition de loi") to amend articles 419 and 420 of the Penal Code, exposé des motifs, *Journal officiel, Documents parlementaires*, annexe no. 6267, p. 1501 (session of 28 June 1923).

85. See the note drafted by the carburier Keller for Judge Coutant on 16 July 1915, in the Albert Thomas papers, AN: 94 AP 109. In the postwar discussion of Article 419, Fernand Engerand was the only deputy to propose that the law forbid price raises but not price cuts, though the latter were equally monopolistic, *Journal officiel, Débats, Chambre*, session of 6 March 1924, p. 1120.

86. Lescouvé, "Examen de la procédure suivie contre les sieurs Giraud-Jordan et autres . . . par M. le procureur de la République," 1 October 1916, p. 23, Albert Thomas papers, AN: 94 AP 353.

87. Henri Hauser stressed these themes more than others. See works cited in notes 59 and 60.

88. Note AT/s 5 837 of 12 March 1917, Albert Thomas papers, AN: 94 AP 109.

89. Note of 15 April 1915 by the directors of the Société commerciale de carbure, AN: BB18 76 BL 58; H. Hauser, "Etude économique," *op. cit.*, p. 5.

90. H. Hauser, "Modifications . . .," *op. cit.*, p. 3.

91. L. Mazeaud, *Le Problème, op. cit.*, p. 109.

92. H. Hauser, "Modifications . . .," *op. cit.*, p. 7.

93. Cf. the arguments of Jules Domergue, Carmichael, and Eugène Touron during the discussion of cartels organized by the Société d'économie nationale in 1903. H. Prévost, *Les Ententes, op. cit.*, p. 213.

94. Text adopted by the Groupement des textiles et du vêtement, *L'Economie nouvelle. Organe de la Fédération des industriels et commerçants français*, 1924, p. 115.

95. Set up at the end of 1915 to encourage exports, particularly to Russia. See H. D. Peiter, "Men of Good Will: French Businessmen and the First World War" (Ph.D. diss., University of Michigan, Ann Arbor, 1973), p. 71.

96. Session of 12 May 1917.

97. *L'Economie nouvelle. Organe de la Fédération des industriels et commerçants français*,

1919, p. 51; 1922, pp. 282–83; 1924, pp. 111–16.

98. See note 84.

99. The FICF opposed this change. *L'Economie nouvelle*, 1924, pp. 111–16.

100. *Journal officiel, Débats, Chambre,* session of 6 March 1924, p. 1123.

101. *Ibid.,* pp. 1131–32.

102. See, for example, Ernest Lafont's amendment, *ibid.,* pp. 1129–30.

103. The results of the vote on the Lesaché amendment may be found in *ibid.,* session of 14 March 1924, p. 1304.

104. Huguenney, *Les Lois nouvelles,* 15 February 1927.

105. "Note sur l'inculpation d'accaparement," unsigned, undated memorandum (in the hand of Maurice Halbwachs), Albert Thomas papers, AN: 94 AP 109.

106. See R. Garraud (law faculty of Lyon), preface to L. Mazeaud, *Le Délit d'altération des prix* (Paris, 1927); L. Polier (Toulouse), in *L'Europe nouvelle,* 25 May 1918, pp. 946–47.

GENDER, CLASS AND NATION

7

The Female Munition Workers of the Seine

Mathilde Dubesset, Françoise Thébaud and Catherine Vincent

In 1974 – seventeen years ago already – we undertook as budding women historians this study[1] of female munition workers during the First World War. They seemed to epitomize the mobilization of women in France and their entry into sectors of the economy traditionally reserved for men. Women's history was just beginning, and we were bursting with enthusiasm to make the role of women visible, though still stumbling on occasion.

We wanted to link the history of female munition workers to the history of the working class in general, which had proved such a rich vein of investigation during the 1960s, to highlight the role of women in that history, and to analyze the belief that outside work is liberating for women. We suspected that the image of the "garçonne,"[2] while perhaps reflecting the experience of young middle-class women, was rather alien to the working class.

Our approach resembled that which Ute Daniel[3] is now suggesting in Germany: refuse to accept as given the view that outside work is liberating and instead set about methodically reconstructing the lives and perceptions of the women involved. This was accomplished in the following way.

First, we studied the origins and patterns of female mobilization in the metal-working industry, examining whether the way in which these women were hired, the work they performed, and the place they occupied in war-time factories could possibly have constituted a positive

Notes to Chapter 7 can be found on page 209.

experience. Second, we examined working conditions in order to determine if mobilized women escaped the ultra-exploitation which traditionally had been the lot of female workers. Third, we studied the conflict between motherhood and factory work. It seemed to us that female labor and its effects could not possibly be adequately analyzed without a close examination of this fundamental contradiction. How were the difficulties perceived and understood during the war? Were any attempts made to resolve them? Finally we studied the social activism of the female workers. What were its manifestations, and how did it square with the struggles of organized labor, whether in the form of strikes, pacifist agitation, or protests against the high cost of living?

The ideological context and the attitudes of the labor movement as a whole were considered throughout the study. On account of the context in which these women went to work, our study of them was necessarily related to many other factors. Their ability to draw all the consequences of their situation depended to a large extent on the attitudes of the labor movement to the mobilization of women in the metal-working industry, to the working conditions they endured and to the fact that these women were also mothers.

We only touched upon the abundance of speeches delivered about women during the four years of the war, without analyzing their function or the ways in which they operated, despite our amusement at all the masculinizing neologisms and the obsession with still being able to detect the little housewife beneath the grinder of shell casings. This kind of rhetoric amused us more than it moved us to deeper thought, even though we were aware of its inhibiting effect on the consciousness of female workers.

Since those early times, the issues under discussion in the history of women in general and of women's relationship to war have evolved. The desire to discover how war redefines the relationship between the sexes, in reality and on a symbolic level – or how the "gender system" changes – is tending to supplant questions of whether war has served the cause of emancipation.[4] Joan Scott even encourages us to study what the history of women can teach us about war policy, gender being a kind of weapon in the conflict.[5]

In addition, international comparisons have become possible, thanks to research that has been undertaken outside France, especially in Great Britain by Arthur Marwick, Gail Braybon, and Deborah Thom.[6] Despite their differing views of the effect of the war on British women, they all describe similar processes. The history of female workers in Britain during the war parallels in many ways the history of the muni-

tions makers in France: belated mobilization, reorganization of the factories and of production techniques, similar types of work, conditions,
and pay rates, and similar reactions by their contemporaries. However,
two key differences stand out in Great Britain: the mobilization of
women was more extensive and was controlled by male-dominated
trade unions which negotiated so-called "dilution" accords. In a recent
dissertation written in the United States, Laura Lee Downs[7] places
these factors in the context of a more long-term view of labor history
and points to the crucial influence of the war on the employment of
women in the British and French metal-working industries of the
1920s and 30s.

Our original article summarized our research under three main head-
ings: female workers on the job, working mothers, and female workers'
social struggles. It remains substantially the same in the present article,
and apart from this introduction we have only extended a few passages
and modified some details.

Let us commence with an image and a few key statistics on which to
base our comments and to justify the choice of the Department of the
Seine:

> France had her munitionnettes, the female munition workers who helped
> make victory possible, her female inspectors, measurers and master iron-
> smiths; she had her female operators who watched over the flowing metal
> and those brave women who risked their lives encasing the tremendous
> power of high explosives.[8]

This was written in 1921 by the feminist historian Léon Abensour in
his history of feminism, where he argues that the war was a major step
forward in the emancipation of women. However, his triumphant list
of all the new kinds of employment henceforth open to women in the
munitions industry is somewhat undermined (unintentionally to be
sure) by the cute diminutive "munitionnette" he cannot resist attaching
to these workers.

France certainly was not deluged by female workers. At their peak in
late 1917, women working in commerce and industry surpassed the
prewar level by only some 20 percent.[9] Female workers represented
only one of several factors in the great diversification of the working
class, which experienced much social and ethnic mixing during the war,
a redistribution of desirable qualifications, and greater mobility.[10]
However, the increase in the female work force was particularly noticeable in the chemical and metal-working industries, sectors of particular
importance to national defense. In the munitions industries, female

workers accounted for one quarter of the work force in 1918, and even more than this in the Department of the Seine, the most important center of arms and munitions manufacturing with a total of some 300,000 workers of both sexes.

It is difficult, however, to obtain precise information on the location of factories, their size, and the extent of the female work force.[11] In June 1916, 58,936 women worked in munitions industries "in the Paris region." In the spring of 1918, approximately 96,000 women were working in munitions industries employing more than fifty women each. The female work force in smaller factories could account for up to one-fifth of the entire female work force in some sectors, and if they are included, the total female work force in defense industries rises to 100,000, or a good third of the entire work force in the munitions industry.

These women were not distributed evenly from the points of view of geography and types of work. Female workers were very common in Boulogne, numbering more than 13,000 (of whom half worked for Renault), and in the 15th *arrondissement* in Paris, where Citroën established itself in the spring of 1915.[12] Women were as likely to work in large factories as in smaller shops, and their proportion of the work force varied considerably. Usually in a minority, they still accounted for a high percentage of the work force in some cases and were even in the majority in certain industries, for instance shell-manufacturing.

Female Workers on the Job[13]

"Our only program is to produce, every day to produce more artillery and munitions," said Albert Thomas in the Chamber of Deputies in February 1916. The organization of war production,[14] an international phenomenon, led to the emergence of war factories which became strategic, closely guarded facilities that devoured labor. In France as elsewhere, women provided a new, ultra-exploited work force.

A New Work Force

In 1914, 8,000 to 9,000 women were employed in metal-working in the Department of the Seine, representing 5 percent of the total work force; by 1918 women accounted for more than 30 percent of workers in war industries. Recruiting did not really begin in earnest until the end of 1915, because industrialists viewed women as a last resort, after some 500,000 conscripted soldiers had been returned to their former jobs, and other civilians, people from the colonies, and foreigners had been taken into the factories. This recruitment of women for war industries was encouraged by the government because it freed more men for service at the front.[15] Official propaganda played on patriotism, while reassuring women that working conditions would be good and industrialists that women possessed adequate technical skills.

Women willing to work in war industries could go to the hiring service of the Undersecretary of State for Artillery and Munitions or to the local employment office. The difficulties they encountered led in April 1916 to the creation of a Board of Female Labor[16] under the Undersecretary of State and the involvement of private women's associations such as the Entente nationale des oeuvres de recrutement féminin, the Office central de l'activité féminine and the Association pour l'enrôlement volontaire des Françaises pour la patrie.[17] However, these initiatives, whether governmental or private, actually affected very few women; most simply took a job on their own initiative after reading a notice or talking to a neighbor. For many, factory work was absolutely essential. Their husbands were at the front, they had no other job,[18] and family allowances[19] were not sufficient to live on. Some newspapers of the day reported dramatic scenes of women racing to acquire certain jobs.[20] Equally important were hopes for a job with a higher salary, in the case of cottage-industry seamstresses for example, or for a certain emancipation, most notably in the case of maids.[21]

Female workers in the war industries varied considerably in their social origins and work backgrounds: there were housewives, including women from the petite bourgeoisie, white collar workers, and laborers.[22] Even though most descriptions emphasize the youth of these workers, physical strength and stamina were the main criteria for employment, and they were not all young. The only thing that united all the women who poured into the war industries was the novelty of the work. The first days on the job were therefore a difficult and anxious time: "They have to hide their aversion, master their fear, keep their nerves under control, and adapt their bodies to precise, quick movements."

Female labor in the war industries was an inescapable consequence of the war. Journalists of the left and right, industrialists, members of labor unions, and socialist or bourgeois feminists all agreed that *munitionnettes* had become a fact of life and that there was no point in discussing the pros and cons, at least so long as the war continued. However, this apparent consensus concealed deeper differences. Despite some reservations,[23] feminists and the political right applauded the entry of women into the war industries. The latter invoked patriotism and praised the heroism of female workers, considering this to be a temporary phenomenon in any case. The special 16 June 1917 edition of *J'ai Vu* dedicated to women working for the victory presents such a woman as smiling and feminine, with an enormous artillery shell under her left hand and a rifle in her right. Feminists were more impressed by the entry of women in sectors of the economy previously closed to them. Léon Abensour's *Les vaillantes héroines, martyres et remplaçantes* celebrated the ability of French women in 1917 to replace men in any position, and through its vocabulary it invited comparisons between the work of these women and that of the male soldiers. *La Vie Féminine* illustrated the advancement of women by placing side by side a little dressmaker and a strong female munitions maker against a backdrop of factory chimneys. On occasion, the descriptions of war factories presented a Dantean vision of an infernal but grandiose world in which women workers took on the allure of fairies or sorceresses taming flame and iron:

> The flames, the smoke and the fusing metal create a hazy, throbbing atmosphere, punctuated by the deafening din of giant lathes . . . ; there, scattered amidst the men and the shooting flames, are young women, grave, clad in leather, with a sculptured air.[24]

Trade unionists and socialist feminists such as Marcelle Capy,[25] however, reacted violently to the torrent of such images and words of praise. They pointed to several studies which emphasized the hardships of the work. "Let us not deliver women unto a holocaust," declared the leader of the Federation of Metal-Workers, Alphonse Merrheim at the Labor Exchange in 1916.[26] However, it was the old fear of feminine competition rather than compassion for female workers which explains most of the reaction of labor unions to the influx of women into the factories. Unions feared that women would drive down wages and allay the militancy of the metal-workers, to the detriment of the soldiers at the front when they returned to their jobs. Many individual male workers were also distrustful and even xenophobic, as Alfred Rosmer points out.[27] The working class was largely in thrall to the image of women as mothers in the home and looked askance at the "masculinization"[28] of the fair sex. None the less, some expressions of surprise at the capabilities of these women should be noted. Pierre Dumas suddenly realized the transformations which the war was working on the condition of women, both economically (women's wages were no longer just a source of a little spare income for the family) and morally (women were now the heads of households).[29]

Even though vast numbers of women were employed in the metal-working industries, they did have their specialties. They usually worked in the manufacture of shells, cartridges, grenades, flares, and rockets, and were relatively rare in iron-foundries, aeronautics, and automobile production, with the exception of some special tasks such as polishing.[30] This was because female work was primarily low skill.

It was often claimed during and after the war that women's participation in the work force tended to increase their skill levels. Inspectors' reports, to be sure, show continual inroads into types of work which women had not performed before the war.[31] However, the army's incessant appetite for more soldiers meant that positions had to be continually refilled, and women became metal-workers without any relevant skills at all. A study of the organization of work and of professional training shows that the work process was revolutionized as a result of the influx of women. This reorganization, sought by Albert Thomas himself and facilitated by the arrival of a fresh work force, was aimed primarily at two essential steps in the rationalization of work: modernization of equipment and, above all, greater division of labor. The imperatives of the war facilitated the emergence of a new class of workers condemned to carry out a limited number of movements all day long – "*usineurs,*" as Pierre Hamp called them in the 7 November 1917 edition of *L'Humanité.*

As a result, women received very little professional training. Factory owners encouraged on-the-job training: quick imitation of one's neighbor on the line and the creation of teams consisting of several women, some male workers, and some skilled workers in charge of setting the lathes and repairing them.[32] The unions did not protest, and only Marcelle Capy demanded for women the right to "work with intelligence and pleasure."

Several categories of female workers can be distinguished: some worked as unskilled laborers – cleaning, tidying and handling; others worked on manual assembly lines and above all on mechanical assembly lines; finally, still others were trained in the manufacture of specialized pieces. These were the production areas where women's output was the highest.[33]

Factory owners compared the production of male and female workers and discussed the attributes of women, their origins, and the best ways to employ their talents. The dominant themes were their patience and their suitability for monotonous tasks as well as their dexterity and attention to detail – the result of the transfer of female workers with textile industry skills to industrial sectors where these skills were not recognized. On the other hand, company managers doubted any "inventiveness" on the part of women workers or any ability to make decisions.[34] Only the Minister of Armaments, eager to cull as many men as possible for military service, argued that men and women had equal skills. Although the tradition of female factories with militaristic chains of command persisted, new management methods were developed to reflect the popular understanding of feminine psychology: vanity, a need for recognition, jealousy, and a desire for promotion. In reality, there were rarely any women on supervisory staffs.

Wartime Exploitation of Labor

"Women have never been so exploited as since the outbreak of the war," proclaimed the newspaper *L'Humanité* on 16 November 1915. The lot of women in the war industries seemed nevertheless rather enviable to some of their contemporaries. Madeleine Pelletier,[35] for example, speaks of their "fantastic wages," and the subject of their generous compensation reappeared regularly in the right-wing press and the café conversations overheard by agents of the Paris police.[36] This impression was based on two factors: first, the wages of women in the war industries were superior to those of women working in other sectors of the economy,[37] and second, the wages of women in the metal-working industry clearly increased in absolute terms after 1917. In this regard, they shared in the generally increasing wages in the metal-working industry during the second half of the war, following the introduction of wage scales by the Ministry of Armaments after wages fell in 1915–16.[38] A quick survey shows that the wages of female workers rose on average by a factor of two or two and a half between 1914 and 1918.

However, this general view requires some modification for four reasons. Smaller workshops need to be distinguished from large factories because the former were clearly much more reluctant to grant the wage increases decreed by the Ministry of Armaments. Even though women in war industries often earned higher wages than women in other industries or than women had earned in metal-working before the war, these wage increases were fragmentary and hard to pin down because they included piecework which was open to many abuses by factory owners. A classic abuse was described in the September-December 1916 issue of *Union des Métaux* referring to a strike by the workers at the Wilcoq-Regnault plant: by manipulating bonuses, the owner was able to increase the 1915 standard production level of 300 bombs per day with a bonus for extra production to a standard production level just one year later of 1,100 bombs per day with no bonuses.[39] The increase in the wages of female workers in the war industries was accompanied by an increase in the cost of living, which at least partially cancelled out its effects.[40] In any event, the "high wages" paid women in the war industries were still always less than men's wages throughout the war.

Within the war industries themselves, women on the whole were always paid less than men. According to the wage scale established in July 1918, for example, a female worker could earn from 7.50 to 12 francs a day while a male worker could earn from 8.50 to 18 francs. Women were always paid substantially less than men for equal work, even though the disparity seems to have diminished considerably by the end of the war.[41]

The question of women's wages was debated throughout the war, with the leading spokesmen being Albert Thomas, the unions, occasionally some female workers speaking out at a union meeting or providing evidence, and finally, the Inter-Union Committee Against the Exploitation of Women Workers.[42] The numerous memoranda about women's wages issued by Albert Thomas are as interesting as they are ambiguous.[43] On the one hand, they endorsed the logic of the factory owners by conceding, for example, that the influx of women into the metal-working industry required modifications to the equipment and therefore imposed higher costs on the owners. On the other hand, Thomas sought to limit the ultra-exploitation of women. He finally proposed the following compromise: women should be compensated according to the principle of "equal pay for equal work"; however, they should have deducted from their wages "the cost of all modifications to equipment, to the organization of work, and to the supervisory system, and in general the additional costs incurred by the substitution of female labor for male labor."

Though the trade union movement often demanded increased wages for women and equal pay for equal work, its reason for doing so tended to be the same old fear of female competition after the war.[44] Most of the positions adopted by the unions seem to us to reflect an essentially defensive attitude to female labor. Only the Inter-Union Action Committee Against the Exploitation of Women occasionally hazarded a more positive approach to female labor. Even though its tracts and brochures aimed at women and calling on them to unionize invoked the theme of unfair competition with men, they also addressed the problems of female workers, emphasizing four points: women who had become heads of households needed wages equal to the former wages of their husbands; a single woman or widow had the same needs as a man and should receive equal pay; to fight for equal pay was to fight for the right to a life based on work and personal dignity; and, women should come together within the union movement in order to defend themselves. In conclusion, although the union movement in general (with the notable exception of the Inter-Union Committee) confined itself to modest demands for increased wages for women, it nevertheless proved tireless in its denunciations of the working conditions of women.

Whether glamorized or presented in its true harsh light, the work these women performed was always described as dangerous and very intensive. The legislation on dangerous and noxious conditions had been practically suspended as a result of the war, and war industry work was often extremely unhealthy. Clouds of dust, toxic gases and smoke were frequent, and the women repeatedly came into contact with such corrosive materials as lead, copper, nickel, and engine oil[46] which required strict, expensive handling procedures which were often lacking. The numerous edicts emanating from the Ministry of Armaments[47] were often poorly implemented, especially in small shops which had recently been quickly created or converted.[48] The likelihood of serious accidents was heightened by flimsy guards on the machines,[49] the cramped working conditions, and the increases, occasionally scarcely credible, in the pace of work as a result of the introduction of piecework and the wartime demand for high productivity. When female workers recounted their experiences, terms like "fatigue," "weariness," and "exhaustion" frequently reappeared. The most gripping account was surely that of Marcelle Capy, who emphasized the haste, the weariness that came from standing on one's feet all day, and the heavy labor assigned to women.[50]

Women also had to work longer hours at these strenuous tasks than during the prewar era. Marcelle Capy evoked the "deadening length of the working day," the "plodding minutes." Prewar labor legislation, which imposed the ten-hour day and a weekly day of rest and forbade the employment of women at night, was suspended in August 1914, and early in the war many women worked up to twelve or even fourteen hours a day with a maximum of two days off a month. However, the situation changed during the war. In the first part of his memorandum of 1 July 1917, Albert Thomas reduced the actual working day to ten hours, forbade nighttime employment of women less than eighteen years old, and reinstituted one day off a week.[51] However, inquiries carried out by the Ministry of Labor showed that these directives were still far from universally applied by the end of the war.[52]

Under conditions such as these, high morbidity and accident rates were reported everywhere, especially among very young girls.[53]

Continuing her report, Marcelle Capy underlined the worrisome physical appearance of female workers, "skinny, exhausted little girls" with "the ravaged faces of old women," extremely vulnerable to infectious diseases and tuberculosis.[54] These conditions taken together explain the high rates of absenteeism and job turnover to which our sources frequently allude.

The government grew concerned about the exhaustion of female workers, because of its impact on productivity and "the future of our race," as it was phrased at the time. As a result, the government and the Committee for Female Workers issued a spate of official circulars and pleas concerning working conditions in factories and their effect on maternity and motherhood. In addition, government and the industry created a number of institutions aimed at reducing the effects of the extreme exploitation of female workers.

The lot of female munitions workers certainly was not made any easier by the life they led outside the factory walls. The industrial belts around Paris in which they lived were overcrowded, regular transportation was expensive and inadequate,[55] and restaurant owners near factories often exhibited their greed by reserving their overcrowded tables for men only, because they ate more and consumed more expensive wines and liquors.[56]

The government therefore sought to create or encourage institutions that improved the daily life of the workers. An Undersecretariat of State for Health was formed in 1915 and it helped to launch nine clinics for women workers only. In the end, these clinics served only a handful of women working in the war industries of the Seine, partly because the women distrusted them and partly because some factory owners and bosses discouraged their use. The main institution remained restaurants, whether operated cooperatively or by the factory management. Those restaurants illustrated the two fundamental approaches taken to health and safety during the war – liberal or paternalistic – and served men as well as women. However, the specific needs of female workers did become an issue in government circles and among feminists, eventuating in the creation of philanthropic institutions such as the *cantines-abris*, or "canteen-shelters," as well as women's centers.[58]

Even more interesting was the emergence of female factory superintendents, at the instigation of the National Council of French Women and in imitation of British factories. Though their official role was not finally codified until November 1918,[59] they were responsible for overseeing the physical and spiritual welfare of the women workers. However, these female superintendents were not overly successful, either *vis-à-vis* the owners, who were suspicious of any initiative which could be seen as undermining their own authority, or *vis-à-vis* workers' organizations, which concluded that "there is an incompatibility between the two roles which the superintendents are expected to fulfill, namely protecting the interests of the women workers on the one hand while maintaining the goodwill of the owners on the other."[60]

Among the reasons for creating these female superintendents, who saw their heyday in the era between the wars,[61] one of the major obsessions of the times can be detected: preserving the ability of French women to bear children.

Working Mothers

"To have women working in factories is in direct conflict with women's role as mothers," wrote Pierre Hamp in September 1918.[62] This is of course obvious and nothing new. The contradiction between motherhood and factory work was an old issue that had often been debated before the war. It was none the less crucial, because it impinged directly women's right to work outside the home. Work outside the home once again became a burning issue when women poured into the war industries at a time when the French were preoccupied by their low birth rate in comparison with other European countries.

Approaches to this issue varied, however, during the war years, and two basic periods can be distinguished. At the beginning of the war, there was an urgent call for female workers and a readiness to create institutions which would help them reconcile "their two duties." The final months of the war were dominated on the other hand by concern about France's demographic problem and industrial reconversion. As a result, the emphasis switched back to women's role as mothers.[63]

Maternity and Factory Work – Are They Incompatible?

Throughout the war, the proponents and adversaries of limiting women's participation in the war industries engaged in an unrelenting debate on women as future mothers, pregnant women, and women as caregivers of young families. Leading medical authorities clashed over the likelihood of voluntary or involuntary sterility as a result of factory work, and the popular press joined in the fray. The various medical opinions can be found in a report of the Paris Academy of Medicine on the protection of women and children in factories published in 1916, and in a report presented by Dr. Bonnaire.

According to a Dr. Pinard, an obstetrician at the maternity hospital of Baudelocque, work in the war industries encouraged women to sterilize or abort themselves, because the time spent raising children was seen as wasted:

> Children, these bothersome hindrances, are seen by some women of little scruple as limiting their freedom to use their time as they wish and as an obstacle to earning maximum profits working at exceptionally well paid jobs.

Furthermore, he wrote that the factory easily lent itself to neo-Malthusian propaganda:

> We know that Malthusian propaganda, already intense before the war, is reaching lower class strata all the more easily because, instead of being scattered, it can now penetrate areas where women are gathered in large numbers. Shops and factories offer incomparable advantages to unhealthy and antisocial suggestions.[64]

So far as the Ministry of Armaments was concerned, these types of arguments could undermine attempts to mobilize female munitions makers. Dr. Bonnaire, a member of the Committee on Female Labor, became the official spokesman of the Ministry of Armaments in charge of refuting the arguments of Dr. Pinard. He wrote:

> The dangers of a decline in population cannot be compared with the sacred requirements of National Defense. . . . In any case, there is no evidence at all that work in the war industries has any harmful effects on the reproductive capacities of women.[65]

So far as Bonnaire was concerned, factory work did not cause sterility; instead, it was the forbidding of pregnant women to work which could drive them to sterilize or abort themselves in order to preserve their source of income.

Opinions differed as well in regard to work during pregnancy. Dr. Pinard called the war industries "baby killers" because they increased the rate of premature births and still-births. Dr. Bonnaire, on the other hand, claimed that among female workers in the war industries "the development of the egg is in no way inferior to what is seen among the working class in general," so long as minimal precautions were taken such as elimination of night work, reassignment to different types of work in case of any danger to the fetus, and a four-week rest period for the mother before delivery.

Once the child was born, the problem became infant mortality, which was related above all to breast-feeding. Everyone agreed at least that mothers needed to nurse their children if they were to survive and grow. Opinions varied, however, about whether it was possible for mothers who worked in factories to nurse properly, depending on whether the working mother dichotomy was highlighted, minimized, or considered solvable. In November 1916, Dr. Pinard suggested to the Academy of Medicine that the following be proposed to the public authorities: "That measures be taken immediately to forbid any woman in France to work in factories if she is pregnant, nursing a child, or gave birth less than six months previously, and to ensure that any French woman who is pregnant or is nursing her child who is less than one year old receive upon demand a daily allowance of five francs."

Dr. Bonnaire riposted by requesting that elementary precautions regarding pregnant workers be enforced and suggesting the creation of special nursing rooms and day-care centers so that female munitions workers could nurse their children.

This controversy soon became public, but the press was no less divided. *La Bataille*, under the direction of A. Hodée, supported Dr. Pinard in the name of protecting pregnant women and the family,[66] while *Le Figaro* embellished the conclusions of the Bonnaire report and did not hesitate to insist that work in war industries was "virtually harmless" on the whole. Some newspapers even claimed it was just "a little puttering around."

Between the one extreme, which wished to protect motherhood by forbidding women to work for long periods or even by returning them to their place in the home once and for all, and the other extreme, which glorified labor in the war industries, some people voiced intermediary views. In view of the indispensable and perhaps irreversible influx of women into the metal-working industry, these people sought to resolve the inherent contradiction in working motherhood by proposing some reforms: the eight-hour day, for instance, or the two-day weekend, or half-time work. Such proposals came from feminists[67] and the left-wing press. "The principle of half-time work is excellent," wrote Jeanine in the 16 November issue of *La Bataille*, "and we very much hope that it will be fully implemented as soon as possible." Marthe Bigot advanced the idea of collectivizing housework in *Le Populaire*:

> In a large six-story block with forty apartments, forty ovens were turned on and forty different women set about the wearisome tasks only too well known to all women who are not independently wealthy. But with a little common sense, it becomes obvious that two or three of these women could have prepared enough food for all forty households without requiring any more time.[68]

In the end, there was little question that the government and factory owners would seek to protect working mothers by adopting those measures which most satisfied the superior interests of National Defense and efficient production.

A "Charter" of the Working Mother?

Some studies and articles written during the war and just afterwards spoke of the reconciliation of work and motherhood effected by the Ministry of Armaments. According to a book entitled *La Française dans la guerre*:

> The right of mothers to work was protected as was the right to life of their children. The former received their wages and the latter their milk! The charter of the working mother followed that of the working woman.[69]

This is a rather rosy view of reality. A more accurate picture of the institutions created to serve working mothers in the Paris region can be gained from an official investigation conducted in the spring of 1918 into "day-care centers and nursing rooms in companies working for National Defense."[70] This study investigated first of all the extent to which the circular of July 1917 on the protection of pregnant women was implemented. While most pregnant workers were indeed relieved of night work and assigned to other positions, the four weeks of rest before delivery were often drastically curtailed or even ignored. Pregnancy and delivery allowances were supposed to be provided to women workers in accordance with two decrees issued in February and November 1917, which mandated the continuance of full salary for four weeks and of 50 percent of full salary for the remaining weeks. The study showed, however, that of the thirty-eight companies investigated, only one camouflage factory in the twentieth *arrondissement* of Paris followed the decrees to the letter. In most cases, the benefits were far less generous, varying from one month of paid leave to a lump sum payment, often very small, complemented by a tiny piece of linen for the baby.[71] The following, for example, is a notice posted in a shop of the Etablissements La Feuillette in Meudon:

> To the Mothers of French Babies.
>   I recall having established several months ago a special fund to help cover the costs incurred by women workers in my factory when they give birth.
>
> Encouragement of Motherhood
>   All female workers forced to leave the factory in order to prepare for maternity shall receive an allowance of fifty francs if they have been in our employ for at least five months.

If they have been in our employ for less than five months, the allowance shall be ten francs a month.

Birth Allowance

An allowance of 100 francs shall be granted upon the birth of a girl.
An allowance of 200 francs shall be granted upon the birth of a boy.

These amounts shall be paid to the mother at the rate of twenty francs a month. The first payment is due within a week of the birth, and the following payments from month to month so long as the mother is employed at the firm.

The allowance will be paid even if the baby should die.

Anniversary of the Birth

If, one year after birth, the child is still alive and the mother is still employed at the firm, a sum of 100 francs shall be paid to her to commemorate the birth.

Babies' Room

A babies' room has been established at the Meudon factory in the forest. All the necessary facilities have been provided for mothers to nurse their babies. A nurse assigned to the room will be available to take care of the babies' needs.

Signed: Feuillette
Long live the children of France![72]

It should be noted in passing that birth allowances were paid in installments, probably in order to discourage workers from quitting their jobs or changing jobs, and – in a telling detail – that the allowance for the birth of a daughter was only half as much as for the birth of a son.

In addition to the pregnancy and birth allowances, a nursing allowance of ten to twenty francs a month was provided at the recommendation of the Ministry of Armaments.

Female munitions makers also needed facilities in which to nurse their babies, and the Engerrand Act of 5 August 1917 required manufacturers employing more than a hundred women to create nursing rooms in their plants and to permit mothers to nurse their babies twice a day during working hours. This measure did not break any new ground, since fifty such nursing rooms were reported in France as early as 1913, most of them at the initiative of northern industrialists.[73] However, the rapid spread of nursing rooms was prompted by an alarming report of Dr. Lesage, the secretary-general of the League to Prevent Infant Mortality, which pointed out to the Committee for Female Labor on 19 December 1916 that there had been a substantial reduction in the nursing rate among female workers in the war industries during 1916. The Committee for Female Labor immediately demanded that the Ministry of Armaments adopt measures to encourage the creation of nursing facilities, resulting in the act of 5 August 1917.

To what extent did these recommendations and acts actually help to create nursing rooms and day-care centers in the munitions plants as well as in other locations such as neighborhoods? According to a study carried out in the spring of 1918, 75 percent of the relevant factories employing more than one hundred female workers were equipped with nursing facilities (though only 20 percent provided day-care facilities). An appendix to this study points out that only 30 percent of women in the Department of the Seine were affected by these benefits for mothers, mostly workers in the largest factories.

The overall effectiveness of these measures is therefore rather doubtful. To be sure, some spectacular facilities were created, such as the working mothers' clinic of Levallois-Perret[74] or the Citroën children's facilities. The latter were described by Dr. Clothilde Mulon, who visited them on 2 March 1918, as containing 60 cribs and 150 day-care places. Citroën had not been niggardly, according to the report:

> Beside the factory there had been a school, whose interior walls were knocked down in order to renovate the facilities. Workers erected partitions, resurfaced the wooden floors, installed baths and dirty laundry shoots, and created patios. . . .[75]

However, only a small minority of factories provided nursing rooms, not to mention day-care facilities. Industrialists often preferred less expensive solutions. Some allowed young mothers to go home twice a day in order to nurse their babies, while others advised mothers to have their babies brought to them twice a day so that they could nurse them in whatever room was available: the porter's room, the lunch room, a storage room, or even the room where the band practiced or the owner's private quarters.[76] Moreover, it is not even clear that a government regulation allowing the Department of Labor Inspection to oblige industrialists to create nursing rooms was even promulgated during the war.

Neglected by many industrialists and often poorly received by working-class organizations and even by female workers themselves,[77] most of these maternal facilities proved ephemeral. Schemes to increase the birth rate were certainly encouraged toward the end of the war and immediately thereafter by the spreading concern about a declining population and the moral crisis. "Children," wrote Marcelle Capy herself, "are unrecognized gods in whom a world of pain and suffering places its hopes."[78] In a work on public health, G.A. Doleris and J. Bouscatel invoked the "duty of motherhood":

> The rights of women are certainly increasing, but what is their great duty? To give birth and give birth and give birth once again. A woman who refuses to bear children no longer deserves the rights she enjoys. The value of a woman lies in her children. If she remains voluntarily sterile, she is no better than a prostitute, a harlot whose organs are mere tools, obscene toys, rather than the venerable mold of all centuries to come.[79]

This campaign for motherhood and a higher birth rate helped to justify the closure of many nursing rooms and day-care facilities after the war, despite the protests of the Committee for Female Labor.

Female Workers' Social Struggles

The four war years were not a very propitious time for social activism on the part of working-class women. Everything was done to facilitate repression, especially in the war industries which came under close police surveillance. Nevertheless, the social truce did not last long. Female munitions workers first went on strike at de Dion in Puteaux in June and July 1916. However, before examining the role women played in the union movement, in the wave of strikes that erupted in the last three years of the war, and in the pacifist movement, one should first recall their daily struggles against war shirkers,[80] rising prices, and brutal or skirt-chasing foremen. Female workers often exhibited contradictory attitudes. When they found themselves in vehement conflict with their supervisors, they were capable of calling upon the factory owner to arbitrate the conflict, as did the women at the Caudron plant for instance in August 1917 by means of a petition sent to the owner's mother.[81] Actions such as this reflect the lack of union experience among female munitions makers.

Female Workers and Unions[82]

Women arrived in the factories with no union experience,[83] and the *Confédération Général du Travail* (CGT) was in turmoil, weak and divided.[84] Women workers in the war industries were concerned with three organizations: the Federation of Metal-Workers, the Confederation of Trade Unions of the Seine, and the Inter-Union Action Committee Against the Exploitation of Women.[85]

The Federation of Metal-Workers was very suspicious of the *union sacrée*. It quickly reorganized itself and resolved to form a union of Seine metal workers which would include trades that had previously been separate (tinsmiths, cutter operators, etc.). Despite the reservations of such skilled workers as mechanics and lens grinders, this union was formed on 2 April 1916[86] and set about organizing women in particular. It became in fact the union of the unskilled ("the *usineur* class") and spread rapidly. Membership rose from 250 at its creation to some 14,000 in 1918, according to *La Vague*.

The departmental grouping of Trade Unions of the Seine supported the *union sacrée* and therefore found itself in constant conflict with the Federation of Metal-Workers. However, it still dispatched many of its members to help the metal workers during strikes or at informational meetings.

The Inter-Union Action Committee Against the Exploitation of Women arose in response to the massive influx of women into jobs from which they had previously been excluded and to the resulting decline in wages. This Committee was extremely active during the first two years of the war and understood its role as educational and complementary to the established unions. For instance, it created a union for women working in industries or at jobs which were not yet organized or whose organizations did not accept female members (which was not the case of munitions makers) and also for men and women who, though already unionized, were particularly interested in the economic emancipation of women.

What was the thrust of the union pitch to women? Besides the traditional issues (improving wages and working conditions), two other subjects were often broached at meetings: first, unionization was necessary because many women would remain the family bread winner after the war, and once the owners were deprived of the enormous profits accruing from the war, they would attempt to reduce wages; and second, women must unionize in order not to pose a threat to the soldiers returning from the front, who could not accept low female wages.

This topic of competition between men and women annoyed Marcelle Capy,[87] for instance, all the more because it was advanced by both the minority and majority wings. The issue of organizing women provoked raucous debates within the Federation of Metal-Workers, as can be seen for instance in the September 1917 meeting of the Confederation Committee of Metal-Workers on "female labor and organizing women."[88] The participants failed to agree on an independent organization for women, and eventually the debate switched from the unionization of female workers to the fundamental issue of whether women should work at all. The final declaration proclaimed that the "systematic introduction of women into workshops is entirely at odds with the establishment and maintenance of homes and family life" and that "the ever-increasing influx of women into all industries is totally inconsistent with the policy of encouraging more births."

This negative attitude greatly hampered the unionization of women, especially since they also had to overcome fierce employer opposition to unions. Union members were even often urged to check memberships at the entrance to meetings so that the presence of owners or supervisory personnel would not intimidate the women into silence. The social policies of certain factory owners (Renault and especially Citroën) posed another major obstacle to unionization. Women were also frequently discouraged by the attitudes of their husbands (even though they were often away at the front) and the strong police presence. If women overcame all these barriers, there were many more obstacles to face: they had families to care for and very little extra time, public transportation was often poor, and many men showed little comprehension of their plight. Marie Guillot spoke, for instance, of the "condescending or even disdainful air that many men adopt when speaking to women."[89] The only issue which the union really succeeded in resolving was the financial one: dues for female workers were set at half the level for men, or twenty-five centimes a month in 1916.

However, circumstances had changed fundamentally in one important regard. Women's wages were no longer a second income used for extras; instead they had become the main support of the family. As a result, women tended to be more motivated than before the war to defend their interests. The strong female presence at union meetings seems to bear this out. In 1915–16, the meetings of the Inter-Union Action Committee Against the Exploitation of Women were very successful. Unfortunately, little information is available about the rate of female participation in the meetings of the Federation of Metal-Workers for the year 1916;[90] for 1917–18, however, police surveillance records show that female workers accounted on average for one third of the crowd at meetings of the metal-workers union. Women usually were more likely to attend local factory meetings than the large meetings at the Labor Exchange. However, though women attended the meetings in large numbers, they rarely spoke out, deferring to the men present unless most of the crowd were women. In conclusion, it appears that fewer than 12 percent of the female workers in the war industries were unionized in 1918, in contrast with 25 percent of the males. This represents some progress, nevertheless, in comparison with the situation before the war.[91]

Who were these new female union members? What age groups did they fall into and had they participated in labor struggles before the war? Were more women unionized in large factories than in the smaller shops? Did the proportion of male workers have a deciding influence on the readiness of women to participate in a union? Only one thing can be said for certain: no woman had the time and the means to rise to the upper echelons of the union. Georges Yvetot stated very forthrightly in the 2 January 1918 issue of *La Voix des Femmes*: "All the good female members remain modestly in the rank and file and allow men to do a very poor job of interpreting their sentiments." However, some women did succeed in becoming shop delegates, at Panhard for example. On the whole, women tended mostly to participate in the union movement during strikes, at climactic moments in working-class struggles.

Strikes – Climactic Moments in the Struggle of Female Workers in the War Industries

"Strikes by female workers are so rare, and those now under way in Paris affect so many industries and workers, that they will mark the beginning of a new era in our social history," commented *La Vie féminine* on 3 June 1917, as waves of strikes swept through the war industries from July 1916 until May 1918.[92] They provide compelling evidence of the discontent and determination of female workers who were ready to risk laying down their tools at a time when the government, most of the press, and a large portion of the public considered such a step to be out-and-out sabotage of the war effort. For most of the female munitions makers, strikes were a new experience, not only for those who had never worked outside the home but even for those who had held outside jobs.[93] The participation rate of these women was very high, and at first – in late 1916 and the first quarter of 1917 – they even constituted a majority of the striking workers.

This mounting militancy of female workers occurred in a general atmosphere of strong political and social tensions during the last two years of the war. Rising prices in 1916 touched off a series of strikes which spread throughout French industry in 1917, especially industries with a high proportion of female workers, before culminating in the great pacifist movement of the spring of 1918. While the press reported in great detail on the strikes of the dressmakers in the spring of 1918, little was said about the strikes in the war industries, because of wartime censorship. These strikes constituted a climactic period when women rebelled against insufficient pay, overwork, and foremen who tormented them. During this short period of time, certain quintessential behavior and, to a lesser extent, a typically female approach became visible, traits which are very important to us and yet extremely difficult to discern during normal working days.

It is impossible to present an exhaustive survey of these strikes, since the statistics are very incomplete.[94] Nevertheless, there were probably around 160,000 people on strike in the war industries of the Seine between 1915 and 1918, some 30 percent of whom would have been women. During the last six months of 1916, women accounted for the vast majority of the strikers, and they continued to dominate during the first half of 1917. In fact, a number of these strikes involved only female workers. However, this tendency was reversed in the autumn of 1917, as a direct result of the types of demands being made. While wage demands were the dominant theme in 1916-17,[95] the slogan "war on the war" grew increasingly prominent in 1918. Women in general were not highly politicized, and this type of demand had less appeal for them. There were several aspects to their economic demands, such as a refusal to accept wage cuts and demands for across-the-board increases of some 20 percent and cost-of-living allowances. In some cases the demands appear surprising, for instance the insistence on maintaining piecework despite the more hectic pace this usually entailed.

In general, strikes for increased wages were successful. Factory own-ers reaped enormous profits during the war and could well afford to yield on this point[96] – though they did attempt to take advantage of the rivalry between male and female workers by according a wage increase to only one sex, in the hope that their common front could be split, a strategy which proved successful in some cases.[97] However, the owners remained intransigent in the face of other demands, such as calls for the dismissal of foremen, for a reduction in working hours, or for improve-ments to equipment, in other words, "qualitative" improvements which the female workers were actually quite willing to forego if they obtained satisfaction in regard to wages.

Was there anything different about the way in which women con-ducted strikes? The strikes called by women or in which they were important participants were almost always abrupt. No warning was given and often the decision was not even taken at a general assembly, while the strikes of men were usually prepared in a more methodical manner. Sometimes women laid down their tools as a result of an inci-dent involving their supervisors. This type of behavior greatly annoyed the government, because it bypassed the arbitration and conciliation procedure which had been established in early 1917.[98] Women's strikes tended to be impulsive, and in the spring of 1917 they began encouraging people at other factories to join them. Processions of strikers from various companies moved from factory to factory in order to stop work there.[99] This type of strike organizing was roundly criticized by the mainstream press, which saw it as the work of outside elements, paid agitators, or even the Germans. Roger Picard even wrote of "*gréviculteurs,*" or strike cultivators. It seems that some women workers, not daring to organize their own job action, did appeal to other strikers to come and help them initiate a strike. At first, most female strikers left the workshops which they perceived as a hostile environment. However, by the end of the war most strikes had become sit-down affairs within the factories, as a safety precaution.[100] Most of these strikes were short-lived, lasting only two days on average, with the exception of some early, longer strikes such as an eleven-day strike at de Dion in June and July 1917 and a one- week strike at Wilcocq-Regnault in November 1916. The negotiations were rarely handled by women when the strikers were mixed; however, when all the strikers were women, they sometimes achieved a remarkable degree of organization.

The example of de Dion is instructive in this regard. The strikers, female rifle makers, participated in regular meetings and sent several letters to management reaffirming their demands:

> We would have liked to yield to our strong desire to bring this conflict to an end . . . however, we do not understand and will not accept that it should be we, the workers, who make the double sacrifice of our health and part of our wages.[101]

Very few women returned to work, despite the pressures exerted by the Marquis de Dion, who announced the end of the strike in *Le Temps* just as it was starting, and who declared through the foremen that "The de Dion company has a fundamental tenet of never yielding in a strike. It did not yield to the men, and it is all the less likely to yield to women."

The strike unfolded in a calm, determined atmosphere. The women were provided solid financial support, thanks to contributions gathered by the Federation of Metal-Workers, *La Bataille,* and numerous other factories (some of which were not even in the Paris region), which collected more than 3,000 francs. In addition, the Inter-Union Action Committee Against the Exploitation of Women organized many support meetings throughout the greater Paris area. This strike was indeed crucial, because it represented the first large strike against an armaments factory, and because it was women who had laid down their tools.

After holding a vote, the women returned to work in an orderly fashion. The next day large numbers joined the metal-workers' union at a meeting, during which it was decided that each woman would make a note of her own production in order to ensure that the compromise agreement with management was respected and that supervisors were informed if the pace of work was accelerated.

Was this strike an exception? The brevity of the other strikes prevented any substantial organization of women, who yielded sometimes to the owners' pressure (intimidating letters at Panhard and the hiring of new workers) and backed down in the face of financial difficulties. Financial solidarity grew increasingly difficult when a number of strikes broke out at the same time. Occasionally violence erupted, though it was always rarer among female workers than among men (clashes with "scabs" and with soldiers in the spring of 1918 at the Caudron and Salmson plants).[102]

A release from the daily grind,[103] these strikes instilled in the women a new boldness and self-assurance which did not always meet with public approval.[104] Male members of the CGT reported on the strikes and came again and again to the same conclusion: "When women are well led, they know what they want and achieve it more rapidly than we do." All this tends to demonstrate that female workers displayed a level of determination that surprised even their male colleagues. According to Pierre Dumas, this can be attributed to the entry of women into formerly all-male industries, where the pay was higher and where women, performing the same work as men, began to claim equal pay. Previously, women had been cloistered in underpaid, largely female industries, where they found less reason to make higher wage claims. Women appeared to have "the energy of beginners," in the words of Roger Picard,[105] which made them both more audacious than their male counterparts and more vulnerable to the counterattacks of the owners.

What were the reactions of the public to these strikes by female workers? According to the December 1916–January 1917 edition of *L'Union des Métaux*, "the workers, and especially those who were women, suffered a barrage of recriminations, insults and slanders." The strike aroused indignation in much of the general public and most of the press, and female workers were most resented. However, it was their manners and behavior that were most strongly criticized, rather than their supposed sabotage of National Defense. Right-wing newspapers denounced the crudeness of their language and complained that their attitudes were "unfeminine."[106] Certain reactions even became total hysteria.[107]

The CGT, anxious to defend its female munitions makers, riposted by emphasizing the organizational prowess which these women had demonstrated. Some female socialist teachers were even enthusiastic, as can be seen in the letters sent to Hélène Brion.[108] The pacifists adopted a rather surprising attitude, some openly displaying their bitterness in 1918 in letters to Alphonse Merrheim that the women workers were only interested in increasing their own wages and not in the struggle for peace. At times the pacifists even spoke of the women strikers with disdain. Why then were female workers so uninterested in pacifism?

Female Workers and Pacifism

According to some pacifist theories, munitions workers occupied a strategic position: an end to production would mean an end to the supply of munitions at the front, which would then supposedly put a halt to the war. Pacifist agitators also broadcast the slogan: we must refuse "to make the shells that smash the faces of proletarians."[109]

However, pacifist propaganda was often maladroit. For instance, Louise Saumonneau[110] distributed a tract that was little more than a long series of insults to working women, who were portrayed as lacking vision and incapable of elevating themselves above the petty concerns of their daily lives in order to fight for peace. Such an approach may have shocked its audience but it was hardly likely to win them over. The same attitude could be found among many other pacifists who adopted an accusatory tone, even reproaching the female workers with having failed to stop mobilization. Marcelle Capy, however, was outraged by such insinuations and advocated instead solidarity between those on the front lines and those in the rear.[111]

On the whole, pacifist appeals remained very vague and ambiguous and most of all failed to offer working women any concrete objective other than renouncing their work and source of income. Not surprisingly, then, pacifism had almost no appeal to working women and remained confined, among women at least, to intellectuals.[112]

Conclusion

When the war industries began dismissing women as soon as the armistice was signed on 11 November 1918, what happened to all that had been gained during the four years of war when women began perhaps to gain some awareness of the female condition? On 13 November, Louis Loucheur put up a notice to "women working in factories and state-operated facilities for National Defence":

> In response to an appeal from the French Republic, you forsook your tradi-
> tional pursuits in order to manufacture armaments for the war effort. The
> victory to which you have contributed so much is now assured; there is no
> more need to manufacture explosives. . . . Now you can best serve your
> country by returning to your former pursuits, busying yourselves with peace-
> time activities·[113]

The demobilization of women was abrupt and often perfunctory.[114]
By the first quarter of 1919, many unemployed female workers found
themselves in dire straits. Industrialists often simply dismissed them *en
masse*, without providing the unemployment benefits recommended by
the government. The anguish of many women was reported in *La
Vague*, which published letters from women workers such as the following which appeared on 1 May 1919:

> My husband has been in the army for the last six years. I worked like a slave
> at Citroën during the war. I sweated blood there, losing my youth and my
> health. In January I was fired, and since then have been poverty-stricken.

What exactly were women to do? People claiming to be concerned
about the birth rate or public health recommended simply that they
return to the role of housewife. But many women had to work in order
to survive. Most unions recognized that female labor was inescapable,
but women were discouraged from working in large metal-working
plants because of the competition this afforded men and because the
work was allegedly too heavy. According to Marcelle Capy, for instance,
women were ideally suited to tertiary industries: "What is needed are
jobs proportional to one's strength. There have been too many athletes
packed onto the employment registers, and too many diminutive
women staggering under loads bigger than they are. The roles must be
changed."[115]

Economists and industrialists, on the other hand, tended to support
the retention of female labor in the metal-working industry at tasks
where it had proved especially profitable.[116] Statistics show in fact that
the war represented a turning point in the employment of women in
the metal-working industries of the Paris region: though the number of
female workers in this industry did decline sharply after the war, they
still remained far more numerous than before the war, and numbers
rose still further between 1921 and 1926.[117]

Should one therefore conclude with Madeleine Pelletier[118] that the
war proved how much "the distinction between male and female jobs is
a question of habit and not of nature," and that it marked a decisive
step forward in the economic emancipation of women? In fact, though

large numbers of working-class and lower-middle-class women worked during the war, the consequences were not the same. Lower-middle-class women may have gained the right to work outside the home as a result of the experience of the war, but this was nothing new for working-class women. Little changed insofar as they were concerned. For the first time, to be sure, their work was recognized for a few years as indispensable and worthy of a higher salary. However, many initiatives which could have contributed to solving the dilemmas of working mothers (day-care facilities, nursing rooms) were not vigorously encouraged and had little impact. The labor movement, sensitive to concerns about the birth rate and still captivated by the traditional ideal of women in the home, did nothing about these issues, even though they were crucial to working women. Insofar as the female munitions makers are concerned, could the strong allure of economic independence transcend the terrible conditions in which they worked and the considerable social pressure of the "return to normalcy" after the interlude of the war years?

The ensuing years provide very little additional evidence in support of Madeleine Pelletier's conclusions. Increasing numbers of women in both France and the United Kingdom did indeed find employment in metal-working industries after 1920, especially light industries, but only in the context of a sexual division of labor which saw women confined to the most repetitive and low-skilled jobs.[119] The result was that the war actually tended to accentuate sexual differences, in the metal-working industry as elsewhere.

Notes to Chapter 7

1. M. Dubesset, F. Thébaud, and C. Vincent, "Quand les femmes entrent à l'usine. Les ouvrières des usines de guerre de la Seine (M.A. thesis, Université de Paris VII, 1974). Copies in the Bibliothèque Marguerite Durand, at the Université de Paris VII, at the BDIC (Nanterre) and at the Centre de recherches d'histoire des mouvements sociaux et du syndicalisme at the Université de Paris I.

2. *La garçonne*, the novel by Victor Margueritte, was a *succès de scandale* in 1922. Only the heroine's amorous adventures are remembered today, not the fact that the book was intended as a "virtuous fable" which led Monique to fidelity to her chivalrous companion.

3. *Arbeiterfrauen in der Kriegsgesellschaft* (Göttingen: Vandenhoeck & Ruprecht, 1989).

4. Cf. *Behind the Lines. Gender and the Two World Wars*. Ed. Margaret Randolph

Higonnet, Jane Jenson, Sonya Michel, and Margaret Collins Weitz (New Haven and London: Yale University Press, 1987).

5. Cf. Joan W. Scott, "Rewriting History," in *Behind the Lines, op. cit.*

6. Cf. Arthur Marwick, *Women at War 1914–1918* (New York-London: Fontana Paperbacks, 1977); Gail Braybon, *Women Workers in the First World War.* (London: Croom Helm; Totowa, New Jersey: Barnes & Noble Books, 1981); Gail Braybon and Penny Summerfield, *Out of the Cage. Women's Experiences in the Two World War* (London and New York: Pandora, 1987); Deborah Thom, "Women and Work in Wartime Britain," in *The Upheaval of War. Family, Work and Welfare in Europe, 1914-1918,* ed. Richard Wall and Jay Winter (Cambridge: Cambridge University Press, 1988).

7. "Women in Industry 1914–1939: The Employer's Perspective. A Comparative Study of the French and British Metals Industry" (Ph.D. diss., Columbia University, 1987).

8. Léon Abensour, *Histoire générale du féminisme, des origines à nos jours* (Paris, 1921).

9. Cf. Françoise Thébaud, *La femme au temps de la guerre de 14* (Paris: Stock, 1986), p. 189.

10. Cf. Patrick Fridenson, "The Impact of the First World War on French Workers," in *The Upheaval of War, op. cit.*

11. There are only two studies. One was carried out in September 1915 in order to list the companies working or likely to work for national defense (AN F22 530). Although it is the only comprehensive study, it has many deficiencies: gaps, dates that are too early, and lack of distinction between male and female workers. The study of day care centers and nursing rooms in the first quarter of 1918 (AN F22 534) gives the number of female workers in the thirty-eight factories where these institutions existed. The supplementary questions concern the number of factories employing more than fifty women in each sector and the total number of women in these factories. In order to calculate the percentage of female labor, the total number of workers had to be discovered elsewhere. Strike statistics and police or newspaper reports occasionally indicate the total number of workers at a factory where there was a strike and the composition of the work force.

12. For these two enterprises, see Patrick Fridenson, *Histoire des usines Renault.* vol. 1: *Naissance de la grande industrie 1898–1939* (Paris: Le Seuil, 1972); Gilbert Hatry, *Renault usine de guerre 1914–1918* (Paris: Lafourcade, 1978); and Sylvie Schweitzer, *Des engrenages à la chaine. Les usines Citroën 1915–1935* (Lyon: Presses Universitaires de Lyon, 1982).

13. For this question, see in particular:

in the French National Archives:

—Series F 22: Work and Social Insurance

—94 AP Fonds Albert Thomas;

among government publications;

—*Le Bulletin du ministère du Travail,* 1914–1918.

—*Le Bulletin des usines de guerre,* 1916–1918.

—The brochure of the *Comité du travail féminin* entitled *Protection et utilisation de la main-d'oeuvre féminine* (1919) (BN 8° F 26748);

among published books:

—those of the Carnegie Foundation and in particular: W. Oualid and C. Picquenard, *Salaires et tarifs, conventions collectives et grèves* (Paris, 1928); M. Frois, *La Santé et le travail des femmes pendant la guerre* (Paris, 1926);

—numerous investigative novels on the lives of women.

among articles appearing in the press at the time:

—*Le Petit Parisien*: a series of articles published in 10, 20, 21, and 27 July 1917 under the heading, "Quinze jours comme ouvrière de la Défense nationale." Written by a "neutral" journalist.

—*La Voix des femmes*: articles published on 28 November and 5, 12, and 17 December 1917 on 2 January 1918 under the heading "La femme à l'usine," by M. Capy.

—*La Française*: 2 March 1918, "Une visite à l'usine de guerre Citroën," by female doctor Clotilde Mulon.

The studies are reproduced in the appendix to our M.A. thesis, pp. 419–37.

Finally, we found the following very informative:

—the M.A. thesis of M.-C. Risacher-Callet, "La main-d'oeuvre féminine dans les usines de guerre," University of Paris X – Nanterre, 1972;

—the eye-witness reports of two former workers whom we met (see our M.A. thesis, pp. 437–42): Mme M., a worker at Ducellier and Renault, and Mme X, a worker at the Société française des Munitions in Issy-les-Moulineaux.

14. See the articles of G. Hardach and A. Hennebicque in this volume.

15. From November 1915 until November 1916 the Undersecretary of State for Artillery and Munitions sent out ten circulars to industrialists and heads of state enterprises to encourage them to hire women. Government appeals were also distributed by the press and by means of posters. On 20 July 1916, it was forbidden to employ mobilized men to perform work which could be done exclusively by women.

16. This committee comprised forty-five people, of whom ten were women: politicians, professors, medical doctors, senior bureaucrats, and trade unionists (only four, of whom two were women from the *Fédération des Tabacs*). Charged with expressing its wishes with respect to all the problems facing female workers, it held inquiries into wages and working conditions. It was seen as a symbol of government concern about female munitions makers, though it was only moderately effective.

17. Wartime encouraged the formation of middle-class women's organizations to support battered women, patriotism and female solidarity. For example, the Association for Voluntary Enlistment appealed to middle-class women to work for free one day a week in factories replacing working-class women who were needed at home.

18. In October 1914, there were 159,000 unemployed women in Paris, or 21 percent of the active female population.

19. Allowances for the unemployed or the wives of mobilized soldiers were very low: only 1.25 francs per day plus 50 centimes per child. This was less than half of a normal female wage.

20. Some women were obliged to work in distant areas where they were placed in lodging with other workers.

21. As a result, there was a shortage of female workers in the garment industry and in domestic service.

22. There is only one precise example, that of a shell-manufacturing plant in Lyon cited by P. Hamp, *La France, pays ouvrier* (Paris, 1916). In this factory there were 4,473 female workers, or 49.9 percent of the work force, of whom 1,326 were housewives and domestic servants, 690 factory workers, 360 clerks, 23 secretaries, 349 dressmakers/weavers/cigarette makers, 143 diverse professions, 16 mechanics, and 238 without profession.

23. Reservations were expressed by the moralists, who were concerned about men and women working together, and those of people worried about health, who were concerned about the difficulty of the work. Their views, occasionally alarmist, had little effect on the official optimism which could be seen, for example, in the *Bulletin des usines de guerre*. In

order to justify the employment of women in metal working, people even went so far as to recognize the difficulty of traditional female jobs. For instance, the *Bulletin des usines de guerre* carried the following in its January 1917 issue: "Before the war, this girl worked as a seamstress in the garment industry, the strength in her body was sapped pushing on the pedal. Now all she has to do is move a lever. Instead of pedaling twelve hours a day, she would rather operate her overhead crane for eight hours."

24. Gaston Rageot, *La Française dans la guerre* (Paris: Petite Bibliothèque de la guerre, 1918) (summary of an American inquiry in Saint-Chamond).

25. For example: "Now there is a war on and the literary clowns are discovering the female working class. They go on forever about the heroism of French women, their self-denial, their grandeur worthy of Corneille," in "Le prolétariat féminin," *La Bataille*, 21 March 1915. Marcelle Capy was a libertarian female journalist who resigned from *La Bataille syndicaliste* in 1915 because she disapproved of the majority positions adopted by the CGT, took a job in a war factory in 1916, wrote in various feminist journals, and then founded *La Vague* in 1918.

26. *L'Humanité*, 7 March 1916.

27. A. Rosmer, *Le Mouvement ouvrier pendant la guerre*, vol. 1 (Paris, 1936). For anti-feminism among workers see Jean-Louis Robert, "Ouvriers et mouvement ouvrier parisiens pendant la Grande Guerre et l'immédiat après-guerre. Histoire et anthropologie," (Thèse d'État, Université Paris I, 1989).

28. Term utilized by Dr. Huot in his work, *De quelques manifestations de l'évolution psycho-passionnelle féminine pendant la guerre* (Paris, 1918).

29. P. Dumas, "Les femmes dans l'industrie, concurrentes ou victimes," *La Bataille*, 7 November 1915. This progressive position was certainly influenced by Dumas' union membership in a largely female industry: clothing. It is evident that the split between the majority and minority wings was not significant in this regard. Dumas, a member of the majority wing, had a more progressive attitude toward working women than many in the minority wing. He certainly was not representative of the labor movement, which, as in the prewar period, was often hostile toward the idea of women working for wages. Cf. M.H. Zylberberg-Hocquard, *Féminisme et syndicalisme en France avant 1914* (Paris: Anthropos, 1978).

30. As a result, the percentage of women in a factory's work force depended on its products. Citroën, which largely manufactured artillery shells, had a work force which was 60 percent female, while Blériot's work force in the aviation industry was only 10 percent female.

31. *Bulletin du ministère du Travail*, July–August 1915, p. 180; January–February 1916; June 1916, p. 192; January-February 1918, p. 7. In January 1916, "women are more and more frequently employed in operating small machines," no longer just in materials handling and checking. By July 1916, in accordance with the recommendations of the inspectors of labor (*Bulletin des usines de guerre*, 17 August 1916), women were utilized in the manufacture of 75 cm shells and of the entire casing and undercut pieces used in rockets. They also worked already on lathes grinding large shells up to 280 cm. Finally, according to a report published in 1918, women were responsible for most operations.

32. Skilled workers exercised enormous power in that the speed that was affected wages based on performance. Besides their technical duties, they could also be very repressive or play the role of Don Juan.

33. This was the case in both France and Great Britain. See Laura Lee Downs, *Women in Industry, op. cit.*

34. In sessions held on 18 October and 25 November 1918 and 6 January 1919, the Académie des Sciences attempted to provide experimental proof of the inferiority of female workers. "If you drop a two-kilogram weight in a shop and measure on a cardiograph the responses of employees, the cardiograms of female machinists show strong fluctuations while those of men show few or none at all." The Academy drew the conclusion that "weaknesses of will, a feeling of physical helplessness or fear have created in women considerable emotional vulnerability." See the reports of J. Amar in *l'Académie de Médecine*: "Les lois du travail féminin et de l'activité cérébrale," 14 October 1918, pp. 560–62; "La fonction mentale dans le travail féminin," 25 November 1918, pp. 788–91; and "Origine et conséquences de l'émotivité féminine," 6 January 1919, pp. 67–69.

35. Madeleine Pelletier, a physician and left-wing feminist, was interned in a psychiatric asylum in 1939 for having performed abortions. She wrote an article published in July 1912 in *La Suffragiste*: "La classe ouvrière et la féminisme." Cf. Felicia Gordon, *Madeleine Pelletier* (Cambridge: Polity Press, 1990).

36. Report on the mood of Paris, 1917–18, in the archives of the *Préfecture de police*, Ba 1587.

37. This, moreover, was one of the reasons that induced women to seek employment in war industries. Mme M, for instance, explained that in 1914 she earned 3 francs a day in a pharmaceutical laboratory, while her neighbor earned 6.5 francs in a shop that manufactured shells. The contrast with wages in the textile industry is even more striking. In November 1916, for example, a woman worker in Saint-Denis wrote to *La Bataille* saying that she was having difficulty earning 1.20 francs a day sewing pillowcases.

38. According to A. Rosmer, *Le Mouvement ouvrier pendant la guerre, op. cit.*, the decline in salaries at the outset of the war reached 20 to 30 percent in some cases. Conditions changed beginning in 1917, the main difference being the implementation by the Ministry of Armaments of a wage schedule applicable to armaments factories in the Paris region. There were two schedules, and the first, issued in January 1917 following the wave of strikes in December and January, fixed the minimum wage at sixty-five centimes an hour for female laborers or, on average, double the hourly wage previously paid female workers in the Paris region and the west. See in this regard M.-C. Risacher-Callet, *La Main-d'oeuvre féminine, op. cit.*, pp. 142–44, and above all, W. Oualid and C. Picquenard, *Salaires et tarifs, op. cit.*, as well as *L'Union des Métaux*, December 1916–February 1917. Rates were revised in November 1917 and again July 1918.

39. It was a bomb finishing shop.

40. See the police report on the state of mind of the Parisian population and appearances in Paris in the archives of the *Préfecture de police*, Ba 1614 and *La Bataille*, which regularly reported the price of basic foodstuffs.

41. See M. Guilbert, *Revue française du Travail*, November 1946, p. 663. According to this article, the wages of female laborers in the Parisian metal-working industry were 45 percent lower than those of men in 1913, 31 percent lower in 1916, 18 percent lower in 1917, and once again, 31 percent lower in 1921.

42. The Interunion Action Committee Against the Exploitation of Women was formed in July 1915 in response to an appeal from the General Union of Undergarment and Linen Workers. The Committee included the Book, Lithography, Performing Arts, Garment, and Metal-Workers' Federations.

43. See the circular of 28 February 1916 from the Undersecretary of State for Artillery and Munitions.

44. See E. Cassin, "La femme dans l'industrie et le principe: A travail égal, "*Union des Métaux*, December 1916: "The exploiters must not be allowed to take advantage of

women to the detriment of men. We must impose conditions on the owners under which we will *tolerate* women working industry."

45. Brochure of the Interunion Action Committee Against the Exploitation of Women: *Le Travail de la femme pendant la guerre* (Villeneuve-Saint-Georges: Imprimerie l'Union typographique, 1917).

46. Repeated contact with engine oil explains the frequent appearance in war industries of a skin affliction known as *bouton d'huile*, or oil pimple, about which government publications carried information and preventive advice. See *Bulletin des usines de guerre*, 17 July 1916, p. 176, for example.

47. Numerous circulars and an article in the *Bulletin des usines de guerre* on 18 September 1916 set forth the public health measures to be followed in factories: ventilation, locker rooms, basins, and the wearing of protective clothing. The latter recommendation prompted the development of a work clothes industry.

48. Two companies were repeatedly singled out as very deficient in the area of public health. The first was the Etablissements Ducellier in the 10th *arrondissement*, where, according to a report of the labor department issued in February 1916 and the 3 February issue of *La Bataille*, ninety workers were squeezed into a space of only 120 sq. meters and provided with only one public health facility: a single tap in a courtyard. The other company was the Etablissements Pathé frères in Vincennes (a gas mask manufacturer) where, according to Dr. Martin, who was charged with conducting an inquiry by the Under-Secretary for Artillery and Munitions, some hundred women spent their entire day "handling with the tips of their fingers gauze impregnated with a nickel-based material. This work produces skin irritations on the hands. . . and in some cases annoying dermatitis and eczema that becomes more or less generalized. Pregnant women who work in this factory usually give birth to still-born babies." See AN F 22 539.

49. The story related by the journalist from *Petit Parisien* attests to this: "There I was a laborer in charge of removing the shells. For the time being, I had my hands full just staying alive amidst a myriad of slapping and snapping belts, twisting and pulling gears, torrents of spurting soapy water, and shaking monsters."

50. See the story related by M. Capy, "La femme à l'usine," in *La Voix des femmes*. According to her, some women workers hoisted up to thirty-five tons a day.

51. These measures were taken after official inquiries. "It has often been noted that any improvement in the conditions of work results in increased productivity," stated the preamble to Albert Thomas's circular of 1 July 1917, contained in the brochure published by the Ministry of Armaments, *Protection et utilisation de la main d'oeuvre féminine dans les usines de guerre, op. cit.*

52. *Bulletin du ministère du Travail,* January–February 1917 and September–October 1919.

53. Mme M. said she lost fifteen kilograms in a few weeks at Renault.

54. *La Revue hebdomadaire* of 6 July 1918 published the fictionalized story of "Bénédicte, a war worker," by Edouard Perrin: "She worked for months, always quiet, always attentive. . . . Little by little, her face grew pinched. . . . Her cheek bones increasingly stood out and began to glow with a touch of fever. . . . Her anonymous grave should bear a simple tombstone engraved with the words: Bénédicte, twenty-two years old, died for France." This novel attests to the frequency of tuberculosis among young female munitions makers, though the only response it proposes is resignation.

55. M. Capy relates in the articles already cited that at her workshop two young female workers rose every morning at 3 o'clock in order to catch a train that enabled them to be at the factory by 6:30. According to the 29 August 1916 edition of *La Bataille*, the

Puteaux workers made the journey "clinging to the steps and coupling buffers of the cars," which resulted in numerous accidents.

56. *La Bataille*, 1 December 1916.

57. See Patrick Fridenson, "The impact," *op. cit.*

58. Examples include the "canteen-shelter" of La Courneuve, founded by the Baronesse de Guinzbourg, and the women's center-canteens founded by Mme Avril de Sainte-Croix (the one in Billancourt had a piano). See Alice La Mazière, "Une oeuvre à généraliser: une cantine-abri modèle pour les ouvrières des usines de guerre" in *La Vie féminine*, 21 January 1917.

59. "Les dispositions générales régissant les surintendantes d'usine," *Bulletin des usines de guerre*, 25 November 1918.

60. Marguerite Martin, *Le Populaire*, 18 June 1918.

61. See Annie Fourcaut, *Femmes à l'usine* (Paris: Maspero, 1982). In Great Britain, on the other hand, where there was little tradition of paternalism, the function disappeared after 1919 (cf. Laura Lee Downs, *op. cit.*).

62. The following were particularly helpful in this regard.

See in the AN:

–boxes F22 444 to 448: Protection of motherhood 1893–1933;

–box F22 534: Organization of day-care 1916–18, especially in regard to the inquiry into day-care and nursing rooms carried out in the first quarter of 1918.

See among academic works:

–P. Magnier de Maisonneuve, *Les Institutions sociales en faveur des ouvrières d'usine* (Paris, 1923), available in the BDIC (B 1871);

See in the press:

–Dr. Clothilde Mulon, "Une visite à l'usine de guerre Citroën," *La Française*, 2 March 1918;

See in government publications:

–Dr. Bonnaire, "Le travail féminin dans les fabriques de munitions dans ses rapports avec la puerpéralité," *Bulletin des usines de guerre*, 25 December 1916.

63. As early as 16 June 1917, Marcelle Tynaire gushed in the pages of the weekly *J'ai vu* over the happy times when "life will return to normal little by little, and women, instead of handling lathes, will rock cradles."

64. AN F22 444. Report in 1916 by the *Académie de Médecine de Paris* on the protection of women and children in factories.

65. Dr. Bonnaire, "Le travail féminin dans les fabriques de munitions dans ses rapports avec la puerpéralité," *op. cit.*

66. *La Bataille*, 8 April 1917.

67. See *La Française*, 5 May 1917. According to this feminist newspaper, one must find "a way to reconcile the professional obligations of working women with their legitimate aspirations as women and the crucial duties of motherhood."

68. *Le Populaire*, 23 June 1918.

69. G. Rageot, *La Française dans la guerre, op. cit.*

70. AN F22 534, *Enquête sur les crèches et chambres d'allaitement*. In order to write this inquiry into day-care centers and nursing rooms, a questionnaire was sent out in the late winter of 1917-18 to all establishments working for National Defense. It contained twenty-six very precise questions on all aspects of female workers and maternity. In the Seine district, only thirty-eight establishments responded.

71. See the Strauss Act.

72. AN F22 538.

73. For the history of nursing rooms see in particular: P. Magnier de Maisonneuve, *Institutions sociales, op. cit.*

74. The Levallois-Perret working mothers' clinic resulted from the initiative of a group of industrialists in western Paris, supported by the Ladies of the Red Cross and Albert Thomas. It was inaugurated on 23 October 1917 in the presence of Thomas and L. Loucheur. The association had 200 members, and the clinic included a day-nursery for 20 babies and two day-care centers for 100 children.

75. Clothilde Mulon, "Une visite", *op. cit.*

76. Inquiry of January–May 1917 into factory day-care centers and nursing rooms, *Bulletin du ministère du Travail,* August–September 1917.

77. For a more detailed examination of the nursing rooms and day-care centers (description of the premises, recruitment of the personnel, and analysis of the day-care center regulations) and of the reactions of the labor movement and the women workers themselves to such initiatives, see "Quand les femmes entrent à l'usine. Les ouvrières des usines de guerre de la Seine, 1914–1918," *op. cit.* pp. 221–41.

78. M. Capy, *Une voix de femme dans la mêlée* (Paris, 1916) passim.

79. G.-A. Doleris and J. Bouscatel, *Hygiène et morale sociale néo-malthusienne, Maternité et féminisme – Education sexuelle* (Paris, 1918). Cf. James F. McMillan, *Housewife or Harlot: The Place of Women in French Society, 1870-1940* (Brighton: Harvester Press, 1981).

80. "Searching for shirkers" was a frequent theme in the union press.

81. AN F7 13366.

82. For the trade unions during the war see, in addition to general works about the labor movement, A. Rosmer, *Le Mouvement ouvrier, op. cit.*, vol. 1 and 2, the thesis of J.L. Robert, *op. cit.*, and above all, the abundant police documents in series F7 (AN): F7 13356; F7 13366, 13367; F7 13569; F7 13574 to 13576.

83. According to the 1913 yearbook of the trade unions of the Seine, fewer than 9 percent of the union members were women, a total which results in part from union distrust of women; cf. M. Guilbert, *Les Femmes et l'organisation syndicale avant 1914* (Paris, 1966).

84. Without going into this in detail, it should be remembered that the confederation majority with Jouhaux supported the *Union sacrée* and opposed the minority, including Alphonse Merrheim, Secretary of the Federation of Metal-Workers (although he returned to the majority viewpoint at the end of the war). Cf. Nicholas Papayanis, *Alphonse Merrheim* (The Hague: Nijhoff, 1985).

85. Cf. M.H. Zylberberg-Hocquard, *Féminisme et syndicalisme, op. cit.*

86. See the long police report on the union movement during 1916, AN F7 13891.

87. Cf. her numerous criticisms of the CGT in *La Vague.*

88. Report of the debates in the May–December 1917 issue of *l'Union des Métaux.*

89. This type of phrase was often heard at meetings: "Instead of spending time daubing your face with talcum powder and lime carbonate, pay attention to your work" – a curious way to rally women's support for the labor movement.

90. The reports of the police informers who infiltrated the meetings are more or less complete. However, they rarely give precise figures on the number of men and women present.

91. The unionization of women became much more widespread in 1917; however, this was a transitory phenomenon. See the thesis of J.L. Robert, *op. cit.*

92. For the strikes see: AN, series F7, Archives of the Préfecture de Police, file Ba 1375; the press which wrote copiously about the strikes of 1916 (though beginning in 1917,

Anastasie – the censors – made deep cuts); and the work by R. Picard, *Les Grèves et la guerre* (Paris, 1917).

93. The number of female strikers in the Seine was low before the war. In 1913, for example, there were only 1,221.

94. Since Ministry of Labor services were very disorganized, statistics on the strikes are very scanty. Many pieces of information collected before the war, such as the sex of the strikers and the course of the negotiations, are no longer extant. There are no records of many strikes which we found elsewhere in archival files. The master's thesis cited in n. 77 contains a table developed on the basis of these different sources, see pp. 415–18.

95. Salary demands were the main issue throughout the war and were the source of 90 percent of the strikes.

96. They could yield all the more in that they were obliged to do so by the arbitration and conciliation procedure established by the Ministry of Armaments in the spring of 1917. See in this regard R. Picard, *La Conciliation, l'arbitrage et la prévention des conflits ouvriers* (Paris, 1918).

97. This was true of the Hispano-Suiza strikes in June 1917 and the Morane-Saulnier strikes in September 1917, when women returned to work before the resolution of the men's strike. The reverse occurred at Salmson in February 1918 (AN F7 13366-13367).

98. One could cite the following words of reproach, reported in R. Picard, *Les Grèves, op. cit.*, although Albert Thomas delivered them in Normandy to women working at Schneider in Honfleur in February 1917, rather than to Parisian women: "Suddenly, without warning, you have stopped work. Have you considered the seriousness of your misconduct? Have you thought of the enemy, who carries on with his work? Why did you not have recourse to conciliation without stopping work? [. . .] I want all of you to be present at the factory tomorrow." The women immediately returned to work.

99. See the police report of 30 May 1917 (AN F7 13366): "In the afternoon of 29 May, women from the Salmson works in Boulogne arrived at the Hanriot plant, leading a group of 200 women comprising strikers from Iris lamps, unemployed workers from Citroën, and laundry workers from the Boulogne region, and attempted to induce the women at Hanriot to go on strike." The next day, a thousand women raising the red flag invaded the Salmson factories. All female trades were in fact paralyzed by strikes in May–June 1917.

100. In late 1917 and 1918, the relations between the government and workers deteriorated with the departure of Albert Thomas, a socialist minister, and the arrival of Louis Loucheur, an industrialist, as minister.

101. The demands of the female munitions makers at De Dion were: refusal of a wage reduction (camouflaged by an increase in productivity since the workers would be required to work three machines instead of two), respect on the part of the foremen, no dismissals in case of illness, and leave when their husbands were on leave. Much was written about this strike at De Dion. *L'Humanité* and *La Bataille* related events on virtually a daily basis. A detailed examination can be found in A. Rosmer, *Le Mouvement ouvrier, op. cit.*

102. AN F7 13367.

103. For the psychology of the strike, see Michelle Perrot, *Workers on Strike. France 1871–1890* (Oxford: Berg Publishers), 1985.

104. This is revealed in various police reports on the mood of Parisians, Archives of the Préfecture de Police, Ba 1614.

105. R. Picard, *Les Grèves, op. cit.*.

106. Similarly, the police reports on the "women ringleaders" show a preoccupation

with the manners of the women. See the police report found in AN F7 13366 which lists the Salmson ringleaders arrested on 31 May (available in our master's thesis, p. 317b).

107. See the letter sent to R. Poincaré on 19 May 1918 by an inhabitant of the XVIe *arrondissement* demanding that a "good police squad be dispatched to take care of these individuals and females," AN F7 13367.

108. Pacifist socialist teacher, who was arrested in 1918. See the material on Hélène Brion in the library of the Institut français d'histoire sociale, 14 AS 183. These letters, intercepted by the police, can be found in file Ba 1561 of the archives of the Préfecture de Police. For Hélène Brion, see Huguette Bouchardeau, *Hélène Brion, la voie féministe* (Paris: Syros, 1978).

109. For pacifism see: AN F7 13370 to 13376; archives of the Préfecture de Police, Ba 1558 to 1562.

110. Another socialist female teacher, member of the Socialist Women's Action Committee For Peace, Against Chauvinism, who participated in the International Conference of Socialist Women in Bern, Switzerland on 28 and 29 March 1915, where an appeal was launched to proletarian women throughout Europe.

111. For example, she opened the columns of *La Vague* to soldiers so that they could report on their experiences to those at home.

112. For this see Françoise Thébaud, *La femme au temps de la guerre . . .* , *op. cit.*, pp. 252–258.

113. The notice promised a departure indemnity of one month's wages to women workers who left their positions before 5 December 1918. The date was significant because the indemnity was reduced thereafter, before being totally eliminated on 5 January 1919. In view of the ensuing difficulties and union protests, the cut-off date was delayed until March 1919.

114. According to the *le Populaire* edition of 25 December 1918, a rumor was started at Citroën to the effect that a corset maker in the area was hiring. Those women who showed up at the corset factory was fired without any indemnity.

115. M. Capy, "Femmes de peine, messieurs de luxe," *La Vague*, November 1918.

116. See for instance the declaration that appeared in *l'Information ouvrière et sociale.*

117. According to the census data of 1911, 1921, and 1926, metal-working factories in the Seine employed 8,572 female workers in 1911 (5.6 percent of the work force), 39,741 female workers in 1921 (14 percent of the work force), and 52,189 female workers in 1926 (14.8 percent of the work force). Cf. Sylvie Zerner, "Travail domestique et formes de travail – Ouvrières et employées entre la première guerre mondiale et la grande crise," Ph.D. thesis, Université Paris X – Nanterre, 1989.

118. See n. 35.

119. Cf. Laura Lee Downs, *Women in Industry, op. cit.*

8

Shop Stewards at Renault

Gilbert Hatry

From the outset of hostilities, the Minister of Labor encouraged his inspectors to close their eyes to violations of the law as it had stood prior to August 1914. This attitude was only aggravated the following year when the Minister of War, Alexandre Millerand, declared before a delegation from the Metal-Workers' Federation: "There is no more labor code and no more social legislation; there is only war."[1]

As a result, the conditions in which workers lived and worked deteriorated sharply: the right to one day of rest a week was suspended, twelve-hour days returned, Taylorism was more fully implemented, and wages were frozen.

Compelled at first to accept these changes by virtue of the *Union sacrée* to which the unions had agreed, the workers soon began to make their dissatisfaction known as the war dragged on. Labor strife spread, and the socialist Minister of Armaments, Albert Thomas, was forced to take action to keep the situation under control. His maxim became "produce, intervene, cooperate,"[2] and to fulfill these goals he sought to develop conciliation procedures and worker representation.

As social tensions escalated after three long years of war, Thomas introduced on 17 January 1917 a conciliation and arbitration procedure designed to forestall labor conflicts that were disrupting production. The provisions of this decree were very clear: according to Section 1, industrialists could not disregard the labor contract if strife erupted, and workers could not lay down their tools "before submitting the questions dividing them to conciliation and arbitration." The standing committees created by Section 2 of the same decree were composed of equal numbers of owners' and workers' representatives, with a minimum of

Notes to Chapter 8 can be found on page 235.

two each. All committee members were exempted from conscription.

The existence of a labor dispute was announced to the labor control officer either by a representative of the owner or his substitute or else by a worker bearing a proxy signed on plain paper by at least twenty workers (Section 3). Upon receipt of this announcement, the inspector of labor was to inform the standing committee and the minister, who would then appoint his representative (Section 4). If a settlement could not be negotiated, an arbitrator was appointed, by the minister himself if he so desired (Section 5).

As soon as standing committees were established in each region or department, this decree proved very effective at stifling labor unrest and preventing it from spreading. What remained was the problem of worker representation – which had actually been a union demand for many years: "This form of worker representation had already been instituted before 1914, notably in the mining industry and some railroad companies. . . . In addition, Millerand had tabled a bill in 1900 designed to establish permanent representatives elected by the workers, but it bogged down in parliamentary manoeuvring."[3] Long before the war, workers had quite naturally appointed some of their fellows to coordinate job action, to represent them, and present their demands to the owners. However, these representatives disappeared as soon as the specific grievance was settled. The unions had long believed it would be helpful to create official, permanent worker representatives, but the owners always opposed any such idea, claiming that "relations between employers and employees are administered through foremen, who, having risen through the ranks, naturally understand the interests of their fellow workers. If the workers wish to follow a different procedure in certain cases, nothing could be easier in practical terms: they simply form a suitable delegation under the particular circumstances, go to the factory manager, and tell him what they want."[4]

Louis Renault, who had been compelled in December 1912 to accept elected worker delegates, took advantage of a strike against strictly timed operations in February 1913 in order to eliminate all worker representatives.[5] In 1917, however, the workers again succeeded in imposing permanent delegates on management, which in fact was probably not terribly opposed to dealing with qualified intermediaries who had the respect of their fellow workers. So long as this delegate system had a delaying function, it was welcomed by management; however, when the delegates began to take a definite class stand in 1918, they were quickly eliminated.

The Establishment of the Delegate System
Development of the Standard Agreement

Heightening social tensions in 1917 allowed the delegate system to emerge. Though not yet officially recognized, the delegate system already existed in essence. Management was tolerating delegates as a necessary evil, and Albert Thomas considered it urgent that their tasks and method of appointment be officially established and regulated.

In his circular of 5 February 1917,[6] he drew the attention of the labor inspectors to the "advantages to be gained from establishing worker delegates in the armaments factories, who would be responsible for maintaining regular contacts with the factory management and the labor inspection division." Furthermore, "the presence of workers who enjoy the confidence of their fellows facilitates negotiations and helps avoid unfortunate incidents."[7] Thomas later pointed to some recent incidents and commented: "In some cases, labor conflict has led to a sudden cessation of work without any previous discussion between the employer, the workers, and my services."[8] In Thomas's view therefore, the worker delegate system would greatly facilitate the application of and adherence to his decree on conciliation and arbitration.

What form could the delegate system take? It could only be instituted by inserting special clauses in the factory rules and regulations; however, these were controlled by the owners, who therefore had to be persuaded to allow special rules in every factory. After excluding factories which employed fewer than fifty people or which had just been established within the previous two months, Thomas submitted several proposals[9] on eligibility requirements to vote for worker delegates (French citizens at least eighteen years of age) and to stand for office (literate workers who had attained the age of majority and had already worked for several months in the factory). Women could vote and stand for office, but foreign workers and colonials were excluded. Finally, the election would be by secret ballot, and each mandate would last for at least six months.

Since Thomas's recommendations imposed no legal obligation, he attempted to appeal to the goodwill of the industrialists. The latter, though tolerating the presence of worker delegates, had little desire to establish them as a permanent feature of their factories. Some business leaders complained bitterly that they had not been consulted in advance "about this change which the authorities want to introduce in the factories of our members."[10] For its part, the Comité des Forges sought to question the minister while assuring him that it "would not adopt a hostile attitude toward the projected system."[11]

Thomas had to negotiate a deal, and he quickly discarded any notion of submitting his proposal to Parliament, which alone could pass a law forcing employers to comply. It was therefore left "to industrialists to establish eligibility requirements for voting and standing for election, the type of representation by job category and work area, the nature of the demands that could be made on management, and the procedures to be followed."[12]

These conditions naturally led to enormous disparities in the way the delegate system functioned in various factories, with some employers not even hesitating to appoint the delegates themselves. Moreover, there were vast differences in understandings of the delegates' role. Albert Thomas wrote:[13]

> During recent negotiations, I have noted enormous differences in views of the delegates' role. Some employers seem to be primarily interested in shop delegates as simple intermediaries, whose services are not necessarily even needed when forwarding various demands from the workers. The workers, on the other hand, often tend to view the shop delegates as thoroughgoing union representatives who should take an interest not only in the particular shop which they represent but also in more general questions concerning the entire factory. For this reason, suggestions are sometimes heard that all the delegates in a factory should come together and elect in turn a committee of delegates to examine disputes that could not be settled separately within each shop. This committee of delegates would in the end play the same role vis-à-vis the industrialists as a union delegation. I think it would be rather dangerous to implant this in the delegate system from the outset. Far from helping to promote cooperative, confidential relations within the factory, the delegate system could quite possibly stir up conflict and, what is more, undermine the development and tasks of the unions which have their own role to play just as the shop delegates have their role.

What then would be the role of the unions and the delegates? Thomas continued:

> The unions should become involved in the choice of the delegates, they should campaign among their members in this regard, they should remain in contact with those shop delegates who are members of their organizations – all this is quite normal and acceptable; however, the unions should not forget that the shop delegates have their own role, distinct from the role of unions, and sufficiently important in its own right. It is incumbent upon the shop delegates to study individual complaints which have not been satisfied within each shop and to take these complaints to the employer, to explain and discuss them.

This was not all, in Thomas's view. The delegates had a further role to play:

Insofar as the technical organization of work is concerned, the delegates can play the role of emissaries from their fellow workers to point out to management how new methods, procedures, or equipment could make work more productive, could better utilize machinery, could economize on primary materials, and reduce worker fatigue. In addition, the delegates can be indispensable interpreters for shop personnel, pointing out to management certain situations which could compromise the dignity of the workers.

In this way, concluded Thomas, "the range of the delegates' activities would be restricted to the shop which elected them, while being broad and extensive enough to give management a good idea of the collective life of the shop in all its manifestations."

The disparities in views of the precise task of the shop delegates and of the ways in which they would be appointed led to the development of a standard agreement to be suggested to employers and unions. The unions advanced their own proposals in this regard, but felt it was ultimately the minister's responsibility to take the initiative. Thomas refused, however, preferring to allow the employers a free hand, in the belief that their support was essential.

It was at this point that Louis Renault made his move.[14] In July 1917 he gathered information from the ministry,[15] and while the unions patiently awaited publication of the official standard agreement,[16] hoping that it would take the workers' desires into account, Renault was busy putting the finishing touches on his own plan. On 22 August Albert Thomas met with him, in the presence of two trade-unionists from the Renault works named Michelet and Bagot. The ensuing discussion immediately foundered on the first three sections setting forth the eligibility requirements for voting and standing for election. Renault supported the inclusion of all trades in the plan, but opposed the requirement of a minimum work force of fifty people. In Renault's view, only French citizens should be allowed to vote, thus excluding large numbers of foreign workers. Finally, he proposed that only "fathers of families, at least twenty-five years of age and working in the same factory and the same trade for at least five years" should be allowed to stand for election.[17] This requirement had the effect of eliminating as possible delegates all workers who had been hired since 1912 and who therefore tended to be the most radical. Thus Renault returned to the argument, already advanced at the time of the strike over strictly timed operations, that only older workers had the necessary experience to represent properly the interests of their colleagues.

Despite their desire to reach an agreement, Michelet and Bagot were not about to accede to such stipulations, especially as the first hint of these proposals were already sparking protests among the rank and file.[18] Renault was therefore forced to back down. All corporations would be represented whatever their size; all workers twenty-one years of age and of French or Allied citizenship who had worked in the factory for at least two months would be eligible to vote; workers who were themselves eligible to vote, were twenty-five years of age, and had worked in the factory for at least one year would be eligible to stand for election.

When all the regulations had been established, they were finally signed on 28 August by Louis Renault and two of his unionized workers, Michelet and Bagot, in the presence of Albert Thomas.[19] On 30 August they were posted in all factory shops.[20] Soon they were being touted by Albert Thomas as a standard agreement and distributed as such to all companies working for National Defense.[21]

The Elections in Billancourt

Even though the trade unionists in the Billancourt works succeeded in obtaining important improvements in Renault's initial proposals, they nevertheless felt obliged to make concessions which the Federation of Metal-Workers considered unacceptable and dangerous for the future: "The Renault agreement includes certain sections against which numerous shops protested when they saw them. Some succeeded in making changes, but it must be said that the original agreement weighed heavily on all the discussions."[22] The parts which raised most objections were sections 15, 16, and 17, dealing with the duties of shop delegates. According to these sections, delegates were "the appropriate intermediaries to help their fellow workers understand the validity and necessity of measures adopted in the shop." They were "not to interfere in the management of other services or shops," and were expected "to make every effort to maintain order and discipline in the shop." The delegates' roles were to reconcile the divergent interests of workers and management, and not to function as spokesmen for worker demands. Delegates therefore seemed like hostages, constantly threatened with disciplining. The delegate system was a far cry from union representation within the company, as demanded by the Federation of Metal-Workers (together with the CGT), in the form of worker delegates nominated by the unions.

It was in this context that the first elections were announced for Billancourt. The announcement was made by means of a notice from management, and candidates had until forty-eight hours before election day to announce their candidacy. However, they had no medium through which they could freely express themselves, because no signs were allowed either within the factory itself or on the surrounding walls. Voting took place throughout 6 September. One hundred and thirty delegates were elected (and an equal number of alternates), among them those men who would turn out to be the leaders: Bagot, Le Bihan, and Michelet.

The biographies of these three men are as follows:[23]

BAGOT (Alexandre-Léon), born on 21 January 1877 in Paris. First mobilized in the 35th territorial infantry regiment, he was given a deferment on 16 October 1915 and assigned on 18 October to the Renault works as a metal-turner for artillery. A member of the 18th section of the Socialist Federation of the Seine, he was a trade unionist belonging to the Syndicat de la Voiture-aviation, where he belonged to the revolutionary minority in the CGT. At union meetings he advocated the resumption of international relations and direct action to oblige the government to conclude a peace treaty without prior conditions. "An orator with the people's unquenchable gift of the gab[!] and highly respected by workers in the Renault plant, whom he is able to lead wherever he desires, he is on very good terms with the deputy Jean Longuet."

Called up once again into the army after the strikes of May 1918, he rejoined the 6th section of the COA at Châlons-sur-Marne. Shortly afterward, he was condemned by a court-martial to four years of forced labor for pacifist agitation.

In 1918 Bagot became a substitute member of the administrative committee of the socialist newspaper *L'Humanité*, and took a seat on the executive committee of the Socialist Federation of the Seine in late 1919. He reappeared in Billancourt on 3 November 1919 at a public meeting, and on 30 November was elected a town councillor in Boulogne on a slate headed by the socialist Morizet. As a Communist Party member, he was elected to municipal office in Châtenay-Malabry in 1945. He died on 18 February 1962.

LE BIHAN (Louis-Georges), born on 8 March 1889, given a deferment on 22 November 1915, and sent to the Renault works as a metal fitter in the automatic lathe shop. A member of the revolutionary wing of the union and a member of the Socialist Federation of the Seine (Clichy section). Was reported in September 1917 for having read to his fellow union members a typewritten pamphlet advocating the formation of a workers' and soldiers' committee, "this mass which is contributing directly to the salvation of the motherland," and demanding the publication of France's war aims.

Belonged to the Mechanics Union of the Seine and to the Federation of State Railroad Unions (Le Havre group). Called up once again into the army after the strikes of May 1918, he joined the sixth section of COA at Châlons-sur-Marne. After the war, he never reappeared in Billancourt.

MICHELET (Anatole), born on 19 September 1884. Was given a deferment and became a fitter in shop 6 at Renault on 10 February 1915. Member of the 20th section of the Socialist Federation of the Seine and a member of the metal-workers' union. Dismissed on 31 May 1918 in the wake of the strikes, he was reinducted into the army and joined the sixth section of COA at Châlons-sur-Marne. After the war, he never reappeared in Billancourt.

The elections certainly did not signify approval of the agreement, quite the contrary. Three days later, the machinists gathered at the Labor Exchange in Paris to protest against Sections 15, 16, and 17, and they appointed twenty delegates "who will form an executive committee to develop a new agreement."[24] The question of a strike also arose,[25] not only in response to the agreement – which had been unfairly imposed according to some workers – but also because of wage demands that had not yet been met. In any case, further cause for discontent had been added, and pressure from the rank and file on delegates grew to the point that they soon ended up performing roles which the original agreement had carefully avoided.

This expansion of the duties of the delegates was discussed at a meeting between Albert Thomas – who then was no longer in government – and the Renault works delegates on 26 November 1917 in the Huyghens gymnasium in Paris.[26] Michelet argued that delegates could "only exercise their role in a useful way if they have the support of their comrades." There was, he said, considerable friction in the Renault works, "where management attempts by every means available to recover from the workers the concessions which the delegates succeeded in extracting." Michelet provided the example of a delegate named Roussel, "who has just received a call-up to rejoin his regiment, despite the promises of the Minister of Armaments who stated last September that delegates could not be penalized in any way as a result of the exercise of their duties." The workers wanted wages that were related to the cost of living, according to Michelet, and "the office employees not included in the schedule should receive a cost of living allowance." Louis Sellier, who followed Michelet on the platform, discussed transportation and emphasized "the influence which the worker delegates from the Renault works have had recently on the Ministry of Armaments and on the public transportation companies which have finally granted certain improvements such as additional streetcar service from the Mirabeau bridge to the Renault works."[27]

Very soon, however, the delegates would burst the bounds of factory issues and the role to which Thomas had attempted to confine them on 26 November: to limit their concerns solely to wages and working conditions, while showing "the prudence to act like a friendly association of delegates and not like this committee which frightened French owners like a Russian soviet."

From Economic Demands to Pacifism

Widespread and Profound Discontent

In early 1918, on 3 January, delegates from the metal-working plants in the Paris region met to discuss the "various reasons for the widespread and profound discontent among their electors."[28] In the agenda approved at the end of the meeting they:

> reiterate their regret that government has lacked sufficient will, that it has so openly expressed its distrust of the workers, by opposing an expansion and clarification of labor union rights at the very time it is providing owners with unlimited power, thanks to special wartime measures, and allowing the most perfidious reprisals;

> affirm that now more than ever their ability to respond, their influence, and their hopes for achieving their goals are totally dependent on the strength of the union movement, outside of which all working class efforts are doomed to sterility and disappointment. Convinced of this necessity, and union members themselves, the delegates undertake to actively and constantly encourage their electors to join their respective unions;

> declare that their actions must always remain under the direction and control of the unions which are the real arbiters and the only true guardians of the interests and rights of workers. Viewing their role in this way, they demand the right to meet and organize on a shop level in order to draw up on behalf of all the personnel proposed solutions that have been jointly developed with the unions.

Furthermore, the delegates could not remain indifferent to "the decisive events that are approaching and that require the utmost unity within working-class organizations." The delegates from the Renault works proposed an addition to the agenda, which, adopted unanimously, called for:[29]

> the preparation by all appropriate means of an inter-Allied conference and an international congress of all representatives of the working class; energetic

measures within the country to compel the government to state its war aims and to obtain a commitment from it to consult with the Allies in order to make a collective declaration of democratic conditions for a peace treaty. These conditions can be summarized in a phrase taken from the Russian Revolution – the "liberty of peoples to dispose freely of themselves" – and they find their practical expression in an honest referendum under the control of the League of Nations. It is understood that the emissaries of the various nations will include direct representatives of their proletariats.

In proposing this text, which also bore the influence of President Wilson's ideas, the Renault delegates were taking their place in the pacifist movement. They thereby joined the wing of the CGT which opposed the war and in which the Federation of Metal-Workers and its leader Merrheim played an important part. The year 1918 at Renault was therefore a time of great agitation, partly on the level of plant issues and partly on the level of larger political issues.

Michelet and Bagot took a very clear position. On 3 February,[30] during a meeting of munition plant shop delegates, Michelet pointed to the attitude of Austrian, German, and Russian workers, who did not hesitate to launch campaigns in favor of peace, and declared that "the French people, who have already carried out several revolutions, cannot remain indifferent to these appeals and could make a good start by taking a stand in favor of pacifism." Bagot said decisions should be taken which would "enlighten the masses of factory workers on the appropriate attitude toward the war," and he praised Lenin and Trotzky as "revolutionaries who have fully accomplished their task and who found the courage to act the same way that they thought." Bagot continued: "Our duty as shop delegates is to make our electors understand that the issue of bigger pay packets should be set aside in favor of a single obsession: peace. We should, if necessary, oppose new call-ups of workers in the shops and demand instead an immediate armistice."

There is no doubt that a great many workers, above all those at Renault, favored measures to accelerate the end of the war. Some, though only a limited number, felt these measures should go beyond mere words. Toward the end of February, there were some cases of sabotage in the "part of the plant that works for the air force."[31] The police report established that there had been "systematic sabotage for a certain amount of time. Recently screws have been found in the casings of motors and a water pump was poorly cottered." However, this type of action could never find widespread support under the general mood prevailing at the time. It soon ceased, and management was able to report that "the situation in the plants is normal."[32]

The Cadière Affair

The situation may have been "normal," but this did not stop the Renault delegates from continuing their efforts to change things. Was it possible at all, however, to mobilize the great mass of workers around pacifist ideals? It seems that Michelet, Bagot, and Le Bihan, who all were syndicalists, quickly realized that if a broad movement was possible it would have to be fueled by more immediate concerns.

The first skirmishes therefore concerned the length of working hours and a wage increase. The delegates immediately adopted a new attitude: they "don't talk to the employers in the same way and evidently intend to be intransigent."[33] Without preliminary notice and with no discussions, the delegates demanded that the lunch break be extended from one hour and fifteen minutes to one and a half hours. The demand was immediately satisfied. One week later, they informed management "that from this day on, workers will only work for ten hours a day, instead of ten and a half."[34] Management acquiesced.

On 11 March, 200 navvies at the Société générale d'Entreprises who were working on a Renault project in Boulogne, 44 quai du Point-du-Jour, laid down their tools to protest the dismissal of a work site delegate who that morning had refused entry to the site to five non-unionized cement workers.[35] At Renault's request, the delegate was rehired, and the cement workers were dismissed. On 17 March, the aviation workers in the O plant demanded "improved regulations governing work and a holiday on Sundays," and threatened to strike "if the improvements they demanded were not conceded."[36] Once again management bowed to the workers' request.

Next the delegates demanded a general wage increase to offset the lost pay resulting from the reduction in the hours of work.[37] This time management dug in its heels and flatly refused. The delegates responded by continuing their efforts to organize a broad movement throughout the factory, not only in favor of wage increases but also "in favor of Peace."[38]

It was at this juncture that the Cadière affair erupted.[39] Cadière had been wounded in the war and reassigned to the Renault works. Although he took part in the various campaigns that swept the works, he was never one of the main agitators. He was simply a former soldier who had seen the horrors of war and decided to combat it by arguing the merits of pacifism with his fellow workers. On 8 April 1918 Cadière was arrested on the job by the works police and taken to the police station in Boulogne, where he was incarcerated for "defeatist propaganda."

The news of Cadière's arrest traveled fast and provoked an intense response that lasted long after he was released without charges. What upset the workers in this affair was the intrusion of the works police into a domain which was none of their concern. Although "management changed certain provisions governing its private police force," the workers "wanted to obtain the dismissal of Dubois, the chief of the force. They also accused the assistant chief, Médard, of having insulted Cadière while taking him to the police station."[40]

Down with War!

The Cadière affair had barely died down when unrest again intensified, "not for more money, but to protest against the conscription of even younger workers and against the war itself."[41]

On 11 May, delegates meeting in the La Victoire restaurant on the Place Nationale in Boulogne adopted in principle the calling of an immediate strike for "the new wage rates and to force the government to take a step toward Peace by announcing its war aims."[42] The delegates supported Michelet when he said: "We must be resolute. They laugh at us and our brothers in the trenches. Our brothers get killed and we are starved to death, not that we too won't be eventually sent to the front to be massacred as well."[43]

The next day, 600 delegates from war factories meeting in the *Maison des Syndicats* voiced their approval of what the Renault delegates had done.[44] The strike was set for Monday, 13 May, and Renault was to give the signal. On the appointed day, the delegates asked the workers to strike as soon as they arrived for the day's work, and "by nine o'clock, everybody had laid down his tools."[45] When the delegates refused to order the workers to start work again by the afternoon at the latest, management posted a sign in the shops informing the personnel "that the plant will be closed until the workers make known their desire to return to work."[46]

By noon, the strikers were in the streets, where they met their comrades from Salmson. The police and the army took up position on the Place Nationale. However, "the news spread like wildfire. Renault and Salmson are out!"[47] The strike movement swept across France, hitting Peugeot, De Dion-Bouton, Chenard et Walcker, Caudron, Morane, S.E.V., Voisin, Hotchkiss, Delaunay-Belleville, Blum-Latil, Darracq, Borrel, Clerget-Blin, Ballot, Ernault, Gnôme et Rhône, Delage, Chausson, Panhard-Levassor, Schneider, Citroën, Hanriot, Clément-Bayard, les Chantiers de la Loire, la Société d'optique, la Compagnie des Compteurs, la Société des Moteurs à gaz, and some twenty other companies of varying sizes. In all, more than 200,000 metal-workers eventually hit the streets.[48]

We can follow the course of the strike thanks to the daily meetings held by the Billancourt workers. Bigot was quoted at the meeting of 14 May as saying that "the real purpose is to compel the government to announce its war aims," and the minutes of the meeting ended with the slogan "Down with the War!"; however, the delegate Décembre admitted at the same meeting that "thirty-five percent of the workers believed they should continue working."[49] Sentiments were therefore far from unanimous, and attempts to prevent "scabs" from entering the plant resulted in violent confrontations on the Place Nationale, where a squad of fifty mounted police were permanently stationed.[50] One delegate named Lucien Morteham was arrested "for having struck a worker on the night shift who wished to return to work."[51]

On 16 May the Metal-Workers' Federation took over control of operations, while Michelet "expressed his satisfaction that the strike had become far larger than ever expected."[52] But was the Metal-Workers' Federation really interested in encouraging the popular uprising? A general German offensive was widely expected,[53] and the Federation was apparently convinced that the rest of society would take a hostile view of any labor agitation under these conditions. The Federation felt it had to find an honorable way out, and it therefore entered into negotiations with the socialist members of the Chamber of Deputies, the Minister of Armaments and the Prime Minister, Georges Clemenceau. The result was unconditional surrender: "noting the declarations that have been made and that the demonstrative nature of the strike has proved successful, adopting the proposal of the unions that work resume in the normal manner on Saturday, 18 May at the usual time in the afternoon."[54] It was the end of all the high hopes.

Repression

The time for company vengeance had arrived. Workers who had not been mobilized and were considered the ringleaders were dismissed, while 146 worker-soldiers were summoned back to the military depots from the factories listed in Table 8.1.[55]

It is evident that the repression was very uneven. There were fourteen call-ups at Renault, which is actually very few in view of the number of workers at Renault and their role in the strike. Dulaunay-Belleville, on the other hand, was even harder hit with nineteen call-ups. The same is true of De Dion-Bouton, Gnôme et Rhône, and above all, Salmson.

Table 8.1

Védrines	1	SACA	2
Peugeot.	6	De Dion-Bouton	10
Renault	14	Chenard-Walcker	3
Caudron	2	Morane	1
S.E.V	7	Voisin	4
Moisant	1	Hotchkiss	1
Chantiers de la Loire	4	Sté de Construction. mécanique	1
Delaunay-Belleville	19	Sté d'Optique.	6
Blum-Latil	1	Darracq	1
Borrel	4	Clerget-Blin	4
Ballot	4	Ernault	2
Gnôme et Rhône	10	Delage	5
Chausson	2	Panhard-Levassor	1
Auto-Livraison	1	Carré	1
Cie des Compteurs	3	Aster	1
Bouhey-Forest	1	Demarçay	2
Schneider	1	Citroën	4
Petit-Vicart-Cousin	1	Pirre	2
S.C.A.P.	1	S.E.A	1
Hanriot	1	Salmson	4
Clément-Bayard	1	Sté des moteurs à gaz	2
Couaillet et Bussoz	1	X	2

The fourteen recalled workers at Renault joined the sixth section of the COA at Châlons-sur-Marne. They were:[56] Franklin Aldiger, class of 1905; Alexandre Bagot, class of 1897; Théodore Beaufort, class of 1894; Bucheron, class of 1901; Antoche Décembre, class of 1900; Paul Decouvrant, class of 1903; Louis Giraud, class of 1898; Louis Le Bihan, class of 1909; Edmond Le Bris, class of 1910; Eugène Letterich, class of 1897; Anatole Michelet, class of 1904; Georges Néron, class of 1890; Nicolas Ritter, class of 1906; and Xavier Violatte, class of 1908. However, a few days later clemency was shown to ninety-three of the recalled workers, including nine at Renault, who were sent back to industry. In this way, the Renault delegates Ritter and Le Bris joined la Cie Générale d'Électricité de Nancy, Violatte joined les Forges and Aciéries de Pompey, Néron joined la Cie générale française des tramways de Nancy, Beaufort joined les Aciéries de Micheville in Marnaval (Haute-Marne), Décembre joined la Société métallurgique de Senelle-Maubeuge in Manis (Haute-Marne), Letterich joined la Société

Châtillon-Commentry in Neuves-Maisons, Giraud joined la Société des distilleries des combustibles in Marnaval, and Bucheron joined les établissements Thuillier et Cie in Précy- sur-Oise.[57]

Only Aldiger, Bagot, Decouvrant, Le Bihan, and Michelet, who were considered the most dangerous, remained in Châlons. Once again in military uniform, they met up with some of their old comrades from other factories in the Paris region, especially Heckenmeyer, who was a member of the *Union corporative des ouvriers mécaniciens de la Seine* and on the Metal-Workers' Federation executive. Beginning on 6 June, they met to "examine together the situation in which we find ourselves in Châlons,"[58] eventually deciding to appoint a committee "to centralize all correspondence of interest to all of us and to respond to it through a secretary."[59] The recalled delegates were eager to avoid isolation and perhaps falling prey to some sort of provocation. Bagot, Le Bihan, and Michelet were already being accused of "going to the city during working hours and making alarmist statements to wine merchants from the surrounding area, though these claims are entirely untrue." In addition, their "comrades are particularly singled out and watched."[60] As a result of an imprudent remark, Bagot was arrested and then sentenced in December 1918 to four years of forced labor. Meanwhile, the police were reporting back at Billancourt that "the morale of the work force is excellent."[61]

By the end of July union members began preparing to hold elections to replace the fourteen men who had been called up. The campaign "revolves entirely around the issue of wage increases, which cannot be supplanted by cost-of-living supplements."[62] Management feared "the election of new agitators."[63] After the election, new faces did appear, in particular Roudet, who became the ringleader, as well as a woman named Mme. Martin. However, the men in Nancy were not forgotten. An emergency fund was established, and in early December 8,600 of the 9,000 francs that were collected were distributed to all their families.[64]

Once the war was over, some former shop delegates who had returned to the Paris region "tried to create a movement to agitate among factory workers."[65] Postcards with pictures of Michelet, Bagot, and Le Bihan were sold on the Place Nationale and demands reminiscent of the prewar era were raised, including:[66] elimination of piecework; abolition of Taylorism, or else timing by the workers themselves rather than by the owners; and elimination of bonuses and of piecework in favor of a fixed wage.

However, peace had returned and people's minds were on other things. The sentencing of Bagot hardly caused a ripple of interest: "In other times, we would have mobilized the workers in the Renault factories, but alas, cowardice still seems to reign supreme among those who benefited from Bagot's devotion. It is all the more incumbent upon us to save him."[67] Péricat, the secretary of the mechanics' union, added in his colorful style: "Bagot is still in prison and you say nothing, you little pussy cats at Renault."[68]

Conclusion

The labor movement, invisible in the Renault plants at the beginning of the war, gradually reasserted itself. The earliest union demands were related to wages and working conditions. Although the first incident occurred in August 1915, the second did not come until almost a year later. Slowly the movement grew, and by late 1916 there were frequent demonstrations of discontent, which grew into virtually incessant agitation at Billancourt, lasting until the end of the war.

The workers elected shop delegates as their spokesmen.[69] These were men of good will, no doubt, but they lacked experience and often were not even union members. Among them to be sure could be found some union militants such as Michelet, Bagot, and Le Bihan, who soon took control. Although these three men exercised enormous influence over their fellow workers, they could not by any means always count on their support. Often they had to bow to the wishes of the mass of workers, which explains most of their equivocations and about-faces. When Albert Thomas paid a visit to Billancourt on 1 September 1917, Michelet, for instance, found himself thanking the minister, his fellow party member, "for the good will that exists between M. Renault and us." Two months later, Michelet was vilifying the same M. Renault – the atmosphere in the plant had deteriorated substantially.

During this period when the labor movement was taking shape at Renault, though without the benefit of a strong, well-organized union organization, since only the Executive Committee of Delegates was functioning on a regular basis, the delegates clearly found themselves under constant pressure from the mass of workers. This pressure radicalized the delegates, and some of them even went on later to join the CGTU or the Communist Party.

Notes to Chapter 8

1. Georges Lefranc, *Le mouvement syndical sous la IIIe République* (Paris: Payot, 1967), p. 202.

2. See Jean-Louis Robert, "Ouvriers et mouvement ouvrier parisiens pendant la grande guerre et l'immédiat après-guerre" (thèse d'État, Université Paris I, 1989), p. 811.

3. Jean-Louis Robert, *op. cit.*, p. 809.

4. *Bulletin du syndicat des mécaniciens, chaudronniers et fondeurs de France* (May-June 1917), letter to Louis Loucheur, Under-Secretary of State for War Production, 27 June 1917.

5. Gilbert Hatry, *Louis Renault, patron absolu* (Paris: Lafourcade, 1982).

6. Circular No. 1584 5/0.

7. *Bulletin des usines de guerre* 48, p. 380 (24 March 1917).

8. *Ibid.*, 8, p. 61 (18 June 1917).

9. Circular no. 4647 5/0 of 24 June 1917.

10. *Bulletin du syndicat des mécaniciens, chaudronniers et fondeurs de France*, previously cited.

11. French National Archives (AN), 94 AP 141, note for the minister, 26 June 1917.

12. *Idem.*

13. Circular no. 5592 5/0 of 5 September 1917.

14. For Renault during this period see G. Hatry, *Renault usine de guerre* (Paris: Lafourcade, 1978) and *Louis Renault, op. cit.*

15. AN 94 AP 141, note of the minister to F. Simiand, 4 July 1917.

16. "Un conflit: notre projet de règlement et celui des usines Renault," *L'Union des Métaux* 67, May–December 1917.

17. AN 94 AP 141, Regulations for appointing delegates; Louis Renault's plan, (n.d.).

18. Notably, this occurred during a meeting of aviation workers from Nieuport, Caudron et Voisin, held in Issy-les-Moulineaux on 22 August 1917, AN F7 13366. For similar criticism in the Loire region, see Kathryn E. Amdur, *Syndicalist Legacy* (Urbana: University of Illinois Press, 1986), p. 74.

19. The full text of the agreement is in AN 94 AP 141.

20. AN 94 AP 141, letter from Automobiles Renault to Mario Roques, 30 August 1917.

21. The brochure published by the Ministry of Armaments is in AN 94 AP 141.

22. *L'Union des métaux, op. cit.*

23. Sources: AN F7 13367; Archives of the Régie Renault, Billancourt; J.P. Depretto, "Les Communistes et les usines Renault (1920–1936)," master's thesis, Université Paris IV, 1974; and for A. Bagot, J. Girault, *Militants de Châtenay-Malabry entre les deux guerres* (Paris: CNRS/GRECO 55 "Travail et travailleurs en France au XIXe et XXe siècles," 1985), p. 12; J. Maitron, *Dictionnaire biographique du mouvement ouvrier français* (Paris, Éditions Ouvrières), vol. 18 (1982), vol. 34 (1989), vol. 36 (1990) adds only a little to our information.

24. Archives of the Préfecture de Police (APP),B a/1375, Renault mechanics' meeting at the Labor Exchange on 9 September 1917. At this meeting, a delegation from the Panhard works declared that they would refuse to adopt the standard agreement of the Renault factory.

25. AN F7 13366. A police report on a threatened strike in the Renault works, dated 20 September 1917, singles out "several worker delegates likely to become ringleaders:

Michelet, Giraud, Decouvrant, Gaudrillière, and Bagot, all of whom are worker-soldiers."

26. The agenda of this meeting is in APP B a/1386. Cf. G. Hatry, "Albert Thomas à Billancourt," *De Renault frères constructeurs d'automobiles à Renault Régie Nationale* (December 1973), pp. 30–36.

27. Louis Sellier was a post-office employee and a socialist organizer. In 1923 he became the Secretary General of the Communist Party. J. Maitron, *Dictionnaire, op. cit.,* vol. 15, p. 151.

28. AN F7 13367, agenda of the shop delegates' representatives meeting for the Department of the Seine, 3 January 1918.

29. *Ibid.*

30. APP B a/1375, meeting of armament industry shop delegates at Grange-aux-Belles, 3 February 1918.

31. APP 327 420 A, the Minister of Armaments to the prefect of police, note of 24 February 1918.

32. APP B a/1375, report on the situation in Boulogne-Billancourt and Issy-les-Moulineaux, 4 March 1918.

33. *Ibid.*

34. *Ibid.*

35. *Ibid.,* strike of navvies working for the Renault company, 11 March 1918.

36. *Ibid.,* threats of a strike at Renault, 17 March 1918.

37. AN F7 13367, note of 18 March 1918.

38. APP B a/1375, from remarks by Bagot at the Boulogne-Billancourt armament factories workers' meeting held on 20 March 1918 at the Mignon-Palace.

39. Born on 13 June 1883 in Oraison (Alpes-de-Provence) and conscripted into the third colonial artillery regiment in Toulon, he was assigned to the Renault works on 3 April 1916 as a fitter in shop 54. He left the works on 7 April 1919.

40. AN F7 13367, police report of 25 April 1918. Dubois, who had entered the factory on 2 April 1917 in the personnel department run by Muzet at the time, left the company on 8 March 1919. In so far as Médard is concerned, he joined on 23 May 1916 and quit at the same time as his chief.

41. *Ibid.,* note of 18 May 1918.

42. *Ibid.,* note of 31 July 1918.

43. *Ibid.*

44. *Ibid.,* note of 12 May 1918.

45. *Ibid.,* note of 13 May 1918.

46. *Ibid.*

47. J. Couergou, "Histoire d'un bagne," *Le Métallurgiste* (February–March 1927).

48. AN F7 13367, Statistics on the May strikes. The figure of 200,000 is taken from J. Couergou, *op. cit.* For the interpretation to give to the series of strikes in Paris in 1918, see above all J.L. Robert, *Ouvriers,* and J.J. Becker and S. Berstein, *Victoire et frustrations 1914–1929* (Paris: Le Seuil, 1990).

49. *Ibid.,* note of 14 May 1918.

50. *Ibid.,* note of 15 May 1918.

51. *Ibid.*

52. *Ibid.,* note of 16 May 1918. For the attitude adopted by the Federation, see as well the little-known memoirs of H. Dubreuil, *J'ai fini ma journée* (Paris: Librairie du Compagnonnage, 1971) and N. Papayanis, *Alphonse Merrheim* (The Hague: Nijhoff, 1985).

53. It occurred on 27 May.

54. AN F7 13367, agenda adopted by the assembly of worker delegates, 18 May 1918.

55. *Ibid.*, statistic on the mobilized workers recalled to military depots, May 1918.

56. *Ibid.*, list of mobilized workers turned over to military authorities, May 1918.

57. *Ibid.*, list of mobilized workers reassigned to industry after the strikes in the Paris region, May 1918.

58. *Ibid.*, letter from Heckenmeyer to Merrheim on 7 June 1918. This letter was seized by the police and never reached its destination.

59. *Ibid.*

60. *Ibid.*

61. *Ibid.*, note of 12 July 1918.

62. *Ibid.*, note of 31 July 1918.

63. *Ibid.*, meeting of Renault workers on 1 December 1918.

64. *Ibid.*

65. *Ibid.*, note of 12 December 1918.

66. *Ibid.*

67. *Ibid.*, letter sent by G. Roussel, of the Mechanics' Union, to Merrheim on 17 December 1918.

68. AN F7 13367, meeting of the Boulogne-Billancourt section of the Mechanics' Union on 25 March 1919, cited by Jean-Louis Robert, *op. cit.*

69. For a national survey of shop delegates' evolution, see John Horne, *Labour at War* (Oxford: Clarendon Press, 1991), pp. 14, 181, 183, 189–95, 206, 217, 280, 294, 380; and in addition, see Judith Eisenberg Vichniac, *The Management of Labor: The British and French Iron and Steel Industries, 1860–1918* (Greenwich, CT: JAI Press, 1990).

THE POLITICS OF
DAILY LIFE

9

The Comité d'Action (CGT-Parti Socialiste) and the Origins of Wartime Labor Reformism (1914-1916)

John Horne

The role of the First World War in renewing the revolutionary vitality of the French Labor movement is a familiar subject. Less well known until recently, but no less important in explaining the divisions and later the schisms which occurred in French socialism and trade union- ism (or syndicalism), is the role played by the war in remodelling and reinforcing reformist orientations.[1] Merely asking the question of how a "total" war encouraged labor movements to use existing economic rela- tionships and the institutions of the state in order to promote reforms is to open a very broad field of investigation. But by limiting the discus- sion to trade union (or syndicalist) leaders at the national level and to their attempts to come to terms with the war as an economic and social, rather than a military, phenomenon, it is possible to suggest the outline of an answer.

When, in late July–early August 1914, the majority of the leaders of the Socialist Party and the Confédération Générale du Travail (CGT) switched from opposing war to supporting the *Union sacrée*, they were responding to a state of emergency. Their behavior is explained above all by the priority given to national survival in the face of invasion, which took precedent over the normal concerns and perspectives of organized labor. But the national emergency did not stop labor leaders responding to the mobilization at a second, economic and social, level, particularly as it affected labor and the working class. A new, composite

Notes to Chapter 9 can be found on page 271.

organization was created in order to confront the emergency at this level – the Comité d'Action.

A Pragmatic and Defensive Reformism

The committee was the result of an initiative taken on 3 September 1914 by the Confederal Committee (or national executive) of the CGT. This resulted in a meeting on 6 September with various socialist organizations – the Commission Administrative Permanente (CAP), or national executive, of the Socialist Party, the parliamentary Socialist Group, and the socialist Fédération de la Seine (covering the Paris region). Perhaps at the outset there lingered a trace of fear at the possibility of punitive measures which, it was felt, the government might still decide to take against labor and anti-militarist activists.[2] But the main function of the Comité d'Action was to ensure the economic, rather than political, protection of workers and of the labor movement.

> The Commission (as it was initially known) has as its function to strengthen the links between activists and their organizations, and in that manner to let them be of maximum use in present circumstances and in aiding . . . the authorities in all the questions which concern the working class population (provisioning, unemployment, relief kitchens, military separation allowances, etc.) and in the national defense.[3]

The composition of the Comité d'Action was subsequently enlarged to include members of the Fédération Nationale des Coopératives de Consommation (FNCC), the national consumer cooperative organization, doctrinally aligned with socialism since 1912. It was thus constituted on a broad base with the deliberate intention of establishing a coalition of working class interests and organizations.[4] Day-to-day administration was in the hands of a secretary,[5] but the full committee met often, and in order to structure its activities, it soon set up subcommittees covering a whole range of objectives.[6]

The Comité d'Action responded to four types of upheaval caused by the onset of hostilities: physical and psychological difficulties experienced by individuals; the rapid increase in prices; the inadequacy of prevailing social welfare arrangements; and unemployment.

The disruption of communications between civilians and the front was a feature of the autumn of 1914. In the confusion born of mass military mobilization, invasion, and heavy, mobile fighting, the Comité d'Action (along with many other organizations) sought to provide information on soldiers who were presumed to be dead or prisoners of war. In late October, for example, the socialist leaders Pierre Renaudel and Jean Longuet went to the headquarters of the Red Cross in Geneva to this end.[7] The committee also sought to channel the aid sent by the labor movement to its mobilized members – an activity which it pursued throughout its existence. By November 1916, 3,425 parcels had been sent to prisoners of war, 3,870 to the trenches, along with the 250 cases of books and brochures and over 1.3 million copies of *La Bataille (syndicaliste)* and *l'Humanité,* the daily papers associated respectively with the CGT and the Socialist Party.[8] The committee equally responded to the influx of refugees in late 1914 (especially Belgians) by creating three shelters in the east of Paris.[9] All this reminds us that the labor movement participated in its own fashion in the more general feeling of national cohesion between civilians on the one hand and soldiers and civilian victims of the war on the other.

If the responsibility for the outbreak of war and disruption of individual lives was blamed essentially on causes outside France, this was not the case for other aspects of the initial chaos. Inflation and transport difficulties led the Comité d'Action to demand government controls over prices and provisioning. Marcel Sembat (moderate socialist and minister of Public Works) was applauded merely for having conserved slender stocks of sugar, and similar measures were demanded for wheat, meat, and coal.[10]

More serious still was the breach made by the war in social welfare arrangements, which were already fairly meager in prewar France. The Comité d'Action campaigned for more generous separation allowances for soldiers' wives, and also for their more liberal application (i.e., to the self-employed, small peasants, sharecroppers, and common-law wives). It also demanded major increases in central government subsidies to the unemployment relief funds administered by the communes.[11] Yet despite criticisms of the government, the committee was ready to envisage the problem of social protection in the spirit of civilian voluntaryism and national solidarity which characterized 1914. It publicly endorsed the Comité de Secours National – the principal national charitable organization dealing with the social emergency, in whose work labor militants enthusiastically participated (with more than a million "popular meals" supplied by the socialists and syndicalists of the Paris region alone in October 1914.)[12]

Perhaps the severest upheaval to which the civilian population was subjected in 1914 was the unprecedented level of unemployment, as investment and production plummeted with the military mobilization. In October 1914, unemployment averaged 35 percent and it was still 20 percent in January 1915.[13] The Comité d'Action called for increased levels of unemployment relief, while at the same time condemning the attempts by employers to use the huge, temporary surpluses of labor in order to reduce wages. This elicited the sharpest criticism yet heard from labor since the beginning of the war.

The question of unemployment was posed especially acutely in Paris by the slump in the building industry, and by the possibilities for relief presented by the construction of a vast fortified camp around the capital. General Gallieni, commander of Paris, envisaged a mass, improvised civilian mobilization for the defense of the city. With the government's withdrawal to Bordeaux, much of the middle class population of the city had melted away, leaving a more proletarian Paris which, to many, suggested a parallel with the siege of 1870. The heightened visibility of labor and the role of a well known socialist on Gallieni's staff, Paul-Boncour, as intermediary between the trade unions and the military government, resulted in the employment of 15,000 to 20,000 unionized building workers on the fortified camp. By this accord, signed by Hubert, the old revolutionary syndicalist leader of the building laborers, these latter were to be paid the union rate.[14] The Comité d'Action entirely approved this approach to the problem. But by the beginning of November, it was clear to its labor subcommittee (and especially to its chairman, Merrheim, the leader of the Fédération des Métaux, or Metal-workers' Federation) that private employers also working on the fortified camp were recruiting non-unionized labor at well below the union rate, by means of "strike-breaking agencies."[15] This flagrant violation of the spirit in which the camp was officially meant to be built (a continuation of the *Union sacrée*) was symptomatic of a much wider onslaught by employers against wage levels and conditions prevailing in the capital's building and engineering industries.

The Comité d'Action protested. Its labor subcommittee declared:

> [These abuses] prove that the immense sacrifices, moral and material, currently accepted by the proletariat, both in its homes and on the field of battle, neither touch nor move the great majority of the patronat (i.e., employers).[16]

But the committee also sought other solutions to the unemployment crisis. A consideration of these leads us to the national political options of the CGT, with which the Comité d'Action was closely associated. In late November 1914, the CGT asked the Government to establish a national system of temporary joint commissions (*commissions mixtes*), which would link syndicalist and employer representatives at the level of each *département*, under the presidency of government delegates, and allow them to explore ways of restimulating economic activity and encouraging an "industrial renaissance." Their brief was to extend as far as the economic preparation of a peace which was still assumed to be fairly imminent. In February 1915, Sembat created "Joint Commissions for the Revival of Work" (*commissions mixtes pour la reprise du travail*), which functioned in nearly every *département* until the end of the war.[17]

Thus, in the eyes of syndicalist leaders, the most effective means of solving unemployment was by creating bodies where organized labor could present its ideas on new projects for reactivating the economy – involving the use, naturally, of unionized labor at union rates. The Comité d'Action displayed the same faith in labor's capacity to administer and plan production by organizing its own workshops in Paris, contracting directly with the army – an example which was followed in the provinces.[18]

In the same vein, the CGT continued its campaign – begun before the war – for a system of labor placement exclusively organized by the state, and according a privileged role to trade unions. Syndicalist leaders (and especially those on the Joint Commission for the Revival of Work of the Seine, which created an extremely effective labor placement office for the Paris region) considered this development one means for regulating the labor supply in the face of the abnormally sharp fluctuations of the wartime labor market, and also as a means of strengthening more permanently, at a new level, the influence of trade unions over wages and conditions of work.[19]

In fact, the rapid growth of industrial production for the war in 1915 soon replaced the problem of unemployment with that of acute labor shortages. But the two principles formulated by the Comité d'Action and the Confederal Committee of the CGT in response to the initial economic chaos – that the wages and working conditions of skilled labor should not be adversely affected by the war and that the representatives of organized (which meant principally skilled) labor should be consulted on the adaptation of the economy to the constrains of wartime – were both to be applied to the host of problems raised by the industrial mobilization.

With the industrialization of the war, syndicalist leaders were no longer the passive witnesses of a process which had relegated them to the sidelines. On the contrary, they were the spokesmen for a group which had become vital for national success. Although the syndicalist movement had been decimated by the military mobilization, local bodies began to revive from 1915, while in 1917 numbers in many industrial federations and departmental organizations surged past prewar peaks. But the influence of syndicalist leaders is not to be measured only by size of membership. Wartime governments were acutely aware of the importance of morale and thus of the need continuously to mobilize political support for the organization and objectives of the national effort. This was nowhere truer than in the case of Albert Thomas, the moderate socialist deputy who was the virtual architect of the French munitions effort from September 1914 until his departure from government in September 1917.[20] Part of that process of trying to preserve a consensus on the war involved government consulting labor leaders, and listening to their criticisms, to an unprecedented degree.

Faced with the lengthening – indeed the virtual normalization – of the war, of which the industrial effort was one of the major signs, and faced, too, with the ramifying problems which the industrial effort entailed, the Comité d'Action no longer had quite the importance which it had known as the coordinator of an emergency labor response at the beginning of the conflict. The return of official political activity to Paris in December 1914 breathed life into the central organizations of the syndicalist and socialist movements, notably the parliamentary Socialist Group. The industrial problems which appeared in 1915-16 due to the munitions effort and strain which it imposed on manpower resources (withdrawal of skilled workers from the trenches, modification and deskilling of the labor process, introduction of compulsory arbitration in war industries in January 1917, etc.) directly concerned various bodies within the CGT (notably the Confederal Committee and the Fédération des Métaux). Nonetheless, the Comité d'Action confronted a number of the fundamental problems raised by the economic mobilization and, through them, reflected on the war itself and its longer-term consequences. It remained an important organization, working in close and sometimes conflictual contact with more established labor and socialist bodies, and as such it contributed to the orientation of the *majoritaires* (the majority) within the CGT, who remained committed to the war effort until the end.

The Comité d'Action was concerned above all in 1915–16 with the cost of living. The explosion of prices (from July 1914 to October 1916, 38 percent in Paris and 46 percent in provincial towns, according to official figures) was compounded by wartime restrictions on normal syndicalist activity to raise wages. Mobilized workers in mines and munitions factories remained subject to military discipline, even though they earned civilian rates of pay, and from January 1917 strikes were illegal for all workers in the defense industries. This placed a particular, and unaccustomed, onus on labor organizations to protect workers and the working class family *as consumers*.[21] The Comité d'Action revived the demand already outlined in the autumn of 1914 that the state should control stocks and fix prices for vital necessities. In October 1915, in response to a working class sense of crisis over the soaring cost of living, the committee requested its relevant subcommittee to draw up a series of reports on provisioning problems – especially concerning meat, coal, sugar, milk, and cereal production.[22]

Two fundamental principles were defined. The first was that the government should actively seek to increase supplies, whether by imports or by raising national production. Various means for achieving this were proposed. The cost of living subcommittee insisted that frozen meat (until the war, practically unknown in France) should be imported on a huge scale and distributed through local government and the cooperative movement. Daudé-Bancel, of the FNCC, was "given the task of demonstrating to the working class how to prepare this produce,"[23] and the Comité d'Action, along with labor papers like *La Bataille*, mounted a veritable propaganda campaign to convince skeptical working class consumers of the virtues of frozen meat. The committee also contributed to the national debate on how best to raise cereal production. In December 1915, it sent a joint delegation, together with the parliamentary Socialist Group, to pressure Méline, minister of Agriculture, into making the cultivation of abandoned farmland compulsory, suggesting that this might best be achieved under the aegis of joint commissions for every commune, in which agricultural laborers would participate.[24]

The Comité d'Action took it for granted, however, that whatever measures might be employed by the government to increase stocks, the gulf between supply and demand was bound to widen (given shortages of agricultural labor, import restrictions, the deterioration of equipment, etc.). This development necessarily encouraged speculation, and like a good deal of public opinion, the committee held the greed of middlemen and small-traders in large part responsible for the rise in prices. Consequently, the second principle adopted by the committee was that market forces must be subject to strict price controls (*taxation*) and to their necessary corollary, the power to requisition stocks from producers and suppliers who refused to sell at the established price.

In this, the Comité d'Action was simply articulating the labor version of a demand common to the broader French left during the war. Thus, it endorsed the law of 16 October 1915 which authorized the requisitioning of wheat and flour for civilian use. It also actively supported the bill of Malvy, minister for the Interior, which provided for drastic price controls of vital necessities. When the bill emerged emasculated from a long battle with the *laissez-faire* Senate (20 April 1916), the committee protested vehemently to the government.[25]

In the same way, the Comité d'Action raised its voice in the acrimonious debate over coal. Coal prices rose above average inflation, reaching dramatically high levels in working class centers such as Roanne.[26] There were several reasons for this. The German occupation of the north-east and the initial mobilization of miners to combat service contributed to the sharp fall in an already inadequate production. France depended on Britain for the balance. Shortages became acute from the second winter of the war, producing municipal price controls in Paris and elsewhere by 1916. Dearth was aggravated by the fact that domestic coal was sold more cheaply than imported British coal, but tended to be monopolized by big industrial enterprises, leaving the already hard-pressed domestic consumer to pay the higher import price.

In response to this price differential, the Mines Commission of the Chamber of Deputies proposed at the end of 1915 that prices should be fixed by the government at two levels, with the domestic consumer paying the lower price.[27] The Comité d'Action accepted this proposal and accompanied it with a substantial report drafted by Luquet, a leading syndicalist and Parisian socialist. The committee was thus understandably furious when once again the Senate emptied the Chamber of Deputies' bill of all substance.[28] The committee also turned its hostility onto Sembat, as the minister responsible, and his principal aide, Léon Blum, both of whom opposed the double price solution. When they appeared before the Comité d'Action in August 1916 in order to defend a government policy premissed on getting the British to reduce their coal prices, they found themselves unable to convince their audience. Jouhaux, general secretary of the CGT and a key figure in the Comité d'Action, replied:

> I know that the question is rather difficult to resolve, but I also know that the working class population, which has made so many sacrifices, is beginning to grumble about the excessive increase in coal prices.[29]

The Committee continued to demand the generalized application of price controls and requisitioning, as shortages and price increases produced a deeper sense of crisis at the end of 1916 and beginning of 1917 (with the cumulative effect of declining domestic production and the impact of unrestricted German submarine warfare). It continued to advocate the raising of national levels of production – notably through the return of skilled workers to the mines and railways. It brandished the specter of violent popular protest movements if the government failed to follow its advice.[30] And it is no accident that it should have been during this third, and very severe, winter of the war that the *majoritaires* of the CGT began calling for a complete reorganization of the mining industry and the railways, extending as far as their nationalization.[31]

Gradually, and with a good deal of hesitation, the government took some steps in the direction urged by the labor movement. Fifty thousand miners were withdrawn from active service in 1917, while little by little general powers of price controls and requisitioning were introduced, eventually to be codified in the law of 10 February 1918. Economic necessity pushed the authorities down this path. But the Comité d'Action and the socialist deputies, jointly the source of the most radical proposals, played a role in this process, which was by no means an automatic one.

The protection of working class consumers was only one of the wartime domains in which the Comité d'Action proposed solutions. No less important were the changes in the composition of the labor force, which had substantial longer-term consequences for the labor movement. Here, the committee served as one of the instruments used by the CGT in order to counteract the potential threat to the position of French male workers which came from women and foreigners.

It was widely held by the leadership of the CGT that the incursion of women into areas of traditional male employment was, on the whole, temporary and reversible with the return of peace (though ensuring this posed many problems).[32] The question of immigrants during, and above all, after the war was a more difficult matter. Nearly half a million foreigners worked in France before 1914 (18 percent of the metal working and 11 percent of the building labor force). Not all left in 1914. But more importantly, new immigrants arrived from three sources. Firstly, substantial numbers of Belgian refugees entered the industrial work force (many coming from industrial regions in their native country). Secondly, large numbers of Spanish, constituting for the first time the biggest single ethnic category, flooded over the Pyrenees from their neutral homeland to work in French industry and agriculture. Finally, from 1915 the government systematically recruited foreigners – from European countries such as Italy and Greece, and (again for the first time on a significant scale) from the French colonies, especially North Africa and Indo-China, as well as from China. In all, well over 600,000 immigrants came to France during the war. In the

light of French war losses and traditional labor shortages, it was clear
that immigration would be a permanent feature of the postwar economic and social landscape.[33]

The CGT accepted this reality, but continued nonetheless to criticize
and pressure the government over the way in which immigrant labor
was used. There was real anxiety, especially in the Fédération des
Métaux, that immigrants would take work away from French males and
allow them to be "combed-out" for the front.[34] Foreign labor also
embodied the threat to skill within the changed wartime labor process
in the engineering industry – hence the emphasis placed by the CGT
on a munitions effort based on the recognition of the vital role of the
skilled worker. *Majoritaire* leaders kept close watch over the introduction of foreign labor and obtained assurances that this would never be
used directly to replace French skilled labor.[35] Labor leaders also tried to
gain some degree of control over the whole process, so that foreign
workers might be economically integrated into the national labor force
without threat to their own members. At the beginning of 1916,
Jouhaux sketched out a plan for the international regulation of migrant
labor flows by means of a strict system of contracts between states, in
the administration of which syndicalists were to play a major part. This
system was designed to restrict immigration to levels which the labor
market seemed to warrant, and also to guarantee equality of treatment
for immigrants with nationals for their mutual protection – including
the right to trade union membership.[36]

The Comité d'Action debated this question many times during
1916. Jouhaux felt it was essential to influence government plans
(notably Albert Thomas's direct negotiations with the Italian government) in order to avoid the menace of permanent and unprecedented
importation of cheap foreign labor by the government itself.

> Of all the questions [facing us] it is incontestably the one which concerns
> the labor movement the most . . . [If] we are unable to insist on, and obtain,
> serious guarantees on the conditions of importation of quantities of workers
> of a culture different from our own, the interests of French workers will be
> sacrificed and exploitation by big business (*haut patronat*) will be made all
> the easier.[37]

Jouhaux did not succeed in utilizing the Comité d'Action to coordinate his approach to immigrant labor with that of the socialist deputies.
Nonetheless, government ministers feared widespread rejection of foreign labor by the French working class and were open to the arguments
and pressure of the labor movement.[38] Jouhaux participated in the

establishment of a national commission to examine this question along with others touching on the manpower crisis, and at least some of his ideas influenced government policy.[39]

The male skilled worker was not only threatened by female and foreign labor. The changes in the engineering production process to which we have alluded – and which centrally involved the "dilution" of skilled jobs, mechanization, "scientific management" (or taylorism), and payment by piece rates rather than time rates – threatened his status. So, too, did the accompanying reduction in wage differentials from the semi-skilled and unskilled. And the abrogation of prewar limits on the working day was a burden oppressing all workers during the war. The Comité d'Action acted as a labor pressure group on all these issues (indeed the notorious observation by Millerand, as minister for War early in 1915, that "there are no longer any social laws, national defense takes precedent over everything," was in reality his reply to a delegation from the Comité d'Action which had tried to get one Sunday in two made a day of rest).[40]

Later in the war, the CGT *majoritaires* as well as the minority trade union opposition approved the emergence of shop stewards (*délégués d' atelier*) in order to exercise local control over these questions.[41]But this was foreshadowed in 1915 by an experiment in which the Comité d'Action took part. The process by which vital mobilized workers had been withdrawn from the front for the unanticipated industrial effort in 1914–15 was chaotic. Many of those withdrawn were not genuine skilled workers, and some were not workers at all, resulting in a popular hostility to the *embusqués* (shirkers) which threatened to taint the entire munitions labor force. The Dalbiez law of 1915 sought to restore order and justice to this process, and established regional joint commissions to vet all munitions workers. Once again, the Comité d'Action served as a pressure group whereby CGT leaders, especially Merrheim and Jouhaux, pressed for the commissions to have trade union delegates and real powers in order to assure *bona fide* skilled workers their central place in war production. The Comité d'Action therefore protested when these aims (despite the inclusion of syndicalists) were flouted, especially in the Paris region. This was largely because Albert Thomas and his staff, though sympathetic to the CGT on many issues, were anxious to retain their entire labor force, whatever its provenance, in the interests of maximizing production, and thus did their best to ignore the Dalbiez law.[42] At the beginning of 1916, the syndicalist delegates on the joint commission for the Seine resigned in protest at their own impotence, thus fuelling the emergence of tighter forms of worker influence at the shopfloor level. Merrheim summed up this process in the Comité d'Action's debate on the Dalbiez law on 30 November 1915:

> The militants [of the Vincennes cartridge factory], fearing that the call-up of the younger military service classes would be used to take away their strongest elements, the good producers, leaving behind only the shirkers (*les protégés*), have decided themselves to demand what the Fédération des Métaux has already asked for, a workshop commission.[43]

So far, we have seen the Comité d'Action (closely linked to the national leadership of the CGT) responding to the war by means of a reformism which was essentially pragmatic and defensive. Labor leaders, in cooperation with socialist parliamentary deputies, pressured politicians and civil servants by criticizing government policy and advancing counterprojects for a variety of problems. This was done first and foremost to defend workers as wage earners (especially the skilled) and to protect the working class consumer. But the full significance of the economic and social questions raised by the industrialization of the war went beyond the war itself. Concretely, labor leaders began to take into account the eventual problems of demobilization and the reconversion to a peacetime economy. Symbolically, this transition raised a more fundamental question still, namely whether the changes wrought by the war would permanently alter the postwar world, including labor and the labor movement. In order to establish some intellectual hold on a war which had turned into a semipermanent state, people in many walks of society sought to interpret the longer-term future by the light of the unfamiliar present. Numerous plans, predictions, and projects appeared in diverse sectors of French opinion. In the case of the Comité d'Action, they became its major preoccupation.[44] Labor leaders used the committee as one of their principal means (though not the only one) for exploring the long-term effects of the war.

A Coherent and Combative Reformism

The reconstruction of the north-east of France, devastated in 1914, and much of it occupied or fought over for the remainder of the war, was the bridgehead of the Comité d'Action's postwar projects. It was a problem which threatened to assume major proportions following the war, but most of the debate (which was lively, in parliament and elsewhere) turned on the rights and obligations of private property. Should the state indemnify war destruction? Were those indemnified under any obligation in the use of what amounted to reconstruction capital?

Government policy during the war did little to go beyond such issues and plan the content and administration of reconstruction.[45]

The Comité d'Action, by contrast, took a much broader view. From the outset, it saw the reconstruction of the devastated zones as the microcosm of changes which it hoped would become the permanent legacy of the war to society and the economy at large. In June 1915, the eighth commission, created especially for this purpose, provided an exhaustive report on "the reconstruction of the destroyed towns," which subordinated the question of indemnities to that of the social responsibility of the state to the region as a whole.[46] The report urged the government to turn wartime destruction to good account by eliminating the worst social scourges in what had been one of the country's most highly industrialized regions before the war, by reforming housing, town planning, and public health. But the goal was not simply greater social justice. The reconstruction of the north-east was also seen as one of the means of resolving the problem of reconversion to a peacetime economy. It was hoped that it would restimulate economic activity in the postwar period while at the same time encouraging the modernization of French industrial production.

> It is not enough purely and simply to repair the damage caused by acts of war. . . . We must use the great destruction of a large number of towns and villages in order to reconstruct these urban areas in conformity with new needs, and according to modern standards of street planning, hygiene, and aesthetics. . . . Our generation would never by forgiven if . . . it did not raise up healthier, finer, and gayer towns. . . . [This reconstruction] would soon draw the entire country in its wake . . . toward a new and intensive development of our national prosperity, toward new economic progress, in turn engendering political and social progress.[47]

It was to be the responsibility of new regional and local organizations – joint commissions on a grand scale – to represent the principal elements of the economy, including labor, in planning this reconstruction. Trade unions were to play a major role – with an unfettered right for workers to join unions, the compulsory recognition of unions by industrialists, and a union monopoly on the supply of labor which would give them a powerful hold over wages.

The Comité d'Action vigorously defended these ideas. Jouhaux and Picart (secretary of the architectural draftsmen's union within the federation of building workers, and one of the moving spirits of the CGT majority) outlined them before the war damages commission of the Chamber of Deputies in March 1916, to some effect. A report in 1921, however, by the Conseil économique du travail (a kind of successor body to the Comité d'Action) showed that the actual process of reconstructing the north-east of France from 1919 took little account of the Comité d'Action's original proposals.[48]

In 1916, however, the Comité d'Action's interest in postwar reform spread well beyond the question of the "devastated regions." The committee sought nothing less than the elaboration of a program which would introduce some doctrinal coherence and future perspectives into organized labor's response to the war as a whole and into the specific demands which it had already put forward. According to the second annual report, this was the "most important question of all those which have come to our attention as a consequence of the war."[49]

In January 1916 the committee discussed "the question of the organization of labor following the war and of the means which should be envisaged as of now for intensifying industrial production and the commercial development of the country."[50] The syndicalists dominated the debates on the different questions involved – the distribution of labor, the reorganization of industrial production, and (articulated by Merrheim) the potential threat from cheap female labor during the demobilization. It was decided to sketch the broad outlines of a general plan of postwar reforms.[51] In mid-April, the committee created a special subcommittee on the "economic reorganization" of postwar France, charged with providing an "overview" for the benefit of the parent body.[52]

At this point the evolution of the committee's plan becomes inseparably bound up with the relationship between the CGT and the Socialist Party. The initial collaboration of socialists and syndicalists in the Comité d'Action was a novel departure in a country where party and trade unions were organizationally independent of each other. Revolutionary syndicalism, the libertarian-inspired creed still formally predominant in the CGT, expressed a deep sense of working class autonomy and an often overt hostility to parliament and politics. The Guesdist (marxist) current of French socialism, on the other hand, sought to subordinate unions to party, an approach which, outside the Guesdist heartland in the north-east, provoked union resentment and fed the anti-political bias within the CGT. Some socialist tendencies were more sympathetic to the decentralized, *ouvriériste* traditions of the CGT, notably the Allemanist and Blanquist currents (the latter exemplified by its veteran leader, Edouard Vaillant), which were both particularly well represented in the capital. Nonetheless, the distinction between a trade unionism embodying the economic defense and particular culture of the (mainly skilled) worker, and a socialism which, while encompassing working class politics, claimed a larger role as the advance guard of the Republican tradition or (in the Guesdist case) as the harbinger of a revolutionary state, remained a fundamental one. This made the Comité d'Action all the more remarkable as an experiment in institutional cooperation.[53]

Throughout 1915 and 1916, however, the Comité d'Action became disproportionately important to the CGT. For numerous socialists, and especially for the socialist deputies, the reopening of parliament offered an alternative and more familiar means of making their views known. The committee in 1916 was increasingly dominated by syndicalist delegates. These last furnished half the active members of the committee in 1916 (ten, compared to eight socialists and two from the FNCC).[54] They were also particularly important in developing postwar reform plans. In the course of the April 1916 reorganization, they supplied secretaries for six of the ten subcommittees (Doumenq for family allowances; Luquet for rents; Merrheim for war work; Dumas, in charge of the committee's own workshops; Jouhaux for work and wages; and Chanvin for the reconstruction of the towns of the northeast). The other secretaries were Poisson of the FNCC for parcels sent to soldiers, Lévy and Braemer, delegates of the Socialist Party executive, who were charged respectively with the cost of living and refugees, and Dejeante, socialist deputy, responsible for relations with the Chamber. CGT delegates also furnished five of the seven members of the important new subcommittee on economic reorganization (Jouhaux, Luquet, Merrheim, Bled, and Chanvin, the others being Lévy and the deputy Comprè-Morel).

Under closer scrutiny, it becomes apparent that one of the key elements of the Comité d'Action consisted of figures who were simultaneously active in the Socialist Party and the trade unions within the world of the Parisian labor movement, or who, as socialists from the Allemanist or Blanquist traditions, were particularly sympathetic to the CGT. Into this category came Alexandre Luquet, secretary of the hairdressers' federation and since 1896 an active socialist (originally Guesdist); Gaston Lévy, of the bank employees and secretary of the socialist federation of the Seine; Pierre Dumas, secretary of the clothing workers' federation, close confidant of the ageing Vaillant (himself a stalwart supporter of the work of the committee), and his eventual successor as a parliamentary deputy for Paris; L. Dubreuilh, Blanquist socialist and secretary of the committee; H. Prêté, secretary to Vaillant; and the socialist deputy Dejeante, a former hat worker and Allemanist.

In fact, as L.-L. Robert has shown, the Blanquist organization of the twentieth section of the socialist federation of the Seine (which covered the working class twentieth *arrondissement* in eastern Paris – Vaillant's constituency – and saw itself as a socialist *avant-garde*) was the heartland of this particular component of the Comité d'Action.[55]But if one influence within the Comité d'Action thus came from those whose prewar past predisposed them to pursue that closer socialist-syndicalist cooperation which Jaurès had urged, and who saw in the war an unprecedented chance to achieve it, the other came from syndicalist leaders who before the war had been among the most convinced upholders of syndicalist principles and the autonomy of the CGT – such as Jouhaux, Merrheim, Picart, Chanvin, and Bled – who now found themselves pushed inexorably by wartime events down the path of cooperation with socialists.

The problem, for either current, was in any case the same: how to reinforce cooperation with the parliamentary Groupe Socialiste as a whole. The benefits of such collaboration were by no means clear to many socialist deputies, whereas they were self-evident to *majoritaire* syndicalist leaders, seeking a parliamentary voice by proxy.[56] From October 1915, the whole group of socialist deputies sitting on the Comité d'Action had been attacked vehemently for their lack of interest and assiduousness in attending the committee. In spring 1916, just as the committee was focusing on the issue of postwar reform, the deterioration of its relations with the Groupe Socialiste provoked a crisies. During a meeting on 13 May, it was agreed that the socialist deputies should be invited to work together with the Comité d'Action on this question.[57] Those socialists on the committee who most ardently advocated socialist-CGT collaboration found themselves in the acutely embarrassing position of simultaneously condemning – and trying to excuse – their parliamentary colleagues for not being more enthusiastic about converting the socialist-syndicalist cooperation temporarily achieved at the beginning of the war into something more permanent. Dubreuilh recognized that "it is currently the CGT delegates who are shouldering the bulk of the work on the Comité d'Action, and he conveyed the committee's complaints to the CAP and to the socialist deputies.

As a result of this crisis, the Groupe Socialiste and the Comité d'Action for a time coordinated their efforts rather better on a number of issues, and especially on postwar reform (which the deputies had independently begun to look at). A Joint Commission on Economic Questions (*Commission mixte d' études économiques*) was established on 20 May 1916, made up of the secretaries of the Comité d'Action's subcommittees and of the Groupe Socialiste's own committee on postwar reforms.[58] Several leading socialists (notably Compère-Morel and Renaudel) endorsed Jouhaux's view that the Comité d'Action should transform itself into a coordinating committee for all the fundamental policy questions which confronted the labor and socialist movements, and that it should also provide a conduit for the CGT to inform and influence the socialist deputies.[59] Jouhaux himself summoned a joint meeting of the Comité d'Action and *all* the socialist deputies in early June in order to explain this idea. He urged those present to bury their discord and establish new means of cooperation so as to turn the problems with which the war had faced workers into the basis of a mass working class movement in favor of reforms. Such a movement, he argued, would accumulate the power to produce fundamental social transformations:

> If we wish to emerge from the state of disorganization in which we currently find ourselves, to succeed in turning ourselves into a veritable proletarian force, we can only do so by creating serious links between the diverse organizations which group workers. We shall constantly meet problems which we are going to have to solve in two ways: alongside the affirmation of socialism which envisages a radical transformation of society, we must look for the formula which is applicable within the framework of existing society. Ideal solutions, practical and immediate solutions – that is the dual concern which should stir us. [60]

What Jouhaux sought to formulate was a definition of reformism. He clearly distinguished between minimum and maximum objectives. He hoped that the hitherto fragmentary efforts of the CGT (and the Comité d'Action) to respond in a pragmatic way to the problems and possibilities of the war period might generate a more fundamental reorientation, with substantial doctrinal changes, of both the form and content of labor action. At the same time, war reformism was to bridge the gulf between the political and industrial wings of labor – a gulf only slightly diminished by prewar cooperation in campaigns against war.

The actual work of the Joint Commission on Economic Questions did not produce this result – at least not in the form envisaged. It is difficult to establish precisely the balance of forces within the Joint Commission, but it seems clear that the Comité d'Action was the stronger of the two elements. The socialist deputies' committee on postwar reforms (established on the initiative of Bédouce and Bretin) had drafted a list of questions before the founding of the Joint Commission, but all the evidence suggests that the Comité d'Action's draft plan formed the basis of the joint discussions. A subsequent project of postwar reform presented by the socialist deputies in April 1917 turned out to be narrow in scope (centering on fiscal reform and on the use of munitions factories in the reconversion to a peacetime economy). The sweeping and influential program of postwar reform which the Joint Committee published in November 1916 was considered by Lévy to reflect faithfully the concerns of the Comité d'Action.[61]

This is not to deny that strong socialist interest in postwar reform existed. But it was strongest in precisely those currents most open to syndicalist cooperation and therefore predisposed to work through the Comité d'Action. Many of the ideas in the November program had been anticipated in debates within the Paris labor movement. [62] Lévy and Poisson (secretary general of the FNCC and a leading Parisian socialist) had published an article in April 1916 which anticipated some of the key themes of the November program.[63] At the end of the year the ninth section of the socialist Fédération de la Seine adopted a sweeping program of reforms, including the "mobilization" of capital, the requisitioning of war factories, solutions to the "problems" of foreign and female labor, the "socialization" of production, and cooperation with the CGT in the "economic reorganization" of France.[64] In December, the congress of the Fédération de la Seine passed a resolution, signed by Poisson, Renaudel, Henri Sellier (a key figure in reformist socialist circles in the capital and later minister of Health in the 1936 Popular Front government), and Dubreuil and Prêté (both secretaries of the Comité d'Action), which demanded a range of health and welfare measures which would "realize in peacetime the principles of social solidarity which have governed the action of the working class during the war."[65]

Yet nationally, the postwar plan emerging from the Joint Commission on Economic Questions in November 1916 received a far better reception in the CGT, where it inspired the program which the *majoritaire* leaders presented to the confederation's December 1916 conference, than it did in the Socialist Party. The corresponding socialist congress in December 1916 considered it only superficially.[66] It was the CGT which continued to campaign on postwar reform in 1917–18. Syndicalist leaders did not reject the principle of joint action with the Socialist Party, but they gave up hope of any immediate and dramatic advances on that front. As Jouhaux explained to the Confederal Committee of the CGT in January 1917, the provisioning crisis and the upsurge of industrial unrest gave new relevance and urgency to criticisms of the organization of the war effort and to labor proposals for reform. But in the absence of serious collaboration with the socialist deputies, he proposed that an exclusively syndicalist basis should be found for labor campaigns on these questions.[67] By virtue of its close identification with the CGT, the Comité d'Action's *raison d'être* was undermined, and it became moribund, while the Joint Commission on Economic Questions, marginalized by the lack of interest shown by socialist deputies, led a reduced and spasmodic existence until the end of the war.[68]

The report presented by the Joint Commission on Economic Questions in November 1916 thus represents the culminating point of the Comité d'Action's attempt to examine the effects of the war on French society and to provide a framework for far-reaching postwar reform. It incorporated numerous proposals already made to resolve specifically wartime problems. It drew on the debates in Paris labor and socialist circles on reform issues. It also echoed Jouhaux's reformist formula by identifying an ultimate ideal and suggesting immediately applicable reforms by which the ideal might be progressively attained. The "ideal solution" was the eventual, vague collectivization of the economy and harmonization of economic activity at both national and international levels:

> The disorder caused by the permanent conflict of private interests . . . will persist, inspite of all attempts made at organization for the benefit of particular classes or nations, so long as the working class has not succeeded in making social harmony prevail through the socialization of the means of production and exchange, and through international understanding between workers.[69]

The "practical and immediate" solution rested on two key images or concepts. The first was the vision of a more modern and efficient French industry within the framework of an essentially capitalist economy. Here the experience of the industrial mobilization was central. It wrought significant changes in the organization (and even more in the rhetoric) of production. The mechanization of the metallurgical industry, the installation of more integrated assembly processes, and the application of "taylorism" were themes debated by labor organizations before the war; but the war unquestionably intensified their development and widened awareness of the shift from artisan to mass production. Syndicalist leaders were not necessarily opposed to mechanization nor to more integrated production – only to the ways in which these were commonly implemented. Men like Jouhaux and Merrheim considered such changes an integral part of industrial development. They felt that the war might well stimulate innovation and shake the self-centeredness and inertia allegedly characteristic of French industrialists – who were regularly accused by labor leaders of being technologically conservative and economic "malthusians," shunning the challenge of growth.[70]The industrial mobilization also witnessed unprecedented state intervention in supplying the factors of production and setting output targets. This created the impression in syndicalist circles that capitalism – readily identified as a system with its prewar, essentially *laissez-faire*, variant – now stood accused of incompetence and was ripe for fundamental change. At the very least, a measure of planning and coordination seemed indispensable for future economic growth.

It was only a small step for syndicalist leaders to suggest that if French industry could be mobilized for war it could also be mobilized for peace – and especially for the benefit of the working class, deemed to have superior claims on the nation to any other social group. Here moral claims and political optimism coincided. In particular, the report envisaged increased real wages and the implementation of social reforms as a means of structurally transforming and expanding demand, which would in turn galvanize the productive capacities of the nation – as the plan for reconstructing the north-east had suggested. These different elements combined in the vision of a major "economic" or "industrial reorganization" (the term varied) of post-war France:

> Immediate economic reorganization should have as its basis the uninterrupted development of national and industrial manufacturing equipment and the unlimited spread of general and technical teaching; and its aim should be to allow the employment of all talents, to pursue the utilization of all material resources and the application of all inventions and discoveries, to stimulate private initiatives by removing all the excuses and inertia of a deadly, sterile routine, and to prevent all voluntary restriction of production and all overworking of the producers, which are harmful to production itself.
>
> The working class must direct the national effort in this direction.[71]

The way in which the working class was to do this turned on a second key image – that of the progressive involvement in the economy of a powerful labor movement. Here, the syndicalist (and even Proudhonist) inspiration of the Joint Commission's report is manifest. The characteristic desire to develop labor participation (joint commissions, labor delegates, etc.) extended to an outline for a decentralized economy, much of it in public ownership, which would place a great deal of power in syndicalist hands. The state would have the right to intervene in the economy in two ways: firstly, by imposing social legislation and also a basic planning framework ("of a transitory nature . . . simply in the existing social framework"); and secondly, by enlarging collective ownership through the extension of public control over certain sectors (essential services, the production of goods vital for the national economy, and all cases where economic concentration had created private monopolies). But these two types of intervention were intended much more to restore power to the principal elements of the economy than to develop "bureaucratic" management by the state itself. Workers' and consumers' delegates were to exercise substantial control over the economy as a whole by instituting a form of economic planning. Enterprises in the nationalized sectors were to be characterized by "autonomous management" – a rather ill-defined concept covering a range of possibilities, from cooperatives, or departmentally or municipally run companies, to entirely new public organisms. Representatives of workers and consumers would take their place on the boards of management along with direct delegates of the state or local government. Few details were supplied by the report on how such public enterprises would actually operate, but it was clearly intended that with this approach, and under the leadership of a powerful labor movement, the economy, society, and the state itself would be progressively transformed.

The report concluded with a list of specific reforms, most of which had been developed by the Comité d'Action and the CGT during the two previous years – the regulation of immigration, public works programs to absorb unemployment on demobilization, a jointly administered system of labor exchanges, and international coordination of labor and social reforms.

The plan elaborated by the Comité d'Action and the Joint Commission at the end of 1916 was less a program of reforms than a reformist program, which sought to instill some doctrinal coherence into the experience of war and the multitude of questions which had been the object of specific labor criticisms and campaigns since the autumn of 1914. Herein lies the full significance of the Comité d'Action. It constituted a central element in the gradual emergence of a distinctive war reformism, identified principally (at the national level) with the *majoritaires* of the CGT. It should be stressed that there were other elements of organized labor involved in this reformism, the full analysis of which is beyond the scope of this article. Nonetheless, the Comité d'Action's role was such that it provides insights into the nature of the phenomenon as a whole.

A Permanent Breach

The outbreak of war was experienced by French labor leaders as a rupture. This caesura operated at several levels. The military mobilization decimated both the CGT and the Socialist Party; it also dislocated the economy, adding to the chaos occasioned by the German invasion. The Comité d'Action was established by syndicalist and socialist leaders in self-defense against these two aspects of the disorder brought by the onset of war. But the sense of rupture with the past also showed itself at another level. The mental universe of many socialists and syndicalists faced sudden and acute change. Admittedly, this universe had been under tension before the war, with such apparent verities as working class internationalism or anti-militarism in reality clouded by compromise and contradiction. The circumstances of August 1914, moreover, with Germany blamed for invading France and German socialism accused of collaboration in national aggression, activated the patriotism which had long been part of the left-wing tradition in France.[72] Nonetheless, palpable socialist and syndicalist belief in working class internationalism and opposition to the *bourgeois* state were profoundly shaken by the war, while new problems surfaced which needed considered responses.

For this reason, the Comité d'Action assumed an ideological significance almost from its inception. The reaction of the CGT leadership to the massive unemployment in autumn 1914 resulted in the idea of an "industrial renaissance" which was to open the way to postwar economic development and to provide a central role for trade unions in economic planning (of which the joint departmental commissions were seen as harbingers). But all this was in expectation of an early peace. As the short war evaporated, to be replaced by a grim test of endurance in which the mobilization of the national economy for defense production became vital, fundamental economic and social relationships were progressively affected by the conflict. The Comité d'Action sought explicitly to give sense and shape to these changes by relating them to the postwar world and to the long-term goals of the labor movement. The rupture and abnormality of war were by this means reintegrated into new definitions of normality and continuity.

Inevitably, reconstructing this "continuity" and "normality" involved new orientations. The 1914–16 period marked a decisive step in the evolution of the CGT. The ideas contained in the November 1916 reform program of the Joint Commission and the Comité d'Action were not in themselves necessarily new. The discussion of "joint commissions" was commonplace in reformist syndicalist circles before the war, and even in certain officially "revolutionary" syndicalist organizations such as the foodworkers' federation, which had campaigned vigorously for a jointly administered labor placement system in order to eliminate the worst exploitation of temporary bakery workers.[73] The idea of a decentralized form of nationalization, administered by representative economic groups, as an alternative to state-administered, bureaucratic public ownership, had appeared in the reformist program of the Broussists in the 1880s as well as in the economic thinking of Jaurès in the early 1900s.[74] It resurfaced in reformist socialist and syndicalist circles in the years just before the war. Albert Thomas and the academic and socialist theoretician, Edgar Milhaud, saw the decentralized model of nationalization (administered by representatives of the workers and even the consumers, as well as of the state) as a strategy for progressively installing a socialist economy without recourse to violent revolution or a dictatorship of the proletariat.[75] Their ideas won a ready response in reformist unions which historically relied on state regulation of their industries and thus had close links with socialist deputies – notably the miners and railwaymen.[76] More generally, the idea of "economic federalism" which underpinned the 1916 program was part of a continuous tradition of French labor since Proudhon, which had witnessed a remarkable revival before the war. Parisian socialists and cooperative theorists as well as intellectuals seeking to reformulate revolutionary syndicalism as a more gradualist doctrine, and one less reliant on the chiliastic image of the revolutionary general strike (notably Hubert Lagardelle and a young magistrate and sociologist, Maxime Leroy), had all adumbrated ideas which moved center stage during the war.[77] Finally, even leaders of the dominant revolutionary syndicalist current of the prewar CGT, such as Jouhaux and Merrheim, were seeking a more pragmatic syndicalist approach which would take the confederation out of the impasse into which falling membership, a declining strike success rate, and confrontational industrial tactics had seemingly led it.[78]

It was the experience of war, however, which infused these ideas with a new sense if relevance, and even urgency, and combined them in a single program. War powerfully underwrote the idea of joint commissions and the demand that the state, endowed with a vastly expanded economic role, should be obliged to consult labor organizations. War generated a host of specific problems to which the idea of labor participation in running the economy might be applied – the composition of the labor market, changing processes of production, the physical reconstruction of the north-east, etc. The industrial mobilization engendered hopes of a permanent change in the organization of the economy and of accelerated expansion in peacetime, of which the working class would be the principal beneficiary. And the war seemed to provide a perfect demonstration of the labor and socialist case for the nationalization of coal and the railways, and hence of the possibilities of a gradualist path to the collectivization of the economy. This all amounted to a novel and powerful reformulation of labor reformism.

By the same token, the apparent relevance of war reformism also won it unprecedented influence. In the Comité d'Action and on the Confederal Committee of the CGT, it was embraced not merely by pre-war reformist leaders (Bartuel and Bidegaray, for example, respectively representing the miners' and railwaymen's federations) but also by numerous ex-revolutionary syndicalists (Jouhaux, Bled, Savoie, Chanvin and, after initial hesitancy or hostility, Merrheim and Dumoulin).[79] From 1915 to 1918, war reformism won the support of 60 to 65 percent of the Confederal Committee.[80] At the national level, therefore, the classic revolutionary syndicalism which had flourished from 1904 to the crisis of 1908–9 (i.e., the conflict with the Clemenceau government), and which had confronted mounting difficulties from then until the outbreak of war without being formally challenged, was replaced during the war by a new, reformist hegemony. This new orientation (which was fiercely contested by a "revolutionary" minority) was based on an alliance of prewar reformists and revolutionary syndicalists.

This being the case, it is unlikely that, as some historians have suggested, the genesis of syndicalist war reformism was due essentially to the influence of people and ideas outside the wartime labor movement. Georges Lefranc, for example, sees it as the result of contacts between Albert Thomas and Léon Jouhaux in 1918, and of the influence of Austrian socialist experiments in nationalization in 1919. Martin Fine, in his important thesis, has brought out the full importance of the relationship established during the war between Thomas as minister of Armaments, a group of reforming civil servants (many of them peacetime academics and former colleagues of Thomas at the élite Ecole Normale Supérieure), a cluster of business leaders in heavy industry who played a pivotal role in the munitions effort, and the inner core of CGT leaders.[81] In particular, Fine characterizes Thomas and Jouhaux as pioneering a "corporatist" approach to the organization of the war economy. Lefranc is clearly wrong in situating the genesis of the wartime reformism in 1918–19 rather than 1914–16. The precise influence of Thomas and the network linking industrialists, civil servants, and labor leaders is more problematic. There is no doubt about the corporatist *tendencies* of the munitions effort. The considerable prewar barriers separating the worlds of labor, business and the republican state were substantially breached by the shock of war, leading to new contacts and opening the way to new comportments by syndicalist leaders. But should we locate the principal source of the November 1916 labor program in a functioning wartime corporatism?

Our study of the Comité d'Action suggests not. In the first place, Thomas himself does not seem to have played any significant role in the Comité d'Action or its deliberations in 1916 (which is scarcely surprising, since he was absorbed in maximizing munitions production by whatever means possible). Only when he had left office in September 1917 did he have the time to engage in reflection on postwar reform (notably reviving his interest in railway nationalization and a state-led process of economic demobilization). But in the last year of the war and the first year of peace, Thomas was progressively marginalized on the right wing of the party (though he was re-elected by the coal miners of Carmaux in November 1919 to Jaurès' old seat in the Chamber).[82] On Thomas's own admission it was Jouhaux and the CGT who embodied organized labor's aspirations to major reform as the war reached its close.[83]

Nonetheless, Thomas successfully engaged CGT leaders in his network of corporatist contacts – notably through several official joint commissions dealing with issues such as manpower recruitment, women's work, and working conditions in the munitions industry, and through a number of forums for discussion. Among the latter were the National Committee for Social and Political Studies, a kind of brain trust; the Permanent Committee for Studies on the Prevention of Industrial Unemployment, founded in 1911 by civil servants and re-established in 1917–20 under Thomas's presidency; and a newspaper, *L'Information ouvrière et sociale*, launched in 1918 by Thomas and Charles Dulot, an official at the Ministry of Labor. But important as these forms of contact were for labor leaders, none of them were places where syndicalist policy originated; rather, they promoted the belief in the need for permanent dialogue with business and the state, and allowed CGT representatives to present policies which they had developed quite independently as alternatives to current practice.[84]

The existence of the Comité d'Action itself illustrates clearly that the impulse for wartime labor reformism came essentially from the *autonomous* response of the CGT leadership and of militants involved in both the confederation and the Socialist Party (especially in the capital) who wished to qualify labor and socialist participation in the national effort by considered criticism and the proposal of more radical alternatives. Integral to that process, they believed, was the construction of a more powerful labor movement, beginning with the closer socialist-syndicalist relations which the committee sought to exemplify.

And if the November 1916 program stands as the apogee of the committee's endeavors, its scope, extending well beyond the interest and ideas of industrialists concerned with defending the power of the *patronat* and the principle of private enterprise (albeit in more "organized" forms), marks the fundamental distinction between labor reformism and a functioning corporatism.[85]

This distinction can be amplified by enquiring a little further into the ideological and organizational role of labor reformism – beginning with the meaning of labor *participation* in the war effort. If mobilization for war is thought of as unilaterally orchestrated by the state, *majoritaire* syndicalists and pro-war socialists are, by definition, reduced to the role of puppets – naïve dupes in the best interpretation, cynically self-interested in the worst. This was certainly the view of the syndicalist and socialist opposition movements, and it has colored the predominant historiographical tradition.[86] If, on the contrary, the political mobilization of French society behind the war effort in 1914–16 is seen as encompassing a large portion of civil society, including many non-governmental organizations, and occurring with a considerable degree of autonomy (despite various government measures to control the process – through censorship, propaganda, etc.), then the specific character of the CGT's participation and its relationship with the official version appear more complex. The CGT's role in official state organisms was more limited than that of the Socialist Party and, thanks to its organizational independence, included no responsibility for participation in government or the voting of war credits. Moreover, the CGT took no overall responsibility (as a "social partner") for negotiating wartime labor and social legislation, many aspects of which it sharply criticized (wages policy, the Dalbiez law, the way in which foreign labor was introduced, etc). In this respect it differed somewhat from British and German trade unions.[87] The *majoritaire* leadership of the CGT maintained throughout the conflict its commitment of August 1914 to the war effort – and therefore to the *political* mobilization of French society. But it did so with considerable independence in the *manner* of its support.

The Comité d'Action demonstrates how from the start labor leaders adopted a critical view of the economic and social impact of the war, which they felt to illuminate or heighten pre-existing inequalities and injustices. This gave an independent tone to their support for the political mobilization, and also to their participation in the industrial effort. Having embraced the cause of the nation in 1914, they remained within the general language of national solidarity, while seeking to protect the specific interests of their own members and of the working class in general. They of course identified the working class with the mass of society, thus transforming the labor movement into the real expression of the "national interest," as the 1916 program of the Joint Commission explained:

> The general interests of the country being intimately bound up with those of the workers and peasants, the working class should concern itself more than any other with economic reorganization . . . the need for which has been demonstrated to everyone by the War.[88]

The language of sacrifice – and of the specific sacrifices made by the working class during the war – appear constantly in the speeches of the *majoritaires* in order to underline this moral and political dimension of their reform demands and its indissoluble link with labor support for the national cause.[89] Indeed, one of the fundamental purposes of the reform demands made during the war was to present an idealized, labor version of the official war effort, projected into the postwar future, as a means of criticizing wartime reality. Precisely because this critical function was so central, the concern of syndicalist leaders with reforms can be sharply differentiated from what has been termed an "ideology of the industrial mobilization," incorporating state, business, and labor in a corporatist consensus. Certainly, there were common concerns in all three groups, but this does not necessarily imply a common viewpoint or shared solutions. The syndicalist version of "productivism" – that is, the transforming potential of postwar economic growth, expressed in plans for rebuilding the north-east, in the November 1916 program, and elsewhere – turned on a generalized technological development rather than on a narrow application of taylorist "scientific management." The role which syndicalist leaders envisaged for organized labor in economic management (*gestion*) went far beyond that entertained by the other "corporatist" elements in the munitions effort, as the *patronat* in particular made clear.[90]

Reformism was a matter of practice as well as doctrine, and here the wartime relationship with the state was central. Labor attitudes toward industrialists (dominated by distrust) changed much less during the war than did those toward government. Admittedly, one visage of extended state power was repressive. The coercive possibilities stemming from wartime legislation, from the fact that half a million munitions workers were mobilized men and therefore under military discipline, and from close state control over life in factories and mines working for the national defense, all reinforced the authoritarian state. Yet even this placed a premium on the labor movement's ability to intercede with government in protection of its members. The other visage of the wartime state, however, was its deliberate encouragement of dialogue with labor and the evidence, despite labor criticisms, that it was by no means simply the agent of the *patronat* or the class instrument of the *bourgeoisie*. The reversal of the initial suspension of social legislation, the imposition of wage increases on reluctant employers, and the consultation of syndicalist leaders on broad policy matters were indications of this. With the right to strike highly circumscribed (and, for mobilized workers, banned), syndicalist leaders in effect acted as a labor pressure or lobby group, intervening with ministers, deputies, and senior civil servants for the protection of individuals, the defense of labor's rights (e.g., of *mobilisés* to join trade unions and receive civilian wages), and the proposal of reforms. It was here that the network of "corporatist" contacts acquired its real significance, allowing labor leaders to pursue this function of labor lobby despite the virtual disappearance of official industrial "direct action" – and indeed, up to late 1916, of industrial action of any sort.

One should not imagine the syndicalist leaders engaged in this reformist practice as cloistered in the ante-chambers of power, and out of touch with a larger working class constituency. Contact was constantly maintained with the local level of the labor movement in 1914-16, through provincial tours by syndicalist leaders. In many localities, socialists and syndicalists participated in the administration and helped tackle problems concerning workers, including provisioning, rent controls, aid to soldiers and their families, etc. Frequently, local comités d'Action were set up, paralleling the activities of the national body and in contact with it. From late 1915 to the end of 1916, local labor and socialist organizations sent more than 9,300 letters to the national committee.[91] In this sense, the national labor leadership articulated real difficulties and tensions experienced by ordinary French workers during the war.

Overall, the reform plans elaborated by French labor leaders in 1914–16 envisaged substantial economic changes and a fundamental recasting of the French state. The absence of any lasting alteration in the balance of political power in France arising from the war doubtless helps explain why war reformism did not produce any dramatic improvement in the position of organized labor or the working class in 1919–20. But by the same token, their postwar fate shows labor's reform projects during the war to have been more than a symptom of labor's absorption into the official industrial mobilization.

It remains to suggest something of the broader significance of this wartime labor reformism, especially in the second half of the war. After all, it might be argued that with the effective demise of the Comité d'Action at the end of 1916 and the changing social and political climate of 1917–18, the phenomenon abated rapidly or, indeed, never had more than passing importance.

The tensions of 1917–18 (strike waves, moments of war weariness, growing labor and socialist sympathies for pacifism, right-wing "anti-defeatist" campaigns, and the arrival in power of Clemenceau, the prewar *briseur de grèves* (strike-breaker) in November 1917) certainly modified the political landscape in which moderate labor leaders operated. But such developments were not automatically hostile to reformism.[92] *Majoritaire* leaders of the CGT feared strikes inasmuch as they generated alternative, more radical, rank-and-file leaderships and ran the risk of reinforcing the coercive tendencies of the state. But to the extent that strikes sought to improve wages and material conditions threatened by the war, they endorsed the fundamental criticisms of reformist leaders, namely that the war effort was ineffectively and inequitably administered. Although strikes in the national defense industries were illegal from January 1917, they provided a powerful sanction for the lobbying activities of labor leaders. In fact, national CGT leaders were engaged more or less constantly in 1917–18 in negotiating the settlement of unofficial strikes. The outcome frequently favored labor rather than the industrialists, and indeed many of the strikes concerned the imposition of officially established wage scales (in whose elaboration syndicalist delegates participated) on recalcitrant employers. The process of institutionalized collective bargaining (and hence of union recognition) – both weak in prewar France – were thus significantly reinforced. Together with rapidly rising CGT membership (nearly double the prewar level by 1918), this seemed to promise the disciplined, mass trade unionism on which the CGT counted to implement its postwar reform program once cooperation with the Socialist Party had languished.[93]

The failure of that cooperation, and of the Comité d'Action's attempt to overcome the historic split between unions and party, colored the longer-term significance of war reformism in a negative fashion. Several reasons can be suggested for this failure. Many of the socialists supporting the war effort did so in a spirit of vigorous jacobin-

ism, in which egalitarian proposals sprang more from historical identification with the republican tradition (references to 1792-4 were legion)
than from specifically socialist principles. It was difficult to generalize
this levelling rhetoric beyond the particular circumstances of war which
had given rise to it. Additionally, Guesdist Socialists (including the
grand old man himself, who entered government in August 1914)
claimed that participation in the defense of France, the *patrie* of revolutions, was quite distinct from collaboration with the *bourgeois* state,
which remained anathema. This attempted maintenance of the principles of class conflict in the midst of the *Union sacrée* reinforced the tendency to think of the war as *sui generis*, and without wider lessons for
peacetime.[94] Finally, the issues of a negotiated peace and the resurrec-
tion of international action in the midst of war – though equally central
and divisive in both organizations – were expressed very differently in
the two cases. In the Socialist Party, they were fought out largely in
their own terms, only impinging indirectly on deeper questions of orientation. In the CGT, wracked by a crisis of orientation in the prewar
period, the issues of peace and internationalism were grafted onto fundamental definitions of the theory and action of trade unionism. Hence
the minority which opposed the war condemned the majority not merely for supporting it but also for their "betrayal" of the fundamental class
principles of syndicalism. Conversely, the *majoritaires* from the start
used their war reformism as a means of opposing the *minoritaires*, who
were seen as wedded to an outmoded form of revolutionary syndicalism.

This dynamic developed further as relations between *majoritaires* and
minoritaires grew more strained in 1917–18, thus reinforcing the internal role of *majoritaire* reformism in the last two years of the war as a
bulwark against the revival of a pacifist-tinged, and potentially mass-
based, revolutionary syndicalism. But by the same token, war reformism
now became an almost exclusively syndicalist phenomenon. Although
locally, socialists continued to express interest in the reform issue,
nationally the November 1916 reform plan of the Joint Commission
and the Comité d'Action stirred barely a ripple after its perfunctory presentation to the December 1916 socialist congress. Its influence resurfaced in April 1919 when Léon Blum, drafting a socialist electoral program, sought to rally the deeply divided party around reformist perspectives. But this attempt was short lived, as a more fundamental fracture
opened between those loyal to traditional definitions of class politics
and revolution and those pulled into the orbit of the Bolshevik model.[95]

Reformism was unequivocally marginalized in the Socialist Party, therefore, and it was the CGT which became widely acknowledged as its principal vector. In the closing months of the war, the Confederal Committee drafted the *Programme minimum*, which was approved in December 1918 and, with subsequent revisions, was to guide the *majoritaires* as they presented organized labor's account to the government and the nation in the postwar period. In its essence the *Programme minimum* was a barely revised version of the November 1916 plan.[96] Nothing could illustrate more clearly the lasting significance of the Comité d'Action's work. But the fact that postwar labor reformism took an almost exclusively syndicalist mould was of equally vital significance. For this deprived syndicalist reformists of the political instrument of socialism at a time when the state was disengaging from its wartime role and much of the *patronat* (from mid-1919) was looking for an opportunity to take the counteroffensive against labor's strengthened position. The immediate outcome of the wartime expectations embodied in the November 1916 program was essentially disappointment. But the ideas which had been elaborated and adopted by a major current of organized labor in the first two years of the conflict (joint commissions, nationalization on the anti-bureaucratic model, economic planning, and a decentralized, collectivized economy, institutionalizing syndicalist and cooperative organizations) became an enduring part of French labor and socialist traditions, influencing syndicalist and also socialist policies during the Depression and especially during the second postwar reconstruction.[97]

Notes to Chapter 9

1. This contribution is a revised version of an article originally published in French, "Le Comité d'Action (CGT-PS) et l' origine du réformisme syndical du temps de guerre (1914–1916)," *Le Mouvement social* 122 (Jan.–March 1983), pp. 33–60. On reformism, see B. Georges and D. Tintant, *Léon Jouhaux*, vol. 1: *Des Origines à 1921* (Paris: Presses Universitaires de France, 1962); M. Fine, "Towards Corporatism: the Movement for Capital-Labor Collaboration in France, 1914–1936 (Ph.D. diss. Wisconsin, Madison, 1971); *id.*em, "Guerre et réformisme en France, 1914–1918," in *Le Soldat du Travail* (L. Murard and P. Zylberman, ed.) special no. of *Recherches* 32-3 (Sept. 1978), pp. 305-24; M. De Lucia, "The Remaking of French Revolutionary Syndicalism, 1911–1918: the Growth of the Reformist Philosophy" (Ph.D. diss., Brown, 1971); J. Julliard, ed., *Réformismes et réformistes français*, special no. of *Le Mouvement social* 87 (April–June 1974); N. Papayanis, *Alphonse Merrheim. The Emergence of Reformism from Revolutionary*

Syndicalism 1871–1925 (The Hague: Nijhoff, 1985); J. Horne, *Labour at War: France and Britain. 1914–1918* (Oxford: Clarendon Press, 1991).

2. *Rapport sur l' action générale du comité présenté le 20 novembre 1915* (hereafter *Rapport . . . 1915*), pp. 1–2; *L'Humanité*, 10 Sept. 1914; *La Bataille syndicaliste*, 10 Sept. 1914, Gaston Lévy, however, in a meeting of the committee on 13 May 1916, attributed the original initiative to the socialist Fédération de la Seine (report of 16 May 1916, Archives Nationales [hereafter AN] F7 13571). Lévy also corroborated the suggestion in *Rapport . . . 1915* that the preconditions for the committee were to be found in the defensive collaboration of socialists and syndicalists against the outbreak of war, and then against the threat of persecution, in late July–early August 1914. The principal sources for the study of the Comité d'Action are the reports of meetings in *L' Humanité* and *La Bataille syndicaliste*; documents in the Archives Nationales (notably in AN F7 13074 and F7 13571); and the published reports of the committee (cited below), which are all in the Institut Français d'Histoire Sociale (IFHS), Picart papers, 14 AS 213 (5) 386. Other accounts of the Comité d'Action are H. Dubreuil, *Employeurs et salariés en France* (Paris: Alcan, 1934), pp. 79–81; N. Papayanis, "Collaboration and Pacifism in France during World War I," *Francia* 5 (1977), pp. 425–51; Horne, *Labour at War*, chap. 3.

3. Communiqué of 6 September 1914, published in *L' Humanité* and *La Bataille syndicaliste*, 10 Sept. 1914.

4. The official title was changed from *commission* to *comité* toward the end of September (*L' Humanité*, 29 Sept. 1914). The FNCC joined the committee at the beginning of October (*L' Humanité*, 3 Oct. 1914).

5. Louis Dubreuilh, also general secretary of the Socialist Party, 1905–18. From mid-1915 the burden of work became such that a second socialist, H. Prêté, was made permanent secretary of the Comité d'Action.

6. The list of subcommittees was drawn up on 1 October 1914: (1) unemployment benefits; (2) rents and the moratorium on rents; (3) work; (4) information on dead or wounded soldiers; (5) information on prisoners-of-war; (6) clothes and diverse gifts for soldiers; (7) ambulances and convalescent homes; (8) supply and distribution of food (*L' Humanité*, 3 Oct. 1914). By 1916, the number of subcommittees had risen to eleven, their nature and the balance between them changing in line with the shifting concerns of the committee. The new subcommittees included "working conditions and wages in war factories"; the committee's own professional workshops, contracting with the army; refugees; war damage and destroyed cities; and "economic reorganization" (*Rapport du Comité d'Action, 2e année, octobre 1915 à octobre 1916*, hereafter *Rapport . . . 1916*, p. 2).

7. *L' Humanité*, 28 Oct. 1914.

8. *L' Humanité*, 17 Oct. and 19 Nov. 1914; *Rapport . . . 1915*, pp. 13–14; *Rapport . . . 1916*, pp. 16–19.

9. *Rapport . . . 1915*, p. 15; report of G. Lévy, *L' Humanité*, 22 Nov. 1914; *L' Humanité*, Dec. 1914, various reports. For the specifically Parisian dimension of this activity, see J.-L. Robert, "Ouvriers et mouvement ouvrier parisiens pendant la grande guerre et l'immédiat après-guerre. Histoire et anthropologie" (Doctorat d'État thesis, Université de Paris I, 1989), pp. 1312–17.

10. AN F7 13074, report of 13 Oct. 1914.

11. *Rapport . . . 1916*, pp. 5–6; report of G. Lévy, *L' Humanité*, 22 Nov. 1914.

12. "Déclaration" of Comité d'Action, *L' Humanité*, 21 Dec. 1914.

13. L. Jouhaux, *Réception de Gompers à la Confédération Générale du Travail 24 et 26 september 1918*, (Paris: CGT, 1918), pp. 13–14; G. Olphe-Gaillard, *Histoire économique et financière pendant la grande guerre* (Paris: Rivière, 1923), p. 39; R. Créhange, *Chômage et placement* (Paris: Presses Universitaires de France, 1927), pp. 75–76; B. G. de

Montgomery, *British and Continental Labour Policy* (London: Paul, Trench and Trubner, 1922), chap. 24.

14. Gallieni, *Mémoires du général Gallieni: défense de Paris* (Paris: Payot, 1920), pp. 118–20; J. Paul-Boncour, *Entre deux guerres. Souvenirs sur la IIIe République*, vol. 1: *Les Luttes républicaines, 1877-1918* (Paris: Plon, 1945), pp. 244–46.

15. *Rapport . . . 1915*, pp. 9–12; *L'Humanité*, 2 Nov. 1914.

16. *Rapport . . . 1915*, p. 12.

17. *La Bataille syndicaliste*, 25 Nov. 1914, and AN F7 13574 for the original project; for the commissions created by Sembat, see *Bulletin du ministère du Travail et de la Prévoyance sociale*, July–Aug. 1915, pp. 202–15, and *ibid.*, Aug.–Oct. 1918.

18. *Rapport . . . 1915*, p. 14; *Rapport . . . 1916*, pp. 12–13; AN F7 13571, report of 15 Feb. 1915. In March 1916, the workshops were taken over by the cooperative movement at the request of the Comité d'Action (*Rapport . . . 1916*, pp. 12–13).

19. AN F7 13574, report of July 1915; Créhange, *Chômage et placement*, pp. 4–5; de Montgomery, *British and Continental Labour Policy*, chap. 24; H. Bruggeman, M. Poëte, & H. Sellier, *Paris pendant la Guerre* (Paris: Presses Universitaires de France, 1925), pp. 52–56; P. Izard, *Le Chômage et le placement en France pendant la guerre* (Paris: Sagot, 1920), pp. 46–80.

20. Horne, *Labour at War*, chap. 2. For Thomas, see B. W. Schaper, *Albert Thomas. Trente ans de réformisme social* (Assen: Van Gorcum, 1959); Fine, *Towards Reformism*; P. Fridenson & M. Rebérioux, "Albert Thomas, pivot du réformisme français," *Le Mouvement social* 87 (April–June 1974), pp. 85–97; J. Godfrey, *Capitalism at War. Industrial Policy and Bureaucracy in France 1914-1918* (Leamington Spa: Berg, 1987), chaps. 6, 7 and 10; and the contributions of G. Hardach and A. Hennebicque to this volume.

21. Good summaries of the material impact of the war on the working class are W. Oualid, "The Effects of the War upon Labour in France," in *Effects of the War upon French Economic Life*, ed. C. Gide (Oxford: Clarendon Press, 1928), pp. 139–91; and P. Fridenson, "The Impact of the First World War on French Workers," in *The Upheaval of War. Family, Work and Welfare in Europe* ed. R. Wall and J. Winter (Cambridge: Cambridge University Press, 1988), pp. 235–48. On prices and wages, see *Bulletin du ministère du Travail*, Aug.–Oct. 1918, pp. 440–41; and L. March, *Le Mouvement des prix et des salaires pendant la guerre* (Paris: Presses Universitaires de France, 1925), p. 244. Labor leaders contested the myth of high real wages and claimed the situation to be worse than even the official figures indicated; see, for example, A. Merrheim, "La Vérité sur les salaires fabuleux," *L'Oeuvre économique*, 10 Jan. 1917, pp. 15–22. One close and fairly impartial contemporary observer confirmed that wage increases lagged well behind price increases; see R. Picard, *Les Grèves et la guerre* (Paris: Comité National d'Etudes Sociales et Politiques, 1917), p. 45.

22. The initiative occurred after it had been clearly demonstrated that working class feelings were rising along with the increase in prices. Merrheim declared that "discontent is predominant in the working population, not just in Paris but in the whole country," Bled, secretary of the CGT's Union des Syndicats de la Seine (covering the Paris region), threatened to exercize his organization's freedom of action if the Comité d'Action did not organize a veritable campaign against the high cost of living (AN F7 13571, report of 4 Oct. 1915). In all there were five: on milk (Compère-Morel, Nov. 1915); meat (Henri Sellier and Gaston Lévy, Dec. 1915); sugar (Roldes, n.d., but Dec. 1915); coal (Luquet, Dec. 1915); and a bill on agricultural work during the war (n.d.).

23. *Rapport . . . 1916*, p. 4.

24. *Rapport . . . 1916*, p. 7; *La Voix du Peuple*, 1 May 1916, for support by the CGT's Confederal Committee for the project.

25. P. Pinot, *Le Contrôle du ravitaillement de la population* (Paris: Presses Universitaires de France, 1925), pp. 6–8; C. Meihac et al., *L' Effort du ravitaillement français pendant la guerre et pour la paix, 1914-1920* (Paris: Alcan, n.d.), pp. 22–24; *Rapport . . . 1916*, p. 8; AN F7 13571, report of 20 April 1916; minutes of the executive of the Union des Syndicats de la Seine, (Musée Social, Paris), 12 April 1916, p. 13.

26. A. Roche, "Le problème de la vie dans un ménage ouvrier," *La Clairière*, 15 Dec. 1918, pp. 1656–57.

27. Bruggeman et al, *Paris pendant la guerre*, pp. 31–32; G. Sardier, *Le Ravitaillement en charbon pendant la guerre* (Paris: Larose, 1920), pp. 63–79; *Journal officiel, Chambre des députés. Débats parlementaires*, 1916, pp. 3384–85, for the Commission on Mine's bill.

28. AN F7 13571, report of 23 Oct. 1915; *La Vie chère, Rapport sur la question du charbon* (Comité d'Action, Dec. 1915); *Rapport . . . 1916*, p. 5.

29. AN F7 13571, rep. of 12 Aug. 1916.

30. AN F7 13571, reports of 10 and 19 Feb. 1917. At the first of these meetings, Jouhaux sounded a warning concerning the wheat crisis: "The government must be told that if it fails to act, we are determined to resume our complete freedom of action. In the future, the working masses, faced with a desperate situation, would not pardon us for not having told the truth and engaged in the necessary demonstrations in order to force the hands of the politicians." This theme was taken up by a "Déclaration" of the CGT on 21 May 1917.

31. *La Voix du Peuple*, 1 May 1917.

32. M. Frois, *La Santé et le travail des femmes pendant la guerre* (Paris: Presses Universitaires de France, 1926); Y. Delatour, "Le Travail des femmes pendant la première guerre mondiale et ses conséquences sur l' évolution de leur rôle dans la société," *Francia* 2, (1974), pp. 482–501; J. McMillan, *Housewife or Harlot: the Place of Women in French Society 1870–1940* (Brighton: Harvester Press, 1981), p. 135; J.-L. Robert, "La CGT et la famille ouvrière, 1914–1918. Première approche," *Le Mouvement social* 116, (July–Sept. 1981), pp. 47–66; *idem*, "Women and Work in France during the First World War," in *The Upheaval of War*, Wall and Winter, ed., pp. 251–66; F. Thébaud, *La Femme au temps de la guerre de 14* (Paris: Stock, 1986), pp. 285–91; Horne, *Labour at War*, chap. 3; and the contribution of M. Dubesset, F. Thébaud, and C. Vincent to this volume.

33. Statistique générale de la France, *Statistique du mouvement de la population, années 1914–1919* (Paris: Imprimerie Nationale, 1922), pp. 16–20; B. Nogaro & L. Weil, *La Main-d' oeuvre étrangère et coloniale pendant la guerre* (Paris: Presses Universitaires de France, 1926); J. Vidalenc, "La Main-d' oeuvre étrangère en France et la première guerre mondiale," *Francia* 2, (1974), pp. 524–50; J. van der Stegen, "Les Chinois en France, 1915–1929" (Maîtrise dissertation, Université de Paris X, Nanterre, 1974); G. Cross, "Towards Social Peace and Prosperity: the Politics of Immigration in France during the Era of World War I," *French Historical Studies* 9, no. 4 (1980), pp. 610–32; P. Dogliani, "Stato, imprenditori, e manodopera industriale in Francia durante la prima guerra mondiale," *Rivista di storia contemporanea* 4 (1982), pp. 523–59; J. Horne, "Immigrant Workers in France during World War I," *French Historical Studies* 14, no. 1 (1985), pp. 57–88; *idem, Labour at War*, chap. 3; G. Noiriel, *Le Creuset français. Histoire de l' immigration XIXe-XXe siècle* (Paris: Seuil, 1986); M. Favre-Le Van Ho, "Un Milieu porteur de modernisation: travail et travailleurs vietnamiens an France pendant la première guerre mondiale (thèse de doctorat, Ecole des Chartes, Paris, 1986).

34. AN F7 13569, report of 13 May 1916, and F7 13366, report of 16 May 1916, for

Merrheim's fears; see also *L' Union des Métaux*, Aug. 1916.

35. AN F7 13569, reports of 8 April, 1 May, 13 May, 16 Sept., and 7 Nov. 1916. See also correspondence between Métin, minister of Labor, and Albert Thomas, concerning the fears of Jouhaux and the CGT, and explaining that the latter had received assurances and were to be kept informed of the number of immigrants (AN 94 AP 135).

36. AN F7 13569, report of the Confederal Committee of the CGT, 31 Dec. 1915; minutes of the executive of the Union Générale des Syndicats de la Seine, Musée Social, pp. 31–36; J. Borderel, "La Main-d'Oeuvre étrangère à la commission mixte du département de la Seine," *Le Parlement et l'Opinion*, Nov. 1916, pp. 1108–17. The control of immigrant labor equally figured in a program of international labor reforms devised by the CGT majority in 1916 (Horne, *Labour at War*, chap. 8).

37. AN F7 13571, report of 5 June 1916.

38. AN 94 AP 135, note of the minister for War, 17 Dec. 1915, and the reply of the minister of Labor, 4 March 1916; J. Lugand, *L' Immigration des ouvriers étrangers en France et les enseignements de la guerre* (Paris: Librairie-Imprimerie Réunie, 1919), p. 58; "La Main-d' oeuvre étrangère en France," *Bulletin du ministère du Travail*, Jan.–Feb. 1920, pp. 19–25.

39. IFHS, 14 AS 213a (4) (Picart papers), for the minutes of the Commission Nationale du Placement; Cross, "Towards Social Peace and Prosperity"; Horne, *Labour at War*, chaps. 2 & 3.

40. AN F7 13366, reports of 12 Feb. and 6 April 1915, on Millerand's comments. For changes in the labor process and working conditions during the war, see P. Fridenson, *Histoire des usines Renault*, vol. 1: *Naissance de la grande entreprise, 1898–1939* (Paris: Seuil, 1972), pp. 89–119; *idem*, "Un Tournant taylorien de la société française 1904–1918," *Annales E.S.C.* 5 (1987), pp. 1031–60; *idem*, "The Impact of the First World War on French Workers," J.-L. Robert, "Les Luttes ouvrières pendant la première guerre mondiale," *Cahiers d' histoire de l' Institut Maurice Thorez* 23 (1977), pp. 28–65; G. Hatry, *Renault usine de guerre 1914-1918* (Paris: Lafourcade, 1978); A. Moutet, "La Première Guerre mondiale et le taylorisme," in *Le Taylorisme* ed. M. de Montmollin and O. Pastré (Maspero, 1984), pp. 64–76; G. Cross, "The Quest for Leisure: Reassessing the Eight Hour Day in France," *Journal of Social History* 18 (1984), pp. 195–216. G. C. Humphreys, *Taylorism in France. 1904–1920: the Impact of Scientific Management on Factory Relations and Society* (London: Garland, 1986); Horne, *Labour at War*, chap. 3.

41. R. Picard, *Le Contrôle ouvrier sur la gestion des entreprises* (Paris: Rivière, 1922); K. Amdur, *Syndicalist Legacy. Trade Unions and Politics in Two French Cities in the Era of World War I* (Urbana: University of Illinois Press, 1986), pp. 67, 74; J. Bond-Howard, "Le Syndicalisme minoritaire dans les usines d' armement de Bourges de 1914 à 1918," *Le Mouvement social* 148 (July–Sept. 1989), pp. 33–62; Robert, "Ouvriers et mouvement ouvrier parisiens," chap. 20; Horne, *Labour at War*, chap. 5; G. Hatry's contribution to this volume.

42. AN F7 13366, reports of 21 June and 26 July 1915 (on employer hostility to the commission), 18 Oct. (Merrheim's decision to boycott it), and 30 Nov. and 6 Dec. (general criticisms by the CGT); J. Horne, "*L' Impôt du sang*: Republican Rhetoric and Industrial Warfare in France, 1914–18," *Social History* 14, (1989), pp. 201–23.

43. AN F7 13366 and F7 13571, reports of 30 Nov. 1915.

44. There is still no satisfactory study of the larger phenomenon or Reconstruction thinking in France. But there are useful contemporary bibliographies in H. Carter, "Enquiry into Economic Regionalism in France," *The Sociological Review* 1919, pp. 120–35, and C. Bloch, "The Literature of Economic Reconstruction in France," *The*

Manchester Guardian Commercial, special supplement 4, 4 Jan. 1923. See also R. F. Kuisel, *Capitalism and the State in Modern France* (Cambridge: Cambridge University Press, 1981), chaps. 2 and 3.

45. *Journal officiel, Chambre des Députés, Documents parlementaires*, 1916, no. 2345, pp. 1175–1242; W. MacDonald, *Reconstruction in France* (London: Macmillan, 1922).

46. *Rapport . . . 1916*, p. 15; *Rapport . . . 1916*, pp. 13–14; Comité d'Action, *Reconstruction des cités détruites et dommages de guerre*.

47. *Reconstruction des cités*, pp. 4–5.

48. *Journal officiel, Chambre des députés, documents parlementaires*, 1916, no. 2345, p. 1187; AN F7 13571, report of a meeting of the Comité d'Action, 14 March, 1916; A. Picart, in *La Bataille*, 4 and 6 Nov. 1916; *Rapport de la commission d' enquête du Conseil Économique du Travail dans les régions dévastées* (Paris: Conseil Economique du Travail, 1921).

49. *Rapport . . . 1916*, p. 15.

50. *La Bataille*, 28 Jan. 1916.

51. AN F7 13571, report of 21 Feb. 1916.

52. AN F7 13571, report of 17 April 1916.

53. B. H. Moss, *The Origins of the French Labor Movement, 1830–1914. The Socialism of Skilled Workers* (Berkeley: University of California Press, 1976); J. Julliard, *Autonomie ouvrière. Etudes sur le syndicalisme d'Action directe* (Paris: Gallimard-Le Seuil, 1988); R. McGraw, "Socialism, Syndicalism and French Labour before 1914," in *Labour and Socialist Movements in Europe before 1914* ed. D. Geary (Oxford: Berg, 1989), pp. 48–100; Horne, *Labour at War*, chap. 1.

54. Horne, *Labour at War*, chap. 4.

55. Robert, "Ouvriers et mouvement ouvrier parisiens," pp. 1331–1347; Horne, *Labour at War*, chap. 4.

56. *La Bataille*, 22 May 1916.

57. AN F7 13571, reports of 23 Oct. 1915 and 16 May 1916; *La Bataille*, 27 May 1916.

58. AN F7 13571, report of 22 May 1916; *Rapport . . . 1916*, p. 15.

59. AN F7 13571, report of 5 June 1916; J. Compère-Morel, "Songeons à demain," *L' Humanité*, 14 April 1916; P. Renaudel, "Renaissance économique," *L' Humanité*, 9 June 1916; H. Bourgin, *Le Parti contre la patrie. Histoire d' une sécession politique* (Paris: Plon, 1924), p. 115.

60. AN F7 13571, report of 14 June 1916.

61. *La Bataille*, 8 June 1916, which shows clearly that the proposals of the Comité d'Action served as the basis for the Joint Commission's deliberations. For Lévy's view, see AN F7 13571, report of 16 Jan. 1917. For the more restricted understanding by socialist deputies of postwar reform, see *Journal officiel, Chambre des députés, Documents parlementaires*, 1917, no. 3253, pp. 447–48.

62. Robert, "Ouvriers et mouvement ouvrier parisiens," pp. 1289–1347; J. Horne, "Autorité ou démocratie: le monde du travail et la pensée sociale en 1910–1920," (unpublished paper, Department of Modern History, Trinity College, Dublin, 1989).

63. G. Lévy and E. Poisson, "Le Prolétariat et la 'renaissance' de la France," *L'Avenir*, April 1916, pp. 55–60.

64. "Les Problèmes économiques," *Le Populaire*, 18/24 Dec. 1916.

65. AN F7 13073, copy of the resolution.

66. *La Voix du Peuple*, Dec. 1916; AN F7 13583, account of the CGT conference; Jouhaux's account of the same in *La Bataille*, 4 Jan. 1917; summaries of the socialist congress, *L' Humanité*, 38 Dec. 1916 and *Le Midi socialiste*, 29 Dec. 1916.

67. AN F7 13571, report of 16 Jan. 1917.

68. The Joint Commission continued to meet in the first half of 1917, and *L' Humanité* contains reports of occasional meetings in 1918. In mid-February 1917, it was decided to reduce meetings of the Comité d'Action to one a month, on urgent matters only, with the large economic questions being referred directly to the Joint Commission (AN F7 13571, report of 19 February 1917).

69. *Rapport de la Commission mixte d' études économiques,* p. 1. Copies exist in the private papers of Albert Thomas, AN 94 AP 406, and in the IFHS, Picart papers, 14 AS 213 (5) 386.

70. Eg. Merrheim, "Le Système Taylor," *L'Oeuvre économique,* 10 June 1917, pp. 342–43.

71. *Rapport de la Commission mixte,* p. 1 (italics in the original).

72. J.-J. Becker and A. Kriegel, *1914: La Guerre et le mouvement ouvrier français* (Paris: Colin, 1964); G. Haupt, *Socialism and the Great War. The Collapse of the Second International* (Oxford: Clarendon Press, 1971); J.-J. Becker, *1914: Comment les français sont entrés dans la guerre* (Paris: Presses de la Fondation nationale des Sciences Politiques, 1977); J. Howorth, "French Workers and German Workers: the Impossibility of Internationalism, 1900–1914," *European History Quarterly* 15, no. 1 (1985), pp. 71–97; J. Julliard, "La CGT devant la guerre (1900–1914)," in Julliard, *Autonomie ouvrière,* pp. 94–111; R. Gallissot, R. Paris and C. Weill, "La Désunion des prolétaires," special no. of *Le Mouvement social* 147 (April–June 1989), esp. R. Gallissot, "La Patrie des prolétaires," pp. 11–25; Robert, "Ouvriers et mouvement ouvrier parisiens," pp. 1291–1302; S. Milner, *French Syndicalism and the International Labour Movement 1900–1914* (Oxford: Berg, 1990); Horne, *Labour at War,* chaps. 1 and 2.

73. F. Challaye, *Syndicalisme révolutionnaire et syndicalisme réformiste* (Paris: Alcan, 1909), p. 119; P. A. Carcenagues, *Sur le mouvement syndicaliste réformiste en France* (Paris: Schleicher, 1912); A. Savoie, "La Répartition de la main-d' oeuvre sera-t-elle assurée dans l' avenir?," *La Clairière,* 1 Nov. 1917, pp. 318–24; Fédération Nationale des Travailleurs de l' Alimentation, *Compte rendu des travaux et résolutions du 8e congrès national, 12–13 juillet, Paris 1918* (1918), pp. 30–32 (Savoie's speech).

74. D. Stafford, *From Anarchism to Reformism. A Study of the Political Activities of Paul Brousse 1870–1890* (London: Weidenfeld & Nicolson, 1971), pp. 260–74; A. Philip, "Jaurès et la gestion ouvrière," *Revue d' Histoire Economique et Sociale* (1960), pp. 24–30.

75. A. Thomas, "Déclaration socialiste" to the Chamber of Deputies, 1910, reproduced in *La Revue socialiste, syndicaliste et coopérative* 2 (1910) pp. 5–7; debate between Thomas and Guesde at the 1912 Socialist congress, *Parti socialiste, 9e congrès national tenu à Lyon . . . février 1912* (1912), pp. 238–53; C. Prochasson, "Le Socialisme normalien (1907–1914). Recherches et réflexions autour du groupe d' études socialistes de l' École Normale" (Maîtrise dissertation, Université de Paris, 1, 1981); P. Dogliani, "Edgar Milhaud e la rivista internazionale 'Annales de la régie directe' (1908–1924)," *Annali della Fondazione Luigi Einaudi* 19 (1985), pp. 195–249.

76. J.-C. Dufour, "Les Nationalisations dans l' histoire du mouvement ouvrier français (jusqu'à la deuxième guerre mondiale) (DES diss., Faculté de Droit et de Sciences Politiques, Paris, 1969), pp. 79–87; Horne, *Labour at War,* chap. 5.

77. C. Bouglé, *Socialisme français* (Paris: Colin, 1932), pp. 139–65; A. Kriegel, "Le Syndicalisme révolutionnaire et Proudhon," in *ead., Le Pain et les roses* (Paris: Presses Universitaires de France, 1969), pp. 69–104; Horne, *Labour at War,* chap. 7; *idem,* "Autorité ou démocratie."

78. Georges and Tintant, *Léon Jouhaux,* pp. 65–101; Papayanis, *Alphonse Merrheim,* chaps. 6 and 7; J. Julliard, "Théorie syndicaliste révolutionnaire et pratique gréviste," in

idem, Autonomie ouvrière, pp. 43–68.

79. Merrheim, faced with the contradictions of his wartime pacifism, disillusioned by initial working class indifference to it, and opposed to the more extremist, revolutionary currents of pacifism developing in *minoritaire* CGT circles later in the war, gravitated to the *majoritaire* position in 1917–18, sealing his acceptance of the new reformism with a speech in 1919, published as *La Révolution économique* (Paris: Editions de l'Information Ouvrière et Sociale, 1919). See Papayanis, *Alphonse Merrheim,* chap. 10. Dumoulin, leading revolutionary syndicalist in the largely reformist miners' federation and assistant general secretary of the CGT before the war, returned from the trenches to mining in January 1917, in the Loire. Initially resuming his militantly revolutionary syndicalist views and joining the antiwar opposition, he embraced *majoritaire* reformism in the second half of 1918 (G. Dumoulin, *Carnets de route. Quarante ans de vie militante* [Lille: Editions de "L' Avenir," 1938], pp. 94–95); P. Arum, "Du Syndicalisme révolutionnaire au réformisme: Georges Dumoulin (1903–1923)," *Le Mouvement social,* special no. on *Réformismes et réformistes français* 87 (April–June 1974), pp. 43–44.

80. Figure based on police intelligence reports of meetings in AN, F7, various cartons.

81. G. Lefranc, "Les Origines de l' idée de nationalisation industrialisée en France de 1919–1920," in *idem, Essais sur les problèmes socialistes et syndicaux* (Paris: Payot, 1970), pp. 109–26; M. Fine, "Towards Corporatism," pp. 4–41; *idem,* "Guerre et Réformisme en France"; *idem,* "Albert Thomas: a Reformer's Vision of Modernization, 1914–1932," *Journal of Contemporary History* 12(1977), pp. 545–64.

82. Horne, *Labour at War,* chap. 7.

83. A. Thomas, "La Classe ouvrière et l' affaire Malvy," *L'Information Ouvrière et Sociale,* 11 Aug. 1918; *idem,* "Le Programme confédéral," *L' Information Ouvrière et Sociale,* 15 Dec. 1918.

84. Papers of the Comité National d' Etudes Sociales et Politiques, AN 94 AP 401; Ministère du Travail, *Comité permanent d' études relatives à la prévision des chômages industriels. Compte rendu des travaux. Années 1917–1920* (Paris: Imprimerie Nationale, 1920); M. Lazard, *François Simiand, 1873–1935. L' homme, l' oeuvre* (Paris, Association Française pour le Pregrès Social, 1935), pp. 6–7; B. Lavergne, *Les Idées politiques en France de 1900 à nos jours. Souvenirs personnels* (Paris: Librairie Fischbacher, 1965), pp. 129–33; Fine, "Towards Corporatism," pp. 35–40, and *idem,* "Guerre et Réformisme en France," pp. 318–19.

85. For a full discussion of this distinction, see Horne, *Labour at War,* chap. 7.

86. For the most influential representative, see A. Rosmer, *Le Mouvement ouvrier pendant la première guerre mondiale,* vol. 1: *De l' Union sacrée à Zimmerwald* (Paris: Librairie du Travail, 1936), and vol. 2: *De Zimmerwald à la révolution russe* (Paris: Mouton, 1959). A. Kriegel, in *Aux Origines du communisme français* (Paris: Mouton, 1964; 2 vols.), is a marked exception, though her principal subject for the war period is the socialist and syndicalist *minoritaires,* as is J.-L. Robert's monumental *Ouvriers et mouvement ouvrier parisiens* (1989).

87. G. Feldman, *Army, Industry and Labor in Germany, 1914–1918* (Princeton: Princeton University Press, 1966), pp. 197–249; H. A. Clegg, *A History of British Trade Unions since 1889,* vol. 2: *1911–1933* (Oxford: Clarendon Press, 1985), chaps. 4 and 5.

88. *Rapport de la commission mixte,* p. 1.

89. Jouhaux, for example, remarked to the December 1916 CGT conference that "[It is] because I have the clear feeling that the working class has acquired a moral authority in this country that I want that to be translated into achievements" (AN F7 13583, account

of the conference).

90. Horne, *Labour at War*, chap. 7.

91. AN F7 13571, reports of 15 Feb., 10 April, and 17 April 1916; *Rapport . . . 1916*, p. 3; Dogliani, "Stato, imprenditori e manodopera industriale," pp. 531–39; Robert, "Ouvriers et mouvement ouvrier parisiens," pp. 1317–22.

92. D. R. Watson, *Georges Clemenceau. A Political Biography* (London: Methuen, 1974); J.-L. Becker, *The Great War and the French People*, trans. Arnold Pomerans (Leamington Spa: Berg, 1986); J.-B. Duroselle, *Clemenceau* (Paris: Fayard, 1988).

93. Horne, *Labour at War*, chap. 5.

94. Eg., J. Lebas, *La Guerre et la politique du parti socialiste français* (Paris: L' Avenir, 1916), p. 9.

95. L. Blum, *Commentaires sur le programme d'Action du Parti Socialiste (discours prononcé le 21 avril 1919 au congrès national extraordinaire,* (1919); Kriegel, *Aux Origines du communisme français*, vol. 1, pp. 327–40; R. Wohl, *French Communism in the Making 1914–1924* (Stanford: Stanford University Press, 1966), pp. 114–57; G. Ziebura, *Léon Blum et le parti socialiste, 1872–1934* (Paris: Presses de la Fondation Nationale des Sciences Politiques, 1967), pp. 141–55; T. Judt, *La Reconstruction du parti socialiste 1921–1926* (Paris: Presses de la Fondation Nationale des Sciences Politiques, 1976), pp. 8–13.

96. J.-L. Robert, "Les 'Programmes minimum' de la CGT de 1918 et 1921," *Cahiers d' histoire de l' institut de recherches marxistes* 17, no. 2 (1984), pp. 58–78; Horne, *Labour at War*, chaps. 4 and 5.

97. J. Amoyal, "Les Origines socialistes et syndicalistes de la planification en France," *Le Mouvement social* 87 (April–June 1974), pp. 137–69; J. Horne, "L' Idée de nationalisation dans les mouvements ouvriers européens jusqu' à la deuxième guerre mondiale," *Le Mouvement social* 134 (Jan.-March 1986), pp. 9–36; J.-L. Robert, "Une Idée qui vient de loin. Les nationalisations dans l' histoire du mouvement ouvrier français 1895–1939," in *Les Nationalisations de la Libération. De l' utopie au compromis* C. Andrieu, L. Le Van and A. Prost ed. (Paris: Presses de la Fondation nationale des Sciences Politiques, 1987), pp. 19–39.

10

Cooperatives and the Labor Movement in Paris during the Great War

Jean-Louis Robert

We begin this study by examining prewar consumer cooperatives. The difficulties they faced before 1914 contrasted sharply with their wartime growth and with their new place within Parisian social relations. In the second part of this essay, we explore trade union reactions in particular to producer cooperatives. We show that during the war the cooperative spirit grew among trade unionists, but that this progress was limited. This is especially clear in the case of the cooperative of carpenters. We conclude that the war increased the importance of cooperation within the Parisian labor movement, at a time when the attention of workers was focused, quite naturally, on daily problems of food, fuel, and consumption.

The *Encyclopédie Socialiste syndicale et coopérative de l'Internationale Ouvrière*, completed by Compère-Morel on the eve of the Great War, was designed to survey "the whole of socialist thinking – the whole of worker activity." Cooperative action evidently was seen as one of the three pillars of the labor movement, the other two being the party and the trade union. Unlike sporting, cultural, or tenants' organizations, the cooperative was not one of the host of elements only vaguely associated with the labor movement – it was clearly a central component of its organization and practice, even though the power of the cooperative movement in France never equalled that in English-speaking nations.

This statement may be modified: as with trade unions, the coopera-

Notes to Chapter 10 can be found on page 309.
BMT = Bulletin du Ministère du Travail
BUG = Bulletin des Usines de Guerre

tive narrowly avoided being a mere staging post for socialism in a specific area. It was in this context that the *Bourse des sociétés coopératives socialistes de France* was established at the beginning of the twentieth century. Cooperatives belonging to this Union were to become fundamentally linked with the Socialist Party. The *Union coopérative des Sociétés françaises de consommation* (the cooperative union of French consumer societies), directed by Charles Gide, brought together independent or unaligned cooperatives. In 1913, however, the two organizations joined together to form the *Fédération nationale des coopératives de consommation* (FNCC) – the national federation of consumer cooperatives – on the basis of complete independence from all parties, but established within the terrain of social transformation. These principles were well summarized by Ernest Poisson, the first secretary of the FNCC, in 1920:

> The cooperative movement has kept faith with the 1913 pact of unity; today as previously, it involves independence from all parties, all religious thinking, and all forms of government. Yesterday as today, the French cooperative knows that it is working for a new world, a great social transformation, and that this will be based on a society shaped by consumers and responsible for its own creative production.[1]

The cooperative element has long been neglected in studies of the labor movement – proving that the two strands had become disconnected by the second half of the twentieth century. Cooperatives have not been entirely ignored in historical studies, and many monographs mention the existence of a local cooperative in their supporting lists of worker activity, but they fail to specify its exact place in the workers' way of life or to assess the degree of its significance. Elsewhere, specialist historians of the cooperative movement such as Jean Gaumont, have published specific studies which are frequently erudite, but which exaggerate the isolated nature of cooperation.[2]

The current renewal of interest in social and economic issues, marked by the publication of dynamic historical journals, now places the cooperative in a broader landscape. We would like to show both the evolution of the cooperative movement during the war and how this development altered our perception of Parisian cooperation.

Alongside consumer cooperatives there are producer cooperatives, the *Associations ouvrières de production et de crédit*, or workers' production and loan associations. The lack of precision is much greater here, because there is not always a distinction between a workers' cooperative and a classic capitalist association, particularly because worker associations benefited from financial encouragement from the state.[3] However, the FNCC accepted the membership of certain of these associations as soon as they could be seen to stem genuinely from combined worker activity. In any case, producer cooperatives, although relatively numerous (450) on the eve of the war, were of only minimal importance: there were only 18,254 society workers, whether or not members of the Association (57 percent of society members worked within the association) and 7,373 auxiliary non-member workers.[4] The producer cooperative movement thus appeared very modest on the eve of war, despite the occasional brilliant exception such as the Albi glass-workers' cooperative, and in very perceptible decline. In 1913, for example, there were fifty-one dissolutions against twenty-one newly established associations. Producer cooperatives were not, however, to be ignored in certain sectors, to the extent that they posed considerable problems for the trade union movement; it is from this angle that we will first consider them.

The Expansion of Consumer Cooperatives during the War

Immediately before the outbreak of war the cooperative movement in Paris was struggling. Following its dazzling expansion at the end of the nineteenth century, when the leading cooperatives were established (the "Bellevilloise" in 1877, the "Egalitaire" in 1876, and the "Revendication" in 1865 being the trailblazers) and the fame spread through almost all the Paris *arrondissements* and many suburban communities, the cooperative movement in Paris underwent a severe crisis at the beginning of the twentieth century. Let us consider the picture presented by the number of consumer cooperatives, in France and in the *département* of the Seine between 1893 and 1913:[5]

Table 10.1: Number of Cooperatives from 1893 to 1913

	FRANCE	SEINE
1893	1005	99
1897	1351	118
1901	1597	114
1905	1989	115
1909	2655	104
1913	3261	102

It may be added that while the number of cooperatives doubled again between 1900 and 1915 in France as a whole, in the *département* of the

Seine there was an appreciable decline. The dynamism of the cooperative movement faded even more abruptly than the figures show, particularly because the result does not reflect a policy of concentrating cooperatives which had barely started at the outbreak of war. If we examine
their sales figures, the reality is even harsher. From a figure for sales in
the Seine of 40 million francs in 1913, the fall has been estimated by
one cooperator at 40 percent by volume,[6] a very considerable amount.
We are unable to analyze this phenomenon, which Jean Gaumont
attributes chiefly to the split within the cooperative movement, especially apparent in Paris. It is clear, however, that the movement in this
region undoubtedly appeared on the eve of the war as being in a very
shaky state, although it should still be seen as an element of considerable significance.

The Cooperative Movement in the Seine on the Eve of the War

With its 69,000 members and its turnover of 34 million francs, the
Paris Cooperative movement lay at the national average of size relative
to population. Indeed, the national figures of 880,710 members and
turnover of 321 million francs represent a national ratio very close to
the figures for the Seine in proportion to that *département's* four million
inhabitants. Neither an area of outstanding strength, such as Lorraine,
nor of weakness, such as the Midi, the Paris conurbation lies in the
median range of cooperative representation, after being one of the leading zones at the end of the nineteenth century. This overall position
covers a wide variation, for cooperative sympathies varied within the
Paris area.[7] The effects of "cooperativisation" are difficult to study from
the geographical point of view, for a cooperative might cover an area
extending beyond the *arrondissement* or commune where it was based.
This applied to "La Bellevilloise," extending over the 19th and 20th
arrondissements in north-east Paris, and "La Revendication" in
Puteaux, covering several communes in the western suburbs. Elsewhere
certain cooperatives, and particularly those which were not members of
the FNCC, were business or trade cooperatives drawing on the whole
of their *département;* this was specifically the case of the independent
railway workers' staff stores.

It is impossible not to be impressed by the working-class nature of
the cooperative movement. The strongholds of cooperation were the
old working-class quarters of east Paris and the new working-class quar-

ters of the northern and western suburbs. Once again Saint-Denis and the 20th *arrondissement* seem to be linked in a common destiny, that of the considerable importance that the retail consumer cooperative acquired in a working-class and militant population. Puteaux, with its population of the Arsenal's skilled mechanic workers, constituted the third beacon of this particular geographical pattern. Although the extreme weakness of the cooperative movement in the west of Paris can be explained satisfactorily by the social character of its inhabitants, it should be noted that cooperation did not develop on the eve of war in certain working-class suburbs of south-west Paris (Boulogne, Issy) or of the south-east (Ivry, Vitry).

Geographical factors also affected the sociology of the working-class cooperative society member. In highlighting the names of Paris cooperative members quoted by Jean Gaumont, the importance of railway workers, print workers, mechanics, and old-established crafts can be seen among the militants. More thorough study, however, is needed on this point.

The Paris cooperative movement consisted of 102 societies, of which the majority belonged to the first section of the FNCC – the *Fédération des Coopératives de la Région Parisienne*, covering the *départements* of the Seine, Seine-et-Oise and Eure-et-Loire. Its secretary, Paul Alexandre, was employed in the Parisian Gas Company and was a veteran of the French *Parti Ouvrier*, the Workers' Party.[8] It should be noted here that the cooperative movement in Paris was much less exclusive than the generality of French cooperation. Thus, 84 societies out of 102 in the Seine belonged to the FNCC, against 894 out of 3261 for the whole country; the Seine societies in the FNCC covered 39,384 members out of 69,234, while at a national level the members of the FNCC amounted to only 254,360 out of a total of 890,710 cooperative members. There was the same difference in turnover figures: 20 million francs out of the 34 million francs of the Seine turnover derived from cooperatives in the FNCC, while at a national level the FNCC had only 111 million francs' turnover against the 321 million francs' turnover for cooperatives as a whole. Depending on the parameters, in 1914 the FNCC covered between 56 percent and 82.5 percent of cooperative strength in the Seine, against between only 27 percent and 34 percent nationally.

At this level a major difference is apparent between the city of Paris and its suburbs. The suburban cooperatives belonged almost exclusively to the FNCC: 91 percent of societies and 98 percent of society members and turnover for the suburban cooperatives came from societies belonging to the FNCC; in the city of Paris the figures were 69 percent,

44 percent and 46 percent respectively.

What did these cooperatives do? They must be given full credit for all their activities. We may begin with a brief overview of the activities of the *La Bellevilloise*, the earliest Parisian – and even national – cooperative, on the eve of the war. First, it was a powerful market force, with nine groceries, a haberdashery, a bakery, a flour-mill, and seven butchers. Its headquarters at 19–23 rue Boyer also had a café. Surrounding these trading activities, a whole network of other activities recalled the trade union or socialist model of participation in the whole of human life. This included a band and a choir, a youth club for cooperative members' children, adult education classes (*la semaille*) and a library, classes in drama, singing, and esperanto. A group of cooperative members took care of publicity and training.[9]

Clearly this was the establishment, in a modest form, of a social structure (this time in the broad sense of the word), perhaps an alternative society, if such a concept can be accepted. In any case, the whole substantially outpaced the single shop and social activity.

One should be wary about generalizing from this example, which remained unique in the Paris conurbation and which only *La Revendication* at Puteaux and *L'Egalitaire* in the 10th *arrondissement* could approach; *Le Progrès d'Arcueil*, with its fifty members and its sales figure of 6000 francs had nothing in common with this colossal machine selling over 5 million francs' worth of goods.

The great question debated in the cooperatives on the eve of the war was that of concentration.[10] In effect each *arrondissement* and each commune tended to have its own cooperative – supplied, it is true, from the same wholesale store,[11] but, according to the managers of the Federation, constituting organisms too fragile to be effective or competitive. The earliest regroupings were taking place on the very eve of the war: a "union of Paris cooperators" was to be set up around the old *Egalitaire* – whose headquarters was "sheltered in a sort of dark fortress, at the foot of which the red flag was always flying"[12] – together with "La Famille du XIème" (the family of the 11th arrondissement) and "L'Avenir de Plaisance" (the future of the Plaisance district). The suburbs acquired their own "union of consumers of the eastern suburbs."[13] The war was to give form to this move towards concentration.

Renewal and Centralization during the War

As with other working-class organizations, the cooperatives were initially severely affected by the war; but the scale of problems of ration supplies, of the increased cost of living, and of feeding the workers in war factories was soon to bring fresh vigor to the cooperative movement. A table of cooperative activity in the Seine can be drawn up, comparing 1913 with 1918:

Table 10.2: Movement in the Seine Region

	SOCIETIES	MEMBERS	TURNOVER (FF)	INDEX OF TURNOVER BASE
1913	102	69,234	34,446,014	100
1918	145	166,852	127,267,150	173

Source: *Annuaire de la Coopérative*, 1920.

These figures, which underestimate the growth in members and turnover (because not all cooperatives replied to the FNCC[14] or the Labor Ministry[15] surveys) nonetheless reveal the great resurgence of the cooperative movement in Paris during the Great War. This phenomenon is seldom recognized; the increase during the two years immediately following the war was even greater. Despite mergers, the number of cooperatives increased perceptibly, indicating a fresh cooperative dynamism.[16] The number of society members doubled – an indication of spreading representation – and the turnover quadrupled, yielding a 70 percent growth in sales volume. New society members thus consumed relatively slightly less than those of 1914.[17]

The record was, however, largely positive, to the extent that the golden age of 1900 was appreciably overtaken in 1918 and during the immediate postwar period. Comparing these figures with the national figures makes the growth in Paris cooperation even more dazzling. Of course one of the bastions of the cooperative movement, the Nord (and the Ardennes), was affected by wartime circumstances, and this factor influenced the movement's overall development. Taking a base figure of 100 in 1913, the number of cooperative societies grew by the end of the war to an index figure of 142 for the Seine, against 116 for the whole of France, and 131 for the whole of France excluding the Nord and the Ardennes. The number of society members grew to an index figure of 241 for the Seine, 150 for the whole of France, and 197 for the whole of France excluding the Nord and the Ardennes. Finally, using statistics deflated to eliminate wartime price movements, we can see that the turnover figure grew to an index of 173 for the Seine, 94 for the whole of France, and 118 for the whole of France excluding the Nord and the Ardennes.

Growth was thus evident in the Seine region no matter which indicator is selected, and particularly in turnover – undoubtedly the most important indicator. Paris, with its suburbs, was the stronghold of cooperative growth during the Great War – a somewhat surprising phenomenon, and one which ill accords with an image of Paris as a workers' revolutionary center.

This growth was marked by several significant elements which indicate a structural change in Paris cooperatives. Despite the appearance of small societies which were not part of the federation, the FNCC increased its share in the turnover of cooperatives in the Seine region, a share which grew from 58 percent in 1913 to 70 percent in 1918. This, however, was not the essential element, as can be seen in Table 10.3.

The crucial point is certainly the diminution of local cooperatives – within districts or communes – to the benefit of cooperative unions. The tendency which had begun before the war grew considerably – the cooperative unions were responsible for more than half the sales of 1918. To the "Union of Paris Cooperators," whose turnover reached 10 million francs in 1919, was added in 1917 the "Union of Cooperatives," including the "Union of Consumers in the Eastern Suburbs," the "Union of Consumers of the Western Suburbs," and various Paris cooperatives. The *Union des Coopératives* had a turnover of 30 million francs in 1918. That same year the *Union des Coopératives de la Banlieue Nord* was established; it immediately achieved a turnover close to 7 million francs. This tendency towards unification continued with the merger, in February 1920, of the *Union des Coopérateurs Parisiens* and the *Union des Coopératives*.[19] The ferocious centralization of the Paris cooperative movement thus entailed the disappearance of many local cooperatives. Those local cooperatives which continued to exist, however, increased their sales by only 16 percent, in contrast to more than 100 percent for FNCC cooperatives as a whole.

Cooperative dynamism was much greater in the suburbs. From less than 40 percent of sales of the FNCC in 1913, the suburbs grew to represent more than 50 percent in 1918, a classic shift which would be noted frequently elsewhere.

Thoroughly typical of cooperatives accumulating problems, *La Bellevilloise* only increased its turnover from 5.347 million francs in 1913 to 10.090 million francs in 1918, i.e., at constant prices, from 100 in 1914 to 88 in 1918. At the General Assembly of 2 December 1917 the administrator recognized the cooperative's effective downturn.

Apart from blaming the departure of mobilized men, Lamothe explained this setback by the reduction in the resources of older people:

Table 10:3: Turnover in French Francs in 1913 and 1918, according to type of cooperative belonging to the FNCC[18]

	1913	1918	INDEX AT CONSTANT PRICES (1918=100)
Existing local cooperatives			
Paris	7,409	15,296	97
Suburbs	6,394	18,901	139
Seine total	13,803	34,197	116
New local cooperatives			
Paris		802	
Suburbs		3,748	
Seine total		4,550	
Local cooperatives lost			
Paris	4,652		
Suburbs	1,469		
Seine total	6,120		
Cooperative unions			
Seine total		47,024	
Business cooperatives			
Paris		2,977	
Suburbs	15	460	
Seine total	15	3,437	
All cooperatives			
Paris	12,061	44,400 (est.)	172
Suburbs	7,877	44,800 (est.)	268
Seine total	19,938	89,208	210

"Yet they were the best cooperators, these old people, the faithful of the *Bellevilloise*." The late return home of women from the factories also made it impossible for them to shop, and more generally:

> The 20th *arrondissement* is not one of those where the number of factories corresponds to today's industrial development or the number of metal-workers. Very many metal-workers live in the 20th *arrondissement* but work in Ivry, or Montrouge, or Billancourt.[20]

These workmen, who left early in the morning and returned home late in the evening, ate in restaurants and bought less at the local cooperative. From this precise analysis the author deduced that it would be possible to hope for improvement after the war. It is fascinating to see in operation here the serious falling-off in a working-class institution, the decline of which reflected changes in the spatial character of Parisian workers' lives.

The appearance of the business cooperative was also a novelty for the cooperative movement in Paris – or at least for that part which belonged to the FNCC. On the eve of the war, there were cooperatives of postal workers, of civil servants, of railway workers, but they were not federated. The war brought factory cooperatives, some of which belonged to the Federation, like the cooperatives of the Vedovelli or Peugeot factories; other branch cooperatives, such as those of state education (founded in 1917) and of the Metro (founded in 1918) did likewise. A structure developed which was different from local or union structure, although without achieving major significance; but it was nevertheless an indication of the growth of business as a framework for the labor movement's activities. The question arises: did the cooperative movement of 1918 still spring from the labor movement?

The Social Relations of Consumer Cooperative Societies in Wartime

One of the central problems in the life of a nation at war is the matter of food supplies and distribution. In this area the experience and potential capacity of cooperatives were very significant. In such circumstances it is understandable that the government should turn to the work of the cooperative movement with increasing interest; as so often with research into the social history of France during the Great War, we find Albert Thomas – but first the strengths of the Paris cooperatives during the war should be assessed.

Food Supplies and Distribution

Examination of the accounts of *La Bellevilloise* reveals some reorganization of cooperative sales (see Table 10.4). Interpretation of this table is difficult, for it includes changes arising wholly from the particular circumstances of the war, but apparently without any further consequences – for example, the feminization of consumer activity, seen in the buoyant sales in printed cotton goods and the steep drop in turnover in hardware (and possibly also the coffee). The noticeable turnover in hardware (and possibly also the coffee). The noticeable expansion in food sales at the expense of other sectors (food constituted 78 percent of sales in *La Bellevilloise* in 1913–14, 88 percent

Table 10.4 : An Index of Sales in *La Bellevilloise* by Type of Product, from 1913 to 1919

PRODUCT	1913/14	1914/15	1915/16	1916/17	1917/18	1918/19
Butchery	100	62	92.5	127	171	276
Grocery	100	70	89	110	132	213
Cooked Meats	100	76	77	132	119	130
Coffee	100	44	63	71	81	166
Coal	100	16	31	40	17	23
Haberdashery including –printed cotton goods	100	89	92	113	145	166
goods	100	98	131	155	184	220
Ironmongery (hardware)	100	35	35	41	49	100

in 1918–19) reflects both a situation of restricted purchasing capacity and also a civic policy of coal distribution at low cost. The increased significance of butchery is a mark of the true success of the cooperative system, which was not exclusive to *La Bellevilloise.*

> To quote only the example of Paris, where now the Cooperatives have more than 80 butcheries selling frozen meat – yet previously the butchery section had been a modest cooperative service which did not offer the excellent results it has since attained.[21]

Concentrating less on this specific expansion in cooperative butchery – which does not appear to have had very significant consequences – we must remember that the Paris cooperatives achieved this success by placing themselves at the forefront of changes in consumption by pushing frozen meat onto the market and by giving advice on how to prepare and cook it, with emphasis on its quality.[22] This received official encouragement, from an administration which saw here a way to limit increases in the price of meat.

The second great initiative in the Paris cooperative movement was its participation in the supply and feeding of workers in war factories. Statistics for the Seine are not available, but there is every indication that the Paris cooperative movement played a leading role in this activity, as Table 10.5 shows.

Although the cooperatives experienced some difficulties in entering state-run establishments where (in a circular dated 2 October 1915) the directors were required to supply their workers with meals,[24] their expan-

Table 10.5: National statistics of restaurants and shops established for workers in war-factories in 1917 and 1918

	June-July 1917			July 1916		
	Restaurants	Customers	Shops	Restaurants	Turnover*	Shops
Private Establishments						
Cooperative Institutions	60	24,550	67	119	7.9	813
Employers' institutions	115	70,478	43	161	6.8	167
Various	7	4,545	0	?		
State Establishments Cooperative Institutions	11	7,485	19	16	1.2	24
State Institutions	47	82,433	2	42	4.3	3
Various	2	600	0	0		

*Turnover is for the first half of 1918 in million francs .[23]

sion in private establishments was spectacular. Their significance appeared in the high turnover/restaurant ratio. In the Paris area the great majority of workers in war factories who were taking their meals away from independent restaurants or home could be found by the end of the war in the cooperative restaurants in the factory or group of factories. We have identified about sixty cooperative canteens[25] set up for workers in the Seine war factories.[26] There were significant exceptions, such as Renault and Citroën, which set up their own restaurants, but the weight of cooperation in Paris restaurants was overwhelmingly dominant, especially for shops supplying various elements of workers' meals.

The introduction of a new cooperative 1500-seat restaurant at *L'Union* in Boulogne on 1 December 1918 reveals clearly that the range of these worker restaurant undertakings was considerable. For the cooperative movement it was a means of combatting the impact of the greater distances travelled by workers from their dwelling place to their workplace. By emphasizing the quality of the service as well as the competitive prices, the hygiene, the variety of the menus, and the brightness of the hall, the cooperative movement could also offer a type of social activity different from that of the restaurant or private establishment,[27] even if opinions differed on the availability of wine. The Cooperative was thus one of the centers of social welfare that expanded during the war.

More naturally the cooperatives disseminated propaganda,[28] using some of the most modern methods, such as the cinema.[29] Like other working-class organizations, they organized family festivities, supported their groups of orphans, and gave money to the families of their mobilized men.[30] The cooperatives naturally took part in the great movement of soup kitchens for the people, established at the end of 1914 by Paris working-class organizations; they also increased the sale of milk, severely affected by the looters of the Maggi shops, who were suspected of pro-German sympathies.[31] Cooperatives were also involved in setting up workshops designed to provide work for unemployed men and women at the beginning of the war.[32] They were also concerned with problems of maternity and breast-feeding.[33]

Cultural activities, in the strictest meaning of the term, were, on the other hand, severely affected. Thus in *La Bellevilloise*, although sponsorship was maintained, the band, the choir, the various classes, and advanced adult education ceased.[34] After the war, however, a very large cooperative such as the "Union of Paris Cooperators" sponsored a group of orphans and organized children's group holidays. It ran a sports club, but its cultural activities were reduced to running a library.[35] Nothing could be more revealing than that in the catalogue of books and brochures available in the FNCC, only four volumes out of ninety-nine were educational (another three concerned orphans and child-care; only one book was "cultural" in the more restricted sense, and was concerned with singing).[36]

The economy thus took a more important place in the Paris cooperative activities, and one cannot fail to ponder the implications of this development in the setting of cooperators' thinking, and in the more general setting of the aims of the various social forces contributing to the cooperative movement.

The New Place of Cooperation

The great expansion in the Paris cooperative movement and the partial redirection of its activities cannot be dissociated from a considerable change in its relationship with the state and with employers. Certainly before the war the cooperative movement lay close to French socialism in its directors and its militants, and the whole of the formerly "neutral" current was not without its links with the government. But the state was little concerned with retail cooperatives, and the latter resisted any attempts at subsidies which might threaten their independence.

Study of the means of financing cooperative restaurants highlights the extent of the changes brought about during the war. Two of Albert Thomas's circulars lay behind the expansion and the nature of restaurants opened especially for war-workers. The circulars dated 1 and 31 October 1916[37] stress the full advantage for managers of state-run establishments and industrialists of calling upon cooperative societies for the management of canteens. Among the chief points of these circulars, the most important is perhaps that of "the commitment to supply meals to all workers in the establishment, whether or not they are members of the cooperative."[38] The cooperator yielded to the consumer – a deep-seated revolution which changed the cooperative from a closed micro-society to a receiver of services. Here one is reminded of the later restaurants run by works committees.

Financial aid for cooperatives whose capital was much reduced came from two sources. One was the *Fonds coopératif pour le personnel des usines de guerre* (cooperative fund for war-factory employees), largely financed by the state, and the other was industrial aid. In his circular of 31 October 1916, Albert Thomas sought the establishment of "employer associations" which would underwrite this financing. These associations were set up in the 19th and 20th *arrondissements*, at Boulogne-Billancourt, Suresnes-Puteaux, Saint-Denis, La Courneuve, and the Pré-Saint-Gervais. To quote the first article of the statutes of the model Union of the 19th and 20th *arrondissements*:

> Its principal aim is the organization of cooperative restaurants in the 19th and 20th *arrondissements*, where consumption of alcohol and all political, social, or religious discussion whatsoever is strictly forbidden. Further aims are the examination and implementation of all measures leading to the improved well-being of these workers.[39]

It was deeply humiliating for the cooperatives to be forced to agree to collaboration with the employers on such restrictive lines, compared to the ideal cooperative of pre-1914 days. However, the directors of the large cooperatives accepted them, as can be seen in the Convention signed between the union of industrialists in the 19th and 20th *arrondissements* and Gaston Lévy for the cooperatives' union, and which brought the union a grant of 33,000 francs.[40] In the suburbs, too, there could be seen "cooperation" between industrialists and cooperators in setting up cooperative restaurants. Official openings were opportunities

ches by cooperative or socialist leaders on social harmony.
alists such as Charles Blum, Niepce, and Voisin were present at
itherings. Albert Thomas was able to stress the "mutual interest"
ustrialists and workers in seeing the "development of produc-
...on."[41] Charles Gide was able to declare his pleasure at the development of cooperation for "here is a basis for rapprochement and collaboration between the working classes and the middle classes."[42] There was
the strange sight at the banquet on 1 December 1918 of the President
of the League of the Rights of Man standing among two ministers, two
industrialists (Niepce and Clément), three cooperative directors, four
socialists (Morizet, Longuet, Cachin and Frossard), and the secretary of
the vehicle and aviation trade union, E. Becker. Contradictory positions
abounded, but no one challenged the cooperative operation. Even the
representative of the minority of the CGT Becker declared both that "it
would be logical to hand over to the workers the whole of the product
of their labor," and thanked the industrialists for their help.[43]

Contacts with the government's men, the ministers, also proliferated.
The presence of Picquenard or of Arthur Fontaine, those two loyal servants of the state and of the Ministry of Labor, was not surprising.
More unexpected were the renewed thanks of the secretary of the
Boulogne "Union," Chassagnade, to Loucheur in December 1918,
although the latter was the object of violent attacks from the labor
movement.[44] We should note, however, that the political neutrality
specified in agreements was not always respected. Quotations or mottos
from socialists or other social philosophers (Jaurès, Pressemane, Benoit-
Malon, Fourier, Saint-Simon, Vandervelde, Gide, Bernstein, and even
Marx, after the Armistice) were displayed on the walls of cooperative
restaurant-halls,[45] revealing the contradictions inherent in the practice.

This profound change in practice and in the direction of cooperative
activity was accompanied by a fresh questioning of cooperative identity.
We have a fine illustration in the names of the societies in the Seine
département which belonged to the FNCC. Examination of the names
of cooperatives set up before the war shows a strong lead for styles such
as *L'Avenir, L'Espérance, L'Aurore* and *L'Aube* – "the Future," "Hope,"
"Dawn" and "Daybreak" – (twenty-one cases of which five also included 'social' or 'socialist'); followed by eight image-titles such as "The
Hive," "The Bee," "The Reaper," "Eglantine;" and seven social references such as "The Proletarian Woman," "Worker Strength," "The
Working Woman" or "The Worker's Union," while family-related
names appeared in seven cases. Finally, there came a range of names
such as "Progress," "Emancipation," "The Liberator," "The Egalitarian"

or "The Claim." Only two names related to "The Cooperative" or "Cooperators."

On the other hand, a study of the names of Paris cooperatives founded between 1914 and 1918 reveals a crushing preponderance of "Cooperative" or "cooperators" – twenty-one, against one "Hope," one "Working woman," and one "Solidarity." The reversal is overwhelming. On the eve of the First World War cooperative identity was not defined by self-reference but by reference to working-class aspirations. During the war the movement confirmed its identity and almost entirely lost its broader social and emancipatory agenda.

May one conclude that the Great War saw the cooperative movement distancing itself from the labor movement? This would mean disregarding the marked reservations of certain cooperators or socialists in the face of this development.

It was in relation to the organization of the cooperative movement that discussions were clearest. Reservations relating to bureaucratization and centralization emerged on several occasions. For example, at the Congress of the Paris Federation of Cooperatives in August 1917 the proposition of the new secretary, Ramadier, to increase the number of its managers aroused resistance and was carried by 89 in favor and 19 against.[46] The merger of the management of the FNCC and of the hitherto autonomous wholesale store brought even more reservations and gained only 69 votes in favor with 37 against. At the FNCC national congress of 30 September–1 October 1917 the opponents were all from the old local cooperatives (the "New Family," the "Social Lutetia," and the "Proletarian Woman" of the 5th *arrondissement*, and the 'Bellevilloise'). They saw the merger as a danger to cooperative ideals, losing the distinction between management and propaganda.[47] Thus these reservations concerned the underlying primacy of the economic function over the ideals of the movement.

Other criticisms were aimed at the advantages that cooperative managers gave themselves and their excessive or unnecessary expenses. It was frequently trade union members who put forward such comments, such as Millarat, secretary of the Clothing Workers union, who denounced the employment of members from the same family, in contravention of the statutes, or did not see the point of the expenditure of 5,000 francs to buy a car.[48] Prost, of the mechanics' union, was opposed to the purchase of a housing block.[49] There were similar criticisms relating to staff policy. For example, Millerat expressed surprise at the dismissal of a caretaker. This was an old question that lay behind numerous conflicts between cooperatives and trade union members before the war,[50] and we can further find on the agenda of the Congress of the Paris Federation of Cooperatives on 28 January 1917 and 26 August 1917: [51] "conflicts between cooperatives and their personnel – creation of a commission of arbitration."

Finally, there were reservations regarding the scope of cooperative activity. Although scepticism was expressed at the outbreak of war as to the capacity of the societies to have at their disposal sufficient capital to buy and resell at competitive prices[52] or to set up cooperative restaurants,[53] such observations faded naturally with the expansion already noted. It was in the immediate postwar period that the limits of cooperative activity relating to social change came to the fore. Thus Frossard estimated that one should not be lured by the significance of the advantages offered by the cooperatives while "the social revolution continues to grow and expand from East to West."[54]

Noting in November 1917 the impressive advance of the Paris cooperatives, Ernest Poisson, secretary of the FNCC, foresaw a vast program of "indefinite expansion of shops and services for distribution, cooperatization of wholesale trade through central agencies, and, further ahead, industrial and even agricultural cooperative production."[55] The historian cannot help but note that the word "cooperatization" has not met with the success of either its predecessor, "socialization" or of one of its contemporaries, "nationalization." However, it certainly appears that at the end of the Great War the success of cooperative activity, which continued until at least the time of the division of the labor movement in 1920, supplied a plausible alternative to revolution. The fact that this progression was particularly strong in the Seine and that it accompanied many changes in the Paris area (Paris/suburbs, centralization, workers' canteens) gave it an up-to-date character, keeping pace with the results of militant activity in the war factories.

At the very least, cooperation was a fundamental element in the development of the reformist current of the worker movement in the postwar period, giving consumers a place as the third force alongside capital and labor in the reconstruction of the French economy. Relations between socialism and cooperation were established immediately before the war, and emerged from it largely consolidated; in effect the socialist branches of the Seine were from 1915 to 1917 distinctly active in reinforcing cooperative action, and even if after 1918 the cooperatives were scarcely in need of this support, the working-class interest in the cooperative ideal remained significant. This can be seen in the pattern of development of socialist conferences or discussions with a bearing on the theme (see Table 10.6).

Table 10.6: Number of workers' meetings in Paris where cooperation was discussed [56]

	1915	1
	1916	7
	1917	9
	1918	12
Jan.–June	1919	8

The significance of these figures is increased by the evidence of a decline in interest in economic questions at the end of the war within socialist organizations in the *département* of the Seine.

Still it was apparent that the trade-union/cooperative link, the decisive link in this project, had to function. Trade unionism and cooperation is an essential area to which we must now turn.

Trade Unionism and Cooperatives

It is no doubt helpful to begin by recalling the text of the Amiens motion concerning relations between trade unionism and cooperation, a text entirely overshadowed by the actual Amiens Charter(1906):

> The Congress does not see the advantage, at the present time, of uniting the two bodies, *trade unionism* and *cooperation*, in a definitive understanding. Nonetheless, it invites all trade union members to become cooperators, and only to use those cooperatives that pass on part of their profits to social activity that will help to suppress wage earning. The Congress also invites all cooperators to belong to their appropriate trade union, affiliated to the CGT. It also issues this formal notice, that, at the very least, the cooperatives' administrative boards should in the future be composed wholly of workers who are trade union federated members, the only condition which will assure cooperative employees of some kind of security in the struggles that may arise between them and the administrative boards.[57]

The fact that the text was approved without discussion did not indicate indifference to the question, but lack of time! Pierre Viche's report underlined, however, the economic character common to both organizations, energetically denouncing the cooperativism of the Nimes school as "supporter of the alliance between capital and labor," and concluding with the positive features of the Exchange of Socialist Cooperatives such as their educational efforts and their support of strikes. He even considered making the cooperative "the stronghold of the unions," quoting the case of the Amiens Union, which employed on its staff some twenty union secretaries or treasurers.

The fusion on the eve of the war of these two currents of the cooperative movement would perhaps render the relationship between trade unionism and cooperatives more uncertain than would the declared position in opposition to one of the currents and of alliance with the other. But the war was to pose these problems even more acutely.

Progress of the Cooperative Spirit

In 1918 it was impossible to remain unaware of definite advances in the cooperative spirit among Paris trade unions. Criticisms which had been widespread during the first three years of the war (30 percent of statements were concerned with cooperatives) faded noticeably during that year; this tendency did not continue, however, into 1919, when new criticisms appeared.

The progress of cooperativism was also marked in trade union practice which gave substantial space for the setting up of producer cooperatives, at least in branches where such activity appeared reasonable (construction and tailoring in particular). In 1916 the shoemakers' union planned to set up a producer cooperative.[58] In November 1916, on the initiative of Joseph Jacquemotte, the clothing workers' union adopted the principle of a tailoring cooperative,[59] and in 1917 the military clothing workers' union set in hand a similar cooperative.[60] Cooperative aspirations became so extensive that during the strike of September 1918 the strikers pronounced themselves in favor of putting pressure on the government for the creation of cooperatives after the war.[61] On 11 April 1918 the papermakers' union decided to study the possibilities of creating a cooperative at the end of the war,[62] and in March 1919 the electrical fitters' union, one of the most revolutionary unions in the *département* of the Seine, proposed a similar question for study.[63]

It was in April 1915 that the timber frame workers' union had established its cooperative.[64] Such an aim was regularly referred to at meetings of the bricklayers' union during the war,[65] and in October 1918 the decorators' union also came out in favor of creating a cooperative.[66] Militants of the stonemasons' union set up a cooperative at the beginning of 1918.[67]

Trade unionists were also interested in the creation of consumer cooperatives or cooperative restaurants, particularly railway workers (for whom a producers' cooperative would be meaningless!). The Paris-Nord union set up a cooperative restaurant in 1915 in the rue du Simplon, with the union secretary, Thys, as manager.[68] In December 1918 the

Asnières railway workers' union planned a cooperative for railway workers of the western suburbs.[69] Within the public assistance system a similar establishment was planned, and the principle was approved despite some reservations concerning a creation which would undermine the already existing cooperatives.[70] In March 1918 the vehicle and aviation union set up a cooperative restaurant at Levallois.[71]

Such developments should not be exaggerated; they were not as general as were other areas of union activity. But each one was an indicator of increasing interest in the cooperative movement, and we should attempt to identify their origins.

Giving Primacy to the Economy, or Settling Accounts with the Shark-profiteers?

The production objective was rarely advanced in the arguments of those who favored producer cooperatives. Internally, however, the cooperative appeared as a means of absorbing unemployment in difficult times. In 1915, for example, it was undoubtedly the exceptional circumstances of the war (unemployment in the construction industry, opportunities for works contracts with the military engineers) that led the reluctant to accept the constitution of a timber frame workers' cooperative. One militant, Brochet, thus declared himself opposed to producer cooperatives in principle, but accepted them in fact.[72] Further, the statutes of the Association contained a time limit restricting it to the duration of the war.[73] Among the painter-decorators, the decision to found a cooperative was part of an overview aimed at relaunching production (reliable delivery of materials, ordering).[74] Again, at the beginning of 1919, when a militant of the Clichy branch of the stonemasons' trade union spoke out in favor of large workers' producer cooperatives, the meeting reflected the view that the audience "only wanted work."[75] Faced with a decline within these ancient and threatened trades of timber frame construction and stonemasonry, cooperation looked like an answer to decline, for which there was no precise analysis.[76]

The only clear-cut case we can find of support for cooperatives as an element of productive development is the agreement of the delegates of the Paris railway workers' union to a proposition from Bled, the secretary of the Seine Union, to take part in cooperatives for the reconstruction of the occupied lands of northern France.[77] This participation of the cooperatives in reconstruction, for which Daudé-Bancel adopted the role of propagandist, met with little response in the Paris unions.

"To cut the cost of living" was the title of an article by Léon Jouhaux in his defense of the actions of retail cooperatives, particularly the sale of frozen meat.[78] This concept of the effectiveness of cooperative action in restraining the rise in prices can be found in certain of these gatherings. Ducoussu, secretary of the union of unskilled hospital staff, even saw it as the only effective form of action.[79] The socialist councillor Reisz put forward this success of cooperative action to the Société anonyme des Applications industrielles du Bois(SAAIB) workers.[80] The notion that cooperative participation might result in lower prices was developed again in 1919.[81]

However, the feeling that dominated discussions of this topic was that cooperatives must be sustained "to teach the profiteer-merchants and the government a lesson."[82] Loze, the secretary of the chemical industry trade union, saw cooperatives as the means to boycott small traders.[83] The Panhard shop steward, Lemaitre, considered that the cooperative would be the means of "escaping from the sharp traders claws."[84] These were, moreover, the traders who put pressure on the Minister of Food Supply, according to Desgranges, to slow down the development of the cooperative movement.[85]

Thus it was not to support an economic project, but rather to resist these adversaries – or those who were seen as such, the small traders – that the trade unionists invested in the cooperative. It was a matter of operating the fulcrum of cooperation, whose leverage was acknowledged, to counterbalance the traders' excesses, just as direct action operated on markets or in shops. In this they distanced themselves clearly from those – particularly among the socialists – with no wish to use cooperatives as a weapon against small traders who might be potential allies.[86]

The Cooperative as Emancipator?

For some the cooperative was both a form of proletarian action in the struggle for emancipation and one of the roads to emancipation; indeed, the cooperative was to some extent an anticipation of a new social order.

Joseph Jacquemotte, the future founder of the Belgian Communist party and one of the most positive proponents of establishing a tailoring cooperative, proposed as a leading argument in its favor that it would make it possible to "avoid" the employer. Widows and the war-injured, who were in a position of inferiority in relation to employers, would escape their dependence, and out-working at home would be supplanted.[87] "The working class should fight with every economic means at its disposal," he concluded. It was in the same sense that Charlotte Amsterdamski intervened; the dynamic leader of the sewing machinists' union came out in favor of a "cooperative on a communist basis," which would enable a more effective struggle against the employers.[88]

More broadly, the producer cooperative opened up "the road towards the enfranchisement of the working class;"[89] it was "a step towards the emancipation of the proletariat,"[90] provided it organized itself on a "communist" basis.[91] The cooperative was thus a model, an anticipation of the future society on the model of the old nineteenth-century associative tradition, the "Work Republic" so elegantly described by Jacques Rancière.[92] Cooperatives were thus "proof" of the value of the individual and, like the union, helped to create "awareness."[93] Finally, as indicated in the vivid language of Froment, the secretary of the boxmakers, the "workers will themselves be the employers' in the cooperatives."[94] The cooperative was thus a gleam of light in "the night of the proletarians," a gleam reawakened by the successes of the cooperative movement during the Great War. One cannot help noticing, however, the rarity of such interventions, which often came from middle-ranking activists, branch secretaries, and former leaders. This enlisting of cooperation in the working-class project was secondary to the support cooperatives offered to trade union organization.

The Cooperative, a "Stronghold" of the Trade Union

The criterion of the cooperatives' value to trade union activity, the basis of their approval at the confederal Congress of 1906, remained at the forefront during the war in working-class meetings. With eighteen references, it was well ahead of economic issues, with twelve references, and emancipatory ideas, with eight mentions. The value of the producer cooperative as a creator of competition from above, equal to working conditions, was little mentioned except by the butchers' union, which expressed its "gratitude" to cooperatives maintaining Monday closing;[95] but the cooperative butchery trade was one of the rare sectors where the cooperative was competitive and could affect wages or the hours of work. When Chamoy stressed that the timber frame workers' cooperative paid its workers at trade union rates and operated the "English" working week while still offering benefits,[96] he was in fact putting forward a defensive argument in the face of criticism, to which we will return.

The financial interest of the cooperatives was more obvious. They were a place for the deposit, in various guises, of trade union money. In effect the risks of bank deposits (dependent on the State) or of private deposits with the official treasurer were avoided, provided the trade union trusted the cooperative. Thus in September 1915 the bakery workers' union withdrew its balance of 2,700 francs from the Crédit Lyonnais and decided to deposit it with the "Fraternelle," the bakery workers' cooperative society.[97] The unions of upholsterers, of clothing workers, of wood-gilders, and of vehicle and aviation workers placed all or part of their money with cooperatives.[98] The commercial travellers' union considered doing so in 1917.[99] The unions were particularly attracted to the Cooperative Wholesale Store, with its strong financial base.

Cooperatives were also a source of direct finance. For example, *La Bellevilloise* granted 1,500 francs to the combined trades unions in the Seine in January 1918.[100] The funds of the timber frame workers' cooperative were used to pay out 10 francs per month to the wives of mobilized members, at a time when solidarity was in decline.[101]

Aid to strikers figured in this range of financial services to workers' action, such as the payment of 100 francs by the clothing workers' insurance to SPC strikers in 1916.[102] In June 1919 the cooperatives supplied meals to strikers at very low price.[103] Cooperative restaurants and cooperatives were also a haven for trade union members.[104] The proposed statute for a leather workers' cooperative indicated that its purpose was to provide employment for workers banned by employers.[105] This aspect of the cooperative as refuge was well displayed by the shoemakers' strike committee secretary in February 1918; he hoped for the creation of a leatherworking cooperative which would allow locked-out strikers to continue working.[106]

Here too we must not generalize from the declarations of militants within certain branches, and rarely of the major unions; but one should note that it all formed part of a bundle of key union practices (financing, control of the labor market, protection of militants, and strikes) and which naturally resulted in a positive perception of the cooperative movement.

The drive of the major consumer cooperatives was not without its effect on the union movement, which was already favorable to it in the prewar period. More than their economic weight or their forward-looking aspect, it was their value in the struggle against the employers or traders which was as apparent in speeches as in trade union practice. This revealed a certain distancing from the primarily economic view of cooperatives held by the national leaders of the labor movement, who saw in them a third force of reconstruction of national production. But if there was therefore some ambiguity, this in no way detracts from the fact that there was certainly a link between the cooperative concept and trade unions during the Great War. It made itself evident, however, in reservations and resistance, to which we now turn.

Criticisms and Reservations

In the course of working-class debates, critical statements relating to cooperatives were insignificant during the war, but never wholly absent, even in 1918 at the peak period of the cooperative debate. It is particularly interesting to note that criticism was very clearly more an act of intervention from those who were not in office, of whom 45 percent denounced the cooperatives, or their policies. The percentage of hostile speeches fell to 25 percent among those with some union responsibilities, and to 13 percent among union secretaries; there were too few speeches from federal, departmental, or national on this subject – four – to offer a reliable percentage. There were slight differences between rank and file and activist criticisms, although they overlapped to some extent.

Chief Characteristics of Militants' Criticism

The activists put forward two essential reservations. First, they expressed skepticism regarding the success of cooperatives. Certain leaders would have liked to establish a cooperative, but initially the lack of money to provide the start-up capital financing led them to doubt the possibility of success. Thus early in 1918 the secretary of the paperworkers' union, Rappin, opposed Charlotte Amsterdamski's proposal of a communist cooperative.[107] This skepticism grew with the cooperatives' general problems; in March 1917 Serre, Gauthier, and Alexandre also refused Jacquemotte's proposition to finance the cooperative because, they said, the cooperatives were struggling to survive.[108] In particular they saw the producer cooperatives as vulnerable, and they recalled the setbacks of the two large cooperatives, *La Bellevilloise* and *L'Egalitaire*, in their attempts to set up a tailoring section.[109]

Such skepticism led to concern at wasting the union's money in setting up a producer cooperative and thereafter of hindering general union activity. Chamoy's initial suggestion, of using the surplus from the union's solidarity fund to provide the capital for the timber frame workers' labor association was therefore rejected by the union.[110] But the deposit of the union funds in a cooperative was not always straightforward either. Roux's suggestion of depositing the Sub-Postmasters' union fund in the Wholesale Store was rejected following an intervention by Calvet, the under-secretary of the union, who declared that "he would prefer to entrust it to Messrs Potin."[111] The union decided to place its money in National Defense bonds. There was also opposition in the bakers' union, members preferring the union money to stay within the CGT structure rather than be deposited with a cooperative.[112]

These reservations, these signs of defiance, were not so serious as to affect adversely recruitment to cooperative activity. It is significant to note that Rappin, who expressed reservations at the beginning of 1918, came round a few months later to the creation of a bookbinding cooperative. Criticisms concerning the way the cooperatives operated were stronger and deeper.

Against the Cooperator-Employer

At a meeting of the shoemakers' union in December 1915 the secretary, Goupil, made a plea for the joint work of trade unions and cooperatives; this had in fact taken place within the Comité d'Action between the CGT, the Socialist Party, and the FNCC, as the chapter by John Horne in this book shows. A founder-member spoke up in lively terms: "Cooperatives only operate to enrich those who manage them." And Borsard ended by proposing to give priority to the union and to maintain a gap between union and cooperative.[113] The basis of a recurrent pattern was thus established. The war did not affect this feeling of cooperation as personal enrichment. In many quarters the success and the centralization of cooperative activity tended to accentuate this feeling, through the greater distance from the cooperative manager.

Conflicting circumstances were the object of discussion among the unions: thus in July 1919 the managers of *La Française*, the stonemasons' cooperative, were briskly questioned by their workers during a union meeting,[114] while Victor defended the administrators, considering that it was the cooperative workers who misunderstood their responsibility. A disagreement brought the union of women workers in cafés and restaurants into conflict with the managers of cooperative restaurants over the requirement to employ union staff.[115] Henriot, the butchery workers' trade union secretary, denounced cooperatives managed by socialists who resisted the "English" week and paid low wages.[116] Some cases reached the general council of the Seine trade unions joint committee, which attempted to settle the quarrels.[117]

Criticism was occasionally more personal, such as the four members who denounced Chamoy for having "managed the cooperative like a boss" at a meeting of the timber frame workers' union in December 1918.[118] The former secretary of the military uniform-makers union,

Burquel, was opposed to the cooperative set up by the new secretary, Dumas, because the latter made himself Chairman with a wage of 500 francs per month plus 5 percent of profits, with the manager of the cooperative receiving the same amount. This statement, as one might imagine, set off an indescribable tumult.[119]

The timber frame workers' union meeting on 6 January 1917 was also stormy. Chamoy, the union secretary and administrator of the cooperative, was continually interrupted and criticized by members, no doubt "loud mouths," such as one Faivre, nicknamed "Flashy." The meeting was not even able to begin its agenda. It would seem that these attacks were motivated by the wish of their promotors to share in the cooperative's profits.[120] We are here very far from the "communist" ideal of the cooperative movement. The tone of certain attacks indicates fairly clearly that it was as much personal jealousy as a criticism of principle that lay behind such distressing gatherings. It was doubtless such difficulties that were in Rappin's mind when he declared that "the attitude of trade unionists" to the creation of a cooperative meant that they are "not yet ready for it."[121]

The stakes were certainly big enough: could the cooperatives remain "on communist terrain," as was demanded by the members of the stonemasons' union,[122] or would they be only a solution for individuals? It is apparent, particularly after the war, that the very success of cooperatives reawakened an old debate, which was to come to a head after the period under consideration here.[123]

Finally, observations criticizing the cooperative idea from the clearly revolutionary point of view, on either a practical or a theoretical basis, were extremely rare. The refusal of Lancelo, of the timberframe workers' union, to follow the cabinet-makers in establishing a tool-insurance cooperative – because it was a question of fighting for the suppression of the worker's duty to supply his tools – was an exception,[124] and late in the day. So also was the declaration by Levasseur (not Levasseur the Deputy, but a militant from Puteaux), denouncing *La Revendication* cooperative as a "bourgeois operation."[125] Only the break between the practice of a workers' productive association, in the timber frame workers' and the stone- masons' trade unions, and that of direct management by the union, exercised by the flooring workers' union, denotes a significant difference during the war.[126]

The presentation of workers' debates about cooperatives is not identical to an accurate assessment of the union-cooperative link during the war. Examination of a producer cooperative entirely run by a union enables us to see how the pieces of our puzzle fit together.

The Union of Timber Frame Workers in the Département of the Seine

It was on 14 March 1915 that Chamoy first suggested to a meeting of his union the constitution of a Workers Association to carry out tasks for the military Corps of Engineers; conditions of work would be based on union rates (1.10 francs per hour), and the financing would be assured by the Solidarity Fund. In the face of opposition from Brochet and Gorioux (the timber frame workers' legal adviser) in favor of direct management, Chamoy had to withdraw his suggestion.[127] At the following meeting, however, on 21 March, Chamoy indicated that, at a meeting with Jouhaux at the Ministry of Public Works to seek timber-frame work, he had been told that the union would receive no work unless it established an association that the minister could encourage. Jouhaux supported this proposition, and the principle of the Association was then accepted by the union.[128] The union meetings on 24 March and 11 and 14 April were almost entirely given up to finaliz-ing the statutes of the Association and its funding. Arthur Fontaine, director of Labor in the Labor Ministry, passed a grant of 1,500 francs, and in addition 20 shares of 25 francs were subscribed by the staff. The association therefore began life with a capital of 2,000 francs, three-quarters financed by the State. The statutes mentioned above required members to be unionized, the Association's life was limited to the dura-tion of the war, and the profits were to be divided – 60 percent to aid and 40 percent to official reserve funds. The official headquarters was established at the Labor Exchange.[129] The meetings on 18 and 25 April completed this creation of the Association. A board was designated, with Brochet as Chairman, Brillant as secretary and Chamoy the essen-tial administrative officer. Aumaréchal, Gorioux, and Georg (who undertook the functions of overseer) completed the board.[130]

From this act of giving birth, what can we learn? First, we see the close interdependence between cooperative intent and the wish for work in a body affected by almost universal unemployment. Next, we find the central presence of the trade union that directed and organized the cooperative, the selection of its headquarters being significantly indicative of this initial condition of dependence. Finally, we note the importance of the State, without which the Association would not have seen the light of day, and which maneuvered to avoid direct manage-ment, of a kind which the experience of the fortified Paris Camp, with the flooring workers' union, has left some traces.

It was once again the *Préfet* of the Seine who was to find a site in which to install the cooperative, at 158 rue de Tolbiac, at a rent of 300 francs per year.[131] After a few difficult months in which there were still signs of a certain skepticism,[132] Chamoy was able to visit the cooperative's site on 26 September 1915 and to announce that he had won its first orders from the state (there were several companies) railway company. At the end of his visit, among the timber workers who were then gathered in the next-door café, optimism reigned supreme.[133] Orders were to come flooding in subsequently, for in October 1915 Chamoy was able to announce 40,000 francs-worth of work (including sleeping quarters for a fire station), and in November new building work, at an estimated value of 44,000 francs, for a military guard house. The Association acquired a loan of 15,000 francs from the Ministry of Labor to begin its work.[134] On 1 December 1915 the Union of Timber Workers of the Seine was able to open its first work site.

Here too the pairing of union and state operated fully during this period. Through its loan and its orders the state enabled the producer cooperative to start work. The union continued with regular supervision of the cooperative's functioning.

1916 saw a severe setback. The cooperative was certainly functioning well, making 130,000 francs' profit in the first three months of 1916, part of which it placed in the solidarity fund,[135] but it dropped out of discussions at union meetings. The cooperative thus dissociated itself from the union; without being able to set a precise date on this, we know also that its headquarters was transferred to 158 rue de Tolbiac, further evidence of this distancing.[136]

Chamoy, who fulfilled the double role of secretary of the union and director of the cooperative, moreover refused, in his report at the beginning of 1917, to refer to the cooperative, despite certain interruptions.[137] The balance-sheet of the cooperative remained sound, however. It continued to obtain substantial orders (a barrack building for prisoners in Nanterre for 100,000 francs, a sanitation block in Vanves).[138] On 6 January 1918 Brochet attacked Chamoy for not having respected the 60 percent proportion of profits for the aid fund and demanded the dissolution of the cooperative, supported by Gorioux.[139] The result of this episode was that Chamoy resigned his post as secretary of the union because of fatigue. He was replaced by Gorioux in March 1918,[140] then Duvart.[141] Henceforward the division between cooperative and union was intensified, and the lack of its administrators' answerability to the union was definitive. A further trace of the cooperative may be seen at a union meeting on 5 May 1918, where Gorioux called for subscriptions to complementary shares,[142] and at another on 29 December 1918, already mentioned, when Chamoy was attacked fiercely.[143] In 1919 the

Union of Timber Frame Workers of the Seine vanished completely from the trade union horizon, which had nothing to do with its dissolution because, initially established purely for the duration of the war, it continued after 1919.[144]

The procedures of 1916 were thus continued and accentuated in the following years, to the extent of reaching complete severance from the two organizations.[145] The character of the founder of the Workers Association, Adolphe Chamoy, may well constitute a typical profile of the development of an entire category of activists. A militant trade unionist-active revolutionary before the war, between 1900 and 1910 he had convictions for violence, attacks, and provocation to murder and insubordination, and filled the post of secretary of the joinery workers' union on the eve of war.[146] At the outbreak of war he was forty-seven, and was therefore not mobilized. He devoted himself totally to the policy of National Defense and the *Union sacrée*, which he was to defend throughout the war, placing himself to the right of the majority. Although in 1919 he was still a union activist, his slide toward the preeminence accorded to action in the Workers Association corresponded with a weariness, which can be observed among many militants of the Great War, and with a resistance to the increasingly strong criticisms of trade unionism in war. The weariness, the fact that for two union meetings (16 September and 15 December 1917) Chamoy had to excuse himself for not having had time to send out individual summons to the meeting, is clear evidence to all those who have some experience of the wearisome nature of such tasks.[147]

Set up for a short term and under a very specific set of circumstances, the timber frame workers' producers cooperative survived the war. It thus corresponded well with a movement which went beyond this combination of circumstances; but this cooperative activity rapidly and completely dissociated itself from the union as an organization. The cooperative activity was thus, at the lowest level, much more than an instant in the militant life of the unionist. However the relationships established between the state and the cooperative were privileged and enduring and should be linked to the state's policy concerning cooperatives, marked by a steep increase in grants.[148]

* * *

The great expansion of the Paris retail cooperatives during the war undoubtedly contributed to a relaunching of the cooperative concept among the unions. It found a staging post there, not so much in the application of the CGT's economic project or in the surge to emancipation, as in the feeling that cooperation could be a useful tool for the union, and that it played a part in the development of many militants' lives in the period of the war.

There was thus an effectively functioning link between union and cooperative at the end of the war and during the immediate postwar period, and the cooperative movement may well appear a plausible alternative to revolution or to the minimum plan of the CGT; for the workers' reservations which we have noted stem from opposition that was apparently more personal than theoretical. But this would be to ignore the silences. In the unions, in essential sectors such as metal working, the lack of visible opposition to consumer or producer cooperation arose from indifference: there are only six references to cooperatives out of all the metal industry workers' or union meetings, which is remarkably few. Only tailoring and construction showed true interest in the phenomenon, but almost exclusively in the single element of producers' associations. Out of twenty-five references in construction, one alone concerns retail cooperatives. And a closer look shows that the references relate overwhelmingly only to the two unions of timber frame and stonemasonry workers. Cooperatives were never mentioned at all by the two largest construction unions, those of the flooring workers and of the cement-workers and bricklayers.

A social approach to the economy came out of the war enhanced, as was noted with satisfaction by Charles Gide and Albert Thomas:[149] "one could almost say that the cooperative movement had been one of the great beneficiaries of the war!" wrote Charles Gide.[150] A combination of meetings between the consumer and the producer, between the cooperative and the union, woven into the workers' activity during the war, is evident, without any of the underlying contradictions being seriously resolved.

Notes to Chapter 10

1. *Annuaire de la Coopération,* 1920. For a general overview, see Ellen Furlough, *Consumer Cooperation in France: The Politics of Consumption, 1834–1930* (Ithaca: Cornell University Press, 1991).

2. Two books by Jean Gaumont are of particular interest because of their geographical approach: Jean Gaumont, *Les Sociétés de consommation à Paris: un demi-siècle d'action sociale par la coopération* (Paris: PUF, 1921); Jean Gaumont, *Les Mouvements de la coopération ouvrière dans les banlieues parisiennes* (Paris: PUF, 1932).

3. Cf. "Les Encouragements aux sociétés ouvrières de production de 1839 à 1920," *Bulletin du Ministère du Travail (BMT)*, April-May-June 1921, pp. 129–34.

4. Cf ."Les Associations ouvrières de production et les sociétés coopératives de consommation et de crédit en France au 1er janvier 1914," *BMT*, October-November-December 1914, pp. 606–12.

5. Cf. *Almanach de la coopération française et suisse*, 1910, and *Annuaire de la Coopération illustré*, 1914.

6. Cf. Charles Gide, "Chronique du mouvement coopératif," *Annuaire de la Coopération illustré*, 1914.

7. The list of cooperatives in the Seine can be found in the appendix VI-12 of Jean-Louis Robert, *Ouvriers et mouvement ouvrier parisiens pendant la Grande Guerre et l'immédiat après-guerre. Histoire et anthropologie* (Thèse d'Etat, University of Paris I, 1989).

8. Cf. the biography of Paul Alexandre by Jean Gaumont in the *Dictionnaire biographique du mouvement ouvrier français*, ed. J. Maitron (Paris: Editions Ouvrières, 1973) p. 125.

9. Cf. the various reports published in the journal of the Cooperative, *La Bellevilloise*, no. 81, November 1915; no. 82, November 1916.

10. This question was connected with trade unionism and the problem of orphans, according to Paul Alexandre, in *Annuaire de la Coopération illustré*, 1914, p. 66.

11. Cf. Gide, "Chronique."

12. Cf. Jean Gaumont, "La Concentration coopérative et les sociétés régionales de développement," *Annuaire de la Coopération*, 1920.

13. Gaumont, "Concentration coopérative," and the deposition of Cooperative statutes on 14 May 1914, *Bulletin municipal officiel de la Ville de Paris*, 18 June 1914.

14. In fact the number of societies is relevant to the situation in July 1919. For reasons of homogeneity we have emphasized *Annuaire de la Coopération*, 1920 as our source, although Jean Gaumont estimates the turnover of the Seine cooperatives in 1918 at 140 million francs. Gaumont, *Mouvements*.

15. Cf. "Les coopératives de consommation, les groupements d'achat en commun, les institutions municipales de ravitaillement pendant la guerre," *BMT*, April–May 1919, pp. 167–76. For the first half of 1918 the turnover for the Seine was 70.5 million francs.

16. Dynamism confirmed in the publication of E. Poisson, *Comment fonder une Coopérative?* (Paris: Grasset, 1919).

17. Was this what raised criticisms that consumers were not buying enough in the cooperatives? Cf. Daudé-Bancel, meeting organized by the Clichy inter-union committee on 12 May 1917, AN, F7 13617.

18. All the figures in the table are taken from lists of cooperatives provided in the *Annuaires* quoted above.

19. Cf. Gaumont, article quoted, *Annuaire de la Coopération*, 1920.

20. *La Bellevilloise*, November 1918.

21. Ernest Poisson, "1914–1919 – Le mouvement coopératif," *Annuaire de la Coopération*, 1920.

22. Cf. for example the running publicity in 1916 in *L'Humanité* and *La Bataille*, such as E. Le Guéry, "Les Ménagères affluent à l'étal de la viande frigorifiée à la 'Revendication' de Puteaux," *La Bataille*, 20 January 1916.

23. Cf. "Statistique des institutions de ravitaillement du personnel des usines de guerre," *Bulletin des Usines de Guerre (BUG)*, 8 October 1917; "Les institutions de ravitaillement du personnel des usines de guerre – rapport présenté à la Commission consultative du Travail dans les Etablissements du ministère de l'Armement (session du 8–10 août

1918)," *BUG*, 9 September 1918 and 16 September 1918. The turnover figures of the national establishments do not include sales to colonial workers.

24. In fact rather than "restaurants," these were "ordinaries" (canteens) providing food for the workers.

25. "Union des coopératives de Paris": 15 war factory restaurants; "Union des coopérateurs parisiens": 2; "Union des consommateurs de la Banlieue nord": 5; "Union des consommateurs de la Banlieue sud": 2; "Société des restaurants ouvriers de Suresnes-Puteaux": 8; "La Revendication" de Puteaux: 13; "L'Union" de Boulogne: 3; plus various cooperative factory canteens, Cf. *BUG*, 9 September 1918.

26. According to Charles Gide, *Les coopératives françaises durant la guerre*, course at the Collège de France, 1926–27, "workers do not like the 'ordinaries' and prefer the restaurants."

27. Cf. the intervention of Dr. Tissot at the inaugural dinner of the cooperative's restaurant, on 1 December 1918 at Boulogne with 500 people, AN, F7 13367, or "Un restaurant coopératif," *L'Humanité*, 22 September 1918.

28. Cooperators' groups re-established themselves quite quickly. *La Bellevilloise* re-established itself in 1916, and in 1919 there were 37 groups in the Seine.Cf. *Annuaire de la Coopération*, 1920.

29. The Boulogne cooperative organized a showing of the films "La Coopération" and "Jaurès" in May 1919. Cf. *L'Humanité*, 30 May 1919.

30. Cf. the meeting of the Cercle des Coopérateurs of the "Union des coopérateurs parisiens" on 22 December 1915, APP, BA 1536. Alice Jouenne wrote many articles on orphans in the labor press.

31. Cf. *La Bellevilloise*, November 1915: meeting of the group "L'Union des Coopérateurs parisiens" of 28 November 1915, APP, BA 1536.

32. For example, the *Union* cooperative at Le Bourget and the socialist branches at Le Bourget and Drancy established a shared workshop (*ouvroir*).

33. *La Bellevilloise* opened a room for mothers to breast-feed. The *Union* cooperative in Boulogne planned to open a cooperative maternity hospital. Cf. the dinner mentioned on 1 December 1918.

34. Cf. *La Bellevilloise*, November 1915. Part of these activities, such as the choir, were to begin again at the end of the war.

35. "Une visite à L'Union des Coopératives parisiennes," *L'Humanité*, 19 March 1919.

36. Cf. *Annuaire de la Coopération*, 1920, pp. 242–47.

37. The first related to the state establishments, the second to private establishments. Cf. *BUG*, 16 October and 13 November 1916.

38. Circular dated 2 October 1916. Cf. also the report of the Sûreté M/10718 of 4 October 1916, which shows the links between Thomas, the militant trade unionists Minot, Picard, and Léon Clément, and employers such as Albert Kahn to establish the first cooperative restaurants, AN F7 13617.

39. Statute of the Union des industriels des 19me and 20me arrondissements, *BUG*, 6 August 1917.

40. Cf. Appendix I-38 of my thesis, quoted above.

41. Cf. "L'Oeuvre des Restaurants ouvriers-Albert Thomas à Suresnes," *L'Humanité*, 10 June 1918.

42. Inaugural dinner, 1 December, report quoted above.

43. It was necessary to wait until June 1919, in a particularly polemical context, to see attacks against the subsidizing of the cooperative by the Minister of Armaments. See the report "Encore un bourgeois," meeting of metalworker strikers, 5 June 1919, APP, BA 1407.

44. Cf. note 42.

45. Cf. *L'Humanité*, 10 June 1918 and 2 December 1918.

46. Account of the Congress of the Paris federation of cooperatives, 16 August 1917, in *L'Humanité*, 17 August 1917.

47. Report of the FNCC congress on 30 September and 1 October 1917 in *L'Humanité*, 2 October 1917. The merging of management of the FNCC and the wholesale store was approved by 893 votes in favor and 122 against, with 24 abstentions.

48. Meeting of the union of Paris cooperators, 28 November 1915, APP, BA1536.

49. *La Bellevilloise*, November 1918.

50. Cf. the Cherbourg conflicts, in a study by J. Quellien, "Un milieu ouvrier réformiste: syndicalisme et réformisme à Cherbourg à la Belle Epoque," *Le Mouvement social*, no. 127 (1984), pp. 65–88.

51. *L'Humanité*, 28 January 1917, 26 August 1917.

52. Cf. Ollano, meeting of the "Union des coopérateurs" on 28 November 1915, APP, BA 1536.

53. Cf. report of the annual assembly of the "Union des coopérateurs parisiens," *L'Humanité*, 18 November 1917.

54. Opening on 1 December 1918; Cf. note 27 above.

55. "A La Bellevilloise," *L'Humanité*, 28 November 1917.

56. I have examined the contents of 18,000 socialist meetings. For the development of themes at socialist meetings, cf. Robert, *Ouvriers et mouvement ouvrier parisiens*, chap. 30.

57. *1906. Le Congrès de la Charte d'Amiens*, reissued, Les Congrès de la CGT, Institut CGT d'Histoire sociale, Paris, 1983, p. 195 in the Congrès pagination.

58. Declaration by Mass, meeting of the shoemakers union on 18 September 1916, AN, F7 13697.

59. Meeting of the general clothing workers union on 19 November 1916, APP, BA 1423.

60. Declaration by Dumas, meeting of the military clothing workers union on 29 September 1917, APP, BA 1376.

61. Agenda for the striking dressmakers' meeting on 23 September 1918, APP, BA 1376.

62. Meeting of the paper trades union council on 11 April 1918, AN, F7 13753. The union secretary, Rappin, once more hoped for this creation at the union meeting on 2 March 1919, AN, F7 13753.

63. Meeting of the electrical fitters' union on 30 March 1919, AN F7 13717.

64. Cf. meetings of the timber frame workers' union on 14 March and 14 April, 1915, AN, F7 13653. The statutes of the workers' Association established the headquarters at the Labor Exchange and indicated that all members should belong to a union.

65. Cf. meetings of the bricklayers' union on 23 January 1916, 23 December 1917, and 3 February 1918, AN, F7 13653.

66. Agenda of the meeting on 3 October 1918, AN F7 13656.

67. Cf. meeting of the stonemasons' union on 26 May 1918, AN, F7 13655.

68. Cf. meetings of the railway workers' of Paris-Nord on 22 July 1915 and of the union committee on 12 August 1915, APP, BA 1535.

69. Ducas, secretary of the Asnières railway workers' union, on 18 December 1918, AN F7 13667.

70. Meeting of the union of supervisory staff in public assistance, on 20 May 1917, AN F7 13814.

71. Meeting of Clerget-Blin workers on 5 March 1918, AN, F7 13367.

72. Meeting of the joinery workers' union on 23 May 1915, AN, F7 13653.

73. Cf. meeting of the joinery workers' union on 14 April 1915, quoted in note 64 above.

74. Agenda of the meeting of the painter-decorators' union on 3 October 1918, quoted in note 66 above.

75. Meeting of the Clichy branch of the stonemasons' union on 2 February 1919, AN, F7 13655. Similarly, Lacouque, at the meeting of the union on 12 January 1919, AN, F7 13655.

76. The wish of Jandon, for the shoemakers' union to join the workers' Association against fire, refers to a similar occurrence. Cf. the meeting of the shoemakers' union on 16 October 1916, AN F7 13697.

77. Meeting of delegates of the Paris union of railways on 18 November 1916, AN, F7 13667.

78. Léon Jouhaux, "POUR REDUIRE LE COUT DE LA VIE, Aux tartinades journalistiques, répondons par de l'initiative et des actes," *La Bataille*, 13 January 1916.

79. Meeting of 20 May 1917, Cf. note 70 above.

80. Meeting of SAAIB workers, 14 October 1917, AN, F7 13366.

81. Cf. Leclerc, meeting of metalworking and vehicle-aviation at Levallois-Perret on 28 May 1919, F7 13367 or Montagne, meeting of chemical strikers, 7 June 1919, APP, BA 1408.

82. Bucquoi, meeting of Paris postal workers on 20 January 1918, AN F7 13804.

83. Meeting of Paris unemployed workers on 18 January 1919, AN, F7 13367.

84. Meeting of shop stewards of the 13th arrondissement, 3 March 1918, AN, F7 13367.

85. Desgranges, secretary of the Noisy-le-Sec railway workers' union, meeting of the union on 4 September 1918, AN, F7 13673.

86. Cf. Pages, conference on "Le commerce et la coopérative," meeting of the Jeunes de la Ménagère on 23 September 1915, AN, F7 13719. Pages considered that, in contrast to the large shops, cooperatives were incapable of destroying the small traders.

87. Joseph Jacquemotte, meeting of the general union of clothing workers, 29 June 1916, APP, BA 1423 and BA 1535.

88. Meeting of the stitchers' branch of the general paperworkers' trade union on 26 January 1918, AN, F7 13753.

89. Joseph Jacquemotte, meeting of the general union of clothing workers, 11 March 1917, APP, BA 1423.

90. Fradin, meeting of Clerget-Blin workers on 5 March 1918, quoted in note 71 above.

91. Cf. the declarations of Charlotte Amsterdamski, meetings of the general paperworkers' union Council on 28 March 1918 and of the stitchers' section on 21 April 1918, AN, F7 13753.

92. J. Rancière, *La nuit des prolétaires. Archives d'un rêve ouvrier* (Paris: Fayard, 1981), pp. 310–55.

93. Duras, meeting of the Saint-Denis branch of the stonemasons' union on 9 June 1918, AN, F7 13655.

94. Meeting of the boxmakers' union on 24 May 1919, AN, F7 13702. The cooperative then became the "corporate workshop." Cf. Godart, meeting of the leather-workers and pursemakers' union on 11 August, 1918, AN, F7 13697.

95. Communiqué of the butchers' union, *L'Humanité*, 14 October 1917.

96. Cf. meetings of the councils of the Paris construction unions on 28 March 1918, AN,

F7 13649, and the timber frame workers' union on 1 September 1918, AN, F7 13653.

97. Meeting of the bakery workers' union on 2 September 1915, APP, BA 1536.

98. Meeting of the upholsterers' union on 19 September 1915, AN, F7 13636; meeting of the general union of clothing workers on 11 March 1917, quoted in note 88 above; meeting of the vehicle-aviation trade union on 5 September 1915, AN, F7 13831; meeting of the wood-gilders' union on 2 December 1917, AN, F7 13636.

99. Péronne, meeting of the VRP union on 28 October 1917, AN, F7 13719.

100. General committee of the Union of Seine trades unions on 16 January 1918, AN, F7 13015.

101. Note on 27 March 1916, AN, F7 13653.

102. Meeting of the dressmakers' and ladies' tailoring sections of the general clothing trades union on 24 September 1916, APP, BA 1423. Naturally Jacquemotte used it to back his argument for his tailoring cooperative. The cooperatives also took part in the Communist soupkitchens during the strike of June 1919. Cf. for example Royer at the meeting of striking sawmill workers, 12 June 1919, APP, BA 1408.

103. One franc (without wine) or 1.70 francs (with wine), meeting of strikers in the 14th *arrondissement* on 13 June 1919, APP, BA 1386; one franc in the 12 restaurants of the *Union des Coopérateurs*, meeting of the delegates of striking trade unions on 12 June 1919; 1.20 francs at *la Revendication* at Puteaux, meeting of Arsenal strikers on 10 June 1915, AN, F7 13367.

104. Cf. the meetings of the grocery workers' union on 30 November 1914 and on 14 December 1916, APP, BA 1423.

105. Statute read out by Rosenfeld at the meeting of the leatherworkers' union on 8 December 1917, AN, F7 13697.

106. Meeting of locked-out shoemakers on 6 February 1918, AN, F7 13697.

107. Meeting of the Council of the paper-workers' union on 28 March 1918, quoted in note 90 above; similarly, Mass, at the meeting of the shoemakers' union on 18 September 1916, quoted in note 58 above; Dumercq doubts the possibility of setting up a cooperative restaurant in the 13th *arrondissement*, meeting of the Gnôme and Rhône workers on 12 May 1918 (report SRUG).

108. Meeting of the general clothing workers' union on 11 March 1917; Cf. note 88 above.

109. Meeting of the general clothing workers' union, 19 November 1916, quoted in note 59 above.

110. Meeting of the timber frame workers' union on 14 March 1915, quoted in note 64 above.

111. Meeting of the Council of the sub-postmasters' union on 10 October 1916, AN, F7 13803. Cf. also the meeting of the VRP union on 28 October 1917, cf. note 98 above.

112. Meeting of the bakery workers' union on 2 September 1915, Cf. note 96 above.

113. Meeting of the shoemakers' union on 5 December 1915, AN, F7 13697.

114. Meeting of the stonemasons' union on 26 July 1919, AN, F7 13655.

115. Cf. meetings of the union of women workers in cafés-restaurants, 29 October 1915 and 5 April 1916, APP, BA 1536 and AN, F7 13632.

116. Meeting for cooperative staff organized by the butchery workers' union, 26 August 1918, BA 1536 and AN, F7 13632; similar criticism of "la Famille nouvelle," the restaurant for vehicle workers, by Rieder on 28 October 1917, at the meeting of the vehicle and aviation workers' union, AN, F7 13831.

117. Meeting of the Union's general committee on 24 July 1918, AN, F7 13015.

118. Bernard, Brochet, Loriot, Aumaréchal, meeting of the timber frame workers' trade union on 29 December 1918, AN, F7 13653.

119. Meeting of the union of military tailoring workers on 29 September 1917, quoted in note 60 above.

120. Meeting of the timber frame workers' union on 6 January 1917, AN, F7 13653.

121. Meeting of the Council of the paper trades' general union, cf. note 90 above.

122. Meeting of the union of stonemasons on 26 July 1919, quoted in note 113 above.

123. Discussion which ended in the third and little-known split, that of the cooperative movement with the creation of the ARRCO.

124. Meeting of the cabinet-makers' union on 19 June 1919, AN, F7 13653.

125. Meeting of the Puteaux inter-union committee on 6 August 1919, AN, F7 13015.

126. Cf. the meetings of the flooring workers' union on 2 February and 18 May 1919, AN, F7 13657. The administration refused, moreover, to give the flooring workers' union a demolition lot for direct management.

127. Meeting of the timber frame workers' union on 14 March 1915, quoted note 64 above.

128. Meeting of the timber frame workers' union on 21 March 1915, AN, F7 13653.

129. Meetings of the timber frame workers' union on 11 March, 11 April and 14 April, 1915, AN, F7 13653.

130. Meetings of the timber frame workers' union on 8 and 25 April, AN, F7 13653. Two supervisors are also named: Auchin and Etcheverry.

131. Meetings of the timber frame workers' union on 9 and 23 May, AN, F7 13653.

132. According to the discussion on 23 May "did not augur well for the cooperative's future," AN, F7 13653.

133. Visit to the cooperative site on 26 September 1915, AN, F7 13653.

134. Meetings of the timber frame workers' union on 10 October and 21 November 1915, source note 70.

135. Note of 27 March 1916, AN, F7 13653.

136. It is at this address that it appears in the list of societies featuring in the list of grants from the Ministry of Labor.

137. Cf. meetings of the timber frame workers' union on 7 January and 3 February 1917, AN, F7 13653.

138. Report of the Sûreté générale on Chamoy M/ll,123, 10 March 1917, AN, F7 13653.

139. Meeting of the timber frame workers' union on 6 January 1918, AN, F7 13653.

140. Meeting of the timber frame workers' union on 10 March 1918, AN, F7 13653.

141. Meeting of the timber frame workers' union on 29 December 1918, AN, F7 13653.

142. Meeting of the timber frame workers' union on 5 May 1918, AN, F7 13653.

143. Cf. note 140 above.

144. Cf. "Encouragements aux sociétés coopératives qui ont formulé la demande en 1919," *BMT*, March–April 1920. The Union gained a grant of 5,000 francs, and a loan of 50,000 francs.

145. Developments were even harsher for the stonemasons, whose union excluded, on 26 July 1919, the members of the Management Council of the cooperative founded by the former secretary Duras, AN, F7 13655.

146. Report M/11, 123, quoted in note 137.

147. Meetings of the joinery workers' union on 16 September and 15 December 1917, AN, F7 13653.

148. Cf. the law of 19 December 1915 concerning workers' production cooperative

societies and work loans, *BMT, Actes officiels,* November–December 1915; and the law of 7 May 1917 concerning retail cooperative societies, *BMT,* June–July 1917. Cf. also "Les encouragements aux sociétés ouvrières de consommation de 1893 à 1920" and "Les encouragements aux sociétes ouvrières de 1917 à 1920," *BMT,* April–May–June 1921.

149. Albert Thomas, *La coopération et les usines de guerre,* bibliothèque de L'Ecole coopérative, Paris, 1919; Charles Gide, "L'essor de la coopération devant la guerre," *Christianisme social,* January 1920, pp. 31–43.

150. Gide, *Les coopératives françaises,* p. 4; Cf. also Abel Chatelain, "Géographie sociologique et commerciale du Mouvement coopératif de consommation dans la région parisienne (1913–1956)," *Revue des études coopératives,* no. 117, 1959, pp. 137–65. For biographies of the activists mentioned in this chapter, cf. Jean Maitron, ed., *Dictionnaire . . . ,* 4th series: *1914–1939,* 1977–1992. See also Ellen Furlough, *Consumer Cooperation in France, op. cit.,* pp. 250–58.

Notes on Contributors

Jean-Jacques Becker, University of Paris X-Nanterre.

Serge Berstein, Institut d'Etudes Politiques, Paris.

Mathilde Dubesset, Lycée Jean Monnet, Saint-Etienne.

Patrick Fridenson, Ecole des Hautes Etudes en Sciences Sociales, Paris.

Gerd Hardach, University of Marburg.

Gilbert Hatry (†), Historical Society, Renault Company.

Alain Hennebicque, Lycée Guillaume Apollinaire, Thiais.

John Horne, Trinity College, Dublin.

James M. Laux, University of Cincinnati, emeritus.

Robert O. Paxton, Columbia University.

Jean-Louis Robert, University of Orléans.

Françoise Thébaud, University of Lyons II.

Catherine Vincent, Lycée Lakanal, Sceaux Paris.

Index

and worker delegates, 223–24, 234
Renoult, René, 45, 51
REP aviation engines, 137
Le Rhône co., 141–42
Ribot, Alexandre, 43, 44, 48, 109, 111
Riva-Berni, and Calcium Carbide consortium, 157, 161
Roanne arsenal, 116–18, 120, 121, 123
Robert, Jean-Louis, 9
Rochette Affair, 49
Rochette, Louis, and Calcium Carbide consortium, 157, 161, 165, 169
Rolland et Emile Pilain co., 148
Rossel-Peugeot co., 141
Rousiers, Paul de, defender of Calcium Carbide consortium, 166–67, 170, 171
Russell, Bertrand, 58

Saint-Chamond co., 59, 60, 67, 72
Saint-Gobain co. 123
Salmson co., aviation engines, 142–43, 148, 149, 151 n. 17
strike of 1918, 231
Santos-Dumont, Alberto, aviator, 137
Sarraut, Albert, 18, 32, 43, 172
Schaper, B. W., on A. Thomas, 119
Schneider co., 60, 76-77, 80, 91, 97, 112. *See also* Le Creusot
Secrétan, Eugène, and copper corner, 1887–89, 155, 159
Segogne, Georges de, and Article 419, 170
Seguin, Augustin, 135
Seguin, Laurent, and rotary engine, 136–38
Seguin, Louis, and G & R, development, 135
death, 144, 150
Seguin, Marc, 135

Sembat, Marcel, 82, 243, 245, 248
shop stewards. *See* Renault, shop stewards
Simiand, François, adviser to A. Thomas, 95, 106, 107, 108, 113, 115
Simyan, Julien, opponent of Calcium Carbide consortium, 162, 163, 165
Sloane Aeroplane co., 140
SNECMA, successor to G & R co., 149
Socialist Party (SFIO), 9, 38, 39, 40, 47, 65, 82, 83, 113, 115, 118, 269–71
and Comités d'Action, 241–48, 254–58, 262, 265, 266, 270
Société des Fonderies de Cuivre de Lyon, Mâcon, et Paris, Thévenin Frères, L. Seguin et Cie., 136
solidarity, principle of Radicals, 41
Sopwith aircraft, 138
Soviet regime, attitude of Radicals toward, 1918, 46
Steeg, Théodore, 48
strikes at G & R co., 1918, 148

Taylorism, 3, 6, 62, 83–84, 123, 166, 251, 259, 267
at Renault co., 219, 233
Thévenin, Maurice, 136
Thomas, Albert, wartime policies, 5–6, 8, 61–74 passim, 89–124 passim
appreciation of C. Cavallier, 2
assessment, 118–24
Calcium Carbide consortium, 158, 162–73
chemical industry, 123–24
Comité d'Action, 250, 251, 265
Contracts Commission, 101–8, 110–11, 121
cooperatives, 293, 294, 309
double social tax, 96, 112
economic reform ideas, 263, 264